THE COURSE OF LIFE

Volume V

THE COURSE OF LIFE

Volume V

Early Adulthood

Edited by
George H. Pollock, M.D., Ph.D.
Stanley I. Greenspan, M.D.

INTERNATIONAL UNIVERSITIES PRESS, INC.
Madison   Connecticut

This is a revised and expanded version of *The Course of Life: Psychoanalytic Contributions Toward Understanding Personality Development*, edited by Stanley I. Greenspan and George H. Pollock, published by the U.S. Government Printing Office, Washington, D.C., 1980.

Library of Congress Cataloging in Publication Data

The Course of life.

   "Revised and expanded version"—T.p. verso.
   Includes bibliographies and indexes.
   Contents: v. 1. Infancy —   — v. 5.
Early adulthood.
   1. Personality development. 2. Psychoanalysis.
3. Developmental psychology. I. Greenspan,
Stanley I. II. Pollock, George H.
[DNLM: 1. Human Development. 2. Personality
Development. 3. Psychoanalytic Theory.
WM 460.5.P3 C861]
BF698.C68 1989   155   88-28465
ISBN 0-8236-1123-X (v. 1)
ISBN 0-8236-1127-2 (v. 5)

Contents

vi

List of Contributors

Harold P. Blum, M.D., Clinical Professor of Psychiatry, Downstate Medical Center, New York; Executive Director, Sigmund Freud Archives; Past Editor, *Journal of the American Psychoanalytic Association.*

Bertram J. Cohler, Ph.D., William Rainey Harper Professor, The College, and Departments of Psychology (The Committee on Human Development), Psychiatry, and Education, Co-Director, Center for Health, Aging and Society.

Rex Culp, Ph.D., J.D., Department Head and Professor, Family Relations and Child Development, Oklahoma State University, Stillwater, Oklahoma.

Mark Freeman, Ph.D., Associate Professor, Department of Psychology, Holy Cross College.

Stanley I. Greenspan, M.D., Clinical Professor of Psychiatry and Behavioral Sciences, and Child Health and Development, George Washington University Medical Center, Washington, D.C.; Supervising Child Psychoanalyst, Washington Psychoanalytic Institute.

Paul C. Holinger, M.D., Professor of Psychiatry, Rush Medical College, Rush-Presbyterian-St. Luke's Medical Center, Chicago.

Richard A. Isay, M.D., Clinical Professor of Psychiatry, Cornell Medical College; Faculty, Columbia University Center for Psychoanalytic Training and Research.

Elliott Jaques, M.A., M.D., Ph.D., F.R.C.P., Visiting Research Professor of Management Science, George Washington University, Washington, D.C.; Professor Emeritus, Social Science, Brunel University, England.

Otto F. Kernberg, M.D., Associate Chairman and Medical Director, The New York Hospital-Cornell Medical Center, Westchester Division; Professor of Psychiatry, Cornell University Medical College; Training and Supervising Analyst, Columbia University Center for Psychoanalytic Training and Research.

W. W. Meissner, S.J., M.D., University Professor of Psychoanalysis, Boston College, Chestnut Hill, MA; Training and Supervising Analyst, Boston Psychoanalytic Institute.

Robert Michels, M.D., The Stephen and Suzanne Weiss Dean, and Barklie McKee Henry Professor of Psychiatry, Cornell University Medical College.

Joy D. Osofsky, Ph.D., Professor of Pediatrics and Psychiatry, Louisiana State
    University Medical Center, New Orleans, Louisiana; Adjunct Professor
    of Psychology, University of New Orleans, Faculty, New Orleans Institute
    for Psychoanalysis.
Ethel Spector Person, M.D., Professor of Clinical Psychiatry, Columbia Uni-
    versity; Training and Supervising Analyst, Columbia University Psycho-
    analytic Center for Training and Research.
William J. Polk, M.D., Clinical Assistant Professor of Psychiatry, Georgetown
    University Medical School; Research Psychiatrist, Mental Health Study
    Center, National Institute of Mental Health.

Preface

The transition from adolescence has occurred. The boundaries are as yet not fixed, and there are evidences of earlier psychological, emotional, and behavioral states that can make their appearance in a variety of contexts ranging from the negotiation of more stable patterns of intimacy to patterns stirred up by the development of one's own children. Biologically both genders have achieved what is considered to be completeness. Career, work, occupation, and role are identifiable. There is movement toward or establishment and further development of adult dyadic relationships.

Adult bio-psycho-social organization has taken place. Parenthood and significant and positive intimate relationships may be established. Work trajectories can be identified and responsible social roles may be assumed. There is movement toward psychological maturity, and the resolution of earlier developmental conflicts and possible psychological deficits. The personality organization, expressing what is traditionally known as adult life—work, play and pleasure, sexual competency, a fairly clear definition of self—biologically, psychologically, and morally is in operation. Toward the middle to later phases of this stage of development, we begin to see evidences of the transition to the next life course.

In the phase known as middle age, we find significant transitions occurring: i.e., biologically we find the onset of menopause; we find changing attitudes toward self, significant others, and children who may be leaving home; parental responsibilities are less; and we find role shifts in the genders. Many women, freer in time and care of offspring, may seek to achieve new (or redefine earlier) goals. Socially we find variations in different economic, ethnic, and religious groups, although much research is needed to fill our knowledge gaps in this life course phase. There are concerns regarding financial planning, health care, relations with older parents, children who themselves now are married and have their own families, leisure activities, and health and longevity issues.

Research into the last phase of the life course, old age, is very active: geriatrics, geropsychology, geropsychiatry, and gerontology. This period is now by some investigators and clinicians divided into subphases, based on observations and studies that indicate important changes occur in different parts of the older-adult period: body shape, appearance, energy levels, memory functions, sleep patterns, sexual capacities, wisdom and world views, and abilities to use leisure or free time. The distinctions between the young elderly, the older adult, and very aged individuals are more clearly evident. Relations with children, grandchildren, siblings, and friends evolve, reflecting the passage of a lifetime's knowledge on to others.

Authors from the first edition of *The Course of Life* have been given the opportunity to update their original papers. In addition, new contributions by outstanding investigators have been added for this revised and expanded edition.

1

Adulthood

ROBERT MICHELS, M.D.

The special contributions of psychoanalysis to developmental psychology have emphasized a set of related themes—the interdependence of biological and psychological development, the impact of the earliest interpersonal experiences on later mental life, and the persistence of infantile and childhood themes in the formal structure and unconscious content of adult experience and behavior. These aspects of psychoanalysis have led to its increasing prominence as a developmental psychology. It seems strange today to recall that the early interests of psychoanalysis had nothing to do with the mental life of childhood and that it was many years before psychoanalysis evidenced any interest in the direct study of children, either clinically, experimentally, or in natural settings. However, although psychoanalysis has become a developmental psychology, it has tended to see development as synonymous with the first years of life, and it has continued to view adult life as a product of development rather than a developmental epoch. There are several reasons for this. First, the method of psychoanalysis emphasizes the impact of the past on the present, and since there have been almost no data based on psychoanalytic investigation of the elderly, there has been little opportunity to look back on adult life. Second, the interplay of biological and psychological development is far more dramatic in childhood; in fact, some have questioned whether any psychologically significant biological development occurs during adult life. Recent studies of brain function, endocrine changes, sexual behavior, and more classical studies of the impact of pregnancy and maternity on mental life have challenged this

1

view, but have had relatively little impact on our general theory. Finally, psychoanalysis's exciting new observations concerning how the mental life of childhood persisted into adult psychopathology had to contend with the still-dominant view concerning the central role of contemporary reality in the mental life of the adult. To emphasize its unique contribution, psychoanalysis may have underemphasized the role of adult social roles and relationships, and most students of adult development have focused on those themes (Levinson, Darrow, Klein, Levinson, and McKee, 1978) rather than the more traditional psychoanalytic issues of drive vicissitudes and the development of intrapsychic structure. In spite of this, there is one reason why psychoanalysis must attend to adult development and cannot dismiss it as nonexistent or purely sociobehavioral. It is that any adequate theory of psychoanalytic treatment is a special case of a theory of adult development, a theory of how, at least in the special situation of psychoanalysis, true developmental change, with shifting patterns of conflict resolution and the maturation of psychic structure, can and does occur.

In considering adult development, there are several orienting themes that must be kept in mind in order to balance the prejudice of psychoanalytic thinking that tends to equate "development" and "childhood." First, the subject is development, not libidinal development or even drive development. This is important because one of the first developmental contributions of psychoanalysis was its clarification of the central role of sexual development in the mental life of the child. Since that time, psychoanalysis has gone on to study other developmental themes of childhood—aggressive drives, object relations, cognitive processes, defensive organization, etc., but none of these has emerged with the clarity or the force of childhood sexuality. Yet, as we shift to consideration of adult development, it would be as great an error to "infantopomorphize" adult psychological processes as it was to "adultopomorphize" childhood in the last century. There are developmental processes in adult mental life, and sexuality may not be as central to these as we now know it to be in childhood development. With the maturation of symbolic functioning, the relative importance of organismic factors in determining mental life diminishes along with the role of sexual (and other) drives.

Later in the life cycle, with the reassertion of the organismic limits of behavior—this time because of waning capacity rather than biological-motivational press—and, at the same time, the progressive impairment of symbolic functioning because of this same waning capacity, we may again see a shift toward a greater prominence of drive in the structuring of mental life, a "second childhood." This merely restates the commonplace, that the mature adult is capable of mental life more autonomous from the influence of immediate organismic determinants than either the child or the older adult. This leads us to one of the problems in conceptualization in this area of psychoanalytic theory—our models of development are fundamentally biological models, with psychological development viewed as derivative of organic embryology. However, the psychological development of the adult results primarily from the interaction of mental structures with experience, integrated in symbolic form. The result is a developmental process, but one quite different in form from the development of the hematopoietic system or even of the superego. The relatively minor role of biological maturational determinants leads to a much more individually variable and inconsistent course of development than in early childhood.

One might ask why the concept of development should be employed at all, and here we come to our central point. For the individual experiencing it, adulthood is just as much as childhood a process of becoming, of progressive transformation from one state to another, with critical periods of change and of consolidation; it is not only a state of being. For years we overemphasized childhood as pure becoming, a mere precursor of adulthood, and because of that lost touch with some of its essential features as an epoch of life having its own meaning. The opposite has been true of our theoretical view of adulthood, but any clinician who has treated adult patients knows that their lives can be more richly understood by recognizing a temporal organization of ongoing developmental lines.

Global Issues of Adult Development

Time

The infant lives in the world of the present. With growing capacity for both memory and anticipation, the span of psychologically meaningful time expands in childhood to include at first the immediate past and future and then progressively more and more of the totality of life. Although the cognitive capacity for this expansion is certainly present in adolescence, it is unusual for an adolescent to have any sense of current self as a point on a lifelong developmental trajectory. Indeed, one of the important themes of the psychoanalysis of young adults is the expansion of their experience of current self-representations as continuous with their childhood and as leading to a future that is related to their past while not being pathologically constrained by it. The adult is expected to relate to both past and future, as well as to the present. The limitations stemming from the personal past can no longer be denied (the recognition that omnipotentiality is impossible), while death is real without being imminent and overwhelming. The adult must relate to generations before and after. In old age there may be another shift to a world that once was, viewed either with longing or bitterness, and to a focus on the past.

The clinical psychoanalyst's view of his adult patient tends to focus on the relationship of present to past, with the implicit assumption that, if the conflicts in this relationship can be resolved, the patient can attend to his own future without assistance. However, the patient's mental representation of the future is an important part of his mental life and therefore an important subject for psychoanalytic inquiry. It is rarely discussed directly in the psychoanalytic literature, but the failure to explore it clinically has specific recognizable derivatives. One of these relates to problems concerning termination. The analyst and patient have explored the past and its relation to the present and have resolved many of the distortions or conflicts that interfered with the patient's adaptation. The subject of termination is introduced, and a crisis follows. The exploration of the crisis reveals that while there might have been understanding and agreement on what was and what is, there were very different notions concerning what was yet to come, differences that were concealed by the "timelessness" of the psychoanalytic situation and the patient's acceptance of the treatment as a temporary substitute for concern about the future. This is a kind of problem that rarely occurs in child or adolescent analysis, where the imminent social pressure for developmental progression forces these issues into the clinical arena.

Self and Other

For the infant, self and other are a distinction in experience that has not yet been made. The development of this differentiation and its fate has been the major area of interest in recent years in psychoanalytic speculation about psychological development. For the child, self remains paramount, and the potential pathological persistence of this orientation into adult life has been a major concern in recent years in clinical psychoanalysis. Nevertheless, for most adults there is a developmental shift with greater attention to the outside world and to others than was the case in childhood and adolescence. The psychoanalyst sees this shift as a complex one that may represent an attempt to maintain a fantasized ideal while recognizing the limitations of reality. For example, the child or adolescent is often concerned with fantasies of future success and grandiose triumph. The adult must recognize the extent to which these fantasies can never be realized but, at the same time, may preserve them as displaced to symbolic extensions or substitutes for the self—the family, group, nation, church, science, or, above all else the most direct extension, the child. In effect, the shift from self to other can preserve the even more valued internal image of an ideal self. This is one of the essential mechanisms of the transformation of infantile narcissism into the mature goals of the normal adult.

Stability and Change

Infancy and childhood are periods of change. Indeed, we sometimes think of them as little else. Adult life, by contrast, is a period of relative stability. The most striking difference in the mental life of the child from that of the adult rests in this distinction rather than in the day-to-day content of experience, particularly for psychoanalysis, which has discovered both the complexity of mental development in childhood and the persistence of the themes of childhood into the mental life of the adult.

This difference is important in understanding many of the features of both childhood and adult life. The child often craves stability, constancy, and may withdraw from developmental processes if anxiety leads to a need for greater constancy. At the same time the ever shifting mental life of the child can protect from what might otherwise be overwhelming trauma. It may be true that a scene is a bad scene, but the act will soon be over and another take its place; although every experience leaves its trace, there is a sense of new opportunity, with the possibility of overcoming the legacies of the past.

For the adult, life is different. Stability and the expectation of continued stability replace change and the expectation of continued change. Some of the syndromes of midlife crisis at times represent an attempt to reconstruct the experience of transformation and rebirth so characteristic of youth, as much as an attempt to deal with the persistent wishes and fears of earlier life. In other words, the structure as much as the content of adult experience is different, and regressive behavior in adults can take the form of attempting to re-create the structure as well as the content of the past.

Drives and Psychosocial Reality

Commonsense views explain adult behavior as a rational adaptive response to psychosocial reality. Children tend to be seen basically as little adults, perhaps less rational, perhaps more concerned with inner needs, but basically little adults. Psychoanalysis has revolutionized this view. Behavior is seen as the product of unconscious wishes, themselves largely understood as the psychological derivatives of infantile drives. Adults are seen basically as large children, perhaps more rational, perhaps less concerned with inner needs (or more able to delay or disguise their gratification), but basically large children.

Yet there is a validity to the commonsense view. Adult behavior is less dominated by drives and their immediate derivatives, more influenced by the structures and channels of the mind that are the product of mental development and by the surrounding world and its significant others. For the adult, consideration of ego, superego, and reality is relatively more important in understanding behavior.

There is nothing particularly novel about this view, but it has an important consequence when we consider adult development. The original psychoanalytic theory of development was a theory of drive, specifically libido development. Even the familiar labels of developmental stages are labels derived from libido theory—oral, anal, phallic, etc. This means that as drive is less central to our thinking about adult development, so psychoanalytic concepts originally stemming from the study of children are less likely to fit it comfortably.

Specific Themes in Adult Life

There are a great many themes of development in adult life that could be considered here. We will arbitrarily limit the discussion to four—work, sex, parenthood, and aging.

Work

Children play; adults work. Play has been a major focus of interest among psychoanalysts studying children, in great part because of its value as an expressive equivalent of free association in the clinical psychoanalysis of children. Work has been given little attention by psychoanalysis, in part because of its close tie to reality and its relative distance from the unconscious mental themes that are the central concern of clinical psychoanalysis. The two aspects of work that have received attention are exceptions to this rule. First are the neurotic interferences with work—work inhibitions, success phobias, etc.—in which unconscious fantasies have intruded upon work functioning. The second is creative work—artistic, scientific and, of course, psychoanalytic—in which the capacity to employ unconscious fantasies is essential for success. However, the great majority of adults work and do so without major neurotic interference and, unfortunately, with relatively little creativity. Work does serve as a major organizer of their psychological lives, as is evidenced by the pathological responses to deprivation from it in the clinical syndromes associated with holidays, vacations, and retirement.

There is a strong gender difference in the psychological meaning of work in our society, although it is rapidly diminishing. For the male, a major work role in adult life is assumed, and its absence would lead most to search for psychopathology. Interestingly, this is true even if there is no economic need and is different only in those from deviant subcultures or those whose lives are dominated by some other role—religious, political, etc. Women may organize their lives around work in the same way, but many still choose not to, and the choice is a socially acceptable alternative. The work of being a parent and homeworker has different meaning to most women. Although usually more important, such work is almost always less valued and of lower status. Men work because they want to or because they want the rewards that work will bring; when women work in the home, they work because the work has to be done.

If children play and adults work, adolescents, in transition, go to school. School is work, but it is work for one's own growth rather than work for survival or society or reward. A major task of adult life is to develop and to integrate a work identity, one that is integrated with other adult identities (sexual, parental, pleasure), enriches and is enriched by them, incorporates its developmental precursors of play and school, yet tolerates the constraints of reality that require that work be different from each. Finally, and perhaps most difficult, the successful adult must also integrate a work identity with an aging identity, must be able to diminish the role of work to accord with transient or progressive diminution in capacity, and yet maintain self-esteem and the capacity for pleasure.

Sex

In recent years there has been a great deal written about the sexual behavior of adults, including some beginning data concerning developmental shifts in sexual behavior during adult years. Gender differences in adult sexuality have been studied, as well as nonheterosexual patterns of gratification and the social roles associated with them. This material is much too extensive to review or summarize here, and it stems largely from descriptive studies rather than psychoanalytic ones.

Perhaps one point worth emphasizing, however, is a growing awareness that many adults have widely varying patterns of sexual behavior, often patterns that most traditional psychoanalytic thinking would label pathological or symptomatic. There are disturbances in pleasure capacity, in physiological functioning, in integration of sexual behavior with the rest of psychological life, or in the stability of sexual behavior and object choice over time. In spite of this, it is apparent that many of these individuals manage to derive considerable satisfaction from their sexual lives. One way of viewing this is to see the adult as having two developmental tasks in the area of sexuality: the first, to structure a pattern of sexual behavior that incorporates that person's biological, psychological, and social reality; the second, to integrate that pattern with the rest of the personality and to achieve maximal satisfaction from it. Much of the traditional psychoanalytic thinking about adult sexual behavior has focused on the first of these tasks, the development of a pattern of sexual behavior and the frequent pathological or deviant outcomes. The power of the adaptive and corrective mechanisms implicit in the second task have been underestimated, and their recognition may provide us with a more adequate framework for understanding adult sexuality.

Parenthood

Parenthood is an outstanding psychological, social, and, for the female, biological event of adult life. From the point of view of the species, it is the critical function necessary for survival of the genome. Parenthood is invested with a great many meanings—the culmination of a sexual act; the opportunity for vicarious rebirth and a "second chance" at one's own life; the reversal of roles experienced with one's own parents, with the possibility of failing, equaling, surpassing, defying, or undoing their parenting; the extraordinarily intimate relationship with another human being who is at first helpless and totally dependent and who ultimately becomes one's own caretaker, who represents at the same time one's own helplessness, one's mortality, and even one's potential immortality. The law has recognized parenthood as "emancipating"; certainly, cultural tradition places it second only to puberty as a formal milestone of the epochs of human life.

Of special importance to the meaning of parenthood in contemporary civilization is that it is viewed by many as a voluntary state, one that is selected and that can be avoided, rather than an inevitable event in the normative life cycle. This voluntariness results not only from the availability of contraceptive and abortive technology, but also from social attitudes toward adult lifestyles that do not include the parent role (Veevers, 1973). This means that becoming a parent, like getting married or selecting a career, is a theme of adult life long viewed as inevitable or controlled by external factors, but now seen as the result of individual decision and action. Indeed, some have suggested that this expansion of the sphere of individual choice is about to progress one step further, as modern techniques of antenatal diagnosis have made it possible for prospective parents to determine the sex of their unborn child and by selective abortion to select the gender of their offspring.

However, even though the notion that becoming a parent is a decision is quite recent, it has long been clear that there are many possibilities within the parenting role and that the style of parenting is a major theme of adult life and a major outcome of earlier development. Further, since parenting is not a simple role, but itself a process, becoming a parent is really entering on a new developmental line that continues through the rest of one's life.

These considerations would lead one to expect a major interest in parenthood by psychoanalysts, yet this has not been the case. Most of the early clinical data on which psychoanalytic theory was based stemmed from analyses of young adults who were childless, with parents being seen through the eyes of children who were patients, rather than in terms of the parenting experience itself. One result was a tendency to overemphasize pathogenic parenting, repeating Freud's earlier error of mistaking the child's remembered experience of trauma as an account of historical validity. A second result has been the neglect of parenthood as an organizing theme of adult psychological development.

Perhaps this lacuna is illustrated most clearly by the outline for Metapsychological Assessment of the Adult Personality published by Anna Freud and her colleagues in 1965. The only mention of parenthood is the question of whether the "attitude necessary for" parenthood has been achieved, categorized under Libido Distribution–Cathexis of Objects. The list of examples of specific life situations to be evaluated includes sex life, work, social relationships, etc., but not parenthood! The tendency to neglect the subject is even stronger when we consider the role of the father, although the available evidence suggests that we may have underestimated his role in development (Earls, 1976).

Benedek (1959), in her landmark article on parenthood as a developmental phase, conceptualized it as a postoedipal stage of libido development. Later she modified this view, recognizing it as a developmental process rather than a developmental phase (Parens, 1975). The parent is an actor in a familiar drama, one that he or she has lived before, but in another role. Each stage of the child's life elicits responses related to the corresponding stage of the parent's life and the conflicts and solutions associated with it. At the same time, the drama is a new one, and it is largely determined by a new character, the child. Parents must be empathically sensitive and responsive to the unique individual character of children but at the same time comfortably accept responsibility for their own personal contribution. Finally, they must recognize that the plot evolves and the child develops, as does the role of parent. The task of parenting a newborn is very different from the task of parenting an adolescent or that of an elderly parent parenting a middle-aged child.

The parent–child relationship has been of special interest to psychoanalysis because many see it as a paradigm for the analyst–patient relationship, in part related to their similar developmental characteristics, with the progression toward greater symmetry, differentiation, and a shift from dependency to autonomy in the patient–child. The corollary of this model is the parent–analyst equation, with the shifting role of the analyst at various phases of treatment.

Aging

Aging begins at conception, but it has special characteristics at each phase of the life cycle (Erikson, 1978). For the adult, aging means for the first time some diminution of capacity and potential, rather than the steady progressive increase associated with childhood. Further, the psychological meaning of death shifts in adult life (Jaques, 1965). For the child or adolescent, it is an infrequent and fearful mental image, linked to traumatic experiences and symbolically related to unconscious fantasies of punishment. For the adult, death begins to be more familiar and is gradually accepted. Friends and loved ones die; one's own death is no longer beyond the psychologically meaningful horizon of future time; and the inevitable diseases and disabilities of middle life begin to replace the child's unconscious fantasies as the symbolic equivalents of death.

The adult undergoes biological, psychological, and social changes in aging. The biological changes have been studied intensively in recent years, with particular interest in differentiating those inherent in the aging process itself from those that follow the many pathological conditions that correlate with aging. We are at the very beginning of understanding this area, but the conceptual infrastructure for important progress has been established, and with the increased social priority related to the increased number of elderly in the population, major advances should be anticipated. Some psychological changes in aging are related to the biological, such as a tendency for slower reactions to stimuli. Others are related to the role of earlier experience in determining behavior. The adult is less likely to find himself in a novel situation than the child is and more likely to develop familiar responses to familiar stimuli.

Finally, the social meanings of being an adult and then of being elderly are important features of adult life. The social significance of old age is in a state of rapid flux, joining race, gender, and physical handicap as demographic categories being redefined. There is little doubt that the growing number of elderly will assert their right to be seen as more than the human residue of mid-adult life, just as children are seen as more than the precursor, women more than the support system for men, and ethnic minorities and the handicapped more than discarded seconds. The special significance of this trend for the elderly is that aging is a universal process; a modification of its cultural role will therefore redefine a universal destiny. Cultural shifts that make old age an epoch of life to be experienced in its own right, rather than an epilogue, might well modify adult attitudes toward the aging process.

Conclusions

Adulthood is the longest phase of the developmental sequence of human life. Psychoanalysis has placed increasing emphasis on the developmental aspects of its theory. In spite of this, psychoanalysis has largely ignored adulthood from a developmental point of view. This relates to historic reasons in the origin of psychoanalytic theory; clinical reasons in the data available to psychoanalytic investigators; and scientific reasons in the power of the psychoanalytic method to add new and creative ideas to our understanding of man. However, the need for a richer theory of adult development is apparent, partly as the substrate for a theory of change and for the mechanism of action of psychoanalytic treatment. Psychoanalysis began with the study of adults. Its discovery of the unconscious roots of mental phenomena took it to the childhood origins of adult experience. Now, with this in mind, it can return to a richer understanding of adult mental life in its developmental context.

References

Benedek, T. (1959), Parenthood as a developmental phase: A contribution to the libido theory. *J. Amer. Psychoanal. Assn.*, 7:389–417.

Earls, F. (1976), The fathers (not the mothers): Their importance and influence with infants and young children. *Psychiat.*, 39:209–226.

Erikson, E. (1978), Reflections on Dr. Borg's life cycle. In: *Adulthood*, ed. E. H. Erikson. New York: Norton, pp. 1–31.

Freud, A., Nagera, H., & Freud, W. (1965), Metapsychological assessment of the adult personality: The adult profile. *The Psychoanalytic Study of the Child*, 20:9–41. New York: International Universities Press.

Jaques, E. (1965), Death and the mid-life crisis. *Internat. J. Psycho-Anal.*, 46:502–514.

Levinson, D., Darrow, C., Klein, E., Levinson, M., & McKee, B. (1978), *The Seasons of Man's Life*. New York: Knopf.

Parens, H. (1975), Panel report: Parenthood as a developmental phase. *J. Amer. Psychoanal. Assn.*, 23:154–165.

Veevers, J. (1973), The social meaning of parenthood. *Psychiat.*, 36:291–310.

2

The "Construction" of Femininity: Its Influence Throughout the Life Cycle

ETHEL SPECTOR PERSON, M.D.

> Once a parent or doctor has identified a child, always by the anatomic
> conformation of his genitals (perhaps this is the meaning of "anatomy
> becomes destiny," anatomy in conjunction with social attribution) as male
> or female, there are released the separate cultural syndromes that are
> related to the rearing of male or female children.
> —Gagnon and Simon (1973)

The course of life dictates that all of us will face certain universal developmental dilemmas and will, in the course of resolving them, take our places in the cycle of generations. Though the tools we bring to the task are shared by all of our species, the specific strategies employed will be shaped by gender. In fact, gender identity, one's sense of one's femininity or masculinity, gives rise to differences in adaptive strategies that begin in the first year of life and last throughout life.

The recent psychoanalytic focus on the psychology of women *qua* women is a welcome corrective to a badly skewed perspective dating from Freud's time. In essence, Freud had postulated that masculinity was the natural state from which the girl retreated into femininity upon the fateful discovery that she had no penis (Freud, 1924a, 1925, 1931, 1933). Subsequent to Freud, insofar as the specifics of female development and adaptive potential were considered at all—and generally they were given short shrift—they were presented as deficiencies. Obviously this perspective was not only skewed theoretically but at times injurious to the psychotherapy of women. From a clinical point of view it was therefore essential that those

15

aspects of development relating specifically to femininity be given their due.

But the new focus on the development of women has not just benefited the work done in the consulting room; it has also led to a major theoretical reformulation regarding the nature and origin of gender. As both Chodorow (1978) and Mitchell (1974) have pointed out Freud's theory that man is born while woman is made is both sexist and inconsistent. We now know that masculinity and femininity (as distinct from maleness and femaleness) are parallel constructs, not ordained by nature, but irreversibly patterned in the earliest years of life. The old paradigm that sexuality organizes gender is no longer accepted; today it appears that gender organization precedes the phallic-oedipal phase and to a large degree orders the fantasies that become attached to sexuality. All these new developments, which I will expand upon shortly, redound to the benefit of psychoanalytic theory and practice. Moreover, they confirm and extend the earliest psychoanalytic position on gender—that it is a central organizing schema in personality development. (Though personality theories differ in their understanding and description of the dynamic through which gender asserts itself, all share an implicit and unvarying assumption regarding its importance.) I would agree with Gagnon and Simon's apt for-mulation that there are two "cultural syndromes" that are uni-versal: masculinity and femininity. And I will try to demon-strate some of the ways in which the constructs of gender shape even that which we tend to think of as fundamentally biological: sexuality.

Having applauded these new developments in psychoanalytic theory, I would also urge that we understand that the emphasis on women's psychology poses problems of its own. The first problem is this: while female psychology has been accorded the status of a separate area for study, there is not yet any compara-ble emphasis on *male* psychology, because male psychology is, implicitly, the basis for our understanding of all psychological development—that is, we identify human psychology with male psychology. Inadvertently, then, while the new emphasis is in-tended to redress an imbalance—to pay attention to what has previously been ignored—the corrective in fact perpetuates the erroneous belief that male psychology is the norm and female psychology a variant.

A second and more fundamental problem has to do with the notion of the polarization of the sexes. Because Freud focused so much on sexual (libidinal) development and body ego as the primary forces in personality differentiation and maturation, psychoanalytic theory sometimes appeared to emphasize differences between the sexes at the expense of recognizing their similarities. The more recent literature, perhaps in overreaction to the earlier exclusion of specifically female developmental issues, has focused so much on differences as to suggest that there is, in the words of Marie de Gournay, Montaigne's "adoptive" daughter "not one human race but two" (Barry, 1987, p. 63). Such a view may deflect us from a full valuation and theorization of problems which are fundamentally human, rooted in humankind's nature and condition, with developmental consequences for all. I refer to some general issues of adaptation, among them the consolidation of a separate self, the relationship between self and other, the quest for meaning, and the necessity of coming to terms with one's place in the cycle of generations, including the fact of one's mortality. Solutions to life tasks may vary, but the underlying dilemmas are well-nigh universal.

To recapitulate: there are indeed valuable new contributions to the clinical and theoretical approach to female psychology. These contributions have led to a reconceptualization of the construction not just of femininity but of masculinity as well. Nonetheless our knowledge is far from complete, and our frequent overemphasis on gender differences tends to obscure what is fundamental to all human development.

Reformulating Femininity

Freud relied essentially on a single concept—that of penis envy, which he believed was the girl's inevitable response to her discovery of the anatomical difference between the sexes—to explain female psychology, including the development of sexuality, normal gender development (the acquisition of femininity), and neurotic conflict. Believing masculinity to be the natural state and femininity to be no more than the outcome of thwarted masculinity, Freud naturally assumed the feminine state was somehow deformed and diminished and that women would display life-long infantilism and immaturity as compared to men. Contemporary psychoanalysis, by contrast, takes a multidimensional point of view. In consequence, theories of the acquisition of femininity (gender identity) have been revised and are no longer prejudicial to women.

Freud (1925, 1931, 1933) believed that psychological development, essentially the same for both sexes up until the phallic phase, diverged only with the child's discovery of the anatomical differences between them—the fact that boys have penises while girls do not. Freud derived his theory of masculinity and femininity, what we now call gender identity, from what he believed were contrasts between the behavior (and mental content) of the two sexes after that discovery. In Freud's psychology, penis envy or the masculinity complex was at the center of the female psyche, whereas castration anxiety was central in the male. Freud thus postulated that femininity grew out of frustrated masculinity—the female's desire to be something she is not—and masculinity from the male's drive to preserve and enhance what he already is. Freud suggested that on discovering the sexual distinction the little girl is overcome by a sense of clitoral inferiority and the penis envy that must inevitably follow, and hence she develops the compensatory characteristics of passivity, masochism, narcissism, and dependency. These characteristics represent an attempted adaptation to (and restitution for) a profound narcissistic wound. In this view femininity is no more than a retreat from an inadequate capacity to be male. Because Freud believed that his female patients' problems were derivative of penis envy, he also believed that women's treatment was inherently limited, the cause of their problems—genital inferiority—being irreversible.

With the benefit of hindsight, we now find it puzzling that such a theory had any adherents at all, since it is evident to

mothers, nursemaids, and anyone with even moderate expo-
sure to young children that girls and boys begin to diverge in
behavior, mannerisms, and interests by 12 to 18 months of age,
much earlier than Freud theorized, and prior to the time when
children first conceptualize the difference between the sexes in
terms of a genital difference. Freud's formulation underscores
the danger of deriving developmental theories from adult analyses without validating them by observations conducted
throughout the course of infancy and childhood.

Even early on in the history of psychoanalysis, there were
alternative formulations distinct from Freud's, among them
proposals by Horney (1924, 1926, 1932, 1933) and Jones (1927,
1933, 1935), both of whom observed an early divergence between masculine and feminine behavior before the age when
children were able to conceptualize the anatomical distinction.
(Some have credited Horney's insights, in part, to her being the
mother of daughters and thus able to make observations at first
hand.)

Both Horney and Jones—in stark contrast to Freud—proposed that femininity was primary, not derivative, that it ante-
dated the phallic phase, and that it was essentially biological,
grounded in awareness of the vagina rather than in disappointment over the lack of a penis. As Jones (1935) put it, "The
ultimate question is whether a woman is born or made" (p.
273). He—and Horney—opted for the view that *both* women
and men are "born." These two theorists differed from Freud
in still another, though related, way. Whereas Freud saw the
girl's libidinal turn to the father as defensive, following upon
her defeat in not being able to possess the mother sexually,
Jones and Horney, in contrast, believed that heterosexuality
was instinctive for females as well as males. Consequently, the
girl was motivated by lust rather than envy, desiring the penis
libidinally rather than narcissistically. The claim for innate femininity was grounded in a biological assumption (erroneous, as
it turns out) of innate heterosexuality—a position that surely
has its ironies, as Horney has come to be best known for her
insights as a culturalist.

Over time, theorists have attempted to integrate information garnered in direct observation of children with more

purely psychoanalytic data. Direct observation has confirmed Horney's and Jones's contention of an early divergence between feminine and masculine development. But their explanations, grounded solely in assumptions about biology and genital awareness, have proved incorrect. Restricting ourselves to their explanations, we would be unable to account for the fact that boys with congenital absence of the penis and girls with congenital absence of the vagina are both observed to develop gender roles appropriate to their genetic sex (Stoller, 1968). Moreover, the preponderence of current research suggests that sexual object choice is acquired, not innate (Baker, 1981). This evidence suggests that Horney and Jones, like Freud, gave too much priority to anatomy, to perceptions of genitals and of genital sensations as solely determinative of gender development. While they were right in giving the same weight to "primary" femininity as to masculinity, correctly perceiving them as parallel constructs, to designate them as innate or biological is to obscure the complexity of gender development. We must look beyond Freud, and even Horney and Jones, for a fuller understanding of the sources of gender differentiation.

Some of our crucial information has come from gender studies of intersexed children. Through such studies Money, Hampson, and Hampson (1955a, 1955b, 1956) demonstrated that the initial and indispensable step in gender differentiation is the child's self-designation as male or female. This self-designation (core gender identity) evolves according to the sex of assignment; core gender is the child's resulting sense, unconscious as well as conscious, of belonging to one or the other sex. Because core gender identity is primarily related to sex of assignment it need not always correspond to biological sex. For example, a genetic male—perhaps a male child with a severe hypospadia—mistakenly assessed as female, and labeled as such at birth, will develop along feminine lines. (Because gender and biology generally correspond, it had not always been clear that core gender identity is related more closely to sex of assignment than any other single factor.) Evolving from the sex of assignment, core gender is consolidated well before the phallic phase and the child's knowledge of the anatomical distinction between the sexes: the external genitals will later confirm and symbolize core gender identity, but only after the fact.

It seems that core gender identity is for the most part cognitively and socially constructed, deriving from nonconflictual learning experience, and that it is immutable by the third year of life. (For an exception to the general rule, see a study by Imperato-McGinley, Peterson, Gautier, and Sturlar, 1979.) Once established, core gender locates the appropriate object for imitation and identification, thereby leading to the development of gender identity (masculinity or femininity), manifestations of which are observable to some extent by the end of the first year of life.

As behaviorally expressed, gender identity refers to such culturally and institutionally determined attributes as predominant interests, mannerisms, emotional responsiveness, and aggressiveness. In addition to such outward manifestations of role, the feminine-masculine polarity also organizes the individual's self-image, the belief that "I am feminine," or "I am masculine," as measured against the cultural norm; consequently, it is an important aspect of self-identity. Although its roots are laid down in the first years of life, gender identity is not a static self-representation; it continues to develop and fluctuate well into adulthood. It is a dynamic (or functional) self-representation, modified by sexual (qua sexual) development, conflict, and the self-evaluation of gender performance, which varies with the motivation and capacity to behave in accordance with the prescribed gender role at any given time (Ovesey and Person, 1973; Person and Ovesey, 1983).

There is a growing psychoanalytic consensus, then, that classical formulations failed to theorize the acquisition of core gender identity ("I am female/male") and gender identity (femininity/masculinity) in accordance with the actual chronological facts of development. The child's relatively late discovery of the anatomical differences, while important, is no longer seen as determinative per se. It has been said that it "is the study of gender identity that has offered the most important correction to Freud's theory of feminine development" (Howell, 1981, p. 16).

Gender identity now appears to be more fundamental to personality development than sexual identity is. The beginnings of gender identity are intertwined with the development of self-identity, and consequently gender identity is integral to any well-articulated concept of self. In fact, self-identity and gender identity appear to develop coterminously, to be inextricable from each other. In this sense, one can say that gender precedes sexuality in development and organizes sexuality, not the reverse (Person, 1980).

Only by learning (in the unconscious sense) their gender and identifying with the appropriate parent are children launched into the oedipal period. Freud's contention that the oedipal period is crucial to the divergent development of gender is still considered valid. But, in fact, his account tacitly assumes that the child has already achieved an appropriate core gender identity, and this assumption must now be made explicit, and the process by which it occurs be elucidated.

However, despite recent changes in our understanding of what constitutes femininity, psychoanalysts have not rejected those factors previously considered determinative for gender identity; they have simply reassessed them. Genital sensations, genital self-stimulation, the discovery of the sexual distinction, castration anxiety, penis envy, and the Oedipus complex are all still viewed as important factors, but it is now recognized that chronologically they do not come first, nor do they completely account either for the fact of gender divergence or for the *content* of either femininity or masculinity.

Moreover, other factors are now weighed in for their influence on the shape of gender. (I am focusing here on *psychological* factors; but one must be aware also of the influence of hormones, particularly at critical junctures in the life cycle.) Early object relations are different in the two sexes and appear to influence certain attributes of femininity and masculinity. Object relations are now considered to be operative in the preoedipal identifications and fantasies that emerge as soon as the child has differentiated self from object. Investigators from different disciplines have focused on those differences in infantile object relations implicit in the almost exclusive female monopoly of child care—the fact that girls are raised by the same sex parent, boys by the opposite sex parent. Stoller, following a lead by Greenson, emphasizes the need for the boy, unlike the girl, to disidentify from the mother. Basing his conclusions on his work with transsexuals, he suggests a normal state of protofemininity for both sexes. Consequently, he assumes a greater fragility in the male sense of gender and a tendency to overcompensate by a kind of masculine protest. Feminist theorists, such as Nancy Chodorow, also emphasize the male's defensive posture revealed in his hypertrophied sense of boundaries, but focus more on the vulnerabilities implicit in female individuation. Thus, Stoller and the feminists, both proponents of asymmetrical parenting as critical to the development of gender, come to opposite conclusions about its impact, Stoller focusing on the fragility of male gender identity, Chodorow on the impairment to female individuation and the sense of a separate self. Despite their disagreement as to the precise impact of the asymmetric preoedipal situation, most contemporary theorists recognize that it presents different potential threats and conflicts (as well as strengths) to the two sexes. In sum, then, theorists posit learning, identification, asymmetric preoedipal situations, and still other factors—in addition to the genital difference—as the important building blocks of gender identity.

What, then, of the *content* of femininity in our culture, of its directives and prescriptions? Many commentators have noted the female tendency to communion as contrasted to the male tendency to autonomy, to connectedness over separation, to caretaking over instrumentality, and so forth. And they have assumed that the commitment to relationships—perhaps even specifically to motherhood—may ultimately organize femininity. Yet this formulation, too, seems oversimplistic; even if descriptively true, it does not adequately theorize the *origins* of these central commitments. Are the causal events to be located solely in discrepancies in object relations, as is so often assumed? (Of course, similar questions must be raised about the origins of the masculine commitment to agency, instrumentality, etc.) One must be especially cautious here, because the content of gender identity is so culturally variable.

Naturally, the concept of "normalcy" or appropriate femininity colors how clinicians regard women and how women regard themselves. Our changing conceptualizations of the origins of gender (and the content of gender role) have had many implications for theories of normative femininity and hence for clinical work, and this in two major ways. First, our evaluation of many "feminine" characteristics has been upgraded; take, for example, Gilligan's work (1982) on the differences between men and women in the hierarchy of values informing their moral judgments—a difference which she refuses to reduce to any simplistic notion of better or worse, higher or lower. Second, the range of "acceptable" behavior for women has been enormously expanded. In a classic paper, Broverman, Broverman, Clarkson, Rosenkrantz, and Vogel (1970) convincingly argued that mental health professionals restricted to Freud's theoretical formulations were in the unhappy position of reinforcing popular biases about women rather than challenging them, sanctioning dependency and passivity as normal female qualities and independence and assertiveness as normal male qualities. Accordingly, until recently, mental health professionals sometimes attributed any dissatisfaction women expressed concerning their traditional role to penis envy and psychopathology and naturally enough encouraged their women patients to cleave to paths tried and true.

With the current reformulations, "femininity" has been freed from its stereotypical description as necessarily passive, masochistic, dependent, and narcissistic in content. The content of femininity is now regarded as multidetermined, with major input from cultural prescriptions as well as early object relations. Given that the content of femininity is now seen as shaped by so many external sources, with that portion of it viewed as innate correspondingly reduced, there are no longer any compelling theoretical reasons for seeing any inherent restrictions on women's creativity and autonomy. Consequently, modern theory does not view female prospects (in life or in therapy) as intrinsically limited, as Freud's theory explicitly posited. Nor is femininity any longer viewed as a kind of deficient masculinity. Instead, femininity and masculinity are now seen as parallel constructs. And now, for the first time, we can scrutinize more dispassionately the creative and the constricting aspects of both feminine traits and masculine ones. (We are still only beginning to explore the special problems men face by virtue of those traits characteristic of masculine gender identity.)

Female Sexuality

Theories of female sexuality have been just as radically revised as those of gender. And here, too, as in the case of gender, these changes in theory have operated in tandem with changing social attitudes about sexuality. And these changes have had important practical results in women's lives.

Freud had hypothesized that female sexuality, compared to male sexuality, must necessarily be weak or hyposexual, given the girl's need to switch both object (from mother to father) and organ (from clitoris to vagina) and her disparagement of her own genitals as compared to the boy's genitals. According to Freud, penis envy was decisive not only in the development of femininity but in normal sexual development too. Penis envy was responsible for the girl's turn away from her mother (renouncing the clitoris as inadequate and blaming the mother for her inadequate endowment) and toward her father (to get a penis from him). Such a double switch was believed to result necessarily in diminished libido, in essence, a weak sex drive. This theory appeared to be substantiated by the inability of so many women patients to achieve orgasm. But even in the early years of psychoanalysis, Clara Thompson was able to identify a more pervasive problem for women in obtaining sexual gratification. She believed that woman's major sexual dilemma was not caused by penis envy but by the selectively restrictive culture (1950). Following Thompson's lead, more and more theoretical attention has been paid to the pervasive cultural prohibitions against female sexuality.

Simultaneous with the exposé of the cultural prejudices against female sexuality, theorists and researchers have reformulated their concepts in this area. The crucial role of clitoral eroticism in adult women, as demonstrated by Masters and Johnson (1966) and others, has led to a repudiation of Freud's theory of clitoral–vaginal transfer. Today, very few continue to hold to the view that true femininity depends on achieving vaginal orgasm. Nor is female sexuality any longer viewed as necessarily debilitated.

There is much more recognition that maximum sexual pleasure often depends on adequate clitoral stimulation and that such stimulation is not always (or even most often) an automatic outcome of heterosexual coitus. Together with significant changes in sexual attitudes and behavior, this knowledge has permitted more women to find sexual fulfillment than ever before, a major benefit of the scientific studies of sex.

In addition, sexuality has been freed from the constraints of a stereotypical nineteenth-century view of femininity, with its emphasis on female submissiveness to male preferences. (This submissiveness has been plausible only because of the female commitment to bonding, to relationship, and to identity construed as the self-in-relationship.) Female sexual inhibition was often based on intimidation by the male and deference to him. Inhibitions were manifested in a repertoire of related behaviors and attitudes such as the lack of insistence on adequate stimulation, the practice of faking orgasm, the assumption that the male orgasm terminated the sexual encounter, and the excessive attention paid to pleasing rather than being pleasured (Dinnerstein, 1977; Person, 1980). As it has turned out, many so-called frigid women have no major unconscious conflicts that inhibit either sexual arousal or orgasm. They suffer instead from ignorance about what constitutes appropriate stimulation (often matched by their lovers' ignorance of female sexuality) or from interpersonal intimidation. Apparent sexual inhibitions often begin to resolve themselves when these women achieve a sense of personal autonomy and, as a result, greater self-assertiveness. The result of such an achievement is not simply greater sexual pleasure for women but a significant redefinition of the female-male bond.

Surprisingly enough, some psychiatrists persist in minimizing the benefits of the sexual revolution for women. They suggest that what we see are merely behavioral changes, while the underlying wishes and conflicts remain unchanged. Such an argument denies the importance of orgasm per se, its power to reaffirm the "incontrovertible truth" of the reality of personal existence (Lichtenstein, 1961; see also Eissler, 1958b; Person, 1980). Liberated sexual behavior among women provides both sexual pleasure and a foundation for increased self-esteem. The potential released by changes in sexuality may thus result in a transformation transcending the strictly sexual.

But what have we learned of the basic "nature" of female sexuality? Just as femininity was once viewed as the result of thwarted masculinity, so, too, was female sexuality seen as a kind of inhibited male sexuality. Insofar as female sexuality is now "liberated," we can now better address the question of the degree to which unfettered female sexuality resembles male sexuality or, rather, obeys its own laws.

Feminists themselves are not in consensus about the answers. Some favor the presumably egalitarian view that the sexualities are essentially identical; others contend that they are necessarily disparate. According to Simone de Beauvoir (quoted by Fuchs, 1980), there is more to eroticism than any mere collection of genital facts: "there will always be certain differences between man and woman; her eroticism, and therefore her sexual world, have a special form of their own and therefore cannot fail to engender a sensuality, a sensitivity, of a special nature. This means that her relations to her own body, to that of the male, to the child, will never be identical with those [of] the male . . ." (p. 311). Fuchs suggests that Beauvoir was on the verge of making a necessary connection between woman's body and form and her eroticism, a task she sees as essential to a female erotic. This feminist position comes very close to the psychoanalytic focus on the importance of the body ego in psychological development.

In contrast, the egalitarian view finds support in the discovery by Masters and Johnson that female and male sexual response cycles are similar, even down to the timing of orgasmic contractions, and derives further plausibility from the evidence that androgen is the "libidinal" hormone in both sexes. But this latter view is only manifestly egalitarian. In truth, it sees sexuality as basically masculine; that is, male sexuality is believed to come closer to expressing human sexuality uncorrupted by cultural or psychological constraints.[1]

_____

[1]Such a view tends to obscure the fact that certain aspects of male sexuality, which long were believed to reflect a biological or instinctual impera-

In fact, although there are some strong resemblances between the two sexualities, there are also major differences. Some of these differences are biological, but as contemporary sex theorists know, sexuality is not so completely defined by biology as was once imagined. It obviously has a biology and biological limits, but sex, like gender, shows cultural and historical variability. As Foucault (1978) has demonstrated, the individual's experience of sexuality has a historical component (over and beyond one's personal history). Some of the current changes in the theory and practice of sex permit us a closer look at the way gender shapes the expression of sexuality within the limits biology imposes.

Viable theories of female and male sexualities must recognize and give proper weight to differences that appear to be the result of a biological imperative, but they must also acknowledge differences engendered by gender identity and by the prescriptions of a particular culture. Overall, these differences are so great, at present, as to suggest that there are not only two separate sexual biologies, but two separate sexual "cultures," as well. To some degree, females and males inhabit two separate sexual worlds. In this chapter I can only begin to allude to some of these differences—and the ways in which they appear to be shaped by both biology and the prescriptions of gender.

It is useful, in this regard, to distinguish among the various components of sexuality. The sexes differ in sexual behavior, eroticism, and primacy of sexuality. *Sexual behavior* refers to those formal characteristics which are observable, sometimes measurable, and relatively "objective." (It is in this area that one sees the greatest impress of biology.) *Eroticism* has to do with the realm of the subjective and psychological, of desire and excitement as experienced. According to Beauvoir, it is that dimension of human experience that has to do with the sexual, but in conjunction with a lived experience, not a collection of genital facts (Fuchs, 1980). (And, of course, it is here that one sees the greatest impress from gender identity and

---

tive—just as masculinity was believed to be innate—are, in fact, actively shaped by society's prevailing definitions of masculinity. The assumption that the expression of sexuality—by either sex—is culture-free is naive.

cultural variability.) The *primacy of sexuality* refers to how central sexuality is to the personality, how closely related it is to identity. (And this appears to be heavily influenced by both biology and the psychological aspects of gender.)

Formal Aspects of Sexual Behavior

Certain formal similarities between men's and women's sexual response cycle and the orgasm have been demonstrated: these similarities have been most emphasized by Masters and Johnson (1966). Yet this is not the only dimension of sexual behavior. As Symons (1979) puts it, "Men and women differ far less in their potential physiological and psychological responses during sexual activities per se than they do in how they negotiate sexual activities and in the kinds of sexual relationships and interactions they are motivated to seek"(p. 179).

Specifically, the sexes differ in what is commonly called drive behavior. Female sexuality, often considered less robust than that of the male, is sometimes designated hyposexual. This means that females are thought to display low "drive" or appetitive behavior compared to males or, in another frame of reference, that the male threshold for sexual release is lower. In recent years, however, it has been recognized that the trajectories of "drive" are different in the sexes, the male peak occurring in the teen years, the female in middle life. Females may end up with as much sexual interest or "drive" as males, or even more. But for many this is consolidated later and remains tied to relational preoccupations.

It is during the adolescent years, particularly in the induction into genital sexuality, that the most striking differences in "drive" behavior are manifested. (Although genital activity may begin prior to adolescence, according to Kinsey, only one-fifth of males and one-tenth of females experience orgasm prior to age twelve.) In males, adolescence is characterized by the beginning of overt sexual activity. The hormonal shifts of puberty cause bodily changes which focus attention on emerging sexuality and frequently result in spontaneous arousal and orgasm. The frequency of spontaneous ejaculation in adolescent males almost insures the integration of genital sexuality into male psychosexual development and fantasy life. Thus the male sex drive does seem tied to a biological imperative.

But the situation appears different for girls. Spontaneous orgasm is relatively rare in female adolescents. For them the most explicit manifestation of their developing sexuality is menstruation, and menstruation often tends to inhibit, not enhance, sexual exploration, both for symbolic reasons and because of the threat of pregnancy. Masturbation is not practiced by the majority of adolescent girls prior to their introduction to interpersonal sexuality; whether this is because of cultural inhibitions or biological differences is not clear.[2] (The study of female masturbation in future generations may help to clarify this issue, particularly the study of women who came of age after the advent of the women's movement.)[3]

Low female drive is thought to be demonstrated by the relatively low rates of adolescent masturbation, the tendency for sexuality to be first awakened in the context of an interpersonal relationship and to remain tied to intimacy, the ability to tolerate inorgasmia, and the chronologically late achievement of

---

[2] Typically, males achieve arousal and orgasm earlier. In males over 80 percent have masturbated to orgasm by age fifteen, whereas only 20 percent of females have done so (Kinsey's data reported by Gagnon and Simon [1973]). This discrepancy is still apparent in data collected twenty years later (Gagnon and Simon, 1973). According to this data, masturbation in females is more erratic than it is in males; in females only about two-thirds ever masturbate to orgasm and, of those, half discover masturbation after having been introduced to orgasm in an interpersonal context.

There may be some small shift in recent years toward greater female masturbation, but most studies reveal the same predominance of male masturbation. Sorenson (1979) found that 58 percent of boys and 39 percent of girls of all ages had masturbated at least once and that boys masturbated more frequently. Arafat and Cotton (1979) conclude that "the percentages of both males and females who masturbate appear to approximate the figures given by Kinsey . . ." (p. 113). Hunt (1979) suggests that his figures approximate Kinsey's but that there may be a small overall increase. In contrast, the sexual difference in coital behavior (age and incidence) has tended to disappear.

[3] Ford and Beach (1951) claim that, in all human societies which have been studied, "males are more likely than females to stimulate their own sexual organs" (p. 199). Further, in both lower mammals and primates there is relatively little female masturbation. Consequently, Ford and Beach support an "evolutionary" or biological component. With the same data available, Gagnon and Simon (1973) form a cultural interpretation. Psychological interpretations abound as well.

first orgasm in many women. Further, female sexuality appears relatively fragile because it is so often variable or erratic, and because orgasm may be completely suppressed in such a wide variety of historical and personal circumstances. By these criteria, the female sex drive appears less a biological imperative than that of males, and more a learned dynamic grounded in psychological motivation.

However, drive behavior cannot be the only measure of sexuality. The capacity for responsiveness and orgasmic discharge, usually referred to as consummatory behavior, is greater in women: only women are capable of multiple orgasms, for example. Are we then to conclude that our scientific (and psychoanalytic) bias accords greater weight to drive than to consummatory behavior? It is otherwise difficult to understand how women's sexuality could be considered deficient, or hyposexual, relative to men's.

Hormonal Differences

Insofar as hormonal differences account for sexual differences, they are probably most influential in affecting the formal characteristics of sexuality. In humans, this conclusion is largely based on studies of patients with some characteristics of intersex conditions—for example, the follow-up of girls born with the andrenogenital syndrome (AGS). In AGS girls, the adrenal cortex does not synthesize cortisol but releases too much androgen, which is the hormone believed to account for masculine sexuality. These girls are born with genital masculinization. Even when operated on at birth (surgically feminized), they are different from matched controls in quite specific ways: they display higher physical energy, prefer rough play, live as tomboys, are career oriented, and show low maternal rehearsals (doll play). In other words, there seems to be a hormonal component to some of the behaviors that comprise gender identity. As regards the biologically influenced aspects of sexuality per se, the sexuality of late-treated AGS women is of interest. These women tend toward a sexuality more typically masculine than feminine as regards formal characteristics: they have more erotic dreams resulting in orgasm than control females, they are more responsive to visual stimuli, and they display what investigators have portrayed as high sex drive (for a good summary statement, see Symons, 1979). However, they do not view themselves as masculine in either gender or sexuality. Their erotic fantasy preoccupations correspond more to feminine than to masculine ones and in fact they were disturbed by, and glad to be rid of, those manifestations of typically masculine sexuality that they themselves viewed as masculine—their clitoral hypersensitivity and tendency toward initiating eroticism (Money, 1961). In their ultimate consolidation of gender identity they adapt to "feminine" norms. According to Money (1965), "the imagery of the erotic thoughts and desires is all suitably feminine in keeping with the sex of rearing and the psychosexual identity" (p. 9). These studies seem to demonstrate considerable override of socialization on hormonal predisposition, at least as regards eroticism.

Thus, while some of the studies on pseudohermaphroditic or intersexed patients establish the primacy of endocrines in shaping certain formal characteristics of sexuality (and of personality traits as well), they also establish the primacy of socialization (in its widest sense) in shaping the overall content and direction of gender identity and eroticism.

Eroticism

When we turn to eroticism, particularly fantasy life, we have less rigorous information, but here we are more clearly in the realm of the psychological—the arena in which sexuality is most obviously influenced by gender and personal history.[4]

---

[4]Part of the patterning in sexuality clearly comes from gender socialization and prescriptions of role. Women and men vary along gender lines in cognitive and perceptual styles, predominant defenses, and goals. Lewis (1971) finds women to be field-dependent and more prone to feelings of shame (that is, of not living up to internalized ideals) and to depression, whereas men are field-independent and more likely to transgress and to react with guilt. Women tend to hysterical defenses, men to obsessive and paranoid ones. Women are affiliative, men oriented to status and power. According to Bakan (1966), women are trained to communion, men to agency. These basic differences in thinking and adaptive modalities are reflected in typical sex fantasies and in the meanings that attach to sexual behavior.

Nonetheless, there are differences that may have a biological predisposition. The only major statistical analysis of fantasies was done by Kinsey, Pomeroy, and Martin (1948, 1953). They discovered that not only the content but also the formal attributes of sexual fantasies vary with gender. So, for

Both sexes fantasize predominantly about their erotic preferences, be these heterosexual, homosexual, or sadomasochistic. Since male erotic preferences are more varied (e.g., perversions occur in more abundance and diversity among men), so too are their fantasies, and men appear to generate more sexual fantasies than do women (Person, Terestman, Myers, Goldberg, and Borenstein, 1989; Person, Terestman, Myers, Goldberg, and Borenstein, 1992).

Male erotic fantasies are usually explicitly sexual. They portray domination. In one questionnaire study done by the Fantas Project at Columbia Psychoanalytic, 44 percent of the male subject had domination fantasies (Person et al., 1989). And male fantasies are often impersonal; autonomy, mastery, and physical prowess are central concerns. However, male fantasies may also be submissive or masochistic. In fact, Freud (1924b) first described "feminine" masochism as it occurred in men. A common theme in male sexual fantasies is that of sex with two women; a lesbian scene is almost a prerequisite in heterosexual pornographic films. (For a object relations interpretation of this phenomenon, see Person [1986].) Barclay (1973), in a study on the sexual fantasies of men and women at Michigan State University, noted that "male fantasies sounded like features of Playboy Magazine or pornographic books, and included elaborate descriptions of the imagined sexual partner. . . . They were stereotyped . . . without personal involvement. Women are always seductive and forward, ready to have intercourse at any time . . . [with a] major emphasis on highly visual imagery" (p. 209).

Turning to women, Barclay (1973) reports that, in contrast to men, "all these women reported that the imaginary person in the sexual fantasy was a man whose face resembled someone

---

example, most males both fantasize during masturbation and have nocturnal sex dreams. By contrast, over one-third of the females did not fantasize during masturbation; fantasy occurred more frequently in older females. Perhaps this correlates with the finding that females tend to fantasize about what has actually occurred; males more frequently fantasize about unfulfilled desires. Although fewer women than men have sexual dreams accompanied by orgasm, more can reach orgasm by fantasy alone. Both sexes may use fantasy to control levels of excitement during intercourse.

they knew or were close to" (p. 210). Female fantasies are often thought to be masochistic. The data base to which the label "feminine" masochism is attached has never been fully elucidated, but the term is used loosely to apply to the frequency of slave, prostitute, rape, beating, and humiliation fantasies elicited during analyses (Person, 1974). However, in the data reported by Person et al. (1989) about 10 percent of both sexes reported masochistic fantasies.

Female sexual fantasies generally are more varied than is usually acknowledged. Femme fatale fantasies, for example, often reveal a wish to dominate. Among women, affiliative and romantic fantasies, with or without any manifestly sexual content, are just as common as more obviously and explicitly sexual ones, and should be included in the erotic repertoire. Many fantasies that do not on the surface appear to be sexual—for example, the not uncommon nurse fantasies (taking care of injured or debilitated men)—may be experienced as erotic. Pregnancy and breast feeding fantasies are other examples. As reported by Barclay (1973), ". . . caring for someone was probably the most common of all themes. Our original hypothesis was that caring or nurturant fantasies were not sexual, but so many of our female subjects reported them with masturbatory activity or coupled with intercourse that we were compelled to accept them as having the same degree of sexual connotation as the more explicit sexual fantasies reported by men" (pp. 211–212).

More important, unconscious fantasies reveal the impact of the specific female (or male) oedipal configuration. Women and men present manifestations of different unconscious desires and, thus, different conflicts, rivalries, and longings. These differences in unconscious fantasy are too well known to require further elaboration. Overall, it is in the area of eroticism, in the content of the conscious and unconscious fantasies that elicit and accompany desire, that we see the greatest impact of gender identity on sexuality. This is particularly apparent in the male tendency to domination fantasies, a product of both gender socialization and the male developmental experience (Person, 1986).

The influence of gender identity on eroticism has been demonstrated by pseudohermaphrodite studies, some of them already discussed. It has been observed that the few genetic males who are misdiagnosed and raised as females grow up dreaming the dreams of women; similarly, misdiagnosed women dream the dreams of men. Gender identity launches the individual onto a particular psychosexual pathway; it is decisive for the shape of the oedipal configuration, which is the crucial event in acculturation and provides the content for much of fantasy life (the specific wishes and fears, rivalries, and longings of unconscious life). Biology (genetic sex), as it turns out, is not necessarily determinative for core gender, gender identity, or certain aspects of sexuality.

It seems, then, that in the area of eroticism, the psychological development of gender identity overrides that of biology and may have more to do with organizing sexuality than does biology (Person, 1980; Person and Ovesey, 1983). Only by learning their gender and identifying with the appropriate parent can children proceed into the oedipal period. To say that gender orders sexuality is not to detract from the autonomous qualities of sexuality (some of which are no doubt biologically mandated) or from interactions between sexuality and gender. This formulation emphasizes that gender, itself the result of postnatal events, organizes object choice and sexual fantasies, which then become linked to the experience of genital pleasure.

Primacy of Sexuality

Another major distinction between the sexes is in the primacy of sexuality, the way in which sexuality is tied to perceptions of the self. The male more frequently views sexuality as self-enhancing and self-defining, whereas the female views it as affiliative and imbued with interpersonal meaning. This difference is reflected in the male appetite for pornography, the female one for Harlequin and Silhouette romances. The difference is not between domination and submission, but between the desire for control (for men) and for bonding (for women); between sex first experienced as an autonomous act and sex first experienced as interpersonally meaningful. This difference in the subjective significance of sex may help to explain the common observation that men are more promiscuous and display a greater interest in partner variation. While this particular pattern is shifting, with some women adopting the so-called male pattern, many women still value monogamy. Certain authors have taken this difference as fundamental to the sexes; Symons (1979) goes so far as to claim that it reflects a genetic difference, and there surely may be a biological component. But it is easy to relate differences on the promiscuity–monogamy continuum to sexual meaning, and to investigate the developmental process by which sexuality comes to represent autonomy for males, attachment for females, without resorting to an exclusively biological explanation. Sexuality constitutes but one of the numerous forums in which the female gender prescription toward affiliation asserts itself; and the male interest in "variety" likewise seems to have some psychological roots (Person, 1986).

There is a wealth of clinical evidence to suggest that, in this culture, genital sexual activity is a prominent feature in the maintenance of a sense of masculine gender, while it is a variable one as regards feminine gender (Person, 1980). Thus, an impotent man always feels that his masculinity, and not just his sexuality, is threatened. In men, gender appears to "lean" on sexuality. It is almost impossible to locate a man who has never achieved orgasm, by any route whatsoever, who does not have significant psychopathology. In many males, the value accorded sexual performance is so great that performance anxiety is the leading cause of secondary impotence. However, for a woman, the issue of whether or not she is orgasmic—or sexually active—while extremely important may have fewer implications for her personality organization. Put another way, there is a difference between men and women in the primacy they accord sexuality—at least in this culture. In men, one can say that sexuality is a mainstay of gender and of self-worth. In women, gender identity and self-worth can more easily be consolidated by other means. This difference in the relationship between genital sexuality and gender may be the single most telling distinction between female and male sexuality, and may be another manifestation of the masculine emphasis on performance and the female emphasis on bonding as confirmations of gender identity.

Cultural dictates regarding femininity and masculinity can shape the expression or inhibition of sexuality, as exemplified by the Victorian suppression of female sexuality. The ultimate consolidation of sexual identity (as distinct from gender identity) rests on the attainment of an actualized sex life, characterized both by the assumption of a sociosexual role and the achievement of sexual gratification. Sexual role is most accurately thought of as a sociosexual role, one assumed by the individual to indicate that she or he is following sexual expectations appropriate to the surrounding society or culture. As culturally defined and reinforced by gender identity, sexual role is extremely significant, sometimes even taking priority over subjective desire when the two are in conflict.

The fact that in sex one is both the desiring subject and someone else's desired object makes the attainment of sexual identity necessarily complicated and elusive. And here the difference between the sexes is striking. Whereas both subject and object self-identifications play a role in sexual identity for both sexes, one or the other facet is more typically exaggerated, to the impoverishment of the other—the male more often over-identifying as subject, the female as object (Person, 1985). Both are diminished by these distortions, for extreme self-typing as subject or object leads to a marred or incomplete sexual identity. But for women in many historical periods, our own by no means excluded, the overemphasis on being a desired object, together with culturally selective restrictions, has affected sexual identity so much that the very ability to experience sexual pleasures has often been inhibited. This phenomenon of inhibited sexuality has in turn come to be perceived as peculiarly—and innately—feminine. The result is that an unfortunate misperception is even more unfortunately perpetuated.

The Conceptual Limitations of a Gendered Psychology

Thus far I have described the ways in which the study of women as separate from men has profited us, both clinically

and theoretically. We have seen that biological sex (the male/
female polarity) does not invariably translate out into specific
characteristics of gender identity (the masculinity/femininity
polarity). This is borne out by the fact that though there is
always, in every culture, a dichotomy between what is considered masculine and what feminine, the *content* of what is masculine or feminine is culturally variable. Moreover, even within a
given culture each individual will display a mixture of traits
generally considered either masculine or feminine.

What is still needed, however, is a theory of gender that
integrates object relations, the symbolic investment of the genitals, and sexual differences, along with the cultural perspective.
We have made some progress in that respect. Though we do
not yet have a coherent theory of gender, we have recognized
the importance of factors as diverse as biological differences,
learning, power relations, scripting, socialization, sex-discrep-
ant expectations that shape fantasies, and guiding myths in the
formation of gender role, in addition to what we have already
learned from the standard psychoanalytic formulation about
the importance of body awareness, sexual distinction, and the
vagaries of the Oedipus complex.

But there are issues even more fundamental than how gender is formed and how its specific contents are shaped within
a given culture. The fact that the dichotomy of gender is universal, though its contents are not, raises complex developmental
and psychoanalytic questions that cannot be reduced to a simple
cultural perspective. What is not truly understood is the habit
of mind by which most cultures, perhaps all, acknowledge *two*
genders. The question, then, is why only these two gender possibilities exist. Modern biology has broken down the components that together constitute "sexuality," and it is clear that a
number of intersexes exist; essentially, however, we still regard
sex as either male or female. Similarly, we come to identify
ourselves as *either* and *only* masculine or feminine (though not
always adequately so, as revealed, for example, in the statement,
"I think I'm not really masculine enough"). Though, in fact,
traits associated with gender show different patterning in each
individual, we still think in terms of masculine and feminine as

somehow being opposites. Given the fact that gender is profoundly related to, if not determined by, one's sex, perhaps the question should be not why there are only two genders, but why we are so insistent on choosing between them. It is the *rigidity* of the gender division that is most disquieting, the degree to which we are invested in making black-and-white distinctions as to gender, the insistence within any given culture on maintaining these distinctions (even though their *content* varies greatly from culture to culture). The problem of gender, then, is a question not only of two-ness but of either/or-ness.

Be that as it may, the two most important categories by which young children appear to self-identify are age and sex. Age is mutable (though the young hardly think so), but sex (except for transsexuals) is not. Around the sexual difference we construct rules of fairly strict conformity to our culture's designation of what constitutes appropriate masculinity and femininity (the more so the younger we are). Seeing how sexually determined the range of narratives allowed to people in all cultures is—however much those narratives differ from culture to culture—we are all the more forcibly reminded of the rigidity of gender division. We seem to suffer a cognitive limitation that affords room for two categories only—same and different, male and female, masculine and feminine, either/or.

This dichotomy in the way we view ourselves (and the world) translates into an unfortunate judgmental tendency when we compare the different trajectories in the development of male and female. First one theory, then the other, wants to give the advantage—or disadvantage—to one sex or the other. (Hence, for Freud, the girl suffers because she must switch her libidnal object; for Stoller, the boy suffers because he must disidentify; and so on.) When this happens, too great a focus on gender can come to interfere with our sense of the essential unity of humankind. Our fundamental dilemmas are more alike than different. Each of us is bounded (trapped) by our own subjective experience, yet in need of congress with an other. We all suffer from conflicts, unfulfilled yearnings, embittered defeats, and we all share envy, jealousy, fear, and rage as part of our emotional heritage—along with our capacities for love, altruism, and all the happy outcomes and emotions. The battle of the sexes is often no more than a skirmish in a much larger struggle—the universalized love–hate relationship between the self and the other (of whatever age and gender). The problems of the separate self (and the need for relationship), of autonomy and communion, of the need for meaning, and of the threat of oblivion, ultimately transcend the fact of gender. But gender becomes a scaffolding for self-identity and predisposes to specific adaptive strategies consonant with our "appropriate gender." When such strategies conflict with the fullest expression of our humanity—as they sometimes do—then we are diminished, not simply defined, by gender.

References

Arafat, I.S., & Cotton, W.L. (1979), Masturbation practices of college males and females. In: *Human Autoerotic Practices*, ed. M.F. DeMartino. New York: Human Sciences Press, pp. 104–115.

Bakan, D. (1966), *The Duality of Human Existence: Isolation and Communion in Western Man*. Boston: Beacon Press.

Baker, S. (1981), Biological influences on human sex and gender. In: *Women: Sex and Sexuality*, ed. C.R. Stimpson & E.S. Person. Chicago: University of Chicago Press, pp. 175–191.

Barclay, A.M. (1973), Sexual fantasies in men and women. *Medical Aspects of Human Sexuality*, 7(5):205–216.

Barry, J. (1987), *French Lovers: From Heloise and Abelard to Beauvoir and Sartre*. New York: Arbor House.

Beach, F.A. (1976), Cross-species comparisons and the human heritage. In: *Human Sexuality in Four Perspectives*, ed. F.A. Beach. Baltimore: Johns Hopkins University Press, pp. 296–316.

Broverman, I.K., Broverman, D.M., Clarkson, F.E., Rosenkrantz, P.S., & Vogel, S.R. (1970), Sex-role stereotypes and clinical judgments of mental health. *J. Consult. & Clin. Psychol.*, 34:1–7.

Chodorow, N. (1978), *The Reproduction of Mothering: Psychoanalysis and the Sociology of Gender*. Berkeley: University of California Press.

Dinnerstein, D. (1977), *The Mermaid and the Minotaur: Sexual Arrangements and Human Malaise*. New York: Harper Colophon.

Eissler, K. (1958a), Notes on problems of technique in the psychoanalytic treatment of adolescents: With some remarks on perversions. *The Psychoanalytic Study of the Child*, 13:223–254. New York: International Universities Press.

—— (1958b), Problems of identity. *J. Amer. Psychoanal. Assn.*, 6:131–142.

Ford, C.S., & Beach, F.A. (1951), *Patterns of Sexual Behavior*. New York: Harper.

Foucault, M. (1978), *The History of Sexuality: Vol. 1. An Introduction*. New York: Random House.

Freud, S. (1923), The ego and the id. *Standard Edition*, 19:12–66. London: Hogarth Press, 1961.

———— (1924a), The dissolution of the Oedipus complex. *Standard Edition*, 19:173–179. London: Hogarth Press, 1961.

———— (1924b), The economic problem in masochism. *Standard Edition*, 19:157–170. London: Hogarth Press, 1961.

———— (1925), Some psychical consequences of the anatomical differences between the sexes. *Standard Edition*, 19:248–258. London: Hogarth Press, 1961.

———— (1931), Female sexuality. *Standard Edition*, 21:223–243. London: Hogarth Press, 1961.

———— (1933), Femininity. *Standard Edition*, 22:112–135. London: Hogarth Press, 1961.

Fuchs, J.P. (1980), Female eroticism. *The Second Sex: Feminist Studies*, 6:307–313.

Gagnon, J.H., & Simon, W. (1973), *Sexual Conduct: Social Sources of Human Sexuality*. Chicago: Aldine.

Gilligan, C. (1982), *In a Different Voice: Psychological Theory and Women's Development*. Cambridge: Harvard University Press.

Horney, K. (1924), On the genesis of the castration complex in women. *Internat. J. Psycho-Anal.*, 5:50–65.

———— (1926), The flight from womanhood: The masculinity-complex in women, as viewed by men and women. *Internat. J. Psycho-Anal.*, 7:324–339.

———— (1932), The dread of women: Observations on a specific difference in the dread felt by men and by women respectively for the opposite sex. *Internat. J. Psycho-Anal.*, 13:348–360.

———— (1933), The denial of the vagina: A contribution to the problem of the genital anxieties specific to women. *Internat. J. Psycho-Anal.*, 14:57–70.

Howell, E. (1981), Women from Freud to the present. In: *Women and Mental Health*, ed. E. Howell & M. Bayes. New York: Basic Books.

Hunt, M. (1979), Changes in masturbatory attitudes and behavior. In: *Human Autoerotic Practices*, ed. M.F. DeMartino. New York: Human Sciences Press, pp. 231–248.

Imperato-McGinley, J., Peterson, R.E., Gauthier, T., & Sturla, E. (1979), Androgens and the evolution of male gender identity among male pseudohermaphrodites with 5a-Reductase deficiency. *New Engl. J. Med.*, 300:1233–1237.

Jones, E. (1927), The early development of female sexuality. *Internat. J. Psycho-Anal.*, 8:459–472.

———— (1933), The phallic phase. *Internat. J. Psycho-Anal.*, 14:1–33.

———— (1935), Early female sexuality. *Internat. J. Psycho-Anal.*, 16:263–275.

Kinsey, A.C., Pomeroy, W.R., & Martin, C.E. (1948), *Sexual Behavior in the Human Male*. Philadelphia: Saunders.

———— ———— ———— Gebhard, P.H. (1953), *Sexual Behavior in the Human Female*. Philadelphia: Saunders.

Lewis, H. (1971), *Shame and Guilt in Neurosis*. New York: International Universities Press.

Lichtenstein, H. (1961), Identity and sexuality. In: *The Dilemma of Human Identity*. New York: Aronson, 1977, pp. 49–126.

Masters, W.H., & Johnson, V.E. (1966), *Human Sexual Response*. Boston: Little, Brown.

Mitchell, J. (1974), *Psychoanalysis and Feminism*. New York: Pantheon Books.

Money, J. (1961), Sex hormones and other variables in human eroticism. In: *Sex and Internal Secrets*, Vol. 2, ed. W.C. Young & G.W. Corner. Baltimore: Williams & Wilkins, pp. 1383–1400.

——— ed. (1965), *Sex Research: New Developments*. New York: Holt, Rinehart & Winston.

——— Hampson, J.G., & Hampson, J.L. (1955a), An examination of some basic sexual concepts: The evidence of human hermaphroditism. *Bull. Johns Hopkins Hosp.*, 97:301–310.

——— ——— ——— (1955b), Hermaphroditism: Recommendations concerning assignment of sex, change of sex, and psychologic management. *Bull. Johns Hopkins Hosp.*, 97:284–290.

——— ——— ——— (1956), Sexual incongruities and psychopathology: The evidence of human hermaphroditism. *Bull. Johns Hopkins Hosp.*, 98:43–57.

Ovesey, L., & Person, E.S. (1973), Gender identity and sexual psychopathology in men: A psychodynamic analysis of homosexual, transsexualism and transvestism. *J. Amer. Acad. Psychoanal.*, 1:53–72.

Person, E.S. (1974), Some new observations on the origins of femininity. In: *Women and Analysis*, ed. J. Strouse. New York: Grossman, pp. 250–261.

——— (1980), Sexuality as the mainstay of identity: Psychoanalytic perspectives. In: *Women: Sex and Sexuality*, ed. C.R. Stimpson & E.S. Person. Chicago: University of Chicago Press, pp. 36–61.

——— (1983), The influence of values in psychoanalysis: The case of female psychology. In: *Psychiatry Update: The American Psychiatric Association Annual Review*, Vol. 2, ed. L. Grinspoon. Washington, D.C.: American Psychiatric Press, pp. 36–50.

——— (1985), Female sexual identity: The impact of the adolescent experience. In: *Sexuality: New Perspectives*, ed. Z. DeFries, R.C. Friedman, & R. Corn. Westport, CT: Greenwood Press, pp. 71–88.

——— (1986), The omni-available woman and lesbian sex: Two fantasy themes and their relationship to the male developmental experience. In: *The Psychology of Men: New Psychoanalytic Perspectives*, ed. G. Fogel, F.M. Lane, & R.S. Liebert. New York: Basic Books, pp. 236–259.

——— Ovesey, L. (1983), Psychoanalytic theories of gender identity. *J. Amer. Acad. Psychoanal.*, 11:203–227.

——— Terestman, N., Myers, W., Goldberg, E., & Borenstein, M. (1989), Gender differences in sexual behaviors and fantasies in a college population. *J. Sex & Marital Ther.*, 15(3):187–198.

——— ——— ——— ——— ——— (1992), Associations between sexual experiences and fantasies in a non-patient population: A preliminary study. *J. Amer. Acad. Psychoanal.*, 20(1):75–90.

Sorenson, R.C. (1973), *Adolescent Sexuality in Contemporary America*. New York: World.

Stoller, R.J. (1968), *Sex and Gender*. New York: Science House.

Symons, D. (1979), *The Evolution of Human Sexuality*. New York: Oxford University Press.

Thompson, C. (1950), Some effects of the derogatory attitudes toward female sexuality. In: *On Women*. New York: Mentor & Plume Books, 1964, pp. 142–152.

3

The Maternal Ego Ideal and the Regulation of Maternal Qualities

HAROLD P. BLUM, M.D.

The biological evolution of *Homo sapiens* permitted the evolution of human civilization and culture. The emergence of humans marked a break from the stereotyped instinctual domination of life to the flexible and highly individual patterning of personality characteristic of humans. Survival was no longer governed by instinctual guarantees, although the instinctual drives have survival value. Survival was dependent upon high level functions of learning, reality testing, judgment, and perception, with degrees of autonomy from instinctual control. Humans, however, with all their marvelous new evolutionary capacities for intelligence and imagination and for eventual alloplastic alteration of their natural environment, were born the most dependent of creatures. For survival, the human infant requires nurturance, protection, and all the essential ingredients of maternal care and love.

Motherhood, in its biological sense, or in the formal sense of being the legal guardian of a child, does not require elaborate preparation and psychological resources. Biological parenthood may be achieved by stuporous drug addicts or disorganized psychotics who are out of contact with reality. The achievement of psychological parenthood may be a uniquely human development, and although in this chapter I am emphasizing the development and importance of the maternal ego ideal, much of the discussion would also apply to the paternal ego ideal. Furthermore, the sources of mature psychological parental attitudes derive from both parents, from mothers and

43

fathers, so that the superego, which includes the ego ideal, is also bisexual and biparental.

The gradual acquisition of moral, legal, and ethical codes of complex culture and social organization was a most important force in human history which also contributed to the personality development, the superego formation, the childrearing practices, etc., in a given culture. All societies regulate parent–child interactions and favor certain types of parenting and childrearing and certain attitudes toward mothers.

Different mothers and different patterns of childrearing in different cultures could still produce "ordinary devoted mothers" or "good enough mothers" (Winnicott, 1965) who could foster a child's growth and development consonant with the particular culture in which they lived. How are these extraordinary achievements possible, and how do we explain the manifold immaturity and pathological deviations in maternal attitudes and behavior?

The sources of motherliness are manifold and complex, and they involve a woman's entire personality. In this chapter, from the many important components of motherliness, e.g., devotion and empathy, and of the structure and resources necessary for responsible and responsive parenthood, I single out for discussion the formation, consolidation, and function of the maternal ego ideal. I also consider certain forms of arrest and pathology of the maternal ego ideal in particular relation to destructive attitudes toward children. It is recognized that normal ego ideal and superego function will not insure maternal attachment and affection.

Mothers were sometimes unable to achieve maternal attitudes and behavior, but the idealizations of motherhood developed and persisted through the ages, however sentimental, defensive, exaggerated, and overevaluated. The ideal mother also represented the idealization of motherly qualities.

These qualities remained linked to maternal figures and functions of fecundity and reproduction but transcended biological procreation. They are idealizations, not only stemming from the children but also from within the mothers in their own development, supported by parents (fathers) and by society. When we look at the extraordinary plasticity and flexibility of mothering, the capacity to adapt to the needs of different children with different rates and rhythms of development and to deal with competing obligations and responsibilities, the strength and resources of "the good enough mother" become dramatically apparent. The adaptive qualities of confident, dependable nurturance which mothers normally impart to their children have much to do with the ego resources of the child and the ultimate capacity of the children to become mature parents rather than to remain overgrown children. Maternity became a civilized ideal protected by law and custom; mothers were revered and even worshipped; motherhood was socially sacrosanct. Apart from the irrational and defensive sources of this idealization, there was probably always some intrinsic recognition of the fundamental importance of mothering and of the continued dependence of the child on the maternal figure. That the child owed so much that was necessary for survival and development to the mother evoked not only gratitude but also eternal ambivalence. This ambivalence was expressed in covert cultural devaluation of mothering and lack of status accorded to maternal activity.

Freud (1926) called attention to the human child's prolonged dependence and helplessness, a dependence which exceeds that of all other mammals. The great danger situations of early childhood which Freud elucidated were the loss of the object and of the object's love, a formulation which inevitably highlighted the crucial importance of the mother. Mothers would empathize and understand their infants and could respond appropriately or at least adequately under trying circumstances, even under states of duress and stress.

Concurrent with the advance of civilization, there has been recognition of the rights of children and increasing protection of children and of mothers. To this process of recognizing the child as a person in his own right (A. Freud, 1972), psychoanalysis has contributed enormously. Reconstructions of childhood from adult analysis and direct studies of children through psychoanalysis and analytic observation depicted the challenges and struggles of children in growing up and the importance of adequate, enlightened, and responsible parents capable of love, protection, and nurturance of their children. Studies of parents and children revealed all sorts of developmental challenges and conflicts. Parenthood is one of the impossible professions, subject to widespread differences in practice and accomplishments.

Biological motherhood was known from the dawn of time, but millennia may have passed before biological fatherhood was understood. Full psychological parenthood with concern, consideration, and empathy for the child at different stages of development has been a still later acquisition in the history of humanity. Doubtless there were always protection and nurturance, or the human race would have long ago approached extinction. It is clear that children have been sufficiently protected and adequately reared so as to maintain the species and even produce creative individuals who have enriched and advanced civilization and have improved the lot of their fellow man and of succeeding generations.

Understanding the importance of the maternal ego ideal requires consideration of the desire to nurture, protect, and assume the care of the dependent and initially helpless infant. Doubtless, different children have different capacities to elicit mothering or to elicit a necessary adaptation of mothering. In other mammals, a maternal instinct is assumed, although it is not entirely preformed and depends upon releasing responses from the offspring and the environment. Nevertheless, the exquisite maternal care seen, e.g., the licking and nursing of the offspring in other mammals, their feeding, protection, and education for independent existence in their own umwelt, is practically taken for granted as instinctive maternal behavior.

The higher the position in the evolutionary scale, the greater the influence of learning and flexible response and the less the dependency on stereotyped, relatively innate reactions. The loss of instinctive patterning implies a loss of instinctive controls and preformed maternal impulses. Is there such a deep-rooted instinctual force, a phylogenetic heritage of maternal instinct in the human female? Deutsch (1945) and Benedek (1970) have postulated deep-seated instinctual forces as physiological influences that support the development of motherliness and represent the biological-constitutional factors that foster the psychological tendency toward motherliness in the human female. These impulses and biopsychological tendencies are postulated as relatively independent of other instinctual drives, and sometimes as reciprocal to attachment drives in the infant (Balint, 1949).

Biochemical, physiological, and neuroendocrine findings and assumptions are used to justify the theory of a maternal instinct. Benedek (1970, p. 139) described an all-pervading instinct for child survival that is the primary organizer of the woman's sexual drive and her personality. Rather than masochistic sacrifice in the service of the species, the source of motherliness, as proposed by Benedek, was to be found as a specific attribute of femininity in the indwelling quality of the female psyche resulting from the central organization of receptive and retentive tendencies.

Hormonal, neurophysiological, and other biological influences are significant in the evolution of the human mother, concomitant with decreasing instinctual domination and patterning of maternal response. Female primates show much less aggressive behavior than the male and a great deal more interest in infants. The early formation of the so-called cyclic female brain which may predispose toward maternal interests is probably reinforced by the psychosomatic effects of the later menstrual cycle and of the vast hormonal and physiological upheaval of pregnancy, delivery, and lactation. However, what appears to be the innate maternal behavior of animals, in primates increasingly involves social processes and experiential learning. Harlow, Harlow, Dodsworth, and Arling (1966) found that monkeys, who were deprived of mothering, rejected both mating and motherhood. If they were impregnated, they abused and neglected the baby. Normal female primates who have been mothered show tenderness, patience, concerned care, and extended play and education of their offspring. Primate mothering is a highly developed organization, but still significantly removed from human motherliness.

Human maternal attitudes and behavior depend upon ego and superego functions which have no direct parallel among nonhuman species. Biological factors and the biological role of the human female inescapably influence female psychology. But they do not determine or sufficiently account for the formation of human maternal attitudes and aspirations. Homologies drawn between humans and even their closest evolutionary relatives may be both informative and subject to biogenetic fallacies. Vestiges of a maternal instinct may exist in the human female, but they are not well defined and are subordinate to acquired trends in female personality development. In addition, the complexity of the mother–child relationship goes beyond and differs radically from the instinctually determined maternal behavior of other mammals and even primates.

The human mother continues mothering long after the child's abject dependence has ended, into the adult life of the next generation, and the mothering qualities of grandmotherhood. The ties between the human mother and her offspring persist and are also expressed throughout the woman's life in other qualities of motherliness toward other individuals, groups, and causes. There may be substitutions via displacements of maternal interests onto other activities such as the care of plants or pets, or the conservation of wildlife, or the sublimation of maternal interests into new creative satisfactions such as in studies of child development or genetics.

The human mother's relationship with her infant is unique and is associated with the unique evolutionary changes and adaptations. The helplessness of the human infant exceeds that of other primate infants whose brains are at least half grown at birth and who have greater motor ability to cling to the mother. The period of human helplessness exceeds that of any other species. At birth, the human infant's brain is only 25 percent of its adult size, compared to 60 percent for the chimpanzee. The infant has to be held physically by the mother who must also provide (with the father) a psychological holding environment (Winnicott, 1965; Kaufman, 1970). Single births, birth spacing due to inhibition of fertility during lactation, and hormonal priming of the central nervous system are all biological factors that favor human maternal orientation and adaptation.

But maternal orientation and interest in humans are not biologically guaranteed or regulated. Guided by her superego, the mother is able to satisfy her own emotional needs to mother, concurrent with her nurturance of the baby. Maternal attitudes, e.g., toward breast feeding or response to crying, are always overdetermined and reflect unconscious fantasy, cultural custom, and education in motherhood. The mother's own childhood fantasies, satisfactions, and conflicts are revived. The mother may become more dependent in other relationships, seeking nurture, support, and guidance from other mother and parental figures. Archaic mother–child relationships are reactivated, while new identifications also occur as the mother strives toward superior maternal competence and confidence. The nine months of pregnancy, and actually carrying and bearing the child, help with the psychological preparation for motherhood and motherliness and propose and propel developmental challenges and changes (Benedek, 1970; Jessner, Weigert, and Foy, 1970). However, the fact that adoptive mothers who have never experienced childbearing, childbirth, or lactation may be excellent mothers, the long, vulnerable preadult preparation to be a parent, the extraordinary range and variability of maternal competence and pathology, the spectrum of different reactions at different times to the same child, and different responses to different children are all indicative of the plasticity of human maternal function.

I shall comment, in passing, that fathers can in many instances be excellent substitute mothers and certainly foster the child's separation–individuation. Despite adaptive flexibility and bisexuality, it is, nevertheless, a serious question whether most fathers are endowed and organized to be able to respond to infants as optimally as mothers. The mother would seem particularly psychobiologically predisposed, prepared, and attuned to nurture the infant and to engage and participate with her child in the developmental phases of symbiosis and separation–individuation. The developmental line leading to nurturant motherhood is hardly identical to fatherhood, although there are much overlap, intersection, and mutual identification in the human bisexual personality. Sex differences do not have to be either denied or obliterated, or exaggerated with value judgments of differences. The maternal ego ideal is not identical in structure or content with the paternal ideal, but concordant and flexible identification facilitates harmony and cooperative, shared parental care and responsibilities.

The ascent of "man" to moral and ethical development and the peaks of creative imagination rests upon the foundation of adequate maternal care and stimulation during childhood. The games between mother and children, the protection and education of the child's autonomous functions and skillful acquisitions, the growth and expansion of language, the richness of communication in the mother tongue with exponential increases in information processing as verbal communication increases between mother and child, lead to extraordinary adaptive possibilities for the human offspring. The freedom from instinctive, stereotyped, preformed, and relatively rigid patterns of maternal behavior have the most far-reaching consequences for the complex development of the human personality. Along with the evolution of the instinctual drives, the lack of relatively innate biological coordination of mother–child bonds and adaptations to each other is in no small measure related to both human creativity and developmental disturbance. The influence of experience, learning, and socialization have made possible the growth of human culture. At the same time, the loss of instinctual guarantees of motherliness has contributed to man's propensity for personality disorder and for arrests and deviations in personality development. The lack of powerful maternal instincts in the mother and the lack of survival instincts in the relatively helpless human offspring are major forces determining the formation and malformation of human personality. The freedom and flexibility of human motherliness from the strictures of biological programming facilitate new levels of development and are also the source of a unique frailty and vulnerability in the early mother–child relationship and interaction. The "natural" nurture and protection of other mammalian mothers have been replaced by varying degrees of confidence and concern associated with an almost unlimited range of human maternal cues and responses. Beyond inevitable mother– (and father–) child conflict, the long history of parental abandonment, abuse, and even murder of children, the repeated regressive breakthroughs of primitive parental irresponsibility, the frequency of postpartum depression, and inability to nurture dramatically testify to the vulnerability of mature parenthood. In the absence of well-defined and maternal instincts, the human female has a longer, richer, and a far more complicated development toward motherliness. The oldest profession is "female," and it is most probably mother-hood (rather than promiscuous childhood). It is bound to ambivalence and to an original relationship not only of succor, but of "devouring and depletion."

Between the poles of overindulgence of the infant and maternal depletion, overprotection of the child and maternal enslavement, lies the mother's healthy adaptation to her child and her own life. Mothers have needs, feelings, and strivings of their own. Some autonomy as a person in her own right is necessary for mothering without excessive resentment, and for the woman's personal gratification and growth. Mothering, in the absence of other activities, may be defensively used to avoid other challenges and to compensate for other internal and external frustrations and disappointments. Women also have nonmaternal interests, ideals, and aspirations.

Given the vagaries and vulnerabilities of human development, the ordinary devoted mother cannot be regarded as a naturally occurring phenomenon, or as anything ordinary, or to be taken for granted. The capacity for devoted mothering depends upon the total personality resources of the mother and is inextricably interrelated with appropriate environmental support and the positive response of the child. The child's responses stimulate and elicit the mothering process, and the child's positive development becomes a barometer of the mothering process for the mother in her own cultural milieu. The child's "nature" and the mother's nurture are reciprocal influences. Mothering requires ever-changing adjustments and coordinations toward successful resolutions of each of the challenges and conflicts posed in the rearing of an ever-changing child. To become a "devoted mother" is thus a developmental achievement that will insure basic support for the growth and development of the child. The child's healthy development is a narcissistic gratification which heightens maternal self-esteem and enriches the evolving object relationship with the child.

Motherliness also implies the capacity for altruistic self-sacrifice and for setting aside personal interests and attitudes in the service of object love of the child and the ego ideals of motherliness. This ability to persevere in the face of frustration and hardship, to endure distress and privation when necessary for the child's nurture and protection, is by no means an attribute of masochism, though masochistic elements will inevitably enter into the picture of devoted self-sacrifice. (This is also true of the hardship and overwork endured by many fathers in support of the family.) It is important to distinguish maternal capacity for delay of gratification and frustration tolerance from the goal of pleasure in pain or the search for suffering as a precondition for pleasure. Masochism is also fostered if there is an ego and cultural ideal of feminine-maternal sacrifice. It is a maternal ideal to place the child's interest before self-interest, analogous to the nurturant maternal patterns of mammal mothers. The loving mother who comforts and consoles the crying and distressed child is not being primarily masochistic if her interest is in the child's care. Her pleasure normally lies in the child's welfare and not in his or her pain. Her endurance of hardship may be related to her ideals, her love, and capacity for sublimation rather than self-seeking or her own joy in discomfort. Ordinary, devoted mothering, then, is not an example of masochistic renunciation or gratification but of sublimated ideals and commitments, object love, and confident nurture. Having powerful maternal ideals and the ability to live up to and to live out these ideals in the mothering process is a precondition for effective motherliness. I regard the maternal ego ideal as a special structure within the female superego which organizes and regulates maternal interests and attitudes (Blum, 1976).

The maternal ego ideal has its roots and precursors in the child's earliest development. It has narcissistic sources which are different from later superego structures. It is also rooted in primary identification with the mother and the experience of maternal empathy during separation–individuation. Precursors of the superego, idealizations of the mother and maternal role, and identification with the comforting mother and comforted baby can be observed in the symbolic play of the later phases of separation–individuation (Mahler, Pine, and Bergman, 1975). Reciprocal identifications between the little girl and her mother foster the development of the maternal ego ideal and maternal ego attitudes. Identifications, learning, social and biological role shape the maternal dimension of feminine identity. Budding maternal interests can already be observed in the girl's emerging separation–individuation. The girl's identification with her mother is supported and encouraged in the normal interaction with her parents. Benedek (1970, p. 157) observed exquisite motherliness in little girls and noted that "a three-year-old girl holds her doll more securely, arranges the equipment of the baby carriage with more natural skill, than her mother had ever taught her or her siblings." These observations are indicative of the powerful early influence of identifications, evolving feminine individuation and self representation (Blum, 1976). Masculinity is repressed and sublimated, and the girl predominantly identifies with her mother as model, mentor, and rival. When children create illusory idealized babies out of dolls, designs, etc., they help stabilize self and object representations (Kestenberg, 1971).

Paternal identifications and the parental relationship also influence girls' idealization of the parents, the maternal role, and maternal objects and objectives. Maternal developmental attainments are themselves the outgrowth of complex processes which are transformed with further learning experience and later identifications. The regulation of maternal attitudes under the domination of the maternal ego ideal as a substructure within the female ego ideal is in itself an advanced development in the history of the individual and the species.

Freud accounted for the ontogenesis of the superego, including the ego ideal, and laid the foundations for an understanding of the superego as the internalization of regulatory authority and the carrier of the culture. Freud (1923) noted that superego function comprises precepts that you ought to be like this and prohibitions that you may not be like this. Freud related the twofold aspect of the ego ideal to ambivalence, bisexuality, and the negative and positive Oedipus complex and stated, "This double aspect of the ego ideal derives from the fact that the ego ideal had the task of repressing the Oedipus complex; indeed, it is to that revolutionary event that it owes its existence" (p. 34). He further noted, "What had belonged to the lowest part of the mental life of each of us is changed, through the formation of the ideal, into what is highest in the

human mind by our scale of values" (p. 36). The ego ideal will
be a major determinant of values and convictions, morality, and
esteem.

The Oedipus complex is resolved by the child's identification with the parents and, with that, the development of powerful interests in becoming parents with parental attitudes and
precepts. The mature sublimation and transformation of infantile narcissism and unbridled instinctual demands depend upon
the development of the ego ideal and the capacity for ego
growth and regulated regression. Maternal sublimation of the
woman's own infantile demands is essential to mature motherhood and in the service of the maternal ego ideal; otherwise,
every child would be exposed to the untamed impulses of primitive mothers. The ego ideal of the mother may permit controlled childish regression to promote empathy, communication, identification with the child. Freud (1914, p. 91) had of
course earlier noted the narcissistic goals and satisfactions in
parenthood, the wishes for immortality and for self-replication.

> The child shall have a better time than his parents; he shall not be
> subject to the necessities which they have recognized as paramount in
> life. Illness, death, renunciation of enjoyment, restrictions on his own
> will, shall not touch him; the laws of nature and of society shall be
> abrogated in his favour; he shall once more really be the centre and
> core of creation—'His Majesty the Baby,' as we once fancied ourselves.
> The child shall fulfill those wishful dreams of the parents which they
> never carried out—the boy shall become a great man and a hero in his
> father's place, and the girl shall marry a prince as a tardy compensation
> for her mother. At the most touchy point in the narcissistic system, the
> immortality of the ego, which is so hard pressed by reality, security is
> achieved by taking refuge in the child. Parental love, which is so moving
> and at bottom so childish, is nothing but the parents' narcissism born
> again, which, transformed into object-love, unmistakably reveals its for-
> mer nature.

The child idealizes the parents, and the parents idealize their
child and their own childhood.

The narcissistic dimensions of the ego ideal were important
not only in the processes of idealization but also in the foundation of the ego ideal to insure narcissistic satisfactions and sup-
plies from within, as it were, independent of external objects

and society. While never losing its narcissistic character, the ego ideal is a fundamental representative not only of the wishful self but also of the idealized parental objects and their ideals.

Freud (1923, p. 35) attributed the origin of the superego to the outcome of two highly important factors: the lengthy duration of childhood, helplessness, and dependence; and the Oedipus complex. He wrote, "We see, then, that the differentiation of the superego from the ego is no matter of chance; it represents the most important characteristics of the development both of the individual and of the species; indeed, by giving permanent expression to the influence of the parents it perpetuates the existence of the factors to which it owes its origin." The superego thus perpetuates the authority and responsibility of the parent and directs the child toward responsible parenthood in accordance with the rearing practices into which the child has been acculturated. That children frequently want to excel over their parents, to be better parents than their own parents, is related to attaining an ideal parenthood and a lost, idealized childhood.

The wish-fulfilling goal of pregnancy and the ideal of biological motherhood have to be differentiated from the goals and ideals of psychological motherhood and being the real caretaker of a real child. Childish fantasies of pregnancy may be lived out by adolescent girls unprepared for actual mothering and child care and very much in need of mothering themselves. The assumption of responsible motherhood is a major developmental challenge which may propel significant regression or progression (Benedek, 1970).

Wishful fantasies of being mother, being like mother, and becoming a mother are organized and integrated at succeeding developmental levels. Each libidinal and developmental phase colors and contributes to later maternal attitudes. In addition to the biological foundations and motivations for parenthood, the psychology of parenthood is itself enormously influenced by the early parent–child relationship. No longer considered from the almost exclusive vantage point of the child's instinctual drives, the motivations and capacities for motherhood have been much more thoroughly explored. The mother's wish to reproduce not only herself but her love object and to see in her

children her own parents and her siblings has been described
and documented. Children in general, and a particular child,
have different meanings for the mother. The mother's identification with her own mother and with other mother figures
will be crucial in the development of her own ideals of motherhood and whether these ideals can and should be realistically
attained. Motherhood becomes a most coveted aspiration of the
maternal ego ideal and conflicts between the maternal ego ideal
and rejecting attitudes toward maternity and children are universal female conflicts. Aspirations for self-fulfillment, sexual
fulfillment, and nurturant motherhood may be in conflict with
each other and with other motives and interests, e.g., wishes to
remain a child or to become a man. The clash betweeen maternal ideals and infanticidal impulses can be observed in the play
and stories of little girls, and the resolution of such universal
conflicts is vastly important for the later development of a mature maternal ego ideal and the requisite quality for mothering
which will be at least "good enough." Struggles may also be
observed between the passive aim of being baby and the active
aim of bearing and rearing children, identifying with the
mother's active maternal attitudes.

Here is an example of such conflicts (described by Brody
[1956, p. 378]) in a 5-year-old girl actively doing with her doll
that which she wishes and fears her mother will do with her:

> A 5-year-old pretended she had a baby and I had to watch how she
> took care of it. She could hardly ask often enough whether I considered
> her a careful and loving mother. At intervals she enumerated all the
> bad things that she would *not* do with her baby—she would not, like
> some mothers, put thousands of clothes on the baby in the summertime,
> or leave it with just a shirt on in the winter! She would never force a
> baby to eat squash! She would never scream at a baby! The child had
> to promise herself, as it were, that she would not do all the many things
> that crowded into her mind. Finally she asked me, "Do you think I
> would kill my baby? I wouldn't ever. I wouldn't be a murderer, and be
> put in jail! What if I got very, very angry? I would break its head
> open—that would be the worst thing! Or the worst would be to kill
> my own self—or my mother—or my grandmother!" Months later, she
> mused on what fun it would be if two girls—even she and
> Mommy—could marry each other—or better still, if Mommy could
> become her own little baby! And soon she divulged fantasies as to how
> her mother might impregnate her.

The child may reproduce the varied attitudes and ideals that it identified with in the parents as well as in the culture. There may be inconsistencies in the values and expectations represented by the parents and the culture, and for various reasons the child may develop inconsistent and even contradictory attitudes toward motherhood. Given special parental objects or different social standards, a female ego ideal might not reflect ideals of motherhood and motherliness (Muslin, 1972).

Paternal attitudes toward the little girl and the father's relationship with her are also significant in the formation and maturation of the maternal ego ideal. The feminine individuation of the girl is guided by both parents, and fathers convey their attitudes toward motherhood in their relationship with their daughter's mother and in their own parental relationship with their daughter. Optimally, both parents convey the conscious and unconscious communication of respect and regard for their daughter as a potential future mother of the next generation. Thus, what Erikson (1968) calls "generativity" represents the concern for establishing and guiding the next generation. Generativity is not achieved by merely having or wanting children. Its success or failure is measured in the harmony between the generations and the regeneration of ideals, values, and responsibilities in the next generation.

Generativity, an imprecise term, is to my mind largely a function of parental values and attitudes and their effective transmission to the next generation. The maternal ego ideal, organizing and consolidating maternal values, attitudes, and attributes, has a central place in generative, motherly (and fatherly) functions. The anticipation of the child's future partially derives from identification with parental attitudes and social values of child survival and growth.

There are multiple motivations and meanings to the reciprocal and mutual parent–child idealization and devaluation. Parents and children inevitably idealize each other to defend against mutual hostility as well as for narcissistic gratification. The children are, however, the actual future and a vital and valued investment for concerned parents. Surmounting ambivalence, mothers (and fathers) transmit positive values for the child's survival and development. The mother's fantasies about

the child's future, her aspirations and ambitions for the child,
are of vast importance and require careful analysis in treatment. Maternal preferences and aversions, beginning in early
fantasy life and activated during pregnancy, will impinge upon
the child's own individuation. The values, ideals, and convictions of the parents are conveyed to the future mother who, in
turn, transmutes and transmits these value systems beginning
with the first directives and admonitions. The future mother
has identified with her parents' superego, especially with that
of the mother.

The earliest identifications, which go back to the infant's
identification with the feeding, comforting, and prohibiting-
sensitive mother, are easily discerned in doll play. Ego ideals,
based upon identifications with idealized objects and self-images are modified, abstracted, and depersonified in later life.
The girl's ideals are reshaped, especially in adolescence, influenced powerfully by her society and culture. Changing cultural
attitudes toward marriage and motherhood may lead to different ego ideals. The deep unconscious maternal ideals may be
inconsistent or in conflict with prevailing or still-changing cultural ideals. The ongoing influence of planned parenthood and
careers, overpopulation, and high divorce rate remains to be
seen.

I am in accord with Jacobson (1964) in affirming the capacity for early and eventually autonomous ego-ideal development
in the girl. The female superego may be less harsh and punitive
(Schafer, 1974), but it has all the authority necessary for strict
enforcement of ideals and obligations. Many dangers and
threats in addition to castration are involved, and the many
threats that may be internally invoked are more than sufficient
to propel superego formation. The development of guilt and
self-reproach in the girl is neither less intense nor less internalized than in the boy.

One area of defined difference between male and female
superego lies in ideals and values, e.g., with respect to being a
"good mother." Not being a harlot also means love and loyalty
to her children. The maternal ego ideal has a different set
of contents than other areas of the female superego and of
masculine ego ideals. Its structure, content, and function and

its autonomy, consistency, and integration—all require separate evaluation. High ideals of motherhood may be securely internalized and relatively autonomous from infantile conflict or external pressures. The ego ideal then has a fundamental regulatory role in motherhood and maternal sublimation. The child not only has archaic meaning for the mother but represents a love object and the bond between the parents. The realization of the mature maternal ego ideal transforms the wish for ideal motherhood and an ideal family toward refined motherliness. Self-realization as the mother who can confidently care for her child is also obtained in the confirmation of her maternal efforts in the healthy development of her children and the reciprocity of parent–child love. Maternal ideals and aspirations via displacement and sublimation importantly influence the development of empathy, concern, and caring responsibility in the succeeding generation. If empathy for someone else's feelings is one of the very deep-seated foundations of morality, then the experience of empathy in early childhood, beginning with the mother's empathic response to her infant, promotes structuralization and identification with the qualities of motherliness. The development of discipline and ethics in the next generation and of humanitarian concerns is also related to the child's protracted experience of protection and discipline from a mother who is also self-disciplined and genuinely interested in the welfare of her child (Blum, 1976).

The internalization of maternal qualities leads to moral connotations and ultimately to morality and ethics. Moral training is impossible for children who are deprived of maternal attachment and starved of affect (Valenstein, 1972). Developmental limitations occur in the functions of self-judgment and self-criticism, in the capacity to identify with empathic concern and responsibility. It is of interest that Freud (1895) stated, "and the original helplessness of human beings is thus the primal source of all moral motives," and that A. Freud (1965, p. 168) described the caretaking mother as the child's first external legislator: "The first external laws with which she confronts the infant are concerned with the timing and rationing of his satisfaction." Internalization of regulating structures begins in infancy, is organized in the agency of the superego in the oedipal phase resolution, and continues through life. Once the ego ideal begins to function, it serves as the standard for winning affection, approval, and self-respect, or feeling failure, shame, and humiliation (Muslin, 1972).

The Psychopathology of the Maternal Ego Ideal

The psychopathology of mothering has often been expressed in such dramatic terminology as the overanxious, overprotecting, intrusive, engulfing, suffocating, rejecting mother. Historically, there have been shifting attributions of malevolence in the mother–child relationship to either the "witch-mother" or the "bad seed." These terms were usually drastic distortions or oversimplifications of the complexities of mother–child problems. Mothers may be more or less competent with different children at different phases in the child's and their own development. Children have different capacities to cue and elicit mothering (Mahler et al., 1975), and particular areas or functions may be affected in mother and child in different and interrelated ways. The discussion of the maternal ego ideal necessarily deals with a particular major area of structure and function apart from many other considerations of mothering and childrearing tasks.

In the vicissitudes of mothering and childrearing, the maternal ego ideal is a significant influence, and it is necessary to understand this dimension of the feminine superego in order to fully comprehend normal mothering and disorder and deviance in motherhood.

The regressive threat to maternal ideals and attitudes of loving nurturance aroused by the child's demanding and devouring behavior with the eruption of infanticidal impulses has been articulated by Shakespeare's Lady Macbeth (in *Macbeth*, Act I, Scene vii): "I have given suck and know, how tender 'tis to love the babe that milks me/ I would, while it were smiling in my face/ Have pluckt my nipple from his boneless gums,/ and dasht the brains out."

Freud (1916) assumed that Lady Macbeth was childless, at least in her marriage to Macbeth, as a punishment for her violation of the laws of geniture, the crime of infanticide. Abortion and infanticide are central themes in the play. The childlessness is thus not only an expression of infanticide; it also represents the punishment for infanticide asserted by the maternal superego.

Lady Macbeth's infanticidal attitudes could be considered a response to her oedipal guilt, with a need to conceal and cover her oedipal crimes and eliminate her incestuous offspring (Calef, 1969). However, pre-oedipal and narcissistic problems are often prominent in abusive and infanticidal mothers. Like Lady Macbeth, such mothers display untempered need, greed, and entitlement, at least in transient states of uncontrolled regression.

Whatever motives are proposed for Lady Macbeth's childlessness and infanticide, she is represented in the play as being driven by ruthless ambition, insufficiently tempered by maternal ideals and tenderness. As an ambiguous psychological portrait, she is partly sketched as one of the untamed female furies, the fearsome and dangerous, castrating and devouring mother. The murderous mother is the feared and hated mother of the child's primitive aggressive fantasies, but also the childish and abusive mother who is really capable of acting out these fantasies toward children or helpless individuals. The development of the maternal ego ideal has been deformed or stunted, and the sublimation of infanticidal impulses has not been achieved under the direction and domination of the maternal ego ideal. She is unable to sustain benevolent, nurturant, and protective attitudes and often also demonstrates the shame and guilt or unconscious need for punishment associated with archaic ideals and sadistic superego function. The qualities of the superego thus decisively influence the capacities for "good mothering" or the miscarriage of motherliness.

Since all moral and ethical codes are an admixture of ideals and admonitions and may be regarded to some degree as external codifications of superego contents, the ego ideal is interwoven with and cannot be considered apart from other areas of superego content and function (Hartmann and Loewenstein,

1962). The Ten Commandments contain exhortations and interdictions, and there are actually four "do's" and six "don't." Of course, the external moral or religious code and the individual conscious system of ideals and values are not necessarily concordant with the largely unconscious superego system. There may be wide discrepancies between conscious and unconscious parental aspirations and ideals. However, certain commandments are basic to almost all moral and religious codes and would seem to be fundamental to the development and survival of human society. One particular commandment of the Ten Commandments is addressed directly to the parent–child relationship under consideration in this paper. I refer to the commandment to "Honor They Father and Thy Mother." This commandment has been the subject of much discussion, and the child's acceptance of parental authority was to be associated with the incorporation of an ideal of responsibility to and reverence for the parents. The commandments imposed obligations on the child toward the parent, and both parents were owed obedience and reverence. These expectations extended to parental authorities and especially toward the idealized parent, the God-parent. God was immortal and promised the narcissistic bliss of reunion with the perfect parent in Paradise, or omnipotent perpetual punishment in Hell.

But where was the commandment for the parent to honor and respect the child? There was no commandment to "Honor Thy Son and Thy Daughter," reciprocal to the child's obligation to honor the parents. The codes were probably written by older scribes and also reflect the origins of morality. It seems as though the ethical codes which have been formed in early childhood and which have undergone progressive abstraction, depersonification, and developmental transformation still retain their childlike qualities and indicate the importance of the taming of the child's impulses and passions for the survival of the family and civilization. The superego is never totally internalized nor completely autonomous, and many people require social and religious reinforcement to sustain superego regulation. Moreover, the superego varies considerably with the culture and with particular groups and leadership. This will influence parental ideals, and maternal attitudes may be more or less autonomous from group pressures. A particular leader and group may be sought as a parent and family. The group superego and ideals may foster constructive cooperation and concern, or mutual antagonism and suspicion, or even the ruthless rampage of the mob or the violent cult. The social surround which protects mothering and children may sanction filicidal impulses under conditions of destructive leadership and group repression.

The repression of childish impulses under the domination of the superego may be a partial explanation for the curious omission of parental responsibility in the commandments, a concern and responsibility which is essential for civilized human survival. It is as if counteroedipal wishes, parents' animosity, child neglect, and even outbreaks of cannibalistic behavior toward children were not acknowledged in the parent. The parent is not supposed to be childish or immature. The child needed to be socialized but was also a ready target of the parents' antisocial impulses. Parental authority could also be used to conceal or justify the psychological and physical abuse of children. Child abuse had been an unacknowledged abuse of parental power and authority.

This line of thought may also help to explain the long history in which the child has not been regarded as a person in his own right. The child was the property of the parent, under obligation to obey the parent. For centuries, disobedience of the parent was considered a heinous crime for which the child could be punished brutally, seemingly without legal or social stricture or restriction of the parents' authority. The history of social and legal protection of the child is one of very slow advance and of relatively recent development in Western civilizations. It may also be significant that the improvement of the lot of women seems to have gone hand-in-hand with increased social responsibility toward children. Children may need protection from their own parents and guardians. In this gradually acquired social sensitivity to the needs of children, we may discern the rise and assertion of the parental ego ideal and, in particular, the embodiment of the maternal ego ideal for the survival and welfare of the child. Contemporary social standards and legal codes are beginning to consider the child's mental health and psychological needs.

Intergenerational tensions have been observed from the beginning of recorded history, and they cannot be understood without an examination of those factors which permitted the succession of generations, that is, with true parental protection and concern. However, the history of the relations of parents and children, beginning with the riddle of the Sphinx and the legend of Oedipus, has often been a sorry testimonial to the thin veneer of civilization and the fragility of responsible parenthood. History and legend are replete with stories of child abandonment and murder. Child-threatening witches abound in fairytale and myth, and these fantasies have derivatives in actual behavior. Oedipus had his ankles pinned together after birth, deriving his name from these infantile injuries which were the cause of his "swollen foot" (oede-pes). Oedipus' symbolism has the meaning of an erect phallus. These cradle injuries, inflicted by his parents, may have additional significance. This myth of the primal family has multiple meanings deriving from different developmental and historical phases. The "cradle injuries" may also be considered on the manifest level of crib death and child abuse. The oedipal myth begins with parental distrust and abandonment of the child. The newborn infant is injured and scarred at the hands of its parents. Oedipus is given away by his mother, Jocasta, to both kill and save him.

Behind and beside the murderous oedipal conflicts of father and son lie the infanticidal impulses of the mother. It is clearly the mother who protects or neglects the newborn, who "recognizes" or rejects her own child, and who cradles the child with varying forms and admixtures of love and hate, protection and neglect.

Although the sacrifice of the first-born male is dominant in the Judeo-Christian heritage of the proposed sacrifice of Isaac and the proclaimed sacrifice of Jesus, infanticide was by no means culturally restricted to males. Other cultures emphasize the sacrifice or destruction of unwanted females or rival sons. Children of both sexes may be mistreated or murdered to appease the terrible gods who embodied the projected aggression and jealousy of both parents.

The murderous rivalry of father and sons was elaborated by Freud (1913) in the theory of the Primal Horde as a historical dramatization of oedipal conflict. The son wishes to murder the father, and the father wishes to murder the son, and these wishes have been ritually defended against and subjected to the most extraordinary variety of compromise formations. Like Oedipus, Christ is pinned, but he represents child sacrifice, crucified at the order of the father, and then secondarily saved and a savior of others.

The story of Abraham and Isaac is said to represent the triumph of paternal love over aggression. The infanticidal urge is constantly reasserted and religiously repudiated and repressed. The sacrificial victim or scapegoat could be an animal substitute or an alien group as, e.g., the Jews came to be. The Jews were then accused of acting out the repressed murderous wishes toward children. As La Barre (1972) notes, Abraham symbolizes a great prehistoric revolution in religion and morality, the abjuring of human sacrifice. Behind the legend of Abraham and Isaac lies the practice of child sacrifice. Abraham's first impulse, presented as God's command to kill the child, is countermanded by the injunction not to kill the child. Infanticide must have been a specific object of a Biblical commandment, "Thou Shalt Not Kill."

Children need the protection of, and may need protection from, their own parents and guardians. The parable of Abraham and Isaac represents the rise and assertion of the parental ego ideal. Parental affection and responsibility are asserted, and Abraham becomes the great patriarch who permits child growth rather than destruction. Abraham's seed will multiply because he permits his seed to multiply. The child is wished for and awaited, as in primal fertility rites, but is also ambivalently welcome as a future parent and survivor of the parent. This acceptance of the child is ultimately dependent upon maternal attitudes and functions, and behind the Abraham parable is the embodiment of the maternal ego ideal for the parenting, survival, and welfare of the child.

Ritual child sacrifice and derivative muted forms of child abuse have been discerned in many cultures. The skeletal remains of thousands of children have been discovered in the archaeological uncovering of Phoenician graves. The cannibalistic and sadistic impulses of these people found religious and cultural acceptance in ceremonial infanticide. The sacrificial remains of the children testify to their systematic filicidal slaughter and the astonishing inference that it is possible for mass murder of children to coexist with an apparently viable social organization and culture, at least for some time. The Phoenician infanticides "appeased" a bloodthirsty goddess, again indicating maternal participation not only in abortion but in child sacrifice.

In Papua, infanticide was an acceptable method of population control, a limit of three children per family was set, and those born after the third were killed. Children could be killed for fees by unscrupulous nurses, and kings would arrange to eliminate the heirs who would replace them. The Greeks and Romans killed defective and deformed infants. In Florence in the Quatrocento, the Bishops forbade taking children into bed with the parents, apparently not because of the primal scene, but because of the high rate of children suffocated by their ostensibly sleeping parents (Bakan, 1971). In this center of the Renaissance, a little arch called an "arcuccio" was fitted over a crib to prevent smothering by the covers or the nurse. The nurse could breast-feed the infant through a hole on the side of the crib. At one time nurses were required to use this type of crib or face excommunication for possible infanticidal behavior. Infanticide was the most common crime imputed to the aged witches of Europe (Trexler, 1973). Abortions of unwanted and out-of-wedlock pregnancies and the murder of illegitimate children were rampant. As late as the sixteenth century in Germany, children were buried alive beneath the doorsteps of public buildings.

These problems have persisted side-by-side with human love, morality, and ideals, and the repression of these impulses and the suppression of human sacrifice are essential cornerstones in the foundation of human civilization and culture. Civilized society could not openly tolerate human sacrifice, which was often particularly directed at the helpless and the defenseless children as it was with unwanted captives and chattels. The ritual slaughter of the innocent was replaced by ritual animal sacrifices and eventually by religious rituals and social ceremonials which were designed to regulate those barbarous impulses and to bind the group together in ways that would be lifepreserving and protective of social needs and ideals. The hostility, jealousy, devouring, and other threatening attitudes of parents toward children were repudiated and disowned with all the defenses that could be mobilized. Infanticidal impulses and attitudes became too abhorrent and atrocious to be accepted and, later, even to be acknowledged. That "civilized" parents might harbor homicidal intentions toward children was considered almost unthinkable. The tendency toward denial was so great that it would be a long time before modern medicine confronted the hidden filicidal motives of pathological parents in the etiology of many injuries, crib deaths, and fatal "accidents" of children (Kempe, Silverman, Steele, Droegemuller, and Silver, 1962).

The ancient practice of filicide recalls the regressive loss of civilized behavior in various upheavals and the periodic massacres of the innocent and the helpless throughout human history. It seems probable that the ritualized murder of youth in recurrent utterly irrational wars is also related in part to the untempered ambivalence of the parents. These remarks, of course, should not minimize the complexity of the forces involved in these destructive social upheavals or the role of the individual victim in provoking or seeking his own destruction. Christ was not only foreordained to die for the sins of humanity, but he offered himself up as a willing self-sacrifice. The sacrificial scapegoat is the martyr for the group, achieving group redemption and reconciliation, and turning punitive parents back into protective and supporting parents. Suffering would win forgiveness, and sacrifice would lead to salvation. The child who was the gift of the gods was sometimes seen as lent by the gods. The borrowed child certainly had to be returned and sometimes asked to return to the gods.

The full historical and psychological implications of infanticide and of derivative expressions of child sacrifice in mistreated babies and battered children have probably only been thoroughly studied in this century, the century of the child and the century of psychoanalysis.

The century of the child and the discoveries of psychoanalysis are no doubt related. Psychoanalysis first demonstrated the importance of childhood for all later personality development and the importance of the parent/child relationship for child development. It may be recalled that Freud's first formulations of the origins of neurosis concerned child abuse. He postulated the sexual seduction of children by their parents. Psychoanalysis actually began with the study of child abuse prior to the discovery of universal incestuous conflicts in children and their parents. The discovery of the universality of the Oedipus complex and primal scene fantasy tended to eclipse the formulations of actual child abuse by deviant parents. "A Child is Being Beaten" (Freud, 1919) can also be understood literally. Beating fantasies may have various derivatives and, if untamed, may tragically influence parental attitudes and actions. Parental abuse or misuse may be psychological and/or physical.

I do not wish to indicate a false equivalence between socially sanctioned harsh discipline and erratic individual acts of child abuse. Also, the boundary between discipline and abuse may be blurred, especially in infantile parents. Where child sacrifice was culturally condoned or a religious rite, certain groups of children were protected, and individual parents were expected to conform to the social-religious rules.

Within a culture that safeguards the lives and welfare of children, there is a spectrum of inappropriate parenting and mistreatment of children. Not all acts of abuse are necessarily derivatives of murderous impulses. Also, excessively punitive or violently hostile actions may focus upon one particular child and not necessarily toward all children. The mother's vital affectionate attachment to that child may be missing or tenuous.

My discussion here will be confined, among the many factors in parental mistreatment of children, to the role of the maternal ego ideal. Both mothers and fathers may mistreat children, and the mother is a passive partner if the father actively mistreats the child or mistreats the child at the mother's instigation. The child who is to be "handed over" to father for a later beating or rape still feels maternal malevolence, as does the child who is used as a weapon to punish the spouse and other objects. Abused wives often become abusive mothers, "taking it out on the child," in what becomes familial sadomasochism. The child responds to direct or devious maternal mistreatment, as well as to the lack of maternal protection and concern.

An infantile ego ideal may be in conflict or concert with an archaic punitive superego. The more obvious "sadistic superego" may be associated with untamed parental ideals and impossible perfectionistic demands. High ideals may be paradoxically paired with tyrannical commands and controls. Excessive expectations and impossible, premature demands may lead to further parental assault and criticism of the child. The infantile mother may react to her infant as if he harbored insatiable demands and withholds love and nurturance from her. The disavowed "overgrown infant" is herself identified with her child and her frustrating mother image. The mother, submitting to her own superego and identifying with the aggressor, her own punitive mother, may then attack the disappointing and depriving child (Steele, 1970). This is rationalized frequently in terms of living up to maternal ideals, of not spoiling the child. The child may have been conceived for purposes of compensation, restitution, or hostile rivalry.[1] The maternal ideal may sanction loss of control as well as the absence of guilt associated with the mother's professed righteous indignation. Guilt may be alleviated if punitive reactions are also self-punitive and simultaneously serve appeasement and atonement. Omnipotent demands and punitive narcissistic rage color maternal responses and may permit mistreatment of the child upon slight frustration or provocation or may invite the child or others to punish the parent. The omnipotent parent can be assured of victory in power struggles with the child. The abuse of parental power over the child reverses the parents' infantile helplessness and victimization and the deprivation of protection, inflicting them upon the relatively helpless child. To paraphrase the Bible, the sins and punishment of the parents are visited upon the children, through the generations. Any helpless victim may be substituted for the relatively defenseless,

---

[1]The motives for parenthood include a spectrum of infantile and mature aspirations, and this chapter highlights only some prominent wishes for parenthood.

traumatized child. In the case of the child, however, the parent may not fear retaliation, and the child may have no other source of protection or support. Traumatic abuse may also be repeated and perpetuated in self-destructive syndromes.

Uneven development of the ego ideal and conscience also makes such parents prone to inconsistent attitudes of permission and prohibition, punishment and seduction, engaging and rejecting the child, etc. Withdrawal from, and neglect of, the child may defend against physical seduction or attack, yet still express abusive attitudes. Poor internalization may leave the mother dependent upon external controls, while tending to project blame onto the child. The superego can be harsh and strict, yet weak in internalization, integration, and autonomy. In isolation from other adults, these mothers may be unable to control primitive impulses and punitive tendencies. Children may be reared in a sadomasochistic milieu of violence and perversion.[2]

The traumatic abuse these children have experienced predisposes to later traumatic repetition, often under the influence of a sadistic and unreliable superego. The aggression may be internalized rather than externalized, and the abuse may be perpetuated and repeated in self-destructive syndromes in the child and the guilty parent. The mother who avoids actual abuse but who is tormented by thought of child abuse may also have suicidal ideas and feelings of worthlessness.

Rather opposite values of protection and punishment, based upon different unintegrated identifications, may coexist with defensive denial, splitting of self and object representations, isolation, etc. In fact, different identifications may be used

---

[2]Some maltreated children show remarkable resilience. Charles Dickens is an example of an abused child who developed a powerful social conscience and artistic ideals. He mastered trauma in his writing, leaving sensitive, vivid descriptions of child abuse. This is probably one historical derivation of the punitive expression "to beat the Dickens." "Dickens" also means "devil."

This chapter does not encompass the role of the child's father and the actual relationship between the parents. I only mention that the father may represent a protective or punitive external superego and a positive or negative parental ideal. The parental relationship has a powerful influence on the parenting process and the child, and the parenting process reciprocally influences the parental relationship.

for pathological defense, and selective standards of the ego ideal may undergo defensive regression (Lampl-de Groot, 1962). Stunting, malformation, disharmony, splitting, and regressive proclivity are characteristic in varying degree of the ego ideal of abusive or infanticidal mothers. The punitive parent may be defensively idealized or split off from a "good object" image (Kernberg, 1975, p. 25). The "denigrated, bad self" identified with the denigrated punitive parent image is often repressed. Contradictory ego ideals may be maintained in consciousness in a "vertical split" in which full awareness of the inconsistencies is defensively avoided.

The mistreated child may represent not only alien aspects of the self but the mother's mother in a reversal of roles (Morris and Gould, 1963). The child's comfort or criticism of the mother will repeat her own experience of parental reward or punishment, as if the child were her own parent or authority. Children differentially elicit motherliness or provoke alienation and abuse. A "good child" and successful parenting may soften a harsh parental superego; and a disturbed child may intensify superego sadism and ego-ideal demands in conjunction with lowered parental self-esteem (Benedek, 1959). The lack of a stable, integrated, relatively autonomous maternal ego ideal is a major contribution to serious maternal psychopathology that cuts across psychiatric, educational, and social classification.

The ego ideal may also betray its narcissistic origins in exaggerated idealizations of mothering or utilization of the child for the mother's infantile narcissistic gratifications. The child may have to be a source of maternal approval or pride, an aggrandized extension of the mother, or the child will represent a narcissistic injury. Nurturance may be used to rationalize the need for nurturance from the child or engulfing attitudes with intolerance of the child's thrust toward separation and independence (cf. Mahler et al., 1975; Stoller, 1978).

Where the cultural attitude or ideal may favor certain child-rearing practices that disregard the child's needs, as in overfeeding or rigidly scheduled feeding, the conflicts engendered in the mother may be constructively influenced by empathy. The maternal ego ideal undergoes cultural and developmental transformations during the life cycle, long after its

consolidation during latency. Motherhood and grandmotherhood frequently engender such changes consequent to the
challenges and demands of those phases of life. Reciprocal experiences of nurturing and being nurtured and mutual "feed-
back" foster 'maturation in motherliness" (Benedek, 1959;
Panel, 1975).

In closing, I will not attempt to outline all the various pathologies of the ego ideal that impair or all the positive attributes that foster and guide motherliness. The mother's own
childhood and the relationship and identifications with her own
parents are perpetuated in her own maternal attitudes, values,
fantasies, and behavior. Primates who have not been adequately
mothered are often unable to become good enough mothers
and may neglect or abuse their offspring. The human female
is more liberated from instinctual domination than her primate
forebears, but her mothering is governed by far more variable
conflicts and maternal ideals and injunctions deriving from her
identifications and experience as well as her innate endowment.

Maternal precepts and values are essential for the development of motherliness. While influenced by the "supporting surround" and the total personality and the particular child, the
maternal ego ideal normally "inspires" and "aspires" toward
motherhood and motherliness. The renunciation of motherhood may imply inner conflict, but also the transformation,
substitution, or sublimation of maternal interests and goals.
Maternal sublimation and fostering sublimation in her child are
in the service of the maternal ego ideal. Without impulse control and sublimation, every child would be the object of its
mother's narcissistic needs and primitive impulses and tensions.
Regression in the service of the child and the child's regressive
"pull" on the mother are ego and ego-ideal modulated. The
normal mother who is at the limit of her patience or tolerance
experiences not only exasperation, but regulation and inner
restraint. Her ego ideal promotes empathy and consideration
for the child and taming of the "danger situation" in the tense
mother–child relationship. The mother can then identify and
deal with her child's pain and frustration without being overwhelmed by the revival of her own childhood conflicts. The
maturity and authority of the parental superego system guide

and goal direct the "ordinary devoted" but always conflicted and ambivalent mother–child relationship. With matured expectations and the taming of infantile ideals, parents also recognize their own limitations. Even with optimal parenting, children are conflicted and confused and bring their inevitable problems into their own parenthood.

References

Bakan, D. (1971), *Slaughter of the Innocents*. San Francisco: Josey Bass.

Balint, A. (1949), Love for the mother and mother-love. *Internat. J. Psycho-Anal.*, 30:251–259.

Benedek, T. (1959), Parenthood as a developmental phase. *J. Amer. Psychoanal. Assn.*, 7:389–417.

——— (1970), Motherhood and nurturing; Parenthood during the life cycle. In: *Parenthood: Its Psychology and Psychopathology*, ed. E. Anthony & T. Benedek. New York: Little, Brown.

Blum, H. (1976), Masochism, the ego ideal, and the psychology of women. *J. Amer. Psychoanal. Assn.*, 24:157–191.

Brody, S. (1956), *Patterns of Mothering*. New York: International Universities Press.

Calef, V. (1969), Lady Macbeth and infanticide. *J. Amer. Psychoanal. Assn.*, 17:528–548.

Deutsch, H. (1945), *The Psychology of Women*, Vol. 2. New York: International Universities Press.

Erikson, E. (1968), *Identity, Youth, and Crisis*. New York: Norton.

Freud, A. (1965), *Normality and Pathology in Childhood*. New York: International Universities Press.

——— (1972), The child as a person in his own right. *The Psychoanalytic Study of the Child*, 27:621–625. New York: Quadrangle.

Freud, S. (1895), Project for a scientific psychology. *Standard Edition*, 1:283–397. London: Hogarth Press, 1955.

——— (1913), Totem and taboo. *Standard Edition*, 13:1–164. London: Hogarth Press, 1955.

——— (1914), On narcissism. *Standard Edition*, 14:67–104. London: Hogarth Press, 1957.

——— (1916), Some character-types met with in psychoanalytic work. *Standard Edition*, 14:309–336. London: Hogarth Press, 1957.

——— (1919), A child is being beaten: A contribution to the study of the origin of sexual perversions. *Standard Edition*, 17:175–204. London: Hogarth Press, 1955.

——— (1923), The ego and the id. *Standard Edition*, 19:3–68. London: Hogarth Press, 1961.

——— (1926), Inhibitions, symptoms, and anxiety. *Standard Edition*, 20:77–178. London: Hogarth Press, 1959.

Harlow, H., Harlow, M., Dodsworth, R., & Arling, G. (1966), Maternal behavior of rhesus monkeys deprived of mothering and peer associations in infancy. *Proc. Amer. Philosoph. Soc.*, 110:58–66.

Hartmann, H., & Loewenstein, R. (1962), Notes on the superego. *The Psychoanalytic Study of the Child*, 17:42–81. New York: International Universities Press.

Jacobson, E. (1964), *The Self and the Object World*. New York: International Universities Press.

Jessner, L., Weigert, E., & Foy, J. (1970), The development of parental attitudes during pregnancy. In: *Parenthood: Its Psychology and Psychopathology*, ed. E. Anthony & T. Benedek. New York: Little, Brown.

Kaufman, I. (1970), Biologic considerations of parenthood. In: *Parenthood: Its Psychology and Psychopathology*, ed. E. Anthony & T. Benedek. New York: Little, Brown.

Kempe, C., Silverman, F., Steele, B., Droegemueller, W., & Silver, H. (1962), The battered child syndrome. *JAMA*, 181:17–24.

Kernberg, O. (1975), *Borderline Conditions and Pathological Narcissism*. New York: Aronson.

Kestenberg, J. (1971), From organ object imagery to self and object representations. In: *Separation-Individuation*, ed. J. McDevitt & C. Settlage. New York: International Universities Press.

La Barre, W. (1972), *The Ghost Dance: The Origins of Religion*. New York: Dell.

Lampl-de Groot, J. (1962), Ego ideal and superego. *The Psychoanalytic Study of the Child*, 17:94–106. New York: International Universities Press.

Mahler, M., Pine F., & Bergman, A. (1975), *The Psychological Birth of the Human Infant*. New York: Basic Books.

Morris, M., & Gould, R. (1963), Role reversal: A concept in dealing with the neglected/battered child syndrome. In: *The Neglected/Battered Child Syndrome*. New York: Child Welfare League of America.

Muslin, H. (1972), The superego in women. In: *Moral Values and the Superego Concept in Psychoanalysis*, ed. S. Post. New York: International Universities Press.

Panel (1975), Parenthood as a developmental phase. Reporter, H. Parens. *J. Amer. Psychoanal. Assn.*, 23:154–165.

Schafer, R. (1974), Problems in Freud's psychology of women. *J. Amer. Psychoanal. Assn.*, 22:459–485.

Steele, B. (1970), Parental abuse of infants and small children. In: *Parenthood: Its Psychology and Psychopathology*, ed. E. Anthony & T. Benedek. New York: Little, Brown.

Stoller, R. (1978), Boyhood gender aberrations: Treatment issues. *J. Amer. Psychoanal. Assn.*, 26(3):541–558.

Trexler, R. (1973), Infanticide in Florence. *Hist. Childhood Quart.*, 1:98–116.

Valenstein, A. (1972), The earliest mother/child relationship and the development of the superego. In: *Moral Values and the Superego Concept in Psychoanalysis*, ed. S. Post. New York: International Universities Press.

Winnicott, D. (1965), *The Maturational Process and the Facilitating Environment*. New York: International Universities Press.

4

A Relationship Perspective on the Transition to Parenthood

JOY D. OSOFSKY, PH.D.
REX CULP, PH.D.

The transition to new parenthood involves a major developmental change with important implications for the parents as individuals and as a couple, for the parent-child relationship, and for the child's development. Transitions during the course of development are nodal points, often accompanied by stress, during which disorganization may occur; a new integration then becomes necessary if the individual is to move on to a reorganized level of adaptive functioning.

Review of the Literature

Research on the transition to parenthood has become progressively more systematic in the last ten years. The older studies (Caplan, 1957; Benedek, 1959; Bibring, Dwyer, Huntington, and Valentine, 1961) were based on clinical evaluations of the intrapsychic issues and needs of expectant women, their husbands, and the couple. These clinical studies, while rich in insights, did not allow for generalization of findings; often they used small and atypical samples including women or men in therapy or with emotional problems whose onset occurred during pregnancy or the postpartum period. In addition, the interpretations of outcomes were highly subjective.

The study reported in this chapter was supported by the Center for Prevention Research, Division of Prevention and Special Mental Health Programs, National Institute for Mental Health, Grant No. MH 39487.

Another group of studies (Hicks and Platt, 1971; Shereshefsky and Yarrow, 1974; Lewis and Spanier, 1979; Grossman, Eichler, and Winickoff, 1980; Feldman, Nash, and Aschenbrenner, 1983; Cowan, Cowan, Heming, Garrett, Coyish, Curtis-Boles, and Boles, 1985; Belsky and Volling, 1986) investigated couples at different stages of family life to determine shifts in marital satisfaction during the first fifteen years of marriage. Almost all of these investigations have indicated a decline in marital satisfaction and quality. However, most of them have focused on shifts occurring in the first few years of the child's life.

A review of early and more recent investigations of marital satisfaction suggests the need to study the transition to parenthood as a life transition that must be understood in a broader perspective. This broader developmental focus is found in recent long-term longitudinal studies of the transition to first parenthood (notably the investigations of Belsky and of Cowan and Cowan) and in new theories and empirical data regarding the formation of relationships. The latter may provide insights and understanding about this important transition. In this chapter, we will present data from these longitudinal studies, review relationship approaches to understanding families in transition, present empirical data from our own short-term longitudinal study in this area, and then attempt to arrive at a new understanding of parenthood as a transitional period in development.

Longitudinal Studies of the Transition to Parenthood

In their "Becoming a Family" project, Cowan and Cowan (1987) have pointed out that the normative processes that are part of the formation and development of families may, for some families, place them at considerable risk for problems in their relationship and in their parenting role. As mentioned above, much of the longitudinal research (Grossman, Eichler, and Winickoff, 1980; Feldman et al., 1983; Belsky, Lang, and Rovine, 1985; Huston, McHale, and Crouter, 1986)—including the Cowan study, which has followed the children during the transition period longer than any other—has documented a significant decline in marital satisfaction for both mothers and fathers following the birth of their first child. Interestingly, taking into account a broader relationships perspective, women and men seem to experience "separate journeys" down that road. As the Cowans have so sensitively written, "men and women begin their journeys toward parenthood as if they were on separate trains heading down different tracks, hoping somehow to reach the same destination—the formation of their family" (Cowan et al., 1985, p. 453). For many reasons related to individual differences between men and women, they may have markedly different experiences of marriage and of new parenthood (Cowan and Cowan, 1987). The Cowans have studied 72 couples beginning in late pregnancy and continuing until the children were 66 months old. They have found that the declines in marital satisfaction manifest themselves differently for women and men. The greatest decline in marital satisfaction occurs for women from pregnancy to 6 months after birth, whereas for men a much greater decline is reported from 6 to 18 months postpartum. These discrepancies in satisfaction with marriage may have important consequences for both the marital and the parenting relationship. Essentially, the Cowans have noted that the greater the discrepancy between the partners, the greater the increase in conflict and the more the decline in marital satisfaction from pregnancy to 18 months after birth. Belsky and Volling (1986) have noted further that unfulfilled expectations can have a negative impact on marital quality.

One of the criticisms of some of the transition to parenthood research is that there have been no comparisons with nonparent couples during this developmental period. The Cowans have provided comparative data on new parents and couples not having a baby during a similar period. This comparison indicated that the level of adaptation at the beginning of the study explains much more of the variation in individual and marital adaptation two years later than does the fact of the couple's having a child. The Cowans' most recent report of their longitudinal study (Cowan and Cowan, 1987) shows a consistent set of relations between marital satisfaction during pregnancy and four years later, with links to both couple interaction and parenting style. In addition, how parents treated each other and their child was significantly related to the child's developmental status at 3½ years. (An interesting exception to this general trend was the absence, for fathers with boys, of consistent correlations linking marital quality and parenting styles.) The Cowans emphasize the importance of studying the parents' relationship in order to understand the nature of the parent-child relationship and the child's developmental progress.

The Transition to Parenthood in Context

In considering the transition to parenthood as part of broader relationship development involving family dynamics and environmental factors, other recent research will be reviewed. In studies examining the influence of maternal personal characteristics on subsequent adaptation to parenting (Andersen, 1984; Hobfoll and Lieberman, 1987), it was reported that maternal postpartum adjustment was influenced not only by the self-esteem of the mother but also by the level of support obtained from the husband. Of particular importance was the interaction of these two factors, in that mothers who were both low in self-esteem and received low support from their husbands were at greatest risk for problems in postpartum coping. The level of support from the husband also may be influenced by personal characteristics, in that men who were nurturant and displayed a greater number of feminine traits were also higher on levels of support.

Characteristics of the child also have been discussed as important factors in early parenthood. Sirignano and Lachman (1985) found a positive relationship between infants perceived by their parents as easier to care for and positive changes in parents' personal characteristics. Similarly, the longitudinal research of Cowan and Cowan (1987, Cowan et al., 1985) has shown that the sex of the child relates to patterns of parental behavior, the marital relationship, and the personal characteristics of the parents. At their 42-month assessment, prenatal measures of self-esteem and marital satisfaction were positively related to a more authoritative parenting style, which in turn was related to higher levels of social and cognitive competence in female children. In families of boys, however, higher self-esteem or marital satisfaction during pregnancy was related to more authoritarian parenting, which in turn was related to less favorable child outcomes. These examples from the literature help to illustrate the importance of viewing the transition to parenthood as part of an interrelated system of factors and events. Consideration of one set of factors (e.g., maternal personal characteristics) may require consideration of other sets of factors (e.g., quality of the marital relationship) and their interaction in order to achieve a more comprehensive understanding.

Stability in the Face of Change during the Transition

It is well documented that the transition to parenthood involves personal and marital change. In studies comparing the experiences of young parents to similar nonparent couples, those experiencing parenthood have been found to show increased efficacy as parents, increased gender differentiation, and decreased marital satisfaction (Cowan et al., 1985; Sirignano and Lachman, 1985). Pre- and post-birth measures of young parents also have shown that marital romance, friendship, displays of affection, and sexual adjustment tend to decrease while feelings of partnership and marital conflict tend to increase during this period of time (Andersen, 1984; Belsky, Lang, and Rovine, 1985; Cowan et al., 1985). Interestingly, changes in marital satisfaction have been found to involve different issues as well as to occur at different rates for men and women, as has been mentioned. Cowan et al. (1985) have reported that women tend to become more concerned with the divisions of familial roles, while men increase their time and efforts in the working world. Similarly, as mentioned above, women tend to feel dissatisfaction with the marriage during the early months of parenthood, while men tend to show their dissatisfaction between 6 and 18 months postpartum.

In addition to all of the changes associated with becoming a parent, a number of investigators have found both personal and marital qualities that remain fairly stable from pregnancy to early parenthood. Brunnquell, Crichton, and Egeland (1981) found that four global clusters of prenatal maternal personal characteristics remained stable at 3 months postpartum. In addition to stability, three clusters—psychological complexity,

negative reactions to pregnancy, and hostility-suspicious-
ness—were useful in predicting the quality of maternal care.
Other investigators have found that levels of self-esteem, self-
satisfaction, and positive mood remained consistent over the
transition to parenthood (Feldman et al., 1983; Cowan and
Cowan, 1987). The reported stability in the marital relationship
concerns the relative rank order of the couples in terms of
marital satisfaction. Both Belsky, Lang, and Rovine (1985) and
Cowan and Cowan (1987) have found that although marital
satisfaction declines following the birth of the first child, the
relative rank-order of the couples from high to low remains
stable.

Formation of Relationships

On the basis of this new research on the transition to parenthood, it is important to broaden our perspective and consider theoretical and empirical work on the formation of relationships. The relationships approach provides a context for
understanding the transition to parenthood as creating a new
system beyond husband-wife, mother-father, or parent-child,
one that can be understood as a family system. Parke and Tinsley (1987) stress the importance of recognizing the interdependence of the roles and functions of family members. To understand the behavior of one member of a family, the
complementary behaviors of others must be recognized and
assessed as well. Parke and Tinsley have focused on shifts in
individual, parental, and family roles as well as societal changes,
all of which impact substantially on the definition and functioning of the family as a system.

The development of marital and family relationships depends on individual personality, biological, and cultural factors
(Hinde and Hinde, 1987). When a baby is born, the established
relationship system is upset and changed, resulting in a new
relationship. Further, the "working models" (Bowlby, 1979;
Bretherton, 1985) of old relationships long since put to rest are
revived and renewed as the child is born. Sameroff and Emde
(1989) note that the infant may acquire an enlarged repertoire
of internalized memories, abstractions of memories, and models, all of which lend stability to the relationship with the parents. They have suggested that the stability and coherence of

this relationship may be conserved through time by such structures. However, it is important to recognize that the reemergence, in the parents, of old feelings and ways of relating from earlier "working models" may at times help the emerging new relationship but may at others interfere with the couple's ability to accomplish a positive transition. Reiss (1989) suggests that we need to have a clearer understanding of the relative power of internal models and common practices to predict sustained patterns of relationships, whether competent or maladaptive. He has described two types of systems to elaborate his understanding of contrasting views of family continuity. The first is the "represented family," the core analogy being the concept of a working model. As children develop, they construct and reuse models of how things happen, particularly in terms of relationships that influence the individual. In later relationships, depending on how the child has integrated earlier experience, past internal working models may or may not be activated. The contrasting system, the "practicing family," has as its central analogy the notion of practice. The child will practice something (art, religion, etc.) until it becomes routine. The main perspective here is not of an individual cognition but of a group with the common group practice to sustain the model.

Sroufe (1989) has pointed out that working models of self and others can be modified, particularly in the context of other significant relationships. It is these early models that influence behaviors and reactions during the transition to parenthood. Diverse processes contribute to stability in a relationship. Further, the durability of a relationship, be it marital, parent-child, or family, depends, at least in part, on the partners' reaching reasonable agreement about how they define the relationship. Often stability depends more on the active avoidance of undesirable states than on seeking the ideal (Hinde and Hinde, 1987). If definitions of the relationship are influenced by early working models which are inappropriate, or which interfere with the changes necessary to make a positive transition to parenthood, the result may be problematic for some components of the family system. According to Sroufe (1989), the relationship itself is an organization. The formative aspects of early social relationships with primary caregivers are crucial for the development of personality. From the dyadic organization emerging from the early relationship with the caregiver comes the organization from which the self emerges. From dyadic behavioral regulation comes self-regulation. Sroufe cites Sander's earlier work (1975) in support of this theoretical position, proposing that an organization is present from a very early developmental period, as far back as the infant–caregiver dyadic system. Originally the organizational system is constructed around the infant; over time the behavioral interaction makes room for increasing participation by the infant, leading to increasing recognition of the role the child may play in determining action leading to a "self-regulatory core."

For the infant or child to be competent, there must be a caregiving environment that is alert and responsive to the newborn's reflexive signals (Ainsworth and Bell, 1974; Sander, 1975). The same notion is important for adult men and women—as individuals, as a couple, and as parents. The environment or context must be responsive to their needs, some of which will emerge from past working models. If the environment is unresponsive, the result may be a breakdown in the system, either in individual roles, the couple relationship, or parental competence and sensitivity.

Emde (1983) has proposed that the infant has a preadapted organized basis within the central nervous system, the affective core, that guides and monitors behavior. This affective monitoring system influences all self-regulatory and social activity. Infants' affective expressions guide caregiving from a very early stage of development. For example, the cry indicates distress and beckons the caregiver to relieve the discomfort. A smile or a coo indicates readiness for playful, pleasant interaction. Emde has proposed the salience of affect with each development transformation.

Considering the growth and development of relationships and the importance of emotional availability (Emde and Sameroff, 1989), affect attunement (Stern, 1985), and affect exchanges between caregiver and infant (Hann, Stringer, and Osofsky, 1987; Osofsky, Culp, and Ware, 1988) we propose that affect may be an important monitor for the relationship as well as for individual growth. Certainly in clinical work we use changes in emotional state and feelings as very sensitive indicators of the course and progress of treatment. Most of the research on the transition to parenthood has focused less on observed interactional patterns and more on perceptions of the situation and the relationship. In our ongoing research, we are studying patterns of affective interaction and emotional availability in relation to reports of marital satisfaction and perceptions of the relationship. Based on the usefulness of behavioral observation data for understanding the parent-child relationship and the clinical situation (Emde, 1988; Cramer, 1987; Osofsky, Culp, and Ware, 1988), this may be an important direction for understanding developmental shifts during the transition to parenthood.

In a recent chapter, Emde (Emde and Sameroff, 1989) has focused on the clinical implications of research on the infant and family relationship experience. He questions why many clinicians, practitioners, and theorists have been hesitant to focus on the child's relationship experience in contrast to emphasis on the individual in evaluating adaptive functioning. He suggests that, historically, individual problems, as opposed to relationship disorders, have been stressed in the etiology of developmental problems. A prime example is the common tendency for troubled families to "scapegoat" an individual when the inherent problem resides in the relationship or family system. However, as Winnicott (1960) so pithily observed, "there is no such thing as a baby," thereby pointing to the importance of recognizing the baby or child as embedded in a family or caregiver system. Emde highlights the implications of this broader perspective for understanding relationship disturbances. In our ongoing research (Osofsky, Culp, and Ware, 1988; Ware, Osofsky, and Eberhart-Wright, 1987) on adolescent mothers and their infants, the role of home visitors has had an important impact on outcomes for both infants and mothers. However, most pertinent for this discussion, the home visitor relationship has become an important one that has impacted on the mother's *relationship* with her child. Thus, we have been able to study the impact of the home visitor relationship on the mother–child relationship. An important component of this relation between relationships has been the *quality* of the relationship as determined by the mother's *genuine* involvement with her home visitor. The quality of this relationship seems to be a determining factor influencing meaningful outcomes for the development of both the young mother and her child, and for their relationship.

It is clear that we need careful studies of low- and high-risk couples to determine the important facilitating factors for the marital relationship during this transition period. In the empirical work of Belsky, Lang, and Rovine (1985), Cowan and Cowan (1987), and Osofsky and Culp (1989), some of the important elements have begun to be specified. We will now present data from our longitudinal study to integrate current empirical research with the theoretical material and other studies.

Study of Risk Factors for Parents and Infants during the Transition to Parenthood

Our longitudinal study of the transition to parenthood was designed to learn more about both the normative processes and the risk factors for parents and infants. One hundred seven married couples who were expecting their first child and who were receiving prenatal care at the University of Kansas Health Sciences Center were recruited for the study. The mean age of the men was 27 years (range 18–48 years) and of the women 25 years (range 18–35 years). At the time of the initial prenatal visit, the couples had been married for an average of 2½ years (range 1 month–15 years). They were primarily middle class and well educated. Table 1 presents this information in summary form. Additional demographic statistics on race and income are presented in Table 2.

Overview of Procedure

The couples were recruited through the obstetrical group practice program of the University of Kansas Medical Center. Initial contact with potential subjects occurred at a regularly scheduled obstetrical visit during the third trimester. All

TABLE 1

Summary Statistics for the Maternal and Paternal Variables of Age,
Education, Socioeconomic Status, and Length of Marriage

	N	Mean	SD	Range
Age				
Father	89	27.7	5.2	18 to 40
Mother	91	25.7	4.5	18 to 35
Education				
Father	88	14.7	3.0	9 to 23
Mother	89	14.2	2.5	10 to 21
Socioeconomic Status				
Hollingshead	86	41.7	13.7	11 to 66
Length of Marriage (years)	89	2.7	2.7	0.1 to 14.8

women who were married, primiparous, between 18 and 35 years of age, and willing to participate were enrolled. Approximately 77 percent of the couples who were approached and met these criteria agreed to participate. They were interviewed during subsequent regularly scheduled obstetrical visits. The men were interviewed if they came in with their wives or, if not, a packet of questionnaires was sent home for them to fill out and return. Couples were interviewed again at 3, 6, and 13 months postpartum during a laboratory session.

Measures

Included in the battery of questionnaires were instruments designed to measure individual levels of depression, self-esteem, and family and social support and others that assessed the couple's relationship and style of interaction.

The three individual measures were administered to both the wife and the husband. Self-esteem was assessed using the Index of Self-Esteem (ISE) from the Clinical Measurement Package (Hudson, 1982). This measure is a 25-item scale on which the respondent rates each item (e.g., "I feel ugly," "I feel I am a likable person") on a 7-point scale. A high score indicates

TABLE 2
Frequency Distributions for Race and Income

Race	Maternal		Paternal	
	Frequency	*Percent*	*Frequency*	*Percent*
White	73	80.2	72	79.1
Black	15	16.5	14	15.4
Amer. Indian	1	1.1	0	0.0
Hispanic	1	1.1	2	2.2
Other	1	1.1	1	1.1
Missing	0	0.0	2	2.2
Total	91	100.0	91	100.0

Income	Couple	
	Frequency	*Percent*
None	1	1.1
<3 000	1	1.1
3 000–49 99	3	3.3
5 000–74 99	2	2.2
7 500–99 993	3	3.3
10 000–14 999	12	13.2
15 000–19 999	12	13.2
20 000–24 999	11	12.1
25 000–29 999	7	7.7
30 000–39 999	9	9.9
40 000–49 999	10	11.0
50 000>	11	12.1
Don't know	5	5.5
Missing	4	4.4
Total	91	100.0

a low level of self-esteem. A single score with a possible range from 0 to 100 was computed for each respondent, with the clinical cut-off score being 30 or higher. Depression was assessed using the Center for Epidemiological Studies Depression Scale—CES–D (Radloff, 1977). This 20-item scale measures current levels of depressive symptomatology. Respondents rate each item on a 4-point scale indicating the frequency of contact with the person listed. A single score with a possible range from 0 to 64 was computed.

Assessments of the couple's relationship and their style of interaction were made using two different scales. One measured marital adjustment and satisfaction, and the other measured mutual role arrangements and satisfaction. Marital adjustment and satisfaction were assessed using a 14-item scale, developed by Huston (1983) using questions adapted from the Areas of Change Questionnaire (Weiss, Hops, and Patterson, 1973; Margolin, Talovic, and Weinstein, 1983). The measure assesses satisfaction and dissatisfaction with marital interaction producing three scores: (1) satisfaction with the extent to which positive interpersonal events/activities have been occurring in the marital relationship, (2) satisfaction with the extent to which negative interpersonal events/activities have been occurring, and (3) satisfaction with the extent to which sexual activities have been occurring. Positive activities include, for example, "my partner expresses approval of me or compliments me on something I did," "sharing leisure time with my partner," and "talking with my partner about things that have happened." Negative activities include, for example, "my partner acts bored or uninterested while I am talking," "my partner is critical of me or complains about something I did or didn't do," and "my partner does things knowing that they annoy me." A high score on the positive activities and the sexual activities scales indicates that the respondent would like the spouse to engage in many more of these activities. A low score indicates that the respondent would like their frequency to remain the same. A low score on the negative activities scale indicates that the respondent would like the spouse to engage in many fewer negative activities. A high score indicates that the respondent would like the rate of negative activities to remain the same.

The couple's mutual role arrangements and satisfaction with them were assessed with the "Who Does What?" scale (Cowan et al., 1985). There are three types of scores based on the parents' responses: (1) role arrangement/involvement score, (2) role satisfaction score, and (3) role awareness score. Each of these scores is computed for the two domains of the questionnaire: (1) household and family tasks, and (2) decision making. The role arrangement/involvement score can be interpreted as a relative involvement score, with higher scores indicating greater involvement by the men and lower scores indicating greater involvement by the women. Scores above an average of 5.0 indicate that men are responsible for more than 50 percent of the labor in that domain. The role satisfaction score is a discrepancy score showing the difference between "how it is now" and "how I'd like it to be." Higher scores indicate greater discrepancies, which is interpreted as lower satisfaction (Cowan and Cowan, 1987). The role awareness score indicates the discrepancy between members of a couple on the amount of involvement in each domain. Higher scores indicate greater discrepancies, which is interpreted as lower awareness of the division of tasks in that domain.

The measures described above produced a total of 21 summary scores, which included three individual scores—a depression score, a self-esteem score, and a family and social support score. For each spouse, three marital adjustment scores were derived—a positive activities score, a negative activities score, and a sexual activities score. For each spouse, four mutual role arrangement scores were derived—current status of role division for household and family tasks, current status of role division for decision making, satisfaction with the division of household and family tasks, and satisfaction with the division of decision making. In addition, a household tasks division awareness score and a decision making awareness score were computed comparing each member of the couple's score on the current status of role division in the two domains assessed.

Results

The results focus on several issues: (1) changes in individual psychological measures and marital relationship measures over time, and (2) the relationship between maternal individual psychological measures, marital relationship measures, and mother-infant behavioral interaction during feeding. Two sets of correlations were run to determine changes in individual psychological measures and the marital relationship over time.

The first set addressed the question of how the maternal and paternal responses to the prenatal measures of depression, marital adjustment, and marital satisfaction related to the 3-month responses to these same measures. The second set addressed the question of how maternal and paternal responses to the prenatal measures of depression, marital adjustment, and marital satisfaction related to the 6-month responses to these same measures. Another set of correlations was run to determine the relationships between psychological measures, marital relationship measures, and maternal feeding behaviors during the perinatal period and when the infant was 3 months old.

Prenatal to 3-Month Relationships

The prenatal measures, including maternal and paternal depression and marital adjustment and satisfaction, were correlated with the matching set of 3-month scales. Of the eight comparisons of equivalent scales, six were statistically significant: maternal depression, $r = 0.40$; maternal positive activities, $r = 0.40$; paternal depression, $r = 0.63$; paternal positive activities, $r = 0.52$; paternal negative activities, $r = 0.49$; and paternal sexual activities, $r = 0.38$.

In order to determine whether the mean scores for the six significant correlations were different from the prenatal to 6-month assessment, a series of repeated measures analyses of variance were performed. The results indicated that of the six correlations reported above, the means of three of the scales were significantly different over time. Prenatal maternal depression scores ($M = 13.19$) were significantly higher than 3-month maternal depression scores ($M = 9.90$), $F (1, 77) = 10.64$, $p < 0.002$. Mothers reported being less depressed at 3 months than they reported prenatally. Prenatal maternal positive activities score ($M = 4.52$) was significantly lower than the 3-month score ($M = 4.78$), $F (1, 79) = 4.64$, $p < 0.034$. Mothers reported being less satisfied with the number of positive activities in their marriage at 3 months than they reported prenatally. Prenatal paternal negative activities scores ($M = 3.53$) were significantly lower than 3-month paternal negative activities scores ($M = 3.76$), $F (1, 64) = 9.34$, $p < 0.003$. Fathers reported being more satisfied with the number of negative activities in their marriage at 3 months than they reported prenatally. There were no significant mean differences between the prenatal assessment and the 3-month assessment for paternal depression, paternal positive activities, or paternal sexual activities. These scores remained relatively stable from the prenatal to the 3-month assessment.

Prenatal to 6-Month Relationships

The prenatal scales, including maternal and paternal self-esteem, household task role arrangement, decision making role arrangement, household tasks role satisfaction, decision making role satisfaction, household tasks role awareness, and decision making role awareness scales, were correlated with the equivalent 6-month scales. Of the twelve comparisons of equivalent scales between the prenatal and 6-month assessments, 10 were statistically significant: maternal self-esteem, $r = 0.62$; maternal household tasks satisfaction, $r = 0.51$; maternal decision making satisfaction, $r = 0.63$; maternal household tasks arrangement, $r = 0.60$; maternal decision making arrangement, $r = 0.41$; paternal self-esteem, $r = 0.74$; paternal household tasks satisfaction, $r = 0.55$; paternal household tasks arrangement, $r = 0.67$; paternal decision making arrangement, $r = 0.54$; and decision making awareness, $r = 0.67$.

In order to determine whether the mean scores for the 10 significant correlations were different from the prenatal to the 6-month assessment, another series of repeated measures analyses of variance were performed. The results of three of the analyses of variance indicated significant differences between the prenatal and 6-month means. Prenatal maternal self-esteem scores ($M = 28.53$) were significantly higher than 6-month maternal self-esteem scores ($M = 23.64$), $F (1, 44) = 10.64, p < 0.002$. Mothers reported lower levels of self-esteem prenatally than they did 6 months postpartum. Prenatal maternal household tasks role arrangement scores ($M = 4.84$) were significantly higher than 6-month maternal household tasks role arrangement scores ($M = 4.51$), $F (1, 56) = 9.89, p < 0.003$. Mothers reported doing a greater percentage of the household tasks at 6 months than they reported doing prenatally. Prenatal maternal decision making role satisfaction scores ($M = 0.49$) were significantly lower than 6-month maternal decision making role satisfaction scores ($M = 0.68$), $F (1, 56) = 7.42$, $p <$ 0.009. Mothers reported being less satisfied with the division of decision making at 6 months than they reported prenatally. There were no significant mean differences between the prenatal and 6-month assessment for maternal household tasks role satisfaction, maternal decision making role arrangement, paternal self-esteem, paternal household tasks role satisfaction, paternal household tasks role arrangement, paternal decision making role arrangement, and decision making role awareness. These scores remained relatively stable from the prenatal to the 6-month assessment.

Relationships between Prenatal Questionnaire Measures and Perinatal Feeding

The prenatal individual psychological and marital relationship measures, including depression, self-esteem, marital adjustment and satisfaction, and mutual role arrangement and satisfaction, were correlated with maternal perinatal feeding behaviors including attentiveness, visual stimulation, en face, auditory stimulation, tactile stimulation, and position of the baby. There were no significant correlations among the four prenatal questionnaire measures and the six maternal feeding scores.

The mothers were then divided into two subgroups based on the depression measure using the standardized clinical cut-off point for this scale. Of the six possible correlations, three were significant within the depressed mothers subgroup. Mothers who reported more depression with less attentiveness to their infants ($r = -0.40$) provided less visual stimulation ($r = -0.42$) and held their infants in a position providing less physical contact ($r = -0.48$). There were no significant correlations within the nondepressed mothers subgroup.

The mothers were then divided into two subgroups based on the self-esteem measure. There were no significant correlations within either the low self-esteem or the high self-esteem subgroups.

Relationships between 3-Month Questionnaire Measures and 3-Month Feeding Observations

The 3-month individual psychological and marital relationships measures, including maternal depression and marital adjustment and satisfaction, were correlated with maternal 3-month feeding behaviors including stimulation, tactile stimulation, and position of the baby. There were no significant correlations among the 3-month questionnaire measures and maternal feeding behaviors.

The mothers were again divided into subgroups based on the depression measure using the standardized clinical cut-off point for this scale. Of the six correlations, two were significant. Mothers who reported higher levels of depression demonstrated less en face behavior ($r = -0.52$) and held the infant in a position providing less physical contact ($r = -0.44$). For the mothers reporting lower levels of depression, none of the correlations were significant.

In sum, mothers reported being more depressed and less satisfied with the amount of positive activities in their marriage at 3 months than they did prenatally. At the same time, fathers reported being more satisfied with the amount of negative activities in the marriage at 3 months than they did prenatally. Between the prenatal and 3-month assessment, mothers' satisfaction with the amount of negative activities in the marriage, fathers' depression levels, and fathers' satisfaction with the amount of positive activities in the marriage remained stable.

Mothers reported having better self-esteem, doing a greater proportion of household tasks, and being less satisfied with the division of decision making in the marriage at 6 months than they did prenatally. Between the prenatal and the 6-month assessments, mothers reported that there was a similar division of decision making but that they were less satisfied with the division. They reported doing a greater proportion of the household tasks but had similar levels of satisfaction between the prenatal and the 6-month assessments. They reported higher levels of self-esteem at 6 months as compared to the prenatal assessment. Their higher self-esteem and greater contribution to household tasks but no increased involvement in the decision making in the marriage probably influenced their decreased level of satisfaction with the division of decision making. Between the prenatal and the 6-month assessments, both mothers' and fathers' reports of the division of household tasks and decision making remained stable. Fathers' reports of self-esteem and household task satisfaction remained stable between the prenatal and the 6-month assessments. The decision making awareness score also remained stable between the prenatal and the 6-month assessment. Within the subgroup of mothers who were clinically depressed prenatally as measured on the self-report measure, level of depression was significantly correlated with mothers' attentiveness, visual stimulation, and physical contact with the infant during feeding. Within the subgroup of mothers who reported clinical levels of depression at 3 months, depression was significantly and negatively correlated with mothers' en face behavior and physical contact with the infant during feeding. The more depressed mothers provided less eye contact and physical contact.

Discussion

In understanding normative growth and development during the transition to parenthood, it may be useful to consider some of Erikson's classic ideas (1950, 1954). He has stressed that reactions and upheavals are part of the growth process. Considerable disequilibrium and crisis can herald the beginning of a new growth phase. The inner organization of an individual or a couple is based on a past relationship history in addition to individual developmental components. Bowlby, Ainsworth, Bretherton, Sroufe, and others have provided empirical evidence confirming the link between the relationship history and the emerging constellation of inner organization which is the self. They have pointed to the important continuity of the relationship history, with parallels between the earlier caregiver relationship influencing the content and style of later relationships. In some ways, this empirical research has provided confirmatory evidence for the earlier, more subjective clinical studies of the transition to parenthood (Caplan, 1957;

Benedek, 1959; Bibring et al., 1961) from a broader relationship perspective.

More recent perspectives are also extremely important in
understanding the normative growth and development of relationships. As noted above, Reiss (1989) argues that a clearer
picture is needed of the relative power of internal models and
common practices to predict sustained patterns of both competent and maladaptive social relationships. We need to know
what we can predict from the perspectives of the "practicing"
and the "represented" family as described by Reiss. Further,
we need to know the effects of various types of interventions
(Barnard et al., 1988; Beckwith, 1988; Emde, 1988; Osofsky,
Culp, and Ware, 1988; Ware, Osofsky, and Eberhart-Wright,
1987) in terms of their impact not only on the individuals, but
also on the relationship.

The transition to parenthood and the subsequent changes
in the relationship that take place during the parenthood phase
are only beginning to be understood in any depth. Models for
understanding developmental life changes have more recently
been applied to this area. For example, the family systems approach has enriched our understanding of this transitional
phase, notably through the work of Belsky and the Cowans.
The notion of "working models" proposed by Bowlby (1979)
and elaborated by Bretherton (1985) and Sroufe (1989) has
moved our understanding closer to the clinical realm described
in a different context by Fraiberg, Adelson, and Shapiro (1975),
who emphasize the importance of earlier caregiver relationships and their crucial impact on those that develop in the
course of becoming a parent. The surface has barely been
scratched, however, in gaining a more meaningful understanding of the developmental course of the parenting couple's relationship as well as the caregiver-child relationship. Clearly the
patterns of dissatisfaction that seem to occur following first
parenthood and appear to increase with subsequent parenthood speak to an imbalance in the parenting couple system
that, in most cases, does not return to the same equilibrium
that was present before the child was born. At the same time,
however, the degree of satisfaction or dissatisfaction after the

birth is consistent with earlier patterns of satisfaction and dissatisfaction with the relationship. The finding that mothers who reported being more depressed were less attentive and responsive to their infants highlights the need for early screening and possible preventive interventions to decrease risk for the parenting relationship. It would be very interesting to pursue, empirically, subsequent changes and readjustments in the relationship as the children grow through different phases of their development.

Very little work has been done based on recent empirical knowledge related to early facilitative interventions with parenting couples, with the notable exception of the interesting group work of Cowan and Cowan (1987). The role of intervention, particularly with families at risk (Barnard et al., 1988; Beckwith, 1988; Osofsky, Culp, and Ware, 1988; Emde, 1988), may prove to be extremely important at crucial transitional periods if the individual needs of both mother and father are addressed, as well as those of the couple. The work of Main, Kaplan, and Cassidy (1985), indicating that mothers' reports of their early nurturance were strongly associated with the security or insecurity of the attachment patterns of their children at 1 year of age, may be particularly instructive in facilitating this process. If either member of the couple feels that individual needs are not being met adequately after the birth of a baby, as is often the case (see Osofsky and Osofsky, 1980; Osofsky and Culp, 1989), then such feelings will likely impact on the marital relationship and even the caregiver-child relationship. Thus, particularly with much less availability of an extended family or supportive network during this transitional period, interventions may be extremely important to facilitate positive growth at a number of different levels. All of these areas are interesting ones that may be important to pursue from a developmental–clinical perspective to gain a better understanding of a relationships perspective on the transition to parenthood.

References

Ainsworth, M.D.S., & Bell, S. (1974), Mother–infant interaction and the development of competence. In: *The Growth of Competence*, ed. K. Connelly & J. Bruner. New York: Academic Press, pp. 97–118.

Andersen, I. (1984), Transition to parenthood research. *J. Psychosom. Obstet. & Gynaecol.*, 3:3–16.

Barnard, K.E., Magyary, D., Sumner, G., Booth, C.L., Mitchell, S.K., & Spieker, S. (1988), Prevention of parenting alterations for women with low social support. *Psychiat.*, 51:248–253.

Beckwith, L. (1988), Intervention with disadvantaged parents of sick preterm infants. *Psychiat.*, 51:242–247.

Belsky, J., Lang, M.E., & Rovine, M. (1985), Stability and change in marriage across the transition to parenthood: A second study. *J. Marriage & Family*, 47:855–865.

———— Volling, B.L. (1986), Mothering, fathering & marital interaction in the family triad: Exploring family systems processes. In: *Men's Transition to Parenthood: Longitudinal Studies of Early Family Experience*, ed. P. Berman & F. Pedersen. Hillsdale, N.J.: Erlbaum, pp. 37–63.

Benedek, T. (1959), Parenthood as a developmental phase: A contribution to the libido theory. *J. Amer. Psychoanal. Assn.*, 7:389–417.

Bibring, G.L., Dwyer, T.F., Huntington, D., & Valentine, A.F. (1961), A study of the psychological processes in pregnancy and the earliest mother–child relationship: I. Some propositions and comments; II. Methodological considerations. *The Psychoanalytic Study of the Child*, 16:9–72. New York: International Universities Press.

Bowlby, J. (1979), *The Making and Breaking of Affectional Bonds*. London: Tavistock.

Bretherton, I. (1985), Attachment theory: Retrospect and prospect. In: *Growing Points of Attachment Theory and Research*, ed. I. Bretherton & E. Waters. Monograph 50 of the Society for Research in Child Development, pp. 3–35.

Brunnquell, D., Crichton, L., & Egeland, B. (1981), Maternal personality and attitude in disturbances of child rearing. *Amer. J. Orthopsychiat.*, 51:680–691.

Caplan, G. (1957), Psychological aspects of maternity care. *Amer. J. Public Health*, 47:25–31.

Cowan, C.P., Cowan, P.A., Heming, G., Garrett, E., Coyish, W.S., Curtis-Boles, H., & Boles, A.J. (1985), Transition to parenthood: His, hers, and theirs. *J. Family Issues*, 6:451–481.

Cowan, P.A., & Cowan, C.P. (1987), Couple relationships, parenting styles, and the child's development at three. Paper presented at biennial meeting of Society for Research in Child Development, Baltimore, April.

Cramer, B. (1987), Objective and subjective aspects of parent-infant relations: An attempt at correlation between infant studies and clinical work. In: *Handbook of Infant Development*, 2nd ed., ed. J.D. Osofsky. New York: Wiley.

Emde, R.N. (1983), The prerepresentational self and its affective core. *The Psychoanalytic Study of the Child*, 38:165–192. New Haven: Yale University Press.

———— (1987), The effect of relationships on relationships: A developmental approach to clinical intervention. In: *Relations Between Relationships Within Families*, ed. R.A. Hinde & J.S. Hinde. Oxford: Oxford University Press, pp. 354–364.

———— (1988), Risk, intervention and meaning. *Psychiat.*, 51:254–259.

———— Sameroff, A.J. (1989), Understanding early relationship disturbances. In: *Relationship Disturbances in Early Childhood: A Developmental Approach*, ed. A.J. Sameroff & R.N. Emde. New York: Basic Books, pp. 3–16.

Erikson, E. (1950), *Childhood and Society*, rev. ed. New York: Norton, 1963.

———— (1954), Growth and crisis of the "healthy personality." In: *Personality in Nature, Society, and Culture*, 2nd ed., ed. C. Kluckholm & H.A. Murray. New York: Knopf, pp. 185–225.

Feldman, S.S., Nash, S.C., & Aschenbrenner, B.G. (1983), Antecedents of fathering. *Child Devel.*, 54:1628–1636.

Fraiberg, S., Adelson, E., & Shapiro, V. (1975), Ghosts in the nursery: A psychoanalytic approach to the problems of impaired infant-mother relationships. *J. Amer. Acad. Child Psychiat.*, 14:387–421.

Grossman, F., Eichler, L., & Winickoff, S. (1980), *Pregnancy, Birth and Parenthood*. San Francisco: Jossey-Bass.

Hann, D., Stringer, S., & Osofsky, J.D. (1987), Adolescent mothers: Emotional availability and the quality of attachment. Poster presented at the biennial institute of the National Center for Clinical Infant Programs, Washington, D.C.

Hicks, M., & Platt, M. (1971), Marital happiness and stability: A review of research in the sixties. *J. Marriage & Family*, 32:553–573.

Hinde, R.A., & Hinde, J.S. eds. (1987), *Relations Between Relationships Within Families*. Oxford: Oxford University Press.

Hobfoll, S.E., & Lieberman, J.R. (1987), Personality and social resources in immediate and continued stress resistance among women. *J. Personality & Soc. Psychol.*, 52:18–26.

Hudson, W.W. (1982), *The Clinical Measurement Package: A Field Manual*. Homewood, Ill.: Dorsey.

Huston, T. (1983), The topography of marriage: A longitudinal study of change in husband-wife relationships over the first year. Plenary address to the International Conference on Personal Relationships, Madison, Wisc.

———— McHale, S., & Crouter, A. (1986), When the honeymoon's over: Changes in the marriage relationship over the first year. In: *The Emerging Field of Personal Relationships*, ed. R. Gilmour & S. Duck. Hillsdale, N.J.: Erlbaum, pp. 109–132.

Lewis, R.A., & Spanier, G.B. (1979), Theorizing about the quality and stability of marriage. In: *Contemporary Theories about the Family*, Vol. 1, ed. W.R. Burr, R. Hill, R.I. Nye, & I.L. Reiss. New York: Free Press, pp. 269–294.

Main, M., Kaplan, N., & Cassidy, J. (1985), Security in infancy, childhood and adulthood: A move to the level of representation. In: *Growing Points in Attachment Research*, ed. I. Bretherton & E. Waters. Monograph 50 of the Society for Research in Child Development, pp. 66–106.

Margolin, G., Talovic, S., & Weinstein, C.D. (1983), Areas of change questionnaire: A practical approach to marital assessment. *J. Consult. & Clin. Psychol.*, 51:920–931.

Osofsky, J.D. (1988), Affective exchanges between high risk mothers and infants. *Internat. J. Psycho-Anal.*, 69:221–231.

———— Culp, R.E. (1989), Risk factors in the transition to parenthood. In: *Fathers and Their Families*, ed. S. Cath, A. Gurwitt, & L. Gunsberg. Hillsdale, N.J.: Analytic Press, pp. 145–165.

—— Ware, L.M. (1988), Intervention challenges with adolescent mothers and their infants. *Psychiat.*, 51:236–241.

Osofsky, H.J., & Osofsky, J.D. (1980), *Answers for New Parents: Adjusting to Your New Role.* New York: Walker.

Parke, R.D., & Tinsley, B.J. (1987), Family intervention in infancy. In: *Handbook of Infant Development*, 2nd ed., ed. J.D. Osofsky. New York: Wiley.

Radloff, L. (1977), The CES-D scale: A self-report depression scale for research in the general population. *J. Appl. Psychological Measurement*, 1:385–401.

Reiss, D. (1989), The represented and practicing family: Contrasting visions of family continuity. In: *Relationship Disturbances in Early Childhood: A Developmental Approach*, ed. A.J. Sameroff & R.N. Emde. New York: Basic Books, pp. 191–220.

Sameroff, A.J., & Emde, R.N., eds. (1989), *Relationship Disturbances in Early Childhood: A Developmental Approach.* New York: Basic Books.

Sander, L. (1975), Infant and caretaking environment. In: *Explorations in Child Psychiatry*, ed. E.J. Anthony. New York: Plenum.

Shereshefsky, P.M., & Yarrow, L.J. (1974), *Psychological Aspects of a First Pregnancy and Early Postnatal Adaptation.* New York: Raven Press.

Sirignano, S.W., & Lachman, M.E. (1985), Personality change during the transition to parenthood. *Developmental Psychol.*, 21:558–567.

Sroufe, L.A. (1989), Relationships, self, and individual adaptation. In: *Relationship Disturbances in Early Childhood: A Developmental Approach*, ed. A.J. Sameroff & R.N. Emde. New York: Basic Books, pp. 97–124.

Stern, D.N. (1985), *The Interpersonal World of the Infant.* New York: Basic Books.

Ware, L.W., Osofsky, J.D., & Eberhart-Wright, A. (1987), Challenges of home visitor interventions with adolescent mothers and their infants. *Infant Mental Health*, 8:418–428.

Weiss, R.L., Hops, H., & Patterson, G.R. (1973), A framework for conceptualizing marital conflict, a technology for altering, some data for evaluating it. In: *Critical Issues in Research and Practice: Proceedings of the Fourth Banff International Conference on Behavior Modification*, ed. F.W. Clark & L.A. Hamerlynck. Champaign, Ill.: Research Press.

Winnicott, D.W. (1960), The theory of the parent-infant relationship. In: *The Maturational Processes and the Facilitating Environment.* New York: International Universities Press, 1965, pp. 37–55.

5

Psychoanalysis and the Developmental Narrative

BERTRAM J. COHLER

MARK FREEMAN

Psychoanalytically informed study of the life course has inspired reconsideration of the significance of the personal past in understanding present experience. Central to this consideration of developmental perspectives across adulthood are such theoretical issues as continuity and discontinuity over the life course, the role of earlier experiences in determining later outcomes, and the place of the oedipal or "nuclear" neurosis as the paradigmatic life course transformation, particularly into middle and late life (Cohler, 1982; Cohler and Carney, unpublished). Further, discussion of these issues is closely tied to the problem of method in the study of personality development across the adult years, particularly that regarding the nature of contributions based on experience-near, empathically informed methods characteristic both of interpretive approaches in the social sciences and of the psychoanalytic interview itself, as contrasted with traditional normative inquiry in the social sciences (Kohut, 1959, 1971, 1982; Polanyi, 1965; Gill, 1976; Klein, 1976; Cohler, 1982; Freeman, 1984). Efforts to integrate these two approaches may lead to greater understanding of the course of life than is possible using either approach alone.

The Paradox of Psychoanalytic Study of the Past

Two fundamentally different perspectives regarding the psychoanalytic study of lives may be identified: the genetic or retrospective, and the developmental or prospective (Freud, 1920c). The genetic point of view (Rapaport and Gill, 1959), first outlined by Freud (1896a, 1896b) and later expanded in the 1915 revision of *Three Essays on the Theory of Sexuality* (1905b), the case studies of Leonardo (1910b) and the Wolf Man (1918), the *Introductory Lectures* (1916–1917), the posthumous "Outline of Psycho-Analysis" (1940), maintained that the structure of present experience may be traced to previous structures, the "now" of present life, as seen in the psychoanalytic interview, being simultaneously regarded the "then" of past life (Freud, 1913; Hartmann and Kris, 1945; Rapaport and Gill, 1959; Zetzel and Meissner, 1973; Solnit, 1982). This genetic approach (see also Schafer, 1976) provides psychoanalysis a historical dimension in which persons look backward from present life in order to explain the relationship of present and past. Often regarded as the defining characteristic of psychoanalysis (Freud, 1913), it is less often realized that this genetic approach was derived at least in part from Freud's prepsychoanalytic developmental neurobiological studies, rather than from clinical observation alone (Bernfeld, 1951; Sulloway, 1979). To a large extent, Freud's own intellectual outlook, which provided the basis of the genetic point of view, was shaped by his "bench research" over a period of more than two decades prior to psychoanalytic study, and was further influenced by his reading of Darwin, Ernst Haeckel (1868), Hughlings Jackson (1875), and others working within an evolutionary framework.

Discussing the concept of fixation, for instance, Freud comments in the *Introductory Lectures* on the importance of this early laboratory study in directing his attention to the prominence of archaic states as the basis for later structures. However, nowhere is Freud as explicit regarding the use of this biological analogy to individual development as in his essay on Leonardo (1910b), where he comments that "impressive analogies from biology have prepared us to find that the individual's mental development repeats the course of human development in a modified form; and the conclusions which psycho-analytic research into the child's mind has reached concerning the high value set on the genitals in infancy will not therefore strike us as improbable" (p. 97). These comparative studies had a profound influence upon psychoanalysis as both a theory of personality development and a treatment modality.

Problems arise, however, to the extent that clinical observation from the psychoanalytic setting is used as a means of confirming assumptions regarding the relationship of past and present which may have been derived from a biological analogy. Viewed from a life course perspective, the formulation of metapsychology may have permitted Freud to realize an increased sense of meaning and direction in his own life, integrating his prepsychoanalytic laboratory study with his later clinical work and maintaining a coherent narrative of his career consistent with the biological knowledge available to him at the end of the nineteenth century (Bernfeld, 1941, 1949; Pribram and Gill, 1976; Kovel, 1978; Sulloway, 1979).

At the same time, it is ironic that in formulating metapsychology (Freud, 1896, 1898, 1915b), or realm "behind" consciousness, Freud appears to have repeated precisely the error he sought to correct in his critique of the mechanistic psychology of his time. As George Klein (1976) has observed, Freud while pioneering the study of motivation through his clinical inquiry, as a result of his continuing concern with metapsychology perpetuated a reductionist philosophy of science based on a datum fundamentally different from that of clinical inquiry; this prevented a more adequate appraisal of psychoanalysis as a human science concerned with issues of meaning, symbolization, and interpretation. In spite of his continuing clinical study of meaning, which has had enormous impact on arts and letters over the past century, Freud seemed unable to understand lives except by analogy with biology.

This deterministic biological perspective led to a connection of present and past based on a relationship of necessity, even inevitability, derived from the reconstruction of events early in the analysand's life which, together with present experience, is viewed as determining wishes and intents. The significance of these earlier life experiences for present adjustment is determined through reenactment, in the therapeutic relationship, of wishes initially derived from attempts to resolve the nuclear neurosis (Freud, 1896, 1910a, 1914, 1937; Kohut and Seitz, 1963). Further, it should be noted that the genetic point of view is not limited to anamnestic connections, in the sense that, following Freud's initial understanding of this term (Breuer and Freud, 1893–1895), past memories and associated feelings are recalled in the present, in circumstances experienced as historically similar. Rather, it is genetic in the sense first used by Freud (1954) in his letters to Fliess (especially his letter of November 2, 1896), regarding the implications of early experiences of the erotogenic zones for later development, and most explicitly stated in letters of April 6, 1897, and October 27, 1897, *Three Essays* (1905b), *The Introductory Lectures* (1916–1917), the case study of Da Vinci (1910b), the case study of the Wolf Man (1918), and the later cultural work, *Moses and Monotheism* (1939). Indeed, in cryptic observations in letters to Fliess, Freud anticipated the more detailed formulations later provided by Abraham (1921, 1924), Glover (1930, 1932a, 1932b), Erikson (1950), Spitz (1959), and Kohut (1971).

The genetic point of view both poses problems and offers promise for the study of how the past may be used in understanding present wishes and intents. Despite the undeniable relevance of the genetic point of view for these more detailed works outlining, in effect, the natural evolution of individual development, Freud's concern with the genesis of behavior also reflects concern with a mode of historical understanding distinctive of psychoanalysis. As Freud (1920c) notes, historical explanation is not simply prediction "turned upside down" (Scriven, 1959); rather, it is predicated on an autonomous mode of understanding, one fundamentally different from modes of understanding linked to prospective inquiry. For this reason, although problematic as regards the realization of psychoanalysis as a human science, Freud's concern with the genetic approach provides the conceptual foundation for the study of life history as a narrative of experience.

The Genetic Approach and Findings from Developmental Psychology

Although findings from experimental psychology have led to substantial revision in the dynamic and economic metapsychological approaches (Rosenblatt and Thickstun, 1970, 1977; Holt, 1975; Applegarth, 1977; Gill, 1977; Horowitz, 1977;

Swanson, 1977a, 1977b; Wallerstein, 1977), findings from normative developmental study have had much less impact in fostering revision of the genetic approach (Escoll, 1977; Abrams, 1978). Findings from normative developmental studies have seldom been used as a means of clarifying the assumptions of the genetic approach; most often they have been used in an effort to provide further support for Freud's earliest assumptions regarding the role of the past in the present, namely, those which seem to have been derived by analogy from neurobiological studies (Sulloway, 1979). To the extent that developmental psychology has been viewed as at all relevant to psychoanalytic theory and practice, it has been regarded primarily as providing supposedly scientific verification of specific assumptions (derived from genetic propositions) as to the origins of behavior in earliest infancy (Basch, 1977, 1982, 1985; Lichtenberg, 1983a, 1983b; Silver, 1985) and the consequences of particular early experiences for psychological development and adjustment across the life course (McDevitt, 1973; Tolpin and Kohut, 1980).

Other findings, suggesting that the course of development may not be as predictable or genetically ordered as previously thought (Gergen, 1977, 1982; Grunes, 1980; Kagan, 1980; Kohlberg, Ricks, and Snarey, 1984), have in the main been disregarded. These findings, based on long-term study of lives, suggest both that continuing personality development across the adult years is critical in understanding the experience of self and others so central to psychoanalytic inquiry, and that modes of inquiry believed to be most distinctive of more traditional natural science inquiry in psychology—modes focused on mechanisms and functions—may be less relevant in understanding factors determining this aspect of development than those which are more completely historical, which seek to understand what *has* taken place rather than merely to foretell what *will*.

However, it is not simply that it is easier to understand and explain the course of life by looking backward rather than forward; more important is the consideration that the meanings people attribute to their experience can be gleaned only retrospectively, after the fact. It is for this reason that a focus on these meanings, as exemplified by the human science approach of Habermas (1968, 1983), Ricoeur (1970, 1977), Geertz (1973, 1983), and others, may be more consistent with the interpretive perspective distinctive of psychoanalysis than is the "natural science" approach, at least to the extent that the latter makes assumptions about the relation of past and present based on experience-distant data and assumes the aims of prediction and control.

The seduction hypothesis. Many of the problems in the use of the genetic approach as a means for explaining later life outcomes may be seen in the effort within psychoanalysis to understand the impact of specific early events—e.g., presumed seduction or observation of parental intercourse (the primal scene)—on later life adjustment. Discussion of the so-called seduction hypothesis, from Freud's correspondence with Fliess (Freud, 1954) to the present (Masson, 1984), has assumed a necessary and specific connection between experiences in earliest childhood and adult psychological symptoms. In his early work with hysterical patients, Freud (1895) was struck by the apparent power of remembered incidents of childhood seduction to elicit symptoms among adults.

Applying developmental neurobiological findings to his initial study of hysterical patients, Freud concluded that their psychological distress was the result of a specific traumatic event, experienced in childhood, typically involving sexual stimulation greater than could be mastered or regulated. This stimulation was not directly represented in awareness but only indirectly, through associations or symbols. For example, in his discussion of the psychopathology of hysteria in the *Project for a Scientific Psychology*, Freud (1895) describes the case of a young lady with a phobia about going into shops, dating from an experience at the age of 12 when she had perceived two shopkeepers laughing at her clothes and had hurried from the shop. Associatively connected with this event was an earlier one, taking place at about age 8, when a shopkeeper had tried to touch her genitals; this earlier seduction was a traumatic event symbolized by the later memory. During the period between 1893 and 1898, Freud collected a series of about twenty cases in which he believed seduction during early childhood to be responsible for the later neurosis; this evidence, he thought, indicated a lawful and inevitable relationship between the initial occurrence and later psychological symptoms.

In their discussion of the seduction theory and its modification in psychoanalytic theory, Sadow, Gedo, Miller, Pollock, Sabshin, and Schlessinger (1976) provide a number of reasons both for Freud's original reliance on this theory and for his later abandonment of it. Undoubtedly, the technical practice of pressure applied to the forehead and the accompanying suggestion made it difficult for both Freud and the patient to separate suggestion from reality. In addition, Freud still had no clear understanding of the concept of the transference neurosis apart from psychoneurosis. However, the principal reason cited by Sadow and his colleagues for Freud's maintaining the seduction hypothesis was that he had not yet reached the point in his own self-analysis of realizing the prominence of young children's fantasies of their parents, as distinct from actual experiences.

In a series of drafts and letters to Fliess during the years 1897–1898, Freud's struggle with the problems involved in the seduction hypothesis is clearly seen.[1] It was difficult for him to accept the view that the important factor was not necessarily the actual event, but rather the child's developmentally determined fantasy of this event. In the famous letter to Fliess of September 21, 1897, Freud lists four reasons for abandoning the seduction

---

[1]Over the past several years, there has been renewed discussion of the seduction hypothesis, viewed as a critical event in the history of psychoanalysis. Masson's edition of the complete correspondence of Freud and Fliess (1985) does show that Freud continued to struggle with the problem of the place of early experience for later outcome. Indeed, this issue remains an unsolved problem both for psychoanalysis and for education, as well as for society generally. It is clear that Freud's solution to this problem removes it from the political intrigue portrayed by Masson (1984) and Malcolm (1984). The intellectual question remains one of understanding the determinants of the experience of self and others, founded on developmentally salient understandings or fantasies. It is because the seduction hypothesis speaks to the issue of the construction of a narrative of development—a central issue for the study of development—and not because of the fact that Freud remained troubled about this issue much longer than was once appreciated, that this issue remains significant in the study of lives over time.

hypothesis: (1) the fact that the suggestion of actual seduction drove patients from analysis; (2) his refusal to believe that such seduction was as common as his analysands' fantasies seemed to suggest; (3) his realization that the unconscious is unable to distinguish between reality and fantasy, so that the real event would never be represented in the unconscious; and (4) his realization that conflict evoked by such an event leads to intense conflict and that, consequently, direct expression of the conflict could never succeed in becoming directly expressed in consciousness.

Over the next several years Freud gradually relinquished the seduction hypothesis, suggesting, in the case of Dora (1905a), that neurotic fantasies are not *necessarily* based on memories of actual occurrences and, in the *Three Essays* (1905b), that children learn sexual expression not through a model, either child or adult, but as a result of "spontaneous internal causes" (p. 191). Finally, the following year, with the publication of the paper on sexuality in the etiology of the neuroses, Freud (1906) stated directly that he had changed his views, using as an explanation the reasons he had previously provided in his correspondence with Fliess. He noted that it was necessary to understand the origins of the neuroses, not only in terms of actual experiences but, perhaps more centrally, in terms of the interplay of psychical forces based on developmentally determined fantasies, which were essentially the same for neurotic and "normal" persons. These fantasies, as Freud (1925) describes in his autobiographical account of the development of psychoanalysis, are derived from the Oedipus complex, the outcome of which is seen as having important implications for later development, with much the same power for determining the subsequent course of life as was earlier posited by the seduction hypothesis.[2]

---

[2]It should be noted that his concern with the world of real events as contrasted with the "internal" world continued to trouble Freud in the development of psychoanalysis until the end of his life. In two of his last works, "Constructions in Analysis" (1937) and *Moses and Monotheism* (1939), Freud returns to this issue, now phrased in terms of myth and history. The editors of the *Standard Edition* discuss this parallel between psychical event and external reality and historical and material truth in a footnote to *Moses and Monotheism* (p. 130). The editors remark in another footnote (Freud, 1931, p. 121) that Freud nowhere suggests that external events are the *sole* cause of hysteria,

The seduction hypothesis remains in many ways the classic instance of the concept of critical period within the psychoanalytic study of development: particular events believed to have occurred at particular points in the infantile years (and Freud was never more specific than that when discussing the first years of life) were seen to have a determining effect on drive development and adult psychopathology. With the advent of direct child observation came increased efforts at relating observational findings to expectable later outcomes. Consistent with Freud's pleas for observational study (1895, 1905a, 1909) with the aim of validating the assumptions of both metapsychological and clinical theory, both Anna Freud (1927) and Melanie Klein and their students (Isaacs, 1932) began systematic observation in the consulting room, the nursery, and the classroom.

Findings from clinical observational study clearly influenced Melanie Klein (1928, 1948) in her revision of the psychoanalytic conceptualization of the point in development most fateful for the development of structure, as well as of the sequence of development, particularly the resolution of the paranoid–schizoid and depressive positions across the first year of life. With the formation of the English School of Psychoanalysis (Kohon, 1986) came an increased concern with the impact of infancy, particularly as a function of the quality of maternal care, on the subsequent course of life (Bowlby, 1969, 1973). This concern was amplified first in the work of Winnicott (1960), Greenacre (1960), and others, and then by Mahler and her colleagues (Mahler, Pine, and Bergman, 1975), Kernberg (1975, 1976), and Kohut (1971, 1977), as well as in the research tradition pioneered by Ainsworth and her colleagues (Ainsworth, Blehar, Waters, and Wall, 1978; Sroufe, 1979).

Encouraged by this emerging perspective amplifying the role of infancy as a determinant of the subsequent developmental course, and pointing the way to another means for understanding symptoms not yielding to interpretation based on

---

but that seduction by the father is but one of a number of possible causes. This comment does not entirely fit with the text of Freud's earliest papers or with the discomfort he felt upon realizing that internal events (fantasies) were the sole determining factor. The footnote reflects both Freud's struggle and our own continuing efforts to reconcile the importance of external and internal events in the development of neurotic disorders.

the nuclear or structural neurosis, psychoanalysis undertook clinical study and intervention with persons showing more pervasive psychopathology believed to originate at even earlier periods in the course of life. Persons showing difficulties in tolerating even brief separations from the therapist, unusually sensitive to each nuance of the therapist's actions, often reacting with feelings of rage and unreality, were now believed to show deficits in development difficult to reverse through prevailing psychoanalytic approaches. On the one hand, this "widening scope of psychoanalysis" (Stone, 1954, 1961) led to innovations in technique in an effort to respond to sectors of personality reflecting deficit not easily resolved through the working through of conflict. On the other hand, psychoanalysis sought understanding regarding the possible origins of observed deficits and, consistent with Freud's earlier formulations, used developmental study as a means for buttressing assumptions derived from the genetic approach.

The concept of the critical period. Much of this effort to use developmental study as a means to validate the genetic approach has been based on the use of the "critical period" concept in developmental study. The concept of the critical or sensitive period has been borrowed from ethological studies, primarily those concerned with the imprinting process by which the very young organism develops an attachment to its mother (Lorenz, 1953; Hess, 1959; Hinde, 1963, 1966; Freedman, 1974). This model presumes that the critical period is a biologically determined "moving window" in development open only at particular points, typically in the very first days after birth. If particular phenomena do not occur during these biologically determined intervals, they will never occur. Further, it is believed that the failure of these events to take place within the critical period has profound consequences for the subsequent course of development, particularly for the formation of the mother–child bond, and for the child's later cognitive and socioemotional development (Khan, 1963; Bowlby, 1969, 1973; Colombo, 1982).

This emphasis on critical periods in the development of the mother–child tie has a parallel in psychoanalytic formulations of the course of emotional development during the first year of life (Winnicott, 1960; Parens and Saul, 1971; Mahler, Pine, and Bergman, 1975; Tolpin and Kohut, 1980; Pine, 1985), although little of this perspective is specifically represented in the corpus of Freud's own work. Stemming primarily from Abraham's systematization (1921, 1924) of Freud's developmental paradigm, together with later modifications by Erikson (1950), Spitz (1965), and others, the critical period hypothesis has led to the specification both of particular failures in early development and of their consequences for the formation of adult character; in general, however, it has not been well supported by systematic research (Caldwell, 1964).

The critical period hypothesis has been used in an effort to provide support for assumptions regarding the presumedly inevitable consequences of adversity in early development, particularly those having to do with limitations or deficits in adjustment. However, longitudinal study has suggested that this supposed longer-term impact is less evident than had been presumed, and that the effects of early adversity are more easily reversed than the critical period hypothesis would suggest (Skeels, 1966; Baller, Charles, and Miller, 1967; Dennis, 1973; Clarke and Clarke, 1976; Chess, 1978; Emde, 1981; Emde and Harmon, 1984). Endorsement of the critical period concept in psychoanalysis was part of the zeitgeist of the 1950s and 1960s, when particular emphasis was given to the irremediable consequences of early experiences on later outcomes, such as the effect of early cognitive deprivation, or lack of stimulation, on the later ability to profit from formal academic instruction.

Understood in terms of retrospective and prospective views of development, it appeared that the occurrence of certain events carried specific meanings for the subsequent course of life, in effect rendering the future course of development a foregone conclusion. Further, assumptions regarding the lawfulness of adversity in early experience suggested that there was little reason for intervention after the fact, since the occurrence of adversity was believed to insure a poor outcome. However, in recent years, with the usefulness of the critical period hypothesis being called into question, it appears that there is good reason for thinking these assumptions anew. Rutter

(1972), for instance, examining the literature on maternal deprivation, reports that the effects of such deprivation on the child's later development are not as serious as had earlier been believed, while Lennenberg (1967) has questioned the usefulness of the critical period hypothesis as regards language acquisition. Follow-up studies reviewed in Clarke and Clarke (1976), particularly Dennis's longitudinal research (1973), show that children who had lived in orphanages and who had suffered maternal deprivation, with the consequence of retardation in development during early childhood, did not, when tested as adults, show any greater retardation than their counterparts in a control group. Similarly, a comparative study of American children with Guatemalan children who experienced deprivation for the first year of life shows that by age 10 the Guatemalans performed no worse on a series of cognitive tasks than the Americans did (Kagan and Klein, 1973; Kagan, Klein, Finley, Rogoff, and Nolan, 1979).

In brief, deprivation may not always lead to the poor outcomes that are assumed to be the result of early hardship or difficulty. Indeed, to the extent that such early experiences are included in a subjective biography in which the theme of succeeding over adversity is highly valued, such hardships become perceived not as deprivation but, rather as a kind of advantage, a prevalent theme in American culture (Cawelti, 1965). In fact, in a study of adults in middle age who had been children in the Great Depression, Elder (1974) found that those whose families had suffered deprivation were *better* able to adapt to current life strain than those whose parents had been financially secure. Findings from follow-up research on persons believed to be at increased risk for psychopathology as a result of early life adversity do not suggest any linear correspondence between specific types of adversity and later outcomes (Anthony and Cohler, 1987). Indeed, in a clinical study of the offspring of schizophrenic parents, as contrasted with children of well parents, those who were independently rated as most creative and effective were raised in families in which mothers had been hospitalized for schizophrenia (Kaufman, Grunebaum, Cohler, and Gamer, 1979).

As Zubin and his colleagues have noted (Zubin and Spring, 1977; Zubin and Steinhauer, 1981), vulnerability does not appear to be specific to particular points in the course of life. Rather, all persons have some degree of vulnerability, which, when confronted with unpredictable later adversity, may lead to psychological symptoms in those with increased predisposition (Hanson, Gottesman, and Meehl, 1977). The problem is that we know little about the means used by persons for maintaining the capacity to overcome adversity, or of the reasons why one person is able to cope effectively with adversity while another succumbs (Cohler, 1987). Finally, it should be noted that even the classical studies of social isolation, such as those carried out in Harlow's laboratory at the University of Wisconsin, have been questioned in terms of the assumptions on which these studies were based. Harlow and his colleagues now report that the disastrous effect of such social isolation can, in most instances, be reversed or corrected (Novak and Harlow, 1975). Such findings argue convincingly against the critical period hypothesis and are consistent with conclusions reached in Connolly's review (1972), which suggests that even if true for other animals, including primates, the critical period hypothesis may not be generalizable to human behavior.

Childhood Experiences and Adult Outcomes

Closely related to the problem of critical periods is the issue of generalizing to adult outcomes from specific developmental tasks or issues successively salient in child development. Not just in specific critical periods, such a those believed to be relevant in the development of the capacity for relatedness, but more generally in the life span, specific issues in childhood have traditionally been viewed as the most important determinants of adult personality and adjustment. The use currently being made of Winnicott's concept (1960) of the "holding environment" (Modell, 1984), Mahler's concept of separation-individuation (1968; Mahler, Pine, and Bergman, 1975), and Kohut's concept of the transmuting internalization (1971), for example, all represent instances of generalizing from assumptions regarding the presumed noxious impact of particular early life experiences on adult outcomes. Further, from this idea it has been inferred that early directed developmental intervention will lessen the impact of assumed pathogenic influences on later development; thus is provided the intellectual foundation for the field of infant psychiatry (Rexford, Sander, and Shapiro, 1976; Fraiberg, 1980; Call, Galenson, and Tyson, 1983, 1984).

Life course developmental study, however, suggests that there is little evidence either that *specific* effects of early adversity in development are maintained over time (Emde, 1981) or that particular intervention techniques provide a "buffering" effect (beyond that due to time itself) against the impact of early adversity in development (Cohler and Musick, 1984; Anthony and Cohler, 1987). Even in large-scale intervention efforts such as Head Start, it has been difficult to identify factors associated with gains over time, although the technique of meta-analysis, aggregating results over large numbers of programs, has suggested that increased parental involvement in the child's learning appears associated with increased success in later classroom performance (Lazar, Hubbell, Murray, Rosche, and Royce, 1977; Darlington, 1978).

As important as the paradigms described by Winnicott, Mahler, and other developmental observers may be for the development of a sense of separateness over the first three years of life, they may be less relevant for understanding the experience of others across later stages in the life course (McDevitt, 1973). For example, clinical reports by Boszormenyi-Nagy and Spark (1973) and Cohler and Grunebaum (1981), as well as empirical findings reported in the volume edited by Shanas and Streib (1965), by Cohler (1983) and Cohler and Stott (1987), and by Pruchno, Blow, and Smyer (1984), all suggest that interdependency and "emotional refueling" characterize most adults in their relationship with their own parents. Stated another way, these studies suggest that complex relations among members of modified extended families cannot be "reduced" to the circumscribed situation of the original mother-infant bond and its modification in the first years of life.

These studies also suggest that it is difficult to maintain that adults show problems in tension management or self-comforting comparable to those of early infancy. It is for this reason that efforts to equate the child's experience of the mother with the analysand's experience of the analyst in terms other than metaphor lead to many of the same problems seen in the assumption of a direct correspondence between early childhood and the adult years; findings to date provide little justification for assuming this correspondence. If the life course may be better understood as a series of abrupt transformations, with little necessary continuity over time, then it is difficult to assume a determinate relationship between the experience of self and others in earliest childhood and subsequent experience across the life course.

Nevertheless, much of the interest in findings from developmental psychology continues to be focused on the specific problem of validating certain psychoanalytic interpretations, particularly those concerned with the reenactment of developmental deficits presumed to have been acquired in earliest childhood. Although there is at present some controversy in psychoanalysis regarding the therapeutic efficacy of these genetic interpretations, as contrasted with those limited to the transference itself (Leites, 1977), concern with the possible origins of these later outcomes is always present in the collaboration of analysand and analyst toward understanding the origins of present distress.

To the extent that normative findings from developmental psychology are used in this process of "postdiction," it may be that both psychoanalysis and developmental psychology suffer in the process. Most certainly, it is neither possible nor even necessarily desirable to determine events in infancy and early childhood which, on the basis of retrospective data obtained from clinical psychoanalysis, may be used to provide a comprehensive explanation of adult conduct. The problem involved in reconstructing childhood events on the basis of the analysand's retrospective accounts is that, in the first place, a continuity is assumed between childhood and adulthood which is not warranted on the basis of empirical study in areas such as personality and adjustment (Neugarten, 1969; Rutter, 1972; Brim, 1976; Kagan, 1980; Emde, 1981); in the second place, and of even greater importance, the attempt to reconstruct childhood events may overlook the fact that the analysand's account as an adult is the outcome of a complex process in which the life biography is successively rewritten at transition points in the life course in order to achieve the consistency which is necessary for continued adaptation (Cohler, 1980, 1982).

Although Freud himself makes repeated statements about the problems involved in postdiction (1901, 1910b, 1913, 1920c), ironically, it was the growing influence of psychoanalysis itself, particularly in America after the Clark lectures (Freud, 1910a), which inspired the numerous and, typically, disappointing studies aimed at examining the relationship between childhood events and adult outcomes (Sears, 1943). The advent of learning theory, which also stresses the primacy of early experiences, further supported this research approach (Sears, 1975). This perspective was apparent in the studies at Iowa and, later, Yale, as well as in the longitudinal research undertaken at the Fels Institute and in the several studies in Berkeley and Oakland which were later organized into the Institute of Human Development at the University of California under the direction of MacFarlane, Bayley, and others.

Particularly in the case of the guidance study, where the hypothesis was tested that explicit instruction for parents would result in more successful adult outcomes, it was assumed that earlier life circumstances were closely linked with the quality of adult adaptation. Examination of this assumption, tested in the several Berkeley and Oakland studies (Jones, Bayley, and MacFarlane, 1971; Elder, 1974; Eichorn, Clausen, Haan, Honzik, and Mussen, 1981) and in the Fels longitudinal study in Ohio (Kagan and Moss, 1962), has shown that little of the variance of later outcomes can be explained on the basis of childhood factors, including child-rearing attitudes and practices.

In a manner parallel to the situation with the critical period hypothesis, disappointing findings from longitudinal studies of child development have led investigators to wonder if we have not overstated the case for the continuity of childhood and adult experience in human development (Neugarten, 1969; Brim, 1976). Indeed, as findings from both clinical reports and longitudinal studies across the adult years have suggested (Moss and Sussman, 1980; Colarusso and Nemiroff, 1981; Kohlberg, Ricks, and Snarey, 1984; Nemiroff and Colarusso, 1985), a primary question in the study of adulthood involves the factors accounting for continuity or change in personality and adjustment from early adulthood through oldest age rather than simply assuming one or the other (Neugarten, 1969). Just as maturational factors and changing social context are important determinants in personality development across the childhood years, role changes, including losses and exits of the older years, provide continuing challenges and opportunities for the maintenance of a sense of self and well-being (Bibring, 1959). In sum, while it may not be possible to rule out, a priori, the possibility of continuity, it should be recognized as something that is *achieved*, a function of modes of experience that are *maintained* across the life course. Continuity is not something that just happens, with the present as a natural outcome of earlier discrete, apparently unconnected past effects. Rather, it is the reflection of continuing effort to make the best possible sense out of the totality of life experiences, with the goal of preserving a life history reflecting perceptible meaning.

Child Development and the Psychoanalytic Study of Early Childhood

There has long been interest in the application of findings from psychoanalytic study to developmental inquiry not explicitly tied to intervention (Murphy, 1973; Stern, 1985). Since Freud's earliest work, psychoanalysis has emphasized the importance of studying psychological processes in infancy and early childhood without any necessary reference to adult outcomes (Freud, 1905b, 1913; Spitz, 1950; A. Freud, 1958; Murphy, 1962). Freud's "discovery" of infantile sexuality, in fact, surely remains as a most important contribution, not only for psychoanalytic intervention but also for the field of developmental psychology, with empathically informed observational study of young children (Parens, Pollock, Stern, and Kramer, 1976; Roiphe and Galenson, 1981) showing that infantile sexuality and the formation of gender identity are among the most salient developmental issues of early childhood. Additionally, Freud's more general observations regarding children's psychological development (1905b, 1920a) were continued by Hug-Hellmuth (1913), Bernfeld (1925), Anna Freud (1927, 1930), Melanie Klein (1928, 1948), and Winnicott (1951, 1957, 1958), all of whom were interested specifically in the study of childhood. The numerous reports issuing from Anna Freud's war nursery especially (Freud and Burlingham, 1943, 1944), and the particular focus of these reports on the quality of caretaking in early childhood, provided particular impetus for studies of maternal deprivation, such as the carefully designed study of Spitz (1945, 1946) on the effects of hospitalism, and including both the Yale studies of the course of child development (Kris, 1951; Wolf, 1953; Senn and Hartford, 1968) and more recent, highly sophisticated studies by Wolff (1966), Stechler and Carpenter (1967), Stern (1974, 1985), Emde, Gaensbauer, and Harmon (1976), and others.

Two problems, however, are posed by psychoanalytic studies of childhood: the use of these studies as the basis of a psychoanalytic understanding of the life course, and the use of experience-distant methods in the study of phenomena that more appropriately are the domain of the experience-near methods characteristic of clinical psychoanalytic study (Kohut, 1959, 1971, 1982). A related problem with at least some developmental research, supposedly informed by clinical psychoanalytic perspectives, and also represented by infant psychiatry, is that it is not always clear how this research, interesting as it is in its own right, is actually informed by the methods and findings of clinical psychoanalytic inquiry as contrasted with the more normative approach characteristic of research in developmental psychology. Consistent with the critiques of Holt (1975, 1985) and George Klein (1976) regarding psychoanalysis and ego psychology, it is not always possible to see how the so-called study of the development of ego functions in early childhood can be differentiated from other developmental research not specifically informed by psychoanalysis (Cohler, 1986). Further, and particularly in the infant psychiatry literature, there is too often the assumption that the entire course of life following early childhood is but the generalization of these early childhood experiences. The psychoanalytic study of infancy and early childhood is significant for a better understanding of *childhood* experience and assists intervention where there is evidence of psychopathology. However, the continuity of experience in early childhood and in later life remains a problem to be investigated.[3]

Virtually all interdisciplinary research efforts in developmental psychology and psychoanalysis have focused on childhood; few of these investigations have concerned the lives of children after entry into school. However, there is little reason why the kind of synthesis that has been achieved between psychoanalysis and child development can not also be achieved between the systematic study of adult development and aging and psychoanalytic observations of development across adolescence and adulthood. The studies reported by Vaillant and his collaborators (Vaillant, 1977; Vaillant and Molovsky, 1982), regarding both successful middle-aged adults previously studied in the college years and the adult lives of working class

---

[3]The clinical psychoanalytic method differs from other methods in the human sciences in the use which is made of the analyst as an empathic observer, who is experience-near rather than experience-distant from the phenomena being studied (Kohut, 1971). From the time of Freud's own anecdotal reports, there have been a number of significant efforts employing clinical psychoanalytic perspectives in developmental research, notably observations reported by Winnicott (1957, 1958), Wolf (1953), and Murphy (1962), and the collaborative study of Monica, a fistula fed baby, from infancy to adulthood (Viderman, 1974; Engel, Reichsmann, Harway, and Hess, 1985).

While it might appear that this empathic method would pose problems as regards the reliability of observations, there is little reason to assume that developmental observers trained to use their own empathic processes are necessarily less likely to be reliable than observers not sharing this perspective; reliability reflects clarity in understanding of the phenomena to be observed and not in the disciplinary orientation of the observer. In other words, empathic understanding need not be equated with an idiosyncratic, subjectivistic kind of immersion into the other. In fact, it can be as public as other methods, provided the structure of the "prejudice" unique to this method can be identified.

All interpretation is necessarily taken up from some perspective or structure of prejudice (Gadamer, 1960), no matter how detached and objective the observer/interpreter strives to be; the question is not whether this prejudice can be eliminated, since it cannot, but whether it facilitates the understanding of phenomena or impedes it by making it little more than a function of the prejudice itself. While, from an empiricist perspective, empathic observation may be seen as inevitably biased, from the perspective of interpretive study there is always bias; the question is whether it is "good" bias (a preunderstanding allowing for further understanding) or "bad" bias (a preunderstanding that forecloses this possibility). Observation, striving to make sense of something *as* something, is inevitably rooted in the interpretive strategies that are brought to the task itself.

youth participating in a study of status offenders (juvenile delinquents) (Felsman and Vaillant, 1986), based on psychoanalytic concepts of conflict and defense, illustrate the promise of
collaborative research on the second half of life.[4]

Continuity and the Developmental Narrative

Little is known regarding the many factors that might account for the correspondence between early adversity and later
outcome, factors reported by Brown (1982), who has shown the
impact of parental death in early childhood on depression in
adulthood; by Roy (1985), who has found that separation from
parents during early childhood increases the risk of a later
depressive episode; and by Elder and Rockwell (1979), who
observed the lasting impact of deprivation in the Great Depression on people now in middle age who were young children
then, as contrasted with its lesser impact on those who were
adolescents at the time. Of greater significance, however, is the
fact that the very assumption of continuity over time—of a
direct correspondence between childhood and adult experience—may obscure many of the most interesting questions regarding development across the life course, especially concerning factors accounting for both continuities and discontinuities

---

[4]Ideally, psychoanalytically informed developmental study, focusing on
the course of life as a whole, would provide important information regarding
such issues as change in the use of memory over time. Preliminary findings,
such as those reported by Vaillant and McArthur (1972), suggest that memories of the past may be transformed as a function of place in the life course.
The recollection of adolescence changes in dramatic ways between adolescence and mid-life. Rather than being inherent sources of unreliability, these
changes reflect socially determined changes in the place of self in the life
course, providing developmentally relevant meanings for past experiences.
Changes in the nature of the role portfolio, in the expected duration of life
itself, and in the duration and termination of career or work, unexpected
adversity or fortune, and cohort membership all may relate to changes reported over time in the memory of past events. Focus on the manner in which
persons experience these socio-historical events, uniquely accessible through
empathically informed psychoanalytic observation, will provide increased understanding of factors related to experience of continuity and change over
time.

in adjustment, personality, and sense of self-coherence (Neugarten, 1969, 1977; Kagan, 1980; Livson and Peskin, 1980; Peskin and Livson, 1981; Emde and Harmon, 1984).[5]

Although the clinical psychoanalytic approach, employing empathically informed observational study of lives over time, provides a unique opportunity to study these factors, the approach has been used in relatively few life course reports. Freud's own case studies, particularly his detailed short-term study of the "Rat Man," suggest that "sleeper effects" of the nuclear or oedipal neurosis may be observed which parallel those first described systematically by Kagan and Moss (1962) in their follow-up studies of persons from childhood through the "stable adult" years (Cohler and Boxer, 1984) and demonstrated more recently in reports by Haan and Day (1974) and Livson and Peskin (1980) on adjustment from early adolescence through midlife. The conflict engendered by attempts to resolve the nuclear neurosis, marking the transition from early to middle childhood, are less likely to appear during middle

---

[5]Significantly, findings reported by Maas and Kuypers (1974), following a group of persons from early childhood through old age, and findings from longitudinal studies reviewed both by Moss and Sussman (1980) and Kohlberg, Ricks, and Snarey (1984), suggest that persons showing greater personal distress may also show greater stability in observed adjustment over time. Presumably, these persons show impairment in psychosocial functioning which is sustained over relatively long periods of time, and the very fact of psychopathology serves to provide a developmental narrative of a particular sort, characterized by repetition, stasis, and an inability to freely move through the course of life. To the extent that psychodynamic studies on the life course have focused on these more troubled persons, findings may have been colored by the greater stability at lower levels of psychosocial functioning sometimes observed among these psychiatric patients.

Kohut (1971, 1977) has shown that failure to attain a coherent sense of self is distinctive of personal distress. Indeed, psychopathology may be characterized by failure to integrate presently experienced past, present, and future into a coherent narrative or story. Major psychopathology provides a means for dealing with this lack of experienced coherence, although in ways which markedly lower sense of well-being, and often at the cost of personal adjustment necessary to cope with the social surround. Psychopathology provides a particular kind of narrative (Evans, 1954), albeit one which markedly interferes with the maintenance of well-being and enhances the experience of fragmentation. Further, continued major psychopathology affords the external observer a view of consistency over time which may not be experienced by the psychiatric patient, whose experience of self is of lack of coherence and even fragmentation.

childhood than at some point during adulthood when, confronted by challenges posed by the assumption of new roles, problems are encountered at work or in maintaining ties of intimacy with significant others.

As suggested above, personality development may be better conceived in terms of abrupt transformations than in terms of linear continuity or predictable epigenetic transitions (Emmerich, 1968; Cohler, 1982; Gergen, 1982),[6] with much of what happens over time a consequence of maturational and social factors, together with unexpected, often adverse experiences. A major task, therefore, across the life course, involves efforts to maintain a sense of coherence when confronted by precisely this sort of experience. Additionally, since historical understanding itself holds within it this dimension of fostering coherence among the disparate data of the past (Ricoeur, 1977, 1983, 1985), persons continually rewrite their life stories so as to show the connectedness of past and present. Although there is some variation in the felt coherence resulting from efforts to fashion a narrative out of the presently experienced course of development, with the task inherently more difficult for some than for others, virtually all persons attempt to maintain a coherent narrative of their life, if not in the concrete sense of telling the story of their lives, then at least in the sense of maintaining some semblance of self-consistency. Much of what is assumed to be developmental continuity may be a reflection of this concern with maintaining a narrative which is consistent with prevailing values and standards, including those regarding the self, at particular points across the course of life, and which adequately accounts for the presently remembered past.

------

[6]At present, there is much controversy regarding the issue of continuity in study of adult personality. Much of this controversy may be traced to methods used for the study of personality (Fiske, 1974). While Block, with Haan (1971), and Costa and McCrae (1980) report findings suggesting marked consistency, their findings are based on trait indices derived from structured personality measures, including temperament. Emmerich (1968) has noted that it is important to differentiate between consistency in relative rank order among persons showing particular attributes and consistency experienced in lives over time. Stability in trait measures may be more a reflection of cultural construction of personality, than of actual continuity of personality and adjustment over time.

Life course transformations. Before considering the process by which this narrative of development is constructed and revised over time, it is necessary to review characteristics of the life course which are successively reintegrated into a personally coherent and meaningful narrative of development. Four major life course transformations have been described to date, although it is possible that subsequent study, and the continuing interaction of history with life history (Riegel, 1979), will lead to the identification of additional or different points of transformation. It is also important to emphasize that these transformations are not explicitly age-connected. Although some discussions of the life course (Levinson, 1986) assume the correspondence of age and stage of life, such views tend to confuse chronological and social age. As Freud (1905b) suggested, efforts at connecting age and stage of life may require a degree of precision not actually observed in experience over time. Rather, there appears to be a range of time within which transformations are expectable. With the attainment of adulthood, when social rather than maturational processes are primarily responsible for changes in the sense of self, there is increased variation in the age at which particular transformations may be observed.

The first observable life course transformation has been termed by White (1965) the "5-to-7 shift." As the paradigm for understanding later transformations, and as perhaps the most significant of such changes in sense of time and use of memory, this point in the developmental course, which is reflected both in the resolution of the infantile or nuclear neurosis and the shift from preoperational to operational thought, has clearly been the most carefully studied. This transformation, including the appearance of the nuclear or oedipal conflict characterizing the developmentally salient fantasies of this time of life, is again but one of several such points in the life course at which discontinuity is experienced between past, present, and future.

There are several interconnected components of the primal fantasy (Freud, 1915) accompanying the transformation from early to middle childhood, including wished and feared seductions, the fear of castration as punishment for unacceptable wishes, and the so-called "primal scene." This last term refers both to experiences that are noxious because not developmentally "dosed" (including presumed observation of parental intercourse) and to fantasies based on the imagining of such experiences, even when they have in fact never occurred. The concept of the primal scene first appears in manuscript draft L in the Fliess correspondence (Masson, 1985), where it is viewed as a major element of the hysterical disorders. Further, it is viewed from the outset as a fantasy, the purpose of which is to prevent awareness of the reality of parental intercourse. Mention is made of the concept in the *Interpretation of Dreams* (1900), in "On the Sexual Theories of Children" (1908), and as a factor contributing to the phobia observed in Little Hans (1909), but it is in the Wolf Man case that Freud (1918) focuses most explicitly on the primal scene, including both its expression as a fantasy and its relation to screen memories.

Freud's discussion of the primal scene in this study of an infantile neurosis reveals his struggle to understand both the origins of this fantasy and its role in subsequent development. As early as the *Interpretation of Dreams* he had suggested that the important factor in symptom formation was not a memory as such but rather the fantasy which developed on the basis of the memory. In the critical fifth section of the study of the Wolf Man, interposed between the first sections, reviewing early life and the development of symptoms in childhood, and the later sections, which provide the formulation of the illness, Freud (1918) engages in a lengthy debate, both with himself and with the reader, concerning the significance of the primal scene and, more generally, the role of childhood, including childhood sexuality, as regards later adult outcomes.

> The view, then, that we are putting up for discussion is as follows. It maintains that scenes from early infancy . . . are not reproductions of real occurrences, to which it is possible to ascribe an influence over the course of the patient's life and over the formation of his symptoms. It considers them rather as products of the imagination, which find their instigation in mature life, which are intended to serve as some kind of symbolic representation of real wishes and interests, and which owe their origin to a regressive tendency to a turning away from the tasks of the present [p. 49].

This statement, as important as any Freud ever made on psychological development across the life course, shows clearly that he believed that the meaning of specific events of childhood were successively transformed, first at the time of the transition to middle childhood and then in late adolescence, ultimately appearing as adult fantasy. As Freud observes, this relieves us of attributing to the child developmental achievements that occur only later. Even the regressive fantasies of adults are not actually those of childhood but those whose structure and content refer to preadult conflicts as the adult symbolizes such conflicts (Cameron, 1944).

In contrast to the views of Jung and Adler, this view does not deny the importance of infantile sexuality. It is clear, as Freud repeatedly states, that the child is capable of erotic stimulation, but this is not to be equated with the transformed instinctual expression of adults. Regressive activity that detours adults from the developmentally appropriate tasks of adulthood is not a direct expression of childhood conflicts, but of those conflicts as now transformed and represented in adult fantasy. The content of such fantasy refers to *adult* perception of the forms of gratification and satisfaction associated with childhood sexual expression.

Given this perspective on the fate of childhood sexuality in adulthood, it is necessary to clarify the concept of the primal scene, which is not simply to be understood as the memory, continuing in the adult, of sexual activity among parents and other important caretakers in childhood (Bonaparte, 1945; Bornstein, 1949; Furman, 1956; Escoll, 1977). It is a metapsychological and not a clinical concept referring, as Freud (1916–1917) had already shown in the *Introductory Lectures*, to a particular form of regressive fantasy in adulthood. Indeed, in his discussion in the Wolf Man case, Freud explicitly states that the primal scene as a prototypical fantasy *cannot* be reduced to a childhood experience. How, then, do we explain the existence of the fantasy of the primal scene? Having posed the possibility that children observe animals having intercourse, Freud dismisses this as subject to precisely the same problem as the assumption that the adult directly remembers childhood experiences (not a tenable position precisely because of the role of repression in the developmental process).

The solution Freud adopts is that the primal scene is but a prototypical, developmentally determined fantasy, which is found among all young children and which is later subject to the same transformations as other developmentally determined fantasies across the life course. As Freud comments, in his letter to Fliess of September 21, 1897, "there are no indications of reality in the unconscious, so that one cannot distinguish between truth and fiction that has been cathected with affect (Accordingly, there would remain the solution that the sexual fantasy invariably seizes upon the theme of the parents.)" (Masson, 1985, pp. 264–265). This observation, elaborated in the paper "A Child Is Being Beaten" (Freud, 1919), shows Freud's intrinsic understanding of developmental phenomena. The origins of the primal scene fantasy are innate and appear to be included in the behavioral repertoire of all human children (Esman, 1973). Precisely the same formulation applies to two related primary fantasies which also appear as the oedipal complex is being resolved: seduction by the adult and, in boys at least, castration. Evidence supporting this interpretation of the origins of these childhood fantasies was reported by Anna Freud (1951) on the basis of observations of young children reared in war nurseries apart from their parents. Although these children had been taken to the nursery right from the maternity hospital and had never seen a private home, their play as preschoolers led her to the following tentative conclusion: "With stimulation from outside excluded, play of this nature appears to be the expression of innate, preformed, instinctual attitudes, a suggestion which—if found to be true—would throw doubt on some of our analytic reconstructions of early witnessing of a primal scene" (p. 29).

She noted that when these preschool children were placed in families, jealousy and rivalry with the opposite sex "parent" developed within a matter of days, often more directly expressed than in homes in which children were more accustomed to family life. Indeed, she noted that intense jealousy developed of a magnitude which in ordinary families would appear over the course of many months during the third to fifth years of life.[7] As Melanie Klein (1981) has noted, with clarification of the determinants of the seduction hypothesis, psychoanalysis "changed from being a psychology of memory to becoming a psychology of fantasy" (p. 206). It need only be added that particular developmentally determined fantasies, of which that connected with the primal scene is paradigmatic, do not remain static over time. The meaning of these fantasies can be understood only in terms of particular points in the life course, and is expressed in a particular setting; the effort to understand these fantasies in the shared collaboration of analyst and analysand represents one such setting. The meaning of these fantasies, woven into a narrative which "explains" the presently experienced past, is jointly constructed in this shared space (Winnicott, 1951; Viderman, 1974; Green, 1975); and is distinctive to that collaboration (Schafer, 1981, 1983; Schwaber reported in Malin, 1982). As the paradigmatic life course transformation, resolution of the infantile or nuclear neurosis results in the reordering of memory (the so-called infantile amnesia), together with alteration in sense of time, with memory of the past less important than forgetting it. The consequence of this reordering is to maintain consistency with the socially determined but personally endorsed sense of self, including acting in ways which reinforce learned values and which increase the sense of well-being and coherence.

The use of repression as a defense in resolving the "infantile neurosis" (Freud, 1909; Nagera, 1966; Tolpin, 1970; A.

---

[7]A child's observations during the years of early childhood, of his parents or other caretakers involved in sexual activity, are believed to have a particularly deleterious effect upon his subsequent psychological development. In part, this is because the child is unable to understand the significance of actions which appear to be uncontrolled and even violent. In part, it is because of the excitement that the child feels, and to which he is passively subjected, without the necessary inner controls which have not yet developed. However, as both Klein (1966) and Esman (1973) noted, the assumption about the traumatic impact of observation of the primal scene should be considered in the light of the child's overall development at the time, including the capacity for active mastery. Such fantasies of the primal scene appear to be innate; their expression will be in age-appropriate forms in which such mastery is possible, unless the child is subject to some unusual explicit trauma, such as forced involvement by older children or adults in sexual activity which is totally inappropriate for the child's age and ego development.

Freud, 1971) and the ensuing infantile amnesia, therefore, introduces the first point of discontinuity in the life course, which must be resolved through reinterpretation of the life history in such a manner that a consistent "narrative" or story of one's past is preserved. Again it should be understood that this narrative of the course of development may be less a concrete telling of the past than an experiential reorganization.[8] Most children in our culture appear to dislike thinking of themselves as directly aggressive or competitive (Schafer, 1960; Whiting and Whiting, 1974); the narrative of the developmental course emerging with the resolution of the infantile neurosis is in the interest of preserving close and affectionate ties with the parent of the opposite sex (Freud, 1909). With the advent of infantile amnesia, the remembered past becomes quite different from that previously recalled. Successive transformations of this narrative of the life course across the adult years further modify earlier memories (Gross, 1949; Eisenbud, 1956).

Development from middle childhood to adolescence marks a second life course transformation, once again leading to a reordering of memory and the sense of time. If the major developmental attainment realized with the resolution of the infantile or nuclear neurosis is the forgetting of infantile sexuality, that of adolescence is realizing the actuality of the future.

---

[8]The concept of narrative is one which is well known in the humanities (Booth, 1961; Scholes and Kellogg, 1966). Study of particular genres in literature has led to agreement regarding the structural aspects of the narrative to be examined (Burke, 1950; Bal, 1985). Within psychology and psychoanalysis, there has been an implicit, often unacknowledged adoption of the narrative perspective. In efforts as diverse as Freud's effort to understand mechanisms of censorship in dreams (1900), and Schafer's discussion of the structure of the picture thematic story (1958), there is continuing concern with the manner in which data are narrated as a means for understanding the nature of wishes and intents. Indeed, that perspective provides the basis for interpretation of the transference in the psychoanalytic situation (Freud, 1905b). The concept of narrative, as employed in literary criticism, has been introduced into psychoanalysis by Sherwood (1969) and especially by Ricoeur (1970, 1977), first with his study of Freud and, more recently, applying this concept to the psychoanalytic study of lives. Leavy (1980) has adopted a similar narrative position in portraying the psychoanalytic interchange as a story jointly constructed by analyst and analysand. Additional study is required in order to employ the narrative perspective developed in literary criticism to other kinds of texts such as the life history or the psychoanalytic dialogue.

Perhaps for the first time in the course of life, the present is viewed as situated between past and future. This developmental achievement is fostered, at least in part, by the new capacity for formal operations in the sphere of logic (Piaget, 1933; Flavell, 1963; Cottle and Klineberg, 1974), as well as by ritual preparations for the tasks of adulthood which heighten a concern with understanding the future in terms of the past (Van Gennep, 1906; Turner, 1967). During later adolescence this developmental transformation leads to the capacity to understand a future experienced as meaningfully related to the past, which fosters the achievement of a sense of identity; as Erikson (1968) notes, this "includes a subjective sense of continuous existence and a coherent memory" (p. 61). Erikson observes that this subjective sense of identity involves a quality of sameness and continuity as a person, which is equivalent to a fully formed self. Realization of this transformation leads to integration of the presently remembered past and the anticipated future, and serves to enhance feelings of coherence and well-being.

A third developmental transformation may be observed in midlife, with increased awareness of the finitude of life (Munnichs, 1966) or personalization of death (Neugarten, 1968; Neugarten and Datan, 1973, 1974). As may be noted, the first two of these transformations of the personal narrative of development are governed primarily by maturational forces, including progression toward increased complexity and integration of cognitive functions (Werner, 1926, 1957; Piaget, 1975), first as a result of the "5-to-7 shift" and the capacity for concrete operational thought, and then as a result of adolescence and the capacity for formal thought, which makes possible the anticipation of the future anchored in a definable course of life.

Across the adult years, however, maturation plays a less significant role in personality transformation than it does in childhood. With the realization of a relatively stable portfolio of adult roles, the subjective assessment of self, and of one's position in the course of life, assumes particular importance as a determinant of change. The achievement of expectable social milestones, within the normative time frame for a particular historical cohort (Neugarten and Hagestad, 1976; Nydegger, 1980; Hogan, 1981; Daniels and Weingarten, 1982; Hagestad and Neugarten, 1985), is a major source of adult morale. Persons "off-time" in terms of these expectable changes, particularly those who are early to marry, have children, and achieve career success, report less positive morale than those more "on-time" (Cohler and Boxer, 1984).

Perhaps the most important of all points in the adult life course is the point at which persons are said to be old, and at which death may be expected. As Neugarten, Moore, and Lowe (1965) have shown, there is fairly good agreement among men and women regarding the expected duration of life. At some time during middle age, persons begin to realize that there is less time to be lived than has been lived already. This midlife transformation characteristically results in the increased salience of the past, reflected in increased reminiscence, leading to an increased inwardness or "interiority" (Neugarten, 1973, 1979). What is important to recognize is that this third transformation of the life course functions just as the change from early to middle childhood, and from middle childhood to adolescence, providing the means for integration of a presently remembered past, an experienced present, and an anticipated future, into a narrative of personal development which continues to be coherent and ordered. Nostalgia, not yet full reminiscence, may assist in the process of making sense of the future in terms of the presently remembered past.[9]

Study of very old persons suggests that there may be yet a fourth transformation of the life course (Butler, 1963; Myerhoff, 1979; Myerhoff and Simic, 1979; Lieberman and Tobin, 1983). Much less is known about this transformation of "survivorship" than about the three other major transformations,

---

[9]Benedek (1959, 1970) implicitly suggests that the advent of parenthood represents a transformation similar in significance to that of the nuclear neurosis. While becoming a parent certainly has an important impact on the sense of self, it does not appear to meet the test of changed experience of time and memory which characterizes major transformations in development. Rather it is a role transition (Rossi, 1968) which provides a unique challenge to adjustment (Bibring, 1959), with important implications for mental health across the adult years. As children grow, they present the parents with particular challenges which lead the parents to recall and reenact experiences as children with their own parents. However, these enactments do not necessarily constitute a reorganization of personality.

although with those over 75 now the most rapidly growing segment of the population there is both increased opportunity to study this transformation and an increased need to understand its significance for mental health. Among very old persons, it appears that there is one more reordering of time and memory, in which much of the preceding concern with the passage of time is now viewed from a distance. With the realization of this fourth transformation of the life course, leading to an additional reorganization of time and memory, at least some of the concern with finitude and the personal reality of death may be replaced by sense of quiet acceptance. Erikson, Erikson, and Kivnick (1986) refer to this as a sense of the "life-cycle as completed," reflecting the capacity for recognizing and including formerly unacknowledged and disavowed wishes and intents as part of the self.

At the same time there is often a pervasive sadness associated with being the survivors of a generation, together with a concern for preserving the attainments and contributions of that generation. While there is little evidence that older persons are inevitably more lonely than younger persons (Lowenthal, 1964; Lowenthal and Robinson, 1976), there may be a sense of being alone, as the last members of a generation, a sense which may be difficult to bear. Again, continuity with the remembered past is attained through increased reliance on reminiscence of times past and, at least for some much older persons, the process of "life review" portrayed by Butler (1963).

Maintaining self-coherence. It should be noted that this view of the course of life assumes that issues of coherence and continuity are problems which persons must resolve in order to maintain a sense of well-being. It may not necessarily be the case that successful realization of a particular transformation insures the maintenance of continuity of self at subsequent points in the course of life. Unexpected adversity, together with particular kinds of vulnerability, may have an adverse impact on lives over time. Although within our culture there is a great need to be able to predict the future in order to plan rationally, chance plays a larger role in determining the course of lives over time than has often been recognized within psychoanalysis and the social sciences (Gergen, 1977, 1982; Grunes, 1980).[10] Ironically, psychopathology, while leading to the experience of personal disarray, may lead to the external perception of continuity in lives over time; it becomes another cultural construct useful in efforts to discern sources of continuity and order in the course of lives over time.

Primarily because of the attention paid to the first of these life course transformations, that of the infantile or nuclear neurosis, much more is known about its impact on the sense of self and the experience of others than is the case as regards subsequent transformations. To date, little is known of the content of the developmentally appropriate fantasies accompanying transformations other than that of the paradigmatic nuclear neurosis. While it is assumed that neurotic symptoms, evidence of compromise formations, continue as significant sources of disruption in adult lives, additional sources of misery may be experienced, such as the failure to attain a sense of self-coherence, a failure based less, perhaps, on the experience of fear than on the breakdown of hope.

Maintaining perspective on both the future and the past is a major developmental task of midlife. Fear of fragmentation may have its instinctual components (Zinberg and Kaufman, 1963; Parens and Saul, 1971), but present also is a recognition that time is no longer malleable and that priorities must be reordered and revised; this recognition is developmentally determined, just as fantasies of rivalry and fear of inferiority mark the oedipal phase of development (Goodman, 1977; Shapiro, 1977, 1981; Coltrera, 1979). Fantasies belonging to, and determined by middle age, must be understood as developmental in precisely the same manner as the so-called oedipal fantasies

---

[10]Indeed, it is possible that the transformations of the life course highlighted here, particularly those determined by the social context of adult lives, may be unique to this culture. In cultures differing in the concept of time, and where there are different expectable tasks in the adult years, other transformations may be identified as salient in shaping the sense of self. Ricoeur (1977) notes that time in Western culture is linear and organized in the same manner as stories. This view of life as having a beginning, a middle, and an end is associated with the particular transformations observed in the West. Within Indian culture, where time is circular rather than linear, adult lives are experienced in ways quite different than in the West.

experienced as part of the infantile neurosis (Prosen, Martin, and Prosen, 1972).

Loss of self-coherence is clearly evident in the so-called midlife crisis, so well portrayed in Erikson's study of Martin Luther (1958); while this volume has become a classic because of Erikson's portrayal of the identity crisis of adolescence, it is perhaps equally significant for its portrayal of midlife, and for the effort to understand the determinants of Luther's depression in later life. In this life history Erikson attempts to relate Luther's midlife depression to his earlier failure to resolve the identity conflict of adolescence. However, it is also possible that his depressive disturbance in midlife was independently determined, resulting from problems associated with this unique challenge to adjustment.

As shown in case histories of persons in midlife experiencing their first episodes of psychiatric disturbance (Gutmann, Griffin, and Grunes, 1982), it is not always possible to identify earlier precipitants of such disturbance; little is known about the determinants of psychiatric illness with an onset in middle or later life (Clausen, 1984; Cohler and Ferrono, 1986). While in the case of Luther, a failure of self-integration in midlife may be traced to the earlier failure to attain self-integration during adolescence, in the case histories presented by Gutmann, Griffin, and Grunes (1982) the individuals appear to have functioned successfully until late middle age. Perhaps as a consequence of that life course transformation particular to that time, a transformation associated with increased awareness of finitude, these persons appear unable to maintain a coherent narrative of the course of life, leading to a sense of self-fragmentation accompanied by feelings of depletion and sadness.

Further study of the fourth transformation of the life course, involving issues of survivorship within a cohort among persons living long, may show similar results among persons for whom realization of loss and aloneness becomes an obstacle to the maintenance of self-coherence. Too often, mental health practitioners fail to recognize that just as thumbsucking is a developmental achievement allowing for the self-regulation of tension (Winnicott, 1951; Kohut, 1977), so the capacity to use reminiscence in order to maintain the experience of a life with continuity and meaning is a developmental achievement unique to later life (Pollock, 1961, 1971a, 1971b, 1981; Butler, 1963; Lieberman and Falk, 1971; Tobin and Lieberman, 1976; Lieberman and Tobin, 1983).

Narrative Perspectives and the Psychoanalytic Study of Development

The maintenance of a coherent narrative of the course of life becomes problematic precisely because of the integrative effort required by successive life transformations, during which one's sense of time, current experience of past memories, and anticipated future are reorganized. The problem posed by each of these transformations is the preservation of a sense of continuity and meaning that fosters self-integration, a process wherein persons understand their lives and attribute particular meanings to life events occurring at various points over time (Antonovsky, 1979). This shift away from mechanisms and functions, so characteristic of the genetic approach in psychoanalysis, also leads away from a concern with the impact of particular events on the subsequent course of life. Instead, the developmental approach focuses on the changing manner in which these events are remembered and reenacted over time, and on the changing meaning of these events across the course of life (Steele and Jacobsen, 1977; Steele, 1979; Schafer, 1981, 1982, 1983). This focus on issues of narrative and meaning in the psychoanalytic study of lives parallels a similar shift of focus elsewhere in the human sciences, particularly in historical studies (Wyatt, 1962, 1963; Danto, 1965; Mink, 1965, 1981; Madelbaum, 1967, 1977; H. White, 1972–1973, 1978; Ricoeur, 1984b, 1985; Wallace, 1985).

Just as with history more generally, so a life history is more than a mere collection of fixed, enduring records of the past. Rather, both history and the life history must be viewed as forms of narrative, episodes in a story which is continually in the process of being retold, and for which the meaning shifts with successive recountings. Remembered events change in meaning over time, as a function both of place in the life course and the context of the retelling. As Schafer (1981) has noted, psychoanalysis may be regarded from a temporal perspective; the meaning of events shifts over the course of analysis as a function both of vicissitudes of the transference and of the ever changing context of other memories and experiences. Indeed, just as in all study within the human sciences, the subject matter is embedded within the context within which the study is carried out, and cannot be studied apart from it. The distinguishing characteristic of the psychoanalytic mode of investigation is that the relationship of context and meaning is itself made the focus of study. Psychoanalysis is thus the means par excellence for studying the process by which persons change their narrative of development over time.

From his earliest work, Freud clearly was aware of the complex interrelationship of context and memory. Discussing the concept of deferred action in the 1895 Project, he acknowledges the problem caused by "the case of a memory arousing an affect which it did not arouse as an experience, because in the meantime the change in puberty had made possible a different understanding of what was remembered" (1954, p. 356). Ten years later, in a footnote to "The Neuro-psychoses of Defense," Freud (1896b) observed that "if the sexual experience occurs during the period of sexual immaturity and the memory of it is aroused during or after maturity, then the memory will have a far stronger excitatory effect than the experience did at the time it happened" (p. 167). It is clear then, from the outset, that Freud was well aware of the idea that the meaning of experiences could be reconstituted on the basis of subsequent ones, and that the present is always coequal in determining the experience of the past. The life history can be viewed only as an ever changing personal narrative of the course of development.[11]

---

[11]Discussing the method followed in the case of Dora, Freud (1905a) wrote as follows: "I begin the treatment by asking the patient to give me the whole story of his life and illness, but even so the information I receive is never enough to let me see my way about the case. This first account may be compared to an unnavigable river whose stream is at one moment choked by rock and at another divided and lost among shallows and sandbanks. I cannot help wondering how it is that the authorities can produce such smooth and precise histories in the case of hysteria. As a matter of fact the patients are incapable of giving such reports about themselves. They can, indeed, give the

Psychoanalytic understanding shares, with certain other human sciences, a concern with the process of making history; the life history or developmental narrative is a record of efforts to maintain coherence in a past which might otherwise be fragmented and unintelligible. The practical goal of analysis cited by Freud (1905a)—the removal of symptoms—can be understood as the effort to make the past visible and understandable, leading to increased personal integration. As a result of this "practical" effort, at realizing a sense of "completeness," a disjointed history becomes more comprehensive and more easily followed. This goal is attained largely through analysis of the transference, the particular rules of translation which render symbolic aspects of the past meaningful to both participants in the analytic situation (Freeman, 1985a).

However, as his discussion of the Wolf Man case shows, Freud (1918) was never able to reconcile a narrative view of history with the belief that there is an actual historical past which can be separated out from its later derivatives. Since this historical past was viewed as "overlaid" with later experience Freud (1913, p. 184) suggested that the past is only "buried," later to be recaptured. But this concern with the possibility of recovering and reliving past history may be a reflection more of Freud's philosophy of science, rooted in his mechanistic prepsychoanalytic studies in comparative biology than of his later clinical investigations (Bernfield, 1951; Gill, 1976; Klein, 1976; Kovel, 1978; Sulloway, 1979). As Potamianou (1985) observes, in discussing the use of the past in psychoanalysis,

> complete objectivity and consistency of knowledge recovered in psychoanalytic treatment are only ideal fictions, and as such cannot be the aim of the analyst. What analysis aims at is the knowledge and acceptance of the constant oscillation of the mental apparatus between the manifestations of movements of desire and resistance to these movements. In

---

physician plenty of information about this or that period of their lives; but it is sure to be followed by another period as to which their communications run dry, leaving gaps unfilled, and riddles unanswered: and then again will come yet another period which will remain totally obscure and unilluminated by even a single piece of serviceable information. The connections—even the ostensible ones—are for the most part incoherent, and the sequence of different events is uncertain" (p. 16).

that sense, the analytic process itself, which is caught in this oscillation, constitutes for the analysand an experience par excellence of consecutive motions marking the return of the repressed, followed inevitably by new repression [p. 287].

Consistent with the emerging structural tradition in the human sciences generally, which emphasizes issues of text and language (Levi-Strauss, 1955; Mitchell, 1981), Potamianou notes that the language in which the past is constructed must become the primary topic of study. The important focus of study is the manner in which the past is successively recounted across the course of analysis, rather than the truth or accuracy of accounts of the past (Ricoeur, 1977; Schafer, 1981, 1982, 1983). However, this perspective on psychoanalysis as narrative has been the subject of much controversy over the past few years, particularly as a result of Spence's reluctant endorsement (1982) of a narrative position as a substitute for a "natural science" conception deemed untenable in the light of continued clinical and empirical study, and of the critiques of Blight (1981) and Grunbaum (1984), each of whom maintains that use of a narrative framework obscures the contributions of psychoanalysis and prevents the emergence of a rigorous, verifiable set of findings regarding human behavior.

Ironically, both "sides" of this debate assume that there must inevitably be conflict between a scientific mode of discourse, concerned with explanation, and an interpretive mode of discourse, concerned with understanding. However, as both Habermas (1968) and Ricoeur (1977) have noted, rejection of a natural science approach to the study of the life history need not mean rejection of concern with issues of cause and origin. Discussing the distinction, for instance, between psychoanalytic "texts" and ordinary literary texts, Habermas (1968) notes of the former that "the meaning of a corrupt text of this sort can be adequately comprehended only after it has become possible to illuminate the meaning of the corruption itself. This distinguishes the peculiar task of a hermeneutics that cannot be confined to the procedures of philology but rather *unites linguistic analysis with the psychological investigation of causal connections*" (p. 217).

Acceptance of a narrative perspective, concerned with the manner in which persons understanding issues of continuity and change over time is progressively transformed across the course of life, must not be viewed as a rejection of the search by traditional social science for reasons and causes (Polanyi, 1949, 1965; Holt, 1972; Toulmin, 1984; Freeman, 1985b). What it does mean is realization of both a method and an epistemology different from that customarily employed within positivist science, as initially represented by Freud's formulation of metapsychology. In contrast to this mechanistic approach, the method most appropriate to the study of lives over time is one in which the study of causes and reasons is located within the experience-near context of the person's own life story, including that dramatized in the psychoanalytic situation, rather than the more experience-distant approach characteristic of earlier metapsychological formulations, especially those tied to the genetic approach. Adoption of such an interpretive perspective does not imply the nihilism assumed by "radical hermeneutic" philosophers, or the inevitable failure to genuinely advance our understanding of the life history, as sometimes suggested by those who criticize this perspective (Blight, 1981; Grunbaum, 1984).

From this perspective, in contrast with the position endorsed by Blight, Grunbaum, and others—again including Spence (1982), who reluctantly endorses an interpretive or "narrative" position, largely because he views clinical psychoanalytic data as inadequate by the criteria of positive science—experience cannot be reified as if it were a "thing." Aspects of the past are more than "fragments" or "traces" surviving into the present as if artifacts of a "real" historical past. These aspects of the past which are remembered in the present are remembered in a particular context and assigned particular meanings, being transformed and rearranged over time (Bartlett, 1932; Meacham, 1972, 1977; Loewald, 1976; Riegel, 1977). At the same time, memory is always the memory of a particular person, based on that person's experience of the past, the meaning of which must be understood in the context of the entire course of life up to the present. In other words, there is still something to be explained, although this effort at explanation does not assume a direct linear correspondence between present and past. The problem is that of understanding the role of the past as a factor determining the present experience of self and others, of present wishes and intents, and of presently understood connections between one's personal past, present, and future.

There is always a kind of "backward" reference in the study of lives, with the significance of the life course viewed as a function of the narrative order itself. The meaning of the life history stems precisely from this capacity to look backward, from the standpoint of the present, over the past, seeing the totality of life to the present time in a particular manner. As Walsh (1951, 1974) has suggested, in discussing the concept of "colligation," all the disparate sources of information for the course of life are contained within a pattern, as is generally true in historical modes of understanding; the facts of a life history are not enduring things, apprehended once and for all, but are established in a continuing manner through ascertaining the part played by past events in the narrative account to date. Regardless of the form of history being told, narrativity may be seen as a constituent element of historical perception (Jauss, 1982) or, in the words of Ricoeur (1984a, 1984b), it is the manner in which human time speaks. History is more than the reproduction of experience, even that of the immediate past. Further, history cannot be separated from narrative and still remain history. Mere reproduction of the past does not provide for an understanding of this past, which is always retold from a particular present perspective. This is no less true of reenactments within the clinical psychoanalytic situation.

Psychoanalysis is a method for observing the processes according to which life history or developmental narrative is successively reshaped over time, as well as a "miniature" developmental narrative from the point of first contact to a period beyond termination, when the analysand may mourn the loss of the analyst and try to integrate this experience into the larger narrative. At the same time, the miniature narrative of development is also shaped by continuing changes in the life of each participant, together with the sociohistorical context in which the analysis takes place, including the continuing developmental course itself. The clinical psychoanalytic experience becomes an additional factor influencing the development of each participant, often dramatically altering the manner in which the subsequent developmental narrative is understood.

Development, Narrative, and the Psychoanalytic Process

The perspective presented in this chapter suggests that it is difficult to understand the relationship between past and present except through the meanings in terms of which the past is presently construed. This view of the significance of the past for the present has important implications both for the process of reconstruction in clinical psychoanalysis, and also for understandings of the transference neurosis. Fantasies emerging during the oedipal phase are but prototypes of such developmentally determined fantasies emerging from each of the major developmental transformations occurring across the course of life. It is important to identify the fantasies emerging from subsequent transformations of the life course. While there has been little detailed study of the developmental narrative, findings from the study of personality change across the adult years may provide some insight into the contours of this narrative at particular points in time.

Reconstruction and the Historical Process

Increased emphasis on the personal experience of the past, including the transformation of developmentally determined fantasies over the course of life, has had an impact on the understanding of reconstruction's significance in clinical psychoanalysis and on the manner in which reenactments of the personal past are viewed in the psychoanalytic situation (Novey, 1968; McGuire, 1971). However, despite the fact that Freud clearly recognized the dynamic and changing nature of the personal past—at least some of the time—some contemporary discussions still emphasize a more static view of his description of the process of reconstruction. This more traditional view is associated with an emphasis on reconstruction as a process tied primarily to the infantile neurosis, as well as to genetic reconstruction largely independent of the transference (Reider, 1953; Ekstein and Rangell, 1961; Joseph, 1973; Meyers, reported in Malin, 1982).

Even where there is agreement that reconstruction can encompass preoedipal conflicts (Lewin, 1946; Ekstein and Rangell, 1961; Blum, 1974, 1977), it is still sometimes assumed that the process of reconstruction is concerned with explicit traumatic events themselves, rather than with interpretations or fantasies of such events. McGuire (1970, 1971) most explicitly challenges this position. Calling into question many of the assumptions which are made regarding individual development and the use of the past in psychoanalytic inquiry, he recognizes that memory is most often organized as patterns rather than uncovered as discrete traces.

Consistent with this perspective, it appears that the total configuration of remembrance is successfully reshaped over the life course, so that reconstruction of the same personal past at different ages yields versions of the past which may be quite different from each other. Different concerns become salient at different points in the life course, with different aspects of memory becoming prominent. This perspective follows directly both from changes in the organization of memory across the life course, as well as from the social organization of time discussed by Schachtel (1947) and, more recently, by Neugarten and Hagestad (1976), Seltzer (1976), and Riegel (1977, 1979).

Screen Memories and Reconstruction

A related problem in the study of psychoanalytic reconstruction concerns the role of screen memories. Greenacre (1975) notes that there is a close and important relationship between the process of reconstruction in analysis and the use of screen memories in facilitating this task. As multilayered, overdetermined phenomena are successively analyzed and reanalyzed, important modes of defense become clear, and the source of the conflict becomes evident. Consistent with Greenacre's portrayal of reconstruction, the screen memory is constructed in layers like an onion; as a result of reconstruction, the significance of the original memory is finally understood.

Her formulation follows from Reider's view (1953) that the process of reconstruction acts like an "injunction" to remember what is believed to be the initial nuclear conflict.

Greenacre also notes that she is puzzled by the relative lack of importance attached to the analysis of such screen memories in contemporary psychoanalysis. Perhaps part of the reason that the analysis of screen memories is less often used in psychoanalysis is to be found in the assumption, repeatedly called into question in this chapter, that there is an "original" conflict for which the screen memory serves as a compromise formation. As has been stressed here, echoing Kris's formulation (1956b), and that of Schimek (1975), memory is not static but dynamic; it is continually active in the process of reconstructing the past. Memories of earlier events are not simply photographic representations arranged in such a manner as to enhance self-consistency.

As noted already in this chapter, with the abandonment of the seduction hypothesis, psychoanalysis took a fateful step away from exclusive reliance on external events as the origins of action to reliance on internal events (fantasies, thoughts) based on the totality of life history (Freud, 1914, 1919). This emphasis on the inner or fantasy world rather than the outer or external world differentiates psychoanalysis from other formulations of human development and gives priority to subjective aspects of experience such as remembering, which ordinarily are not subjects of special study.[12] Freud (1899) makes it quite clear that the so-called "screen memories" of adults, disguised representations of infantile wishes, are not mere reproductions of childhood memories but are successively transformed by subsequent life experiences, with memories from

---

[12]This distinction between psychical and historical reality should be differentiated from the distinction between actual neurosis and psychoneurosis. Freud used the term "actual neurosis" primarily in his earlier papers to refer to traumatic neuroses brought about by real-life, temporally related, actual circumstances, as contrasted with the psychoneuroses, which are to be understood in developmental terms based on successive transformations of primal fantasies which were accessible to psychoanalytic modes of understanding (Laplanche and Pontalis, 1967).

Because the actual neuroses did not have this developmental basis, psychoanalytic treatment techniques, which are also developmental in origin, are not appropriate as the treatment of choice.

the period of middle childhood more easily "recovered" than those of early childhood. Regardless of whether these memories are in the service of displacement of repressed conflicts, Freud (1901) cautions against assuming that they *actually* belong to the period of childhood:

> It may indeed be questioned whether we have any memories at all from our childhood: memories relating to our childhood may be all that we possess. Our childhood memories show us our earliest years not as they were, but as they appeared at the later periods when the memories were aroused. In these periods of arousal, the childhood memories did not, as people are accustomed to say, *emerge*; they were *formed* at that time. And a number of motives, with no concern for historical accuracy, had a part in forming them, as well as in the selection of the memories themselves [p. 322].

Screen memories can function both progressively and regressively. Not only can conflicts contemporary with the memory be symbolically represented, but earlier memories can serve to disguise conflicts taking place later in the life course, just as later events can provide a "cover for earlier conflicts" (Freud, 1901). To the extent that the analysand's need to preserve such self-consistency is recognized, it becomes increasingly possible to interpret the past in terms of the present and, particularly, in terms of the variety of transferences which the analysand presents to the analyst.

While recognizing the concern of psychoanalysis with demonstrating the impact of the remembered and forgotten past on the present, Kris (1956b) is pessimistic about the ability of genetic reconstruction in clinical psychoanalysis to provide the data which would be necessary for this task, precisely because screen memories, so important in the process of framing a construction, represent successive transformations of the personal biography in such a manner that the original conflict no longer exists except as interwoven with later affects and experiences. As he observes,

> reconstructive work in analysis cannot aim at such a goal: its purpose is more limited and yet much vaster. The material of actual occurrences, of things as they happen, is constantly subjected to the selective scrutiny of memory under the guide of the inner constellation. What we here

call selection is itself a complex process. Not only were the events loaded with meaning when they occurred; each later stage of the conflict pattern may endow part of these events of their elaboration with added meaning. But these processes are repeated throughout the many years of childhood and adolescence and finally integrated into the structure of the [adult] personality. *They are molded, as it were, into patterns, and it is with these patterns rather than with the events that the analyst deals.* [1956b, pp. 76–77; italics ours].

Kris emphasizes that the analyst must be concerned with the interaction of childhood events with all subsequent events across the life cycle and not simply the analysand's childhood itself. Precisely because we deal with patterns of meanings rather than with discrete memory traces, and because these patterns are continually reworked across the life course, reconstructive activity is subject to perpetual change (Schimek, 1975).

It is precisely because of Kris's understanding of the organization of memory and his appreciation of the developmental process in personal biography (Kris, 1956a) that he is able to avoid the position characteristic of Reider, Greenacre, and others, whose approach to reconstruction as the "fitting" of observation and hypothesis leads to the aim of uncovering the actual events which have provided the basis for an infantile neurosis and which can become apparent during the process of psychoanalysis. The alternative view, presented in this chapter, is that there are a number of developmentally salient conflicts which are called forth at particular transition points across the life course and which have the effect of reorganizing the personal biography in ways which were not possible earlier. The task is to understand this process and the means by which a consistent personal history has been created as a result of these successive transformations. Increased awareness of this process is among the most effective means of fostering the capacity for self-observation and for increased neutralization which Kris (1956b), among others, views as important goals of psychoanalysis.

Although there are important theoretical problems to be resolved in the development of the psychology of the self (Kohut, 1971, 1977; Gedo and Goldberg, 1973), this emerging framework for understanding mental life is perhaps the first to recognize explicitly the significance of adult development for our understanding of personality across the life course (Kohut, 1975). Increased recognition of the significance of the psychological changes taking place across adulthood provides an important opportunity for enriching both psychoanalysis and developmental psychology.

Reconstruction and Interpretation

Remembering is usually viewed as the most essential aspect of the process of reconstruction in clinical psychoanalysis. Since Freud's discussion of this issue (1937), there has been general agreement that reconstructions in clinical psychoanalysis are characterized by generalized formulations, usually on the part of the analyst, concerning the origins of the infantile neurosis. Such reconstructions are contrasted with interpretations, which refer to single elements of behavior in the analysand's life. As Freud (1937) comments,

> "Interpretation" applies to something that one does to some single element of the material, such as an association or a parapraxis. But it is a "construction" when one lays before the subject of the analysis a piece of his early history that he has forgotten, in some such way as this, "Up to your nth year you regarded yourself as the sole and unlimited possessor of your mother; then came another baby and brought you grave disillusionment. Your mother left you for some time, and even after her reappearance she was never again devoted to you exclusively. Your feelings towards your mother became ambivalent, your father gained a new importance for you," . . . and so on [p. 261].

Such reconstructions have the quality of a comprehensive and all-encompassing description of the role of the past in determining present actions, leading to the formulation of what Murray and associates (1937) described as a "unity-thema" for explaining the totality of life.

In contrast with reconstructions, interpretations focus on such discrete aspects of the analysand's life as the significance of dreams, free associations, parapraxes, and transference reactions. In discussing the difference between interpretations and constructions, the Kris study group (Fine, Joseph, and Waldhorn, 1971) concluded that

> interpretations and reconstructions are functionally different, and have different aims. Interpretations aim to further understanding of, and

attempt to explain, phenomena. Genetic interpretations further attempt to explain psychological phenomena causally in terms of the past. Reconstructions aim ultimately to produce integrated recall of (or conviction about) the existence of repressed or otherwise defended against experiences or events [p. 90].[13]

Freud (1937) noted that the test of the validity of reconstructions was not the actual recall of events, for clearly such recall was not always possible. Rather, the test was often the development of a "sense of conviction" on the part of the analysand.

From the perspective of the present approach to the study of reconstruction, there is no single reconstruction or unity-thema which explains the totality of the analysand's life, but only a series of such reconstructions, or interpretations in the larger sense, which make sense in terms of the current state of the transference and the analysand's developmental status. As Schafer (1978) comments,

the analyst uses the general past to constitute the individualized present that is to be explained, while using that present as a basis for inquiry into the individualized past. Thus, while moving with the analysand back and forth through time, the analyst bases interpretations on both present communication and a general knowledge of possible and probable parts. . . . All of which is to say that the psychoanalytic interpretation is circular. Events may be recounted forward or backward, but what counts as an event in this kind of history is established by a circular kind of understanding . . . interpretation is a particularized creative action performed within a tradition of procedure and understanding. It has no beginning and no end [pp. 11–12].

---

[13]Meyers (Malin, 1982) notes the distinction between genetic interpretations and other interpretations of the transference, and suggests that genetic interpretations differ from reconstructions in being focused on discrete segments of the analysand's past. From the perspective of the present chapter, the problem with these genetic interpretations is that they are experience-distant; the realm of interpretation might be more properly limited to the "here and now" (Gill, 1976, 1982), which, if close to the analysand's present experience of particular reenactments in the therapeutic relationship, lead the analysand to making the relevant connections to the past which is experienced in the context of the relationship. As this chapter has consistently argued, there can be no "real" past outside that which is given in the particular meanings of the present analytic situation (Shafer, 1981, 1982; Kermode, 1985).

The test of the validity of that reconstruction is therefore not unlike that for other texts, including both those of literature and culture (Geertz, 1973; Auerhahn, 1979; Freeman, 1985a; Kermode, 1985), only in this case successful reconstructions have the effect of increasing the analysand's involvement in the psychoanalytic process, including the production of additional analytic material.

This perspective, derived from a historical or textual model for the "validation" of the psychoanalytic approach to the study of actions and intents, has important implications for our understanding of the process of reconstruction in clinical psychoanalysis. Although Wetzler (1985), among others, suggests that the analyst actually reconstructs events from a "real" past, the perspective adopted here suggests that not only is it impossible to assume that past events remembered in analysis are separable from the revision of the life biography, but that the reconstructed past relevant to one particular point will not necessarily resemble the reconstructed past at some other point (Schafer, 1981; Ricoeur, 1984a). Again, the view of the personal past which characterizes reconstruction among young adults is quite different from the view of the personal past which emerges among middle-aged and older analysands.

Developmental Narrative and the Analysis of the Transference

This view of reconstruction as a unifying and creative process, rather than as an attempt to uncover some set of supposedly "objective" historical facts, has important implications for understanding of the transference. As Novey (1968) has observed, "historical reconstruction is an intrinsic part of the process of therapy. An attempt is made to see the patient and have him see himself in some continuing context in which his present modes of experiencing and dealing with himself and others are a logical outgrowth" (p. 68). Later in his discussion he observes that

reconstructions are inevitably made from the point of view of the person making them, and they are influenced by what he intends to do with them. This is especially so when the process involves reconstructing not only the actual physical events of the past but, more especially, the psychological status of the participants in the events of the past. Since this latter is the very meat of the reconstructive process in psychiatry and psychoanalysis, reconstructions are heavily influenced by one's theoretical position and one's feeling for what will be most useful therapeutically. There is, in the final analysis, no "true" reconstruction; there are reconstructions of greater or lesser degrees of validity and plausibility and, most importantly, greater or lesser degrees of usefulness and integrative forces [p. 147].

Therefore, while the analysand may be said to have but a *single* past, a single sequence of "somethings" that have comprised the course of life, there may well be *many* histories, especially when these histories require reorganization of the meaning of the past more fully in terms of present and future wishes and intents. As these wishes and intents change, the life history is transformed in order to accommodate both previous interpretations and the reasons why these interpretations are now viewed by the person as inadequate. Particular life histories constructed by persons, and successively revised across the course of life, constitute narratives of personal development containing presently acceptable reasons for the outcome of past experiences, and integrating the totality of these life experiences into a story which can be followed by its narrator.

As this chapter has repeatedly emphasized, the development narrative is changed as a result of subsequent life experiences, including particular transformations of time and memory accompanying maturation and aging, requiring revised explanations of prior experience and present anticipations. Thus, changes observed across the course of a psychoanalysis represent but one instance of a changed personal narrative. Indeed, one of the major accomplishments of the psychoanalytic process is the collaborative revision of the analysand's narrative of development into one which is more readily followed, providing for a less rigidly maintained portrayal of the past than was possible prior to that point. For example, following termination of analysis, adults often see their parents in a more balanced manner than previously, accepting inevitable limitations and being able to relate more comfortably with other family members.

Clearly, the most important force shaping the processes of interpretation and reconstruction in clinical psychoanalysis is the transference itself (Freud, 1914; Strachey, 1934). Yet, with the exception of Novey's work, together with the contributions of Kanzer (1953), Greenacre (1975, 1981), and Schafer (1981, 1983), most discussions of reconstructions fail to consider the importance of the transference, even in the consideration of the process by which the analysand develops a "sense of conviction" regarding these constructions. However, Greenacre maintains that there is little difference between such constructions and reconstructions and interpretations, as they are more generally understood in psychoanalysis, and appears to support Brenman's assertion (1980) that reconstructions consist of valid inferences about the meaning of the past for the analysand, apart from the patient's position in the life course or the nature of the present collaboration between analyst and analysand. Reconstruction arises directly out of the transference, with all the immediacy of the analysand's reactions to the analyst.

Confusion between reconstruction in psychoanalysis as a process by which an interpretation of the personal past is created and the formulation of "genetic" interpretations based on the analyst's own hypotheses about the analysand's past has resulted in the belief, expressed most clearly by Leites (1977), that these genetic interpretations are an aspect of reconstruction and that such interpretations can supplement and perhaps even supplant analysis of the transference. The problem with such genetic interpretations however, as has been noted, is that they may split the experiential quality of remembering from the idea of the past and in some instances may foster increased isolation and intellectualization. In addition, since genetic interpretations may be removed both from the "here and now" of the transference (Strachey, 1934; Gill, 1979, 1982) and the context of the process in which the analysand reconstructs his personal biography, including his place in the life course, they may lack direct relationship to the analysand's actions or intents and may have little relevance to the psychoanalytic process itself.

The singular advantage of psychoanalysis as a means of treatment lies precisely in the opportunity for increasing the analysand's appreciation of wishes and intents resulting from the immediacy of their reenactment in the here and now (Strachey, 1934; Stone, 1954, 1961; Gill, 1979, 1982; Schafer, 1982). Frequency of sessions, the use of the couch, and the analyst's benign, neutral, observational approach, all encourage the analysand to repeat, experientially, modes of being with others which, collaboratively, may be understood through detailed study. Encouragement of the analysand's expression of feelings and thoughts regarding the analyst makes possible the working through of prototypical modes of understanding the self and others engendered principally through the repetition and new solution of the infantile neurosis (Strachey, 1934; A. Freud, 1958; Nagera, 1966), together with fantasies associated with later transformations across the life course.

This view of the process by which salient wishes and needs are reenacted in the psychoanalytic situation has two implications: one is that, as Schafer (1982) has explicitly commented, "transference is a psychoanalytic version of facts that have been told and always could be told in other ways" (p. 77). In a similar manner, Kermode (1985) has observed that "the past is inextricable from the present of the interpreter. There and then cannot be detached from here and now . . ." (p. 7). The other implication is that place in the course of life may often reshape the nature and meaning of these reenactments. It is for this reason that the meaning of reenactments must be understood in terms of the dual time perspectives of the life course (Nemiroff and Colarusso, 1985) and, as Blum (1980) and Schafer (1981, 1983) have noted, the course of the analysis itself.

Use of a transformational rather than a genetic framework (at least to the extent that "genetic" is associated with linearity, lawfulness, etc.) for understanding the course of life suggests that, while the infantile neurosis remains the focus of much psychoanalytic intervention, reenactments observed in the clinical situation are derived from each of those points across the life course at which time, memory, and sense of self are reorganized.[14] Psychoanalytic study of adults to middle age suggests

---

[14]The concept of transference in the present instance refers to all forms of reenactment in the clinical psychoanalytic situation. As is well known, and explicated by Kohut and Seitz (1963), the definition of transference is closely tied to the means by which wishes, stemming from the infantile period, and related to the parental constellation, which are unacceptable in awareness,

that the impact of experiences regarding issues of autonomy and identity, for instance, may be more significant as a determinant of particular reenactments than has sometimes been recognized; and interpretation of reenactments relevant to this developmental transformation may enhance the potency of analysis of the transference. As Nemiroff and Colarusso (1985) have observed:

> The advent of a developmentally dynamic psychology of adulthood now allows reconsideration of the effect of events in adulthood on the nature of transference . . . to place a greater emphasis on adult experience in which psychogenesis takes on a longitudinal dimension, incorporating new developmental conflicts and experiences occurring at each phase throughout the life course. In such a conceptual framework, the adult past can be an important source of transference [p. 63].

Reenactments relevant to transformations of later life, including not just that of adolescence, but also midlife and the associated concern with issues of finitude, as well as later life and the associated issue of survivorship, inspire particular changes in the understanding of self and others in a manner similar to that of the nuclear neurosis. What is required is the extension of the model first developed in the study of the infantile mental conflicts, which might encompass later enactments as well, acknowledging their complex interrelation with the infantile neurosis. While it is certainly likely that residuals of the infantile neurosis will still be observed in later life, adult experiences may precipitate significant developmentally relevant concerns and associated fantasies as well as successively alter the manner in which the infantile neurosis is expressed (Loewald, 1978, 1979); failure to realize expectable transformations of the adult years in such a manner as to maintain a sense of coherence and meaning for the course of life as a whole may lead to additional developmentally relevant concerns and

---

seek gratification, via disguise through displacement and condensation, as first formulated by Freud (1900) in his discussion of the dreamwork. From the perspective of the present chapter, the transference is paradigmatic of a series of reenactments marking life course transformations, each of which may be observed through traces shown in the reenactments characteristic of the psychoanalytic interview.

associated reenactments in a continuing effort to resolve concerns related to the adult years.

Clearly, the psychoanalytic study of older persons may be more complex than that of younger persons, for there is a much larger set of enactments to be observed and interpreted. Memories of the past also have a changed role in the analysand's present life and adjustment; just as the manner in which the analyst may be used may change, both in the enactment of salient concerns and in terms used for attaining satisfying means of merger and idealization, the very significance of past memories may change as well (McMahon and Rhudick, 1967). Again, however, there has been relatively little psychoanalytic study of persons in middle and later adulthood. Where such study has been carried out, and particularly in more recent clinical reports informed by a life course perspective (Sandler, 1978; King, 1979; Cohen, 1982; Nemiroff and Colarusso, 1985), a variety of reenactments have been reported which complement and extend that most often described for the infantile neurosis, and have been marked by expression of the fantasies relevant to that particular life course transformation. While all analytic observers have been children, and are able to empathically employ their understanding of their own past in the struggles of analysands younger than they are, it may be more difficult to understand the struggles of an older analysand facing issues not yet confronted by the analyst. It may be much easier to recognize the analysand's efforts at making the analyst into the critical, seductive, or apparently rejecting parent of childhood than to recognize efforts at making the analyst into a grandchild, a lost spouse, or a fellow survivor of a generation now largely deceased. The analyst may find it difficult to help an analysand complete the process of grief, or to recognize the feelings of relief accompanying the death of a spouse who has lingered with a terminal illness. Since the very meaning of death, and of the personalization of issues of mortality and finitude, change across the second half of life, it may be particularly difficult for younger analytic observers to understand the significance attached to issues of finitude and mortality among older persons. There may even be a tendency to interpret these issues in terms more relevant to the analyst's place in the life course than to that of the analysand.

Younger persons, including empathic analytic observers working with older persons, are at a different point in the course of life and may not be able to appreciate an increased concern with self or changing priorities regarding important sources of morale (Crusey, 1985). For example, the effects of loneliness, so much a concern in the lives of young adults, appear to have quite different meaning in the lives of older persons (Cohen, 1982). In a related manner, reminiscence may effectively supplant continuing contact with others as a major source of satisfaction. As older persons suffer increasing limitation of their own mobility, the capacity for remembering as a substitute for meeting others may become increasingly useful in realizing adjustment.

Pollock (1961, 1971b, 1981) has shown the importance of dealing with issues of mourning and loss in psychoanalysis. This concern is accentuated in the analysis of persons in the second half of life. To date, it is not clear whether psychoanalytic intervention in dealing with this issue differs for younger persons, as contrasted with those for whom losses are expectable and on-time. Findings reported by Lopata (1979) and Bankoff (1982) suggest that where widowhood is on-time, as among women in their late seventies, the process of mourning and readjustment may be somewhat different than among women becoming widows at younger ages. Again, the importance of maintaining a developmental perspective (Goodman, 1977; Colarusso and Nemiroff, 1981; Nemiroff and Colarusso, 1985) is as important in the psychoanalytic study of adult lives as in that of the childhood years.

In Review: Life Course Development and the Problem of Continuity

Many of the concepts believed to be distinctive of psychoanalytic approaches to the study of development have been derived, at least in part, from Freud's developmental neurobiological studies in the decades prior to his first psychoanalytic work, and from the philosophy of science implicit in it. These concepts, providing the basis for the so-called genetic approach, tend to portray the course of personality development in the planful manner associated with the development of organ systems across species. This effort at demonstrating Haeckel's fundamental biogenetic law, elaborated in Abraham's systematic developmental formulation, as well as in later formulations by Glover, Spitz, Erikson, and others describing the development of personality, may have less relevance to clinical psychoanalytic theory, viewed as the study of wishes and intents in lives over time, than has often been realized.

Observations based on experience-near or empathically informed clinical study, particularly expressions of transference and other reenactments in the analytic relationship, provide the basis for a distinctively psychoanalytic study of development. This experience-near study of development represents the unique contribution of psychoanalysis as a method of inquiry in the human sciences and leads to recognition of the significance of the subjective realm of experience for understanding changes in lives over time. While associated primarily with the clinical interview, this empathic or experience-near mode of observation is relevant to inquiry not necessarily addressed to directed intervention in the course of life. Some pioneering work in this area has already been reported, focusing principally upon the preschool years; distinctive contributions resulting from a psychoanalytically based developmental psychology of the adult years are less common, but findings reported to date suggest the manner in which this subsequent inquiry might be directed.

Failing to distinguish the genetic point of view of metapsychology from the clinical approach, which may be seen as genetic in a somewhat different and more transformative manner, psychoanalysis has sometimes sought to support an approach concerning the course of development by recourse to experimental findings in developmental psychology at the expense of the experience-near, empathically derived observations which are the basis for the clinical psychoanalytic study of lives over time. The use of concepts such as that of critical period, borrowed from developmental psychology, fail to make clear the problems inherent in this approach to the study of development. While findings from normative studies may inform the understanding of development based on clinical study, these findings are sometimes assumed to have primacy over experience-near observation and are given unwarranted precedence in developmental study.

This emphasis on normative study continues Freud's initial problem in assuming that mechanistic explanations are equivalent to explanations emerging from the study of meaning in the narrative of development, which is so central to psychoanalytic inquiry. Although through the study of attention he had sought to move away from functional explanations of behavior, his continued reliance on metapsychology compromised this effort. Continued efforts to use findings from normative developmental study, as representing an approach assumed to be superior to that of clinical psychoanalytic inquiry, may impair progress in both areas of study. Findings from clinical study suggest that order attributed to earlier developmental experiences is less a direct consequence of particular events, including aspects of early child care, than of the person's changing experience of aspects of the past across the subsequent course of life. From this perspective, the character of particular life events, including those presumed to occur at so-called critical points in development, may be less important in determining continuity and change in lives over time than the meanings that are figured and refigured across the course of life. Once it is recognized that measurement problems have compounded problems in understanding determinants of continuity and change in lives over time, it becomes clear that the problem of continuity is one of experience.

The issue, then, is less the manner in which particular events were experienced at some point in the past than the mode in which these events are presently experienced, including both how and to what extent these events are included in a narrative of the life course viewed as coherent. Indeed, if the course of life may be better conceived as a series of abrupt transformations, in which the past is successively refashioned in terms of present understandings of self, others, and expectable problems and challenges, then the focus of study shifts from attributes of events and relationships in the past observed in a linear or continuous mode in the present, as implied by the concept of epigenesis, to the sense of coherence or consistency maintained over time in the life history. Since initial psychoanalytic consideration of the relation of past and present focused on continuity in serious psychopathology, and since the presence of psychopathology becomes a particular kind of narrative of the relationship of past and present, albeit one which does not permit an increased sense of well-being, this focus may have further obscured the understanding of both change and continuity in the experience of self and others over time.

Sense of continuity of presently experienced past, present, and future may vary over time; precisely because of its concern with the realm of experience, psychoanalysis is able to provide increased understanding of factors determining variation in this sense of coherence by providing a unique opportunity for understanding the ways in which persons use the personal past in present life, including such issues as the changing significance of particular life experiences, the changing manner in which important present and past relationships are construed across the course of analysis, and, perhaps of greatest significance, the experience of continuity and change in lives over time.

This focus on the clinical psychoanalytic situation as the means for understanding the life course has two important implications for developmental perspectives in the human sciences. In the first place, since analysand and analyst are both involved in the observational process, the life history created across the course of analysis, including that refashioned from the analysand's present experience of the past, is a shared construction (Winnicott, 1951; Schafer, 1981, 1983; Gedo, 1984). It is likely, therefore, that different combinations of analyst and analysand will arrive at differently constructed life histories. However, it is likely also that there will only be a finite number of life histories which will be plausible, explaining the facts of the life as enacted through the transference and as remembered in conjunction with such clinical material as dreams and free associations. It must be emphasized that the inevitability of different histories constructed in psychoanalysis is *not* tantamount to claiming either that "anything goes," with histories created out of nothing, or that the fact of differently constructed histories shows that psychoanalytic evidence regarding the dynamics of development is inherently faulty or lacking in validity.

If the appropriate means for understanding the course of development is that of a constructed narrative rather than of the "recovery" of a supposed set of events which have had a predictable, determined outcome, then the test of validity associated with positive science will not be adequate. As this chapter has emphasized, adoption of an interpretive perspective is not equivalent to claiming that questions of causes and reasons are irrelevant in the human sciences. However, new means of validation are required which are more appropriate than those of positive science to clinical psychoanalytic inquiry. Adoption of an interpretive perspective in the study of lives redefines the problem as one of understanding and explaining the course of particular narratives which persons construct of their own past, and which serve to express important wishes and intents. The focus is on the determinants of these narratives and on the factors accounting for their present structure, with these determinants located in the context both of culture and of life experiences which assume a particular configuration for persons at particular points in this socially defined course of life. Study of the narrative successively constructed across the course of psychoanalysis provides a unique opportunity to observe these determinants, experientially emerging in the analytic setting.

Viewed from this perspective, clinical psychoanalytic study has much to offer to the study of development across the life course, for this mode of study is focused on understanding meanings, including the displaced or derivative modes through which they may be expressed. Foremost among these meanings are those tied to the nuclear neurosis, the paradigmatic transformation for understanding changing experience of self, including both sense of time and memory of the past. However, the impact of subsequent transformations may also be observed, including those of adolescence, where there are not just past wishes to be forgotten, but also future goals to be anticipated; the midlife transformation, leading to a foreshortened sense of time and increased concern with mortality; and that of very old age, including guilt over survivorship. Accompanying each of these transformations are particular developmentally relevant fantasies reenacted once again in the context of the analytic relationship. Study of the appearance and resolution of these transformations as reflected in the developmental narrative may provide both increased understanding of the factors governing continuity and change in the experienced sense of self and others across the course of life, and increased understanding of the role of psychoanalytic intervention in this process.

References

Abraham, K. (1921), Contribution to a discussion on tic. In: *Selected Papers on Psycho-Analysis*. New York: Basic Books, 1953, pp. 323–325.
———— (1924), A short study on the development of the libido, viewed in the light of mental disorders. In: *Selected Papers on Psycho-Analysis*. New York: Basic Books, 1953, pp. 418–501.
Abrams, S. (1977), The genetic point of view: Antecedents and transformations. *J. Amer. Psychoanal. Assn.* 25:417–425.
———— (1978), The teaching and learning of psychoanalytic developmental psychology. *J. Amer. Psychoanal. Assn.*, 26:387–406.
Ainsworth, M., Blehar, M., Waters, E., & Wall, S. (1978), *Patterns of Attachment: A Psychological Study of the Strange Situation.* Hillsdale, N.J.: Erlbaum.
Anthony, E.J., & Cohler, B., eds. (1987), *The Invulnerable Child.* New York: Guilford Press.
Antonovsky, A. (1979), *Health, Stress, and Coping.* San Francisco: Jossey-Bass.
Applegarth, A. (1977), Psychic energy reconsidered. *J. Amer. Psychoanal. Assn.*, 25:599–602.
Auerhahn, N. (1979), Interpretation in the psychoanalytic narrative: A literary framework for the literary process. *Internat. Rev. Psycho-Anal.*, 6:423–436.
Bal, M. (1985), *Narratology: Introduction to the Theory of Narrative.* Toronto: University of Toronto Press.
Baller, W., Charles, O., & Miller, E. (1967), Mid-life attainment of the mentally retarded: A longitudinal study. *Genet. Psychol. Monographs*, 75:235–329.
Bankoff, E. (1982), Response to Widowhood. Unpublished dissertation, University of Chicago.
Bartlett, F.C. (1932), *Remembering: A Study in Experimental and Social Psychology.* New York: Cambridge University Press, 1977.
Basch, M. (1973), Psychoanalysis and theory formation. *Annual of Psychoanalysis*, 1:39–52.

——— (1976), Psychoanalysis and communication science. *Annual of Psychoanalysis*, 4:385–422.

——— (1977), Developmental psychology and explanatory theory in psychoanalysis. *Annual of Psychoanalysis*, 5:229–263.

——— (1982), The significance of infant development studies for psychoanalytic theory. In: *Infant Research: The Dawn of Awareness*, ed. M. Mayman. New York: International Universities Press, pp. 731–738.

——— (1985), Some clinical and theoretical implications of infant research. In: *Commentaries on Joseph Lichtenberg's Psychoanalysis and Infant Research*, ed. D. Silver. Hillsdale, N.J.: Analytic Press, pp. 509–516.

Beilin, H. (1972), The status and future of preschool compensatory education. In: *Preschool Programs for the Disadvantaged*, ed. J. Stanley. Baltimore: Johns Hopkins University Press, pp. 161–181.

Bendedek, T. (1959), Parenthood as a developmental phase: A contribution to the libido theory. *J. Amer. Psychoanal. Assn.*, 7:389–417.

——— (1970), Parenthood during the life-cycle. In: *Parenthood: Its Psychology and Psychopathology*, ed. E.J. Anthony & T. Benedek. Boston: Little, Brown, pp. 185–206.

——— (1973), Discussion: Parenthood as a developmental phase. In: *Psychoanalytic Investigations*. New York: Quadrangle, pp. 401–407.

Bernfeld, S. (1925), *The Psychology of the Infant*. London: Routledge, 1929.

——— (1941), Freud's earliest theories on the school of Helmholtz. *Psychoanal. Quart.*, 13:341–362.

——— (1949), Freud's scientific beginnings. *Imago*, 6:163–196.

——— (1951), Sigmund Freud, M.D., 1882–1885. *Internat. J. Psycho-Anal.*, 32:204–217.

Bibring, G. (1959), Some considerations of the psychological processes in pregnancy. *The Psychoanalytic Study of the Child*, 14:113–121.

Blight, J. (1981), Must psychoanalysis retreat to hermeneutics? *Psychoanal. & Contemp. Thought*, 4:147–206.

Block, J., & Haan, N. (1971), *Lives Through Time*. Berkeley: Bancroft.

Blum, H. (1974), The borderline childhood of the Wolf-Man. *J. Amer. Psychoanal. Assn.*, 22:721–742.

——— (1977), The prototype of preoedipal reconstruction. *J. Amer. Psychoanal. Assn.*, 25:757–786.

——— (1980), The value of reconstruction in adult psychoanalysis. *Internat. J. Psycho-Anal.*, 61:39–52.

Booth, W. (1961), *The Rhetoric of Fiction*. Rev. ed. Chicago: University of Chicago Press, 1983.

Bonaparte, M. (1940), Time and the unconscious. *Internat. J. Psycho-Anal.*, 21:427–468.

——— (1945), Notes on the analytic discovery of a primal scene. *The Psychoanalytic Study of the Child*, 1:119–125. New York: International Universities Press.

Bornstein, B. (1949), The analysis of a phobic child. *The Psychoanalytic Study of the Child*, 3/4:181–226. New York: International Universities Press.

Boszormenyi-Nagy, I., & Spark, G. (1973), *Invisible Loyalties: Reciprocity in Intergenerational Family Therapy*. New York: Harper & Row.

Bowlby, J. (1951), *Maternal Care and Mental Health*. New York: Columbia University Press, 1956.

―――― (1969), *Attachment and Loss: Vol. 1. Attachment*. New York: Basic Books.

―――― (1973), *Attachment and Loss: Vol. 2. Separation, Anxiety and Anger*. New York: Basic Books.

Brenman, E. (1980), The value of reconstruction in adult psychoanalysis. *Internat. J. Psycho-Anal.*, 61:53–60.

Breuer, J., & Freud, S. (1893–1895), Studies on hysteria. *Standard Edition*, 2. London: Hogarth Press, 1955.

Brim, O. (1976), Life-span development of the theory of oneself: Implications for child development. In: *Advances in Child Development and Behavior*, Vol. 2, ed. H. Reese & L. Lipsitts. New York: Academic Press, pp. 241–251.

Bronfenbrenner, U. (1975), Is early intervention effective? In: *Handbook of Evaluation Research*, Vol. 2, ed. M. Guttentag & E. Struening. New York: Academic Press, pp. 241–251.

Brown, G. (1982), Early loss and depression. In: *The Place of Attachment in Human Behavior*, ed. C.M. Parkes & J. Stevenson-Hinde. New York: Basic Books, pp. 232–268.

Burke, K. (1935), *Permanence and Change: An Anatomy of Purpose*, 3rd ed. Berkeley: University of California Press, 1984.

―――― (1950), *A Rhetoric of Motives*. Berkeley: University of California Press.

Burnell, G., & Solomon, G. (1964), Early memories and ego function. *Arch. Gen. Psychiat.*, 11:556–567.

Butler, R. (1963), The life-review: An interpretation of reminiscence in the aged. *Psychiatry*, 26:65–76.

Caldwell, B. (1964), The effects of infant care. In: *Review of Child Development Research*, Vol. 1, ed. M.L. Hoffman & L.W. Hoffman. New York: Russell Sage, pp. 9–88.

Call, J., Galenson, E., & Tyson, R. (1983), *Frontiers of Infant Psychiatry*, Vol. 1. New York: Basic Books.

―――― ―――― ―――― (1984), *Frontiers of Infant Psychiatry*, Vol. 2. New York: Basic Books.

Cameron, N. (1944), Experimental analysis of schizophrenic thinking. In: *Language and Thought in Schizophrenia*, ed. J. Kasanin. New York: Norton, pp. 50–64.

Cawelti, J. (1965), *Apostles of the Self-Made Man*. Chicago: University of Chicago Press.

Chess, S. (1951), Utilization of childhood memories in psychoanalytic therapy. *J. Child Psychiat.*, 2:187–193.

―――― (1978), The plasticity of human development. *J. Amer. Acad. Child Psychiat.*, 17:80–91.

Cicirelli, V., Evans, J., & Schiller, J. (1970), The impact of headstart: A reply. *Harvard Educational Rev.*, 40:105–129.

Clarke, A., & Clarke, A.D.B., eds. (1976), *Early Experience: Myth and Evidence*. New York: Free Press.

Clarke, S.D.B., & Clarke, A.M. (1981), "Sleeper effects" in development: Fact or artifact? *Development. Rev.*, 1:344–360.

Clausen, J. (1984), Mental illness and the life course. In: *Life-Span Development and Behavior*, Vol. 6, ed. P. Baltes & O.G. Brim, Jr. New York: Academic Press, pp. 204–243.

Cohen, J. (1966), Subjective time. In: *The Voices of Time*, ed. J.T. Fraser. New York: Braziller, pp. 257–275.

Cohen, N.A. (1982), On loneliness and the aging process. *Internat. J. Psycho-Anal.*, 63:149–155.

Cohler, B. (1980), Adult developmental psychology and reconstruction in psychoanalysis. In: *The Course of Life, Volume III: Adulthood and the Aging Process*, ed. S. Greenspan & G. Pollock. Washington, D.C.: U.S. Government Printing Office, pp. 149–200.

—— (1982), Personal narrative and life course. In *Life-Span Development and Behavior*, Vol. 4, ed. P. Baltes & O.G. Brim, Jr. New York: Academic Press, pp. 205–241.

—— (1983), Autonomy and interdependence in the family of adulthood. *Gerontologist*, 23:33–39.

—— (1987a), Adversity, resilience, and the study of lives. In: *The Invulnerable Child*, ed. E.J. Anthony & B. Cohler. New York: Guilford Press, pp. 363–374.

—— (1987b), Approaches to the study of development in psychiatric education. In: *The Role of Psychoanalysis in Psychiatric Education*, ed. S. Weissman & R. Thurnblad. New York: International Universities Press, pp. 225–269.

—— (1989), Psychoanalysis and education: Motive, meaning, and self. In: *Learning and Education: Psychoanalytic Perspectives*, ed. K. Field, B. Cohler, & G. Wool. Madison, CT: International Universities Press, pp. 11–83.

—— Boxer, A. (1984), Middle adulthood: Settling into the world—Person, time, and context. In: *Normality and the Life-Cycle*, ed. D. Offer & M. Sabshin. New York: Basic Books, pp. 145–203.

—— Carney, J. (unpublished), Developmental continuities and adjustment in adulthood: Social relations, morale, and the transformation from middle to late life.

—— Ferrono, C. (1986), Schizophrenia and the life-course. In: *Schizophrenia and Aging*, ed. N. Miller & G. Cohen. New York: Guilford Press, pp. 189–197.

—— Grunebaum, H. (1981), *Mothers and Grandmothers: Personality and Childcare in Three Generation Families*. New York: Wiley.

—— Musick, J. (1984), Psychopathology of parenthood: Implications for mental health of children. *Infant Ment. Health J.*, 4:140–164.

—— Stott, F. (1987), Separation, interdependence and social relations across the second half of life. In: *The Psychology of Separation Through the Life-Cycle*, ed. J. Bloom-Feshbach & S. Bloom-Feshbach. San Francisco: Jossey-Bass, pp. 165–204.

Cohn, F. (1957), Time and the ego. *Psychoanal. Quart.*, 26:168–189.

Colarusso, C., & Nemiroff, R. (1981), *Adult Development: A New Dimension of Psychodynamic Theory and Practice*. New York: Plenum.

Collingwood, R.G. (1946), *The Idea of History*. New York: Oxford University Press, 1972.

Colombo, J. (1982), The critical period of concept: Research, methodology, and theoretical issues. *Psychological Bull.*, 91:260–275.

Coltrera, J.T. (1979), Truth from genetic illusion: The transference and the fate of the infantile neurosis. *J. Amer. Psychoanal. Assn.*, 27(Suppl.): 289–314.

Connolly, K. (1972), Learning and the concept of critical periods in infancy. *Devel. Med. & Child Neurol.*, 14:705–714.

Costa, P., & McCrae, R. (1980), Still stable after all these years: Personality as a key to some issues in adulthood and old age. In: *Life-Span Development and Behavior*, Vol. 3, ed. P. Baltes & O.G. Brim, Jr. New York: Academic Press, pp. 65–102.

Cottle, T. (1976), *Perceiving Time: A Psychological Investigation.* New York: Wiley Interscience.

―――― (1977), The time of youth. In: *The Personal Experience of Time*, ed. B. Gorman & A.E. Wessman. New York: Plenum, pp. 163–190.

―――― Klineberg, S. (1974), *The Present of Things Future.* New York: Free Press.

Crusey, J. (1985), Short-term psychodynamic psychotherapy with a sixty-two-year-old man. In: *The Race Against Time: Psychotherapy and Psychoanalysis in the Second Half of Life*, ed. R. Nemiroff & C. Colarusso. New York: Plenum, pp. 147–166.

Cumming, E., & Henry, W. (1961), *Growing Old.* New York: Basic Books.

Curtis, H.C. (1983), Construction and reconstruction: An introduction. In: *Construction and Reconstruction in Psychoanalysis*, ed. M. Bornstein. Hillsdale, N.J.: Analytic Press, pp. 183–188.

Daniels, P., & Weingarten, K. (1982), *Sooner or Later: The Timing of Parenthood in Adult Lives.* New York: Norton.

Danto, A. (1965), *Narration and Knowledge (Including Analytical Philosophy of History).* New York: Columbia University Press, 1985.

Darlington, R. (1978), Methods, issues and some illustrative findings in analyzing the data of the consortium on developmental continuity. Paper presented at the annual meetings, American Educational Research Association, Toronto.

Dennis, W. (1973), *Children of the Creche.* New York: Appleton-Century-Crofts.

Dray, W. (1963), The historical explanation of actions reconsidered. In: *Philosophy and History: A Symposium*, ed. S. Hook. New York: International Universities Press, pp. 105–135.

Eichorn, D., Clausen, J., Haan, N., Honzik, M., & Mussen, P. (1981), *Present and Past in Middle Life.* New York: Academic Press.

Eisenbud, J. (1956), Time and the Oedipus. *Psychoanal. Quart.*, 25:373–384.

Ekstein, R. (1959), Thoughts concerning the nature of the interpretive process. In: *Readings in Psychoanalytic Psychology*, ed. M. Levitt. New York: Appleton-Century-Crofts, pp. 221–247.

―――― Rangell, L. (1961), Reconstruction and theory formation. *J. Amer. Psychoanal. Assn.*, 9:684–697.

Elder, G. (1974), *Children of the Great Depression.* Chicago: University of Chicago Press.

―――― Nguyen, T., & Caspi, A. (1985), Linking family hardships to childrens' lives. *Child Devel.*, 56:361–375.

―――― Rockwell, R. (1979), The life-course and human development: An ecological perspective. *Internat. J. Behav. Devel.*, 2:1–21.

Emde, R. (1981), Changing the models of infancy and the nature of early development: Remodeling the foundation. *J. Amer. Psychoanal. Assn.*, 29:179–219.

―――― Gaensbauer, T., & Harmon, R. (1976), Emotional expression in infancy: A biobehavioral study. *Psychological Issues*, Monograph 37. New York: International Universities Press.

———— Harmon, R. (1984), Entering a new era in the search for developmental continuities. In: *Continuities and Discontinuities in Development*, ed. R. Emde & R. Harmon. New York: Plenum, pp. 1–11.

Emmerich, W., (1968), Personality development and concepts of structure. *Child Devel.*, 39:671–690.

Engel, G., Reichsmann, F., Harway, V., & Hess, D.W. (1985), Monica: Infant-feeding behavior of a mother gastric fistula-fed as an infant: A 3-year longitudinal study of enduring effects. In: *Parental Influences in Health and Disease*, ed. G. Pollock & E.J. Anthony. Boston: Little, Brown, pp. 29–90.

Erikson, E.H. (1950), *Childhood and Society*, rev. ed. New York: Norton, 1963.

———— (1958), *Young Man Luther: A Study in Psychoanalysis and History*. New York: Norton.

———— (1959), Identity and the life-cycle. *Psychological Issues*, Monograph 1. New York: International Universities Press.

———— (1962), Psychological reality and historical actuality. In: *Insight and Responsibility*. New York: Norton, 1964, pp. 159–256.

———— (1968), Identity, psychosocial. *International Encyclopedia of the Social Sciences*, 7:61–65. Rev. ed. New York: Free Press.

———— Erikson, J., & Kivnick, H. (1986), *Wisdom and the Life-Cycle*. New York: Norton.

Escoll, P.J. (1977), Panel report: The contribution of psychoanalytic developmental concepts to adult analysis. *J. Amer. Psychoanal. Assn.*, 25:219–234.

Esman, A. (1973), The primal scene: A review and reconsideration. *The Psychoanalytical Study of the Child*, 28:49–81. New Haven: Yale University Press.

Evans, J. (1954), *Three Men*. New York: Knopf.

Feinstein, A.D. (1979), Personal mythology as a paradigm for a holistic public psychology. *Amer. J. Orthopsychiat.*, 49:198–217.

Felsman, K. & Vaillant, G. (1986), Resilient children as adults: A forty year study. In: *The Invulnerable Child*, ed. E.J. Anthony & B.J. Cohler. New York: Guilford Press, pp. 289–314.

Fine, B., Joseph, E., & Waldhorn, H. (1971), *Recollection and Reconstruction and Reconstruction in Psychoanalysis*. Monograph IV of the Kris Study Group. New York: International Universities Press.

Fink, H. (1957), The relationship of time perspective to age, institutionalization and activity. *J. Gerontol.*, 12:414–417.

Fiske, D. (1974), The limits for the conventional science of personality, *J. Personal.*, 42:1–11.

Flavell, J. (1963), *The Developmental Psychology of Jean Piaget*. Princeton: Van Nostrand.

Fraiberg, S. (1980), *Clinical Studies of Infant Mental Health*. New York: Basic Books.

Fraisse, P. (1963), *The Psychology of Time*. New York: Harper & Row.

Freedman, D.G. (1974), *Human Infancy: An Evolutionary Approach*. New York: Erlbaum/Halsted/Wiley.

Freeman, M. (1984), History, narrative, and life-span developmental knowledge. *Human Devel.*, 27:1–19.

———— (1985a), Psychoanalytic narration and the problem of historical knowledge. *Psychoanal. & Contemp. Thought*, 8:133–182.

————— (1985b), Paul Ricoeur on interpretation: The model of the text and the idea of development. *Human Devel.*, 28:295–312.

Freud, A. (1927), Four lectures on child analysis. In: *The Writings of Anna Freud*, Vol. 1. New York: International Universities Press, 1964, pp. 3–69.

————— (1930), Four lectures on psychoanalysis for teachers and parents. *The Writings of Anna Freud*, Vol. 1. New York: International Universities Press, 1964, pp. 73–133.

————— (1951), Observations on child development. *The Psychoanalytic Study of the Child*, 6:18–30. New York: International Universities Press.

————— (1958), Child observation and prediction of development: A memorial lecture in honor of Ernst Kris. *The Psychoanalytic Study of the Child*, 13:92–116. New York: International Universities Press.

————— (1965), *Normality and Pathology in Childhood: Assessments of Development*. New York: International Universities Press.

————— (1971), The infantile neurosis: Genetic and dynamic considerations. *The Psychoanalytic Study of the Child*, 26:79–90. New York: Quadrangle.

————— Burlingham, D. (1943), *War and Children*. New York: International Universities Press.

————— ————— (1944), *Infants Without Families*. New York: International Universities Press.

Freud S. (1895), Project for a scientific psychology. *Standard Edition*, 1:295–387. London: Hogarth Press, 1966.

————— (1896a), The aetiology of hysteria. *Standard Edition*, 3:191–221. London: Hogarth Press, 1962.

————— (1896b), The neuro-psychoses of defence. *Standard Edition*, 3:45–61. London: Hogarth Press, 1962.

————— (1896c), Letter of 2/13/1896. In: *The Complete Letters of Sigmund Freud to Wilhelm Fliess: 1887–1904*, ed. J. Masson. Cambridge, Mass.: Harvard University Press, 1985, pp. 172–173.

————— (1898), Letter of 3/10/1898. In: *The Complete Letters of Sigmund Freud to Wilhelm Fliess: 1887–1904*, ed. J. Masson. Cambridge, Mass.: Harvard University Press, 1985, pp. 301–302.

————— (1899), Screen memories. *Standard Edition*, 3:299–322. London: Hogarth Press, 1962.

————— (1900), The interpretation of dreams. *Standard Edition*, 4/5. London: Hogarth Press, 1958.

————— (1901), The psychopathology of everyday life. *Standard Edition*, 6:1–279. London: Hogarth Press, 1960.

————— (1905a), Fragment of an analysis of a case of hysteria. *Standard Edition*, 7:1–122. London: Hogarth Press, 1953.

————— (1905b), Three essays on the theory of sexuality. *Standard Edition*, 7:130–243. London: Hogarth Press, 1953.

————— (1906), My views on the part played by sexuality in the aetiology of the neuroses. *Standard Edition*, 7:271–282. London: Hogarth Press, 1953.

————— (1908), On the sexual theories of children. *Standard Edition*, 9:207–226. London: Hogarth Press, 1959.

————— (1909), Analysis of a phobia of a five-year-old-boy. *Standard Edition*, 10:5–152. London: Hogarth Press, 1955.

————— (1910a), Five lectures on psycho-analysis. *Standard Edition*, 11:3–55. London: Hogarth Press, 1957.

———— (1910b), Leonardo da Vinci and a memory of his childhood. *Standard Edition*, 11:63–138. London: Hogarth Press, 1957.

———— (1910c), A special type of choice of object made by men. *Standard Edition*, 11:163–176. London: Hogarth Press, 1957.

———— (1913), The claims of psychoanalysis to scientific interest. *Standard Edition*, 13:165–192. London: Hogarth Press, 1958.

———— (1914), Remembering, repeating and working through. *Standard Edition*, 12:147–156. London: Hogarth Press, 1958.

———— (1915a), A case of paranoia running counter to the psycho-analytic theory of the disease. *Standard Edition*, 14:261–272. London: Hogarth Press, 1957.

———— (1915b), The unconscious. *Standard Edition*, 14:159–195. London: Hogarth Press, 1957.

———— (1916–1917), Introductory lectures on psycho-analysis. *Standard Edition*, 15/16. London: Hogarth Press, 1961/1963.

———— (1918), From the history of an infantile neurosis. *Standard Edition*, 17:1–122. London: Hogarth Press, 1955.

———— (1919), A child is being beaten. *Standard Edition*, 17:179–204. London: Hogarth Press, 1955.

———— (1920a), Beyond the pleasure principle. *Standard Edition*, 18:7–66. London: Hogarth Press, 1955.

———— (1920b), Group psychology and the analysis of the ego. *Standard Edition*, 18:65–144. London: Hogarth Press, 1955.

———— (1920c), The psychogenesis of a case of homosexuality in a woman. *Standard Edition*, 18:145–172. London: Hogarth Press, 1955.

———— (1925), An autobiographical study. *Standard Edition*, 20:3–74. London: Hogarth Press, 1959.

———— (1931), Female sexuality. *Standard Edition*, 21:221–246. London: Hogarth Press, 1961.

———— (1937), Constructions in analysis. *Standard Edition*, 23:255–270. London: Hogarth Press, 1964.

———— (1939), Moses and monotheism. *Standard Edition*, 23:1–208. London: Hogarth Press, 1964.

———— (1940), An outline of psycho-analysis. *Standard Edition*, 23:141–207. London: Hogarth Press, 1964.

———— (1954), *The Origins of Psycho-Analysis: Letters to Wilhelm Fliess, Drafts and Notes (1887–1902)*. New York: Basic Books.

Furman, E. (1956), An ego disturbance in a young child. *The Psychoanalytic Study of the Child*, 11:312–335.

Gadamer, H.-G. (1960), *Truth and Method*. New York: Seabury, 1975.

———— (1963), The problem of historical consciousness. In: *Interpretive Social Science*, ed. P. Rabinow & W. Sullivan. Berkeley: University of California Press, 1979, pp. 103–162.

Gardiner, P. (1959), *Theories of History*. New York: Free Press.

Gedo, J. (1984), *Psychoanalysis and Its Discontents*. New York: Guilford.

———— Goldberg, A. (1973), *Models of the Mind*. Chicago: University of Chicago Press.

Geertz, C. (1973), *The Interpretation of Cultures*. New York: Basic Books.

———— (1983), *Local Knowledge: Further Essays in Interpretive Anthropology*. New York: Basic Books.

Gergen, K. (1977), Stability, change, and chance in understanding human development. In: *Life-Span Developmental Psychology: Dialectical Perspectives on Experimental Research,* ed. N. Datan & H. Reese. New York: Academic Press, pp. 136–158.

——— (1980), The emerging crisis in life-span developmental theory. In: *Life-Span Development and Behavior,* Vol. 3, ed. P. Baltes & O.G. Brim, Jr. New York: Academic Press, pp. 32–65.

——— (1982), *Toward Transformation in Social Knowledge.* New York: Springer.

——— Gergen, M. (1983), Narratives of the self. In: *Studies in Social Identity,* ed. T. Sarbin & K.E. Scheibe. New York: Praeger, pp. 254–273.

Gill, M. (1976), Metapsychology is not psychology. In: *Psychology Versus Metapsychology. Psychoanalytical Essays in Honor of George S. Klein,* ed. M. Gill & P. Holzman. *Psychological Issues* Monograph 26. New York: International Universities Press.

——— (1977), Psychic energy reconsidered. *J. Amer. Psychoanal. Assn.,* 25:581–597.

——— (1979), The analysis of the transference, *J. Amer. Psychoanal. Assn.,* 27(Suppl):263–289.

——— (1982), *Analysis of the Transference: Vol. I. Theory and Technique.* New York: International Universities Press.

——— Holzman, P. (1976), *Psychology Versus Metapsychology: Psychoanalytic Essays in Honor of George S. Klein. Psychological Issues* Monograph 36. New York: International Universities Press.

Glover, E. (1929), The "screening" function of traumatic memories. *Internat. J. Psycho-Anal.,* 10:9–93.

——— (1930), Grades of ego differentiation. In: *On the Early Development of Mind.* New York: International Universities Press, 1956, pp. 112–122.

——— (1932a), On the etiology of drug addiction. In: *On the Early Development of Mind.* New York: International Universities Press, 1956, pp. 187–215.

——— (1932b), A psychoanalytic approach to the classification of mental disorders. In: *On the Early Development of Mind.* New York: International Universities Press, 1956, pp. 161–186.

Goffman, E. (1963), *Stigma: Notes on the Management of Spoiled Identity.* Englewood Cliffs, N.J.: Prentice-Hall.

Goodman, S. (1977), *Psychoanalytic Education and Research.* New York: International Universities Press.

Gorman B., & Wessman, A.E., eds. (1977), Images, values, and concepts of time in psychological research. In: *The Personal Experience of Time.* New York: Plenum, pp. 218–264.

Green, A. (1975), The analyst, symbolization and absence in the analytic setting: On changes in analytic practice and analytic experience. *Internat. J. Psycho-Anal.,* 56:1–22.

Greenacre, P.A. (1949), A contribution to the study of screen memories. *The Psychoanalytic Study of the Child,* 3/4:73–83. New York: International Universities Press.

——— (1954), Problems of infantile neurosis: Contribution to a discussion. In: *Emotional Growth,* Vol. 2. New York: International Universities Press, 1971, pp. 59–67.

——— (1960), Considerations regarding the parent–infant relationship. *Internat. J. Psycho-Anal.,* 41:571–584.

——— (1975), On reconstruction. *J. Amer. Psychoanal. Assn.*, 23:693–712.

——— (1979), Reconstruction and the process of individuation. *The Psychoanalytic Study of the Child*, 34:121–144. New Haven, CT: Yale University Press.

——— (1981), Reconstruction: Its nature and therapeutic value. *J. Amer. Psychoanal. Assn.*, 29:27–46.

Greenson, R. (1971), A dream while drowning. In: *Separation-Individuation: Essays in Honor of Margaret Mahler*, ed. J. McDevitt & C. Settlage. New York: International Universities Press, pp. 377–384.

Gross, A. (1949), Sense of time in dreams. *Psychoanal. Quart.*, 8:466–470.

Grunbaum, A. (1984), *The Foundations of Psychoanalysis: A Philosophic Critique*. Berkeley: University of California Press.

Grunes, J. (1980), Reminiscences, regression, and empathy: A psychotherapeutic approach to the impaired elderly. In: *The Course of Life: Volume III. Adulthood and the Aging Process*, ed. S. Greenspan & G. Pollock. Washington, D.C.: U.S. Government Printing Office, pp. 545–548.

Gubrium, J., & Buckholdt, D. (1977), *Toward Maturity*. San Francisco: Jossey-Bass.

Gutmann, D. (1969), *The Country of Old Men: Cross-Cultural Studies in the Psychology of Later Life*. Occasional papers in gerontology, No. 5. University of Michigan and Wayne State University: The Institute of Gerontology.

——— Griffin, B., & Grunes, J. (1982), Developmental contributions to the late-onset affective disorders. In: *Life-Span Development and Behavior*, ed. P. Baltes & O.G. Brim, Jr. New York: Academic Press, pp. 244–263.

Haan, N., & Day, D. (1974), A longitudinal study of change and sameness in personality development: Adolescence to later adulthood, *Internat. J. Aging & Human Devel.*, 5:11–39.

Habermas, J. (1968), *Knowledge and Human Interests*. Boston: Beacon Press, 1971.

——— (1983), Interpretive social science vs. hermeneuticism. In: *Social Science as Moral Inquiry*, ed. N. Haan, R. Bellah, P. Rabinow, & W. Sullivan. New York: Columbia University Press, pp. 251–270.

Haeckel, E. (1868), *Naturaliche Schopfungsgesichte (Natural History of Creation)*. Berlin: George Reimer, 1968.

Hagestad, G., & Neugarten, B. (1985), Age and the life-course. In: *Handbook of Society and Aging*, 2nd ed., ed. R. Binstock & E. Shanes. New York: Van Nostrand-Reinhold, pp. 35–61.

Hanson, D., Gottesman, I., & Meehl, P. (1977), Genetic theories and the validation of psychiatric diagnosis: Implications for the study of children of schizophrenics. *J. Abnorm. Psychol.*, 6:575–588.

Hartmann, H. (1950), Comments on the psychoanalytic theory of the ego. In: *Essays on Ego Psychology*. New York: International Universities Press, 1964, pp. 113–141.

——— Kris, E. (1945), The genetic approach in psychoanalysis. *The Psychoanalytic Study of the Child*, 1:11–30. New York: International Universities Press.

——— ——— & Lowenstein, R. (1946), Comments on the formation of psychic structure. *Psychological Issues*, Monograph 14. New York: International Universities Press, 1964, pp. 27–54.

Hebb, D.O. (1949), *The Organization of Behavior*. New York: Wiley.

Hendricks, C.D., & Hendricks, J. (1976), Concepts of time and temporal construction among the aged, with implications for research. In: *Time, Roles and Self in Old Age*, ed. J. Gubrium. New York: Human Sciences Press, pp. 13–49.

Hess, E. (1959), Imprinting. *Science*, 130:133–144.

Hinde, R. (1963), The nature of imprinting. In: *The Determinants of Infant Behavior*, Vol. 2, ed. B. Foss. New York: Wiley, pp. 227–234.

——— (1966), *Animal Behavior: A Synthesis of Ethology and Comparative Psychology*. New York: McGraw-Hill.

Hochschild, A. (1975), Disengagement theory: A critique and a proposal. *Amer. Sociol. Rev.*, 40:533–569.

Hogan, D. (1981), *Transitions and Social Change: The Early Lives of American Men*. New York: Academic Press.

Holt, R.R. (1961), Clinical judgment as a disciplined inquiry. *J. Nerv. & Ment. Dis.*, 133:369–381.

——— ed. (1967), Motives and thoughts: Psychoanalytic essays in honor of David Rapaport. *Psychological Issues*, Monographs 18/19. New York: International Universities Press.

——— (1972), Freud's mechanistic and humanistic image of man. *Psychoanal. & Contemp. Sci.*, 1:3–24.

——— (1975), The past and future of ego psychology. *Psychoanal. Quart.*, 44:550–576.

——— (1976), Drive or wish? A reconsideration of the psychoanalytic theory of motivation. In: *Psychology Versus Metapsychology: Psychoanalytic Essays in Memory of George S. Klein*, ed. M. Gill & P. Holtzman. *Psychological Issues*, Monograph 36. New York: International Universities Press, pp. 158–197.

——— (1985), The current status of psychoanalytic theory. *Psychoanal. Psychol.*, 2:289–316.

Horowitz, M. (1977), The quantitative line of approach in psychoanalysis: A clinical assessment of its current status. *J. Amer. Psychoanal. Assn.*, 25:559–580.

Hug-Hellmuth, H. (1913), *A Study of the Mental Life of the Child*. Washington, D.C.: Nervous and Mental Disease Publishing Company.

Isaacs, S. (1932), *The Nursery Years*. London: Routledge, Kegan Paul.

Isay, R.A. (1978), Panel report: The pathogenicity of the primal scene. *J. Amer. Psychoanal. Assn.*, 26:131–142.

Ivimey, M. (1950), Childhood memories in psychoanalysis. *Amer. J. Psychoanal.*, 10:38–46.

Jackson, H. (1875), Evolutional dissolution of the nervous system. In: *J.J. Jackson, Selected Writings*, Vol. 2, ed. J. Taylor. New York: Basic Books, pp. 45–75.

Jaques, E. (1965), Death and the mid-life crisis. *Internat. J. Psycho-Anal.*, 46:502–514.

Jauss, H.R. (1982), *Toward an Aesthetic of Reception*. Minneapolis: University of Minnesota Press.

Jones, E. (1953), *The Life and Work of Sigmund Freud*, Vol. 1. New York: Basic Books.

Jones, M., Bayley, N., & MacFarlane, J. (1971), *The Course of Human Development*. Waltham, Mass.: Xerox College Publishing.

Joseph, E. (1973), Sense of conviction, screen memories and reconstruction: A clinical note. *Bull. Menn. Clin.*, 37:565–580.

Jung, C.G. (1933), *Modern Man in Search of a Soul.* New York: Harcourt, Brace and World, 1935.

Kafka, J. (1973), Panel report: The experience of time. *J. Amer. Psychoanal. Assn.,* 21:650–667.

Kagan, J. (1980), Perspectives on continuity. In: *Constance and Change in Human Development,* ed. O.G. Brim, Jr. & J. Kagan. Cambridge: Harvard University Press, pp. 26–74.

——— Klein, R. (1973), Cross-cultural perspectives on early development. *Amer. Psychologist,* 28:947–961.

——— ——— Finley G., Rogoff, B., & Nolan, E. (1979), *A Cross-Cultural Study of Cognitive Development.* Society for Research in Child Development, Monograph 44.

——— Moss, H. (1962), *Birth to Maturity.* New York: Wiley.

Kanzer, M. (1953), Past and present in the transference. *J. Amer. Psychoanal. Assn.,* 1:144–154.

Kastenbaum, R., & Durkee, N. (1964), Elderly people view old age. In: *New Thoughts on Old Age,* ed. R. Kastenbaum. New York: Springer, pp. 250–262.

——— ——— (1977), Memories of tomorrow: On the interpretations of time in later life. In: *The Personal Experience of Time,* ed. B. Gorman & A.E. Wessman. New York: Plenum, pp. 194–214.

Kaufman, C., Grunebaum, H., Cohler, B., & Gamer, E. (1979), Superkids: Competent children of schizophrenic mothers. *Amer. J. Psychiat.,* 136:1398–1402.

Kennedy, H. (1950), Cover memories in formation. *The Psychoanalytic Study of the Child,* 5:73–84. New York: International Universities Press.

Kermode, F. (1985), Freud and interpretation. *Internat. Rev. Psycho-Anal.,* 12:3–12.

Kernberg, O. (1975), *Borderline Conditions and Pathological Narcissism.* New York: Aronson.

——— (1976), *Object Relations and Clinical Psychoanalysis.* New York: Aronson.

Khan, M. (1963), The concept of cumulative trauma. In: *The Privacy of the Self.* New York: International Universities Press, 1974, pp. 42–58.

——— (1964), Ego-distortion, cumulative trauma, and the role of reconstruction in the analytic situation. In: *The Privacy of the Self.* New York: International Universities Press, 1974, pp. 59–68.

King, P. (1979), The life cycle as indicated by the nature of the transference in the psychoanalysis of the middle-aged and elderly. *Internat. J. Psycho-Anal.,* 61:153–160.

Klein, G. (1966), The several grades of memory. In: *Psychoanalysis—A general Psychology: Essays in Honor of Heinz Hartmann,* ed. R. Loewenstein, L. Newman, M. Schur, & A. Solnit. New York: International Universities Press, pp. 371–389.

——— (1973), Is psychoanalysis relevant? *Psychoanal. & Contemp. Sci.,* 2:3–21.

——— (1976), *Psychoanalytic Theory: An Exploration of Essentials.* New York: International Universities Press.

Klein, M. (1928), *The Psycho-Analysis of Children,* rev. ed. New York: Delacorte, 1975.

——— (1948), *Contributions to Psycho-Analysis: 1921–1945.* London: Hogarth Press.

———— (1981), Freud's seduction theory: Its implications for fantasy and memory in psychoanalytic theory. *Bull. Menn. Clin.*, 45:185–208.

Klineberg, S. (1967), Changes in outlook on the future between childhood and adolescence. *J. Personal. & Soc. Psychol.*, 7:185–193.

Kohlberg, L., Ricks, D., & Snarey, J. (1984), Childhood development as a predictor of adaptation in adulthood. *Genet. Psychol. Monographs*, 110:91–172.

Kohon, G. (1986), *The British School of Psychoanalysis*. New Haven: Yale University Press.

Kohut, H. (1959), Introspection, empathy, and psychoanalysis: An examination of the relationship between mode of observation and theory. *J. Amer. Psychoanal. Assn.*, 7:459–483.

———— (1971), *The Analysis of the Self*. New York: International Universities Press.

———— (1973), The future of psychoanalysis. *Annual of Psychoanalysis*, 3:325–340.

———— (1975), The psychoanalyst in the community of scholars. *Annual of Psychoanalysis*, 3:341–370.

———— (1977), *The Restoration of the Self*. New York: International Universities Press.

———— (1982), Introspection, empathy and the semi-circle of mental health. *Internat. J. Psycho-Anal.*, 63:395–407.

———— Seitz, P. (1963), Concepts and theories of psychoanalysis. In: *Concepts of Personality*, ed. J. Wepman & R. Heine. Chicago: Aldine, pp. 113–141.

Kovel, J. (1978), Things and words: Metapsychology and the historical point of view. *Psychoanal. & Contemp. Thought*, 1:21–88.

Kris, E. (1951), Opening remarks on psychoanalytic child psychology. *The Psychoanalytic Study of the Child*, 6:9–17. New York: International Universities Press.

———— (1956a), The personal myth: A problem in psychoanalytic technique. *J. Amer. Psychoanal. Assn.*, 4:653–681.

———— (1956b), The recovery of child memories in psychoanalysis. *The Psychoanalytic Study of the Child*, 11:54–88. New York: International Universities Press.

Laplanche, J., & Pontalis, J.-B. (1967), *The Language of Psycho-Analysis*, trans. D. Nicholson-Smith. New York: Norton, 1973.

Lazar, I., Hubbell, V., Murray, H., Rosche, M., & Royce, J. (1977), *The Persistence of School Effects: A Long-Term Follow-up of Fourteen Infant and Preschool Experiments*. Washington, D.C.: U.S. Government Printing Office.

Leavy, S. (1980), *The Psychoanalytic Dialogue*. New Haven: Yale University Press.

Lecky, P. (1961), *Self-consistency: A Theory of Personality*. New York: Doubleday Anchor.

Leites, N. (1977), Transference interpretations *only? Internat. J. Psycho-Anal.*, 58:275–287.

Lennenberg, E. (1967), *Biological Foundations of Language*. New York: Wiley.

Levinson, D. (1986), A conception of adult development. *Amer. Psychologist*, 41:3–13.

Levi-Strauss, C. (1955), The structural study of myth. In: *Structural Anthropology*. New York: Basic Books, 1963, pp. 206–231.

Lewin, B. (1946), Sleep, the mouth and the dream screen. *Psychoanal. Quart.*, 15:419–454.

Lichtenberg, J. (1983a), A clinical illustration of construction and reconstruction in the analysis of an adult. In: *Construction and Reconstruction in Psychoanalysis*, ed. M. Bornstein. Hillsdale, N.J.: Analytic Press, pp. 279–294.

——— (1983b), *Psychoanalysis and Infant Research.* Hillsdale, N.J.: Analytic Press.

Lieberman, M. (1964), Adaptation and survival studies. Progress report, National Institute on Child Health and Human Development.

——— Cohler, B. (1975), Constructing personality measures for older people. Final report, Administration on Aging.

——— Falk, J. (1971), The remembered past as a source of data for research on the life cycle. *Human Devel.*, 14:132–141.

——— Tobin, S. (1983), *The Experience of Old Age.* New York: Basic Books.

Livson, N. & Peskin, H. (1980), Perspectives on adolescence from longitudinal research. In: *Handbook of Adolescent Psychology*, ed. J. Adelson. New York: Wiley, pp. 47–98.

Loch, W. (1977), Some comments on the subject of psychoanalysis and truth. In: *Psychiatry and the Humanities: Vol. 2. Thought, Consciousness and Reality*, ed. J.H. Smith. New Haven: Yale University Press, pp. 217–255.

Loewald, H. (1962), The super-ego and the ego-ideal: II. Super-ego and time. *Internat. J. Psycho-Anal.*, 43:264–268.

——— (1972), The experience of time. *The Psychoanalytic Study of the Child*, 27:401–410. New York: Quadrangle.

——— (1976), Perspectives on memory, *Psychological Issues*, Monograph 9. New York: International Universities Press, pp. 299–325.

——— (1978), *Psychoanalysis and the History of the Individual.* New Haven: Yale University Press.

——— (1979), The waning of the Oedipus complex. *J. Amer. Psychoanal. Assn.*, 27:751–775.

Loewenstein, R. (1951), The problem of interpretation. *Psychoanal. Quart.*, 20:1–14.

Lopata, H. (1979), *Women as Widows: Support Systems.* New York: Elsevier North-Holland.

Lorenz, K. (1937), The nature of instinct. In: *Instinctive Behavior*, ed. C. Schiller. New York: International Universities Press, 1957, pp. 129–175.

Lovejoy, A.O. (1939), Present standpoints and past history. *J. Philos.*, 36:477–489.

Lowenthal, M. (1964), Social isolation and mental illness in old age. *Amer. Sociol. Rev.*, 29:54–70.

——— Robinson, B. (1976), Social networks and Isolation. In: *Handbook of Aging and the Social Sciences*, ed. R. Binstock & E. Shanas. New York: Van Nostrand Reinhold, pp. 432–456.

Maas, H., & Kuypers, J. (1974), *From Thirty to Seventy.* San Francisco: Jossey-Bass.

McCarley, R., & Hobson, J. (1977), Neurobiological origins of psychoanalytic dream theory. *Amer. J. Psychiat.*, 134:1211–1221.

McDevitt, J. (1973), Panel report: The experience of separation-individuation in infancy and its reverberations through the course of life: Maturity, senescence, and sociological implications. *J. Amer. Psychoanal. Assn.*, 21:633–645.

McGuire, M. (1970), Repression, resistance, and recall of the past: Some reconsiderations. *Psychoanal. Quart.*, 39:427–448.

——— (1971), *Reconstructions in Psychoanalysis.* New York: Appleton-Century-Crofts.

McMahon, A., & Rhudick, P. (1967), Reminiscing in the aged: An adaptational response. In: *Psychodynamic Studies on Aging: Creativity, Reminiscing, and Dying*, ed. S. Levin & R. Kahana. New York: International Universities Press, pp. 64–78.

Mahler, M. (1968), *On Human Symbiosis and the Vicissitudes of Individuation: Vol. 1. Infantile Psychosis.* New York: International Universities Press.

——— Pine, F., & Bergman, A. (1975), *The Psychological Birth of the Human Infant.* New York: Basic Books.

Malcolm, J. (1984), *In the Freud Archives.* New York: Knopf.

Malin, A. (1982), Panel report: Construction and reconstruction. *J. Amer. Psychoanal. Assn.*, 30:213–233.

Mancuso, J., & Sarbin, T. (1984), The self-narrative in the enactment of roles. In: *Studies in Social Identity*, ed. T. Sarbin & K. Scheibe. New York: Praeger, pp. 233–253.

Mandelbaum, M. (1967), A note on history as narrative. *History & Theory*, 6:413–419.

——— (1977), *The Anatomy of Historical Knowledge.* Baltimore: Johns Hopkins University Press.

Masson, J. (1984), *The Assault on Truth.* New York: Farrar, Straus, & Giroux.

——— ed. (1985), *The Complete Letters of Sigmund Freud to Wilhelm Fliess: 1887–1904.* Cambridge: Harvard University Press.

Meacham, J. (1972), The development of memory abilities in the individual and society. *Human Devel.*, 15:205–228.

——— (1977), A transactional model of remembering. In: *Life-Span Developmental Psychology: Dialectical Perspectives on Experimental Research*, ed. N. Datan & H. Reese. New York: Academic Press, pp. 261–284.

Mink, L.O. (1965), The autonomy of historical understanding. *History & Theory*, 5:24–47.

——— (1981), Everyman his or her own annalist. In: *On Narrative*, ed. J.T. Mitchell. Chicago: University of Chicago Press, pp. 233–239.

Mitchell, J.T. (1981), *On Narrative.* Chicago: University of Chicago Press.

Modell, A. (1984), *Psychoanalysis in a New Context.* New York: International Universities Press.

Moss, H., & Sussman, E. (1980), Longitudinal study of personality development. In: *Constancy and Change in Human Development*, ed. O.G. Brim, Jr. & J. Kagan. Cambridge: Harvard University Press, pp. 530–595.

Munnichs, J. (1966), *Old Age and Finitude: A Contribution to Psychogeriatrics.* New York: Karger.

Murphy, L. (1962), *The Widening World of Childhood.* New York: Basic Books.

——— (1973), Some mutual contributions of psychoanalysis and child development. *Psychoanal. & Contemp. Sci.*, 2:99–123.

Murray, H., and associates (1937), *Explorations in Personality.* New York: Oxford University Press.

Myerhoff, B. (1979), *Number Our Days.* New York: Dutton.

———— Simic, A. (1979), *Life's Career: Aging. Cultural Variations in Growing Old.* Beverly Hills: Sage Publications.

Nagera, H. (1966), *Early Childhood Disturbances, the Infantile Neurosis and the Adulthood Disturbances: Problems of a Developmental Psychoanalytic Psychology.* New York: International Universities Press.

Nemiroff, R., & Colarusso, C., eds. (1985), *The Race Against Time: Psychotherapy and Psychoanalysis in the Second Half of Life.* New York: Plenum.

Neugarten, B.L. (1968), The awareness of middle age. In: *Middle Age and Aging,* ed. B. Neugarten. Chicago: University of Chicago Press, pp. 93–98.

———— (1969), Continuities and discontinuities of psychological issues into adult life. *Human Devel.,* 12:121–130.

———— (1973), Personality change in late life: A developmental perspective. In: *The Psychology of Adult Development and Aging,* ed. C. Eisdorfer & M. Lawton. Washington, D.C.: American Psychological Association, pp. 311–338.

———— (1977), Personality and aging. In: *Handbook of Personality and Aging,* ed. J. Birren & K.W. Schaie. New York: Van Nostrand Reinhold, pp. 626–649.

———— (1979), Time, age, and the life-cycle. *Amer. J. Psychiat.,* 136:887–894.

———— (1984), Interpretive social science and research on aging. In: *Gender and the Life Course,* ed. A. Rossi. New York: Aldine, pp. 291–300.

———— Datan, N. (1973), Sociological perspectives on the life-cycle. In: *Life-Span Developmental Psychology: Personality and Socialization,* ed. P. Baltes & K.W. Schaie. New York: Academic Press, pp. 53–69.

———— ———— (1974), The middle years. In: *American Handbook of Psychiatry: Vol. 1. The Foundations of Psychiatry,* ed. S. Arieti. New York: Basic Books, pp. 592–608.

———— Hagestad, G. (1976), Aging and the life course. In: *Handbook of Aging and the Social Sciences,* ed. R. Binstock & E. Shanas. New York: Van Nostrand-Reinhold, pp. 35–57.

———— Moore, J. (1968), The changing age status system. In: *Middle Age and Aging,* ed. B. Neugarten. Chicago: University of Chicago Press, pp. 5–21.

———— ———— Lowe, Jr. (1965), Age norms, age constraints, and adult socialization. *Amer. J. Sociol.,* 70:710–717.

Niederland, W. (1965a), Panel report: Memory and repression. *J. Amer. Psychoanal. Assn.,* 13:619–633.

———— (1965b), The role of the ego in the recovery of early memories. *Psychoanal. Quart.,* 34:564–571.

Novak, M., & Harlow, H. (1975), Social recovery of monkeys isolated for the first year of life: I. Rehabilitation and therapy. *Devel. Psychol.,* 11:453–465.

Novey, S. (1968), *The Second Look: The Reconstruction of Personal History in Psychiatry and Psychoanalysis.* Baltimore: Johns Hopkins University Press.

Nydegger, C. (1980), On being caught up in time. *Human Devel.,* 24:1–12.

Parens, H., Pollock, L., Stern, J., & Kramer, S. (1976), On the girl's entry into the Oedipus complex. *J. Amer. Psychoanal. Assn.,* 24(Suppl.):79–108.

———— Saul, L. (1971), *Dependence in Man.* New York: International Universities Press.

Peskin, H., & Livson, N. (1981), Uses of the past in adult psychological health. In: *Present and Past in Middle Life*, ed. D. Eichorn, J. Clausen, N. Haan, M. Honzik, & P. Mussen. New York: Academic Press, pp. 154–183.

Piaget, J. (1933), *The Construction of Reality in the Child*, trans. S. Milgram & A. Parsons. New York: Basic Books, 1954.

——— (1975), *The Equilibration of Cognitive Structures: The Central Problem of Cognitive Development*, trans. T. Brown & K.J. Thampy. Chicago: University of Chicago Press.

Pine, F. (1985), *Developmental Theory and Clinical Process*. New Haven: Yale University Press.

Plank, E. (1953), Memories of early childhood in autobiographies. *The Psychoanalytic Study of the Child*, 8:381–393.

Polanyi, M. (1949), The nature of scientific convictions. In: *Scientific Thought and Social Reality*, ed. F. Schwartz. *Psychological Issues*, Monograph 32. New York: International Universities Press, 1974, pp. 49–66.

——— (1965), On the modern mind. *Psychological Issues*, Monograph 32. New York: International Universities Press, 1974, pp. 131–149.

Pollock, G. (1961), Mourning and adaptation. *Internat. J. Psycho-Anal.*, 42:341–361.

——— (1971a), On time and anniversaries. In: *The Unconscious Today: Essays in Honor of Max Schur*, ed. M. Kanzer. New York: International Universities Press, pp. 233–257.

——— (1971b), On time, death, and immortality. *Psychoanal. Quart.*, 40:435–446.

——— (1981), Reminiscence and insight. *The Psychoanalytic Study of the Child*, 36:278–287. New Haven: Yale University Press.

——— Kastenbaum, R. (1964), Delay of gratification in later life: An experimental analog. In: *New Thoughts on Old Age*, ed. R. Kastenbaum. New York: Springer, pp. 281–290.

Potamianou, A. (1985), The personal myth: Points and counterpoints. *The Psychoanalytic Study of the Child*, 40:285–296. New Haven: Yale University Press.

Pribram, K.H., & Gill, M.M. (1976), *Freud's Project Re-assessed*. New York: Basic Books.

Prosen, H., Martin, R., & Prosen, M. (1972), The remembered mother and the fantasized mother: A crisis of middle age. *Arch. Gen. Psychiat.*, 27:791–794.

Pruchno, R., Blow, F., & Smyer, M. (1984), Life events and interdependent lives: Implications for research and intervention. *Human Devel.*, 27:31–41.

Rabinow, P., & Sullivan W.M. (1979), The interpretive turn: Emergence of an approach. In: *Interpretive Social Science: A Reader*, ed. P. Rabinow & W.M. Sullivan. Berkeley: University of California Press, pp. 1–24.

Ramzy, I., & Shevrin, H. (1976), The nature of the inference process in psychoanalytic interpretation: A critical review of the literature. *Internat. J. Psycho-Anal.*, 57:151–159.

Rangell, L. (1961), The role of early psychic functioning in psychoanalysis. *J. Amer. Psychoanal. Assn.*, 9:595–609.

Rapaport, D., & Gill, M. (1959), The points of view and assumptions of metapsychology. *Internat. J. Psycho-Anal.*, 40:153–162.

Reider, N. (1953), Reconstruction and screen function. *J. Amer. Psychoanal. Assn.*, 1:389–405.

Revere, V. (1968), Developmental differences in the remembered past. Unpublished doctoral dissertation, University of Chicago.

Rexford, E., Sander, L., & Shapiro, T. (1976), *Infant Psychiatry: A New Synthesis.* New Haven: Yale University Press.

Ricoeur, P. (1970), *Freud and Philosophy: An Essay on Interpretation.* New Haven: Yale University Press.

——— (1977), The question of proof in Freud's psychoanalytic writings. *J. Amer. Psychoanal. Assn.*, 25:835–872.

——— (1983), Can fictional narratives be true? *Analecta Husserliana,* 14:3–19.

——— (1984a), *The Reality of the Historical Past.* Madison: Marquette University.

——— (1984b), *Time and Narrative,* Vol. 1, trans. K. McLaughlin & D. Pellauer. Chicago: University of Chicago Press.

——— (1985), *Time and Narrative,* Vol. 2, trans. K. McLaughlin & D. Pellauer. Chicago: University of Chicago Press.

Riegel, K. (1977), Toward a dialectical interpretaition of time and change. In: *The Personal Experience of Time,* ed. O. Gorman & A. E. Wessman. New York: Plenum, pp. 60–108.

——— (1979), *Foundations of Dialectical Psychology.* New York: Academic Press.

Ritvo, S. (1974), Current status of the concept of infantile neurosis. *The Psychoanalytic Study of the Child,* 29:159–188. New Haven: Yale University Press.

Roiphe, H., & Galenson, E. (1981), *Infantile Origins of Sexual Identity.* New York: International Universities Press.

Rosenblatt, A., & Thickstun, J. (1970), A study of the concept of psychic energy. *Internat. J. Psycho-Anal.,* 51:265–278.

——— ——— (1977), Energy, information and motivation: A revision of psychoanalytic theory. *J. Amer. Psychoanal. Assn.*, 25:537–558.

Rossi, A. (1968), Transition to parenthood. *J. Marriage & Family,* 30:26–39.

Roy, A. (1985), Early parental separation and adult depression. *Arch. Gen. Psychiat.,* 42:987–991.

Rubenstein, B. (1975), On the role of clinical psychoanalytic theory and its role in the inference and confirmation of particular clinical hypotheses. *Psychoanal. & Contemp. Sci.,* 4:3–58.

Rutter, M. (1972), Relationships between child and adult psychiatric disorders: Some research considerations. *Acta Psychiatrica Scandinavica,* 48:3–21.

Sadow, L., Gedo, J., Miller, J., Pollock, G., Sabshin, M., & Schlessinger, N. (1976), The process of hypothesis change in three early psychoanalytic concepts. *Psychological Issues,* Monograph 34/35. New York: International Universities Press.

Sandler, A.M. (1978), Psychoanalysis in later life: Problems in the psychoanalysis of an aging narcissistic patient. *J. Geriat. Psychiat.,* 11:5–36.

Saul, L., & Snyder, T. (1956), On earliest memories. *Psychoanal. Quart.,* 25:228–237.

Schachtel, E. (1947), Memory and childhood amnesia. *Psychiat.,* 10:1–26.

Schafer, R. (1958), How was this story told? *J. Proj. Tech.,* 22:181–210.

——— (1960), The loving and beloved superego in Freud's structural theory. *The Psychoanalytic Study of the Child,* 15:163–188. New York: International Universities Press.

————— (1976), *A New Language for Psychoanalysis*. New Haven: Yale University Press.

————— (1978), *Language and Insight*. New Haven: Yale University Press.

————— (1980), Narration in the psychoanalytic dialogue. *Critical Inquiry*, 7:29–53.

————— (1981), *Narrative Actions in Psychoanalysis*. Worcester, Mass: Clark University Press.

————— (1982), The relevance of the 'here and now' transference interpretation to the reconstruction of early development. *Internat. J. Psycho-Anal.*, 63:77–82.

————— (1983), *The Analytic Attitude*. New York: Basic Books.

Schaffer, R. (1977), *Mothering*. Cambridge: Harvard University Press.

Schimek, J. (1975), The interpretations of the past: Childhood trauma, psychical reality and historical truth. *J. Amer. Psychoanal. Assn.*, 23:845–865.

Schlesinger, H. (1969), The place of forgetting in memory functioning. *J. Amer. Psychoanal., Assn.*, 17:358–371.

Schmideberg, M. (1950), Infant memories and constructions. *Psychoanal. Quart.*, 18:468–481.

Scholes, R., & Kellogg, R. (1966), *The Nature of Narrative*. New York: Oxford University Press.

Scriven, M. (1959), Truisms as the grounds for historical explanations. In: *Theories of History*, ed. P. Gardiner. New York: Free Press, pp. 443–475.

Sears, R. R. (1943), *Survey of Objective Studies of Psychoanalytic Concepts*. Social Science Research Council Bulletin 41. New York: Social Science Research Council.

————— (1975), Your ancients revisited: A history of child development. In: *Review of Research in Child Development*, Vol. 5, ed. E. Hetherington. Chicago: University of Chicago Press, pp. 1–74.

—————, Maccoby, E., & Levin, H. (1957), *Patterns of Child-rearing*. New York: Harper & Row.

————— Whiting, J., Nowlis, V., & Sears, P. (1953), Some childrearing antecedents of aggression and dependency in young children. *Genet. Psychol. Monog.*, 47:135–234.

Seltzer, M. (1976), Suggestions for the examination of time disordered relationships. In: *Time, Roles and Self in Old Age*, ed. J. Gubrium. New York: Human Sciences Press, pp. 111–125.

Senn, M., & Hartford, C. (1968), *The Firstborn: Experiences of Eight American Children*. Cambridge: Harvard University Press.

Seton, P. (1974), The psychotemporal adaptation of late adolescence. *J. Amer. Psychoanal. Assn.*, 22:795–819.

Shanas, E. (1979), Social myth as hypothesis: The case of the family relations of old people. *Gerontologist*, 19:3–9.

————— Streib, G., eds. (1965), *Social Structure and the Family: Generational Relations*. Englewood Cliffs, N.J.: Prentice-Hall.

Shapiro, T. (1977), Oedipal distortions in severe character pathologies: Developmental and theoretical considerations. *Psychoanal. Quart.*, 46:559–579.

————— (1981), On the quest for the origins of conflict. *Psychoanal. Quart.*, 50:1–21.

Sherwood, M. (1969), *The Logic of Explanation in Psychoanalysis*. New York: Academic Press.

Silver, D., ed. (1985), *Commentaries on Joseph Lichtenberg's Psychoanalysis and Infant Research.* Hillsdale, N.J.: Analytic Press.

Skeels, H.M. (1966), *Adult Status of Children from Contrasting Early Life Experiences: A Follow-up Study.* Monographs of the Society for Research in Child Development, No. 3.

Solnit, A. (1982), Developmental perspectives on self and object constancy. *The Psychoanalytic Study of the Child,* 37:201–220.

Spence, D. (1982), *Narrative Truth and Historical Truth.* New York: Norton.

Spitz, R. (1945), Hospitalism. *The Psychoanalytic Study of the Child,* 1:53–74.

——— (1946), Anaclitic depression. *The Psychoanalytic Study of the Child,* 2:313–342. New York: International Universities Press.

——— (1950), The relevancy of direct infant observations. *The Psychoanalytic Study of the Child,* 5:66–73. New York: International Universities Press.

——— (1959), *A Genetic Field Theory of Ego Formation: Its Implications for Pathology.* New York: International Universities Press.

——— (1965), *The First Year of Life: A Psychoanalytic Study of Normal and Deviant Development of Object Relations.* New York: International Universities Press.

Sroufe, A. (1979), The coherence of individual development: Early care, attachment, and subsequent developmental issues. *Amer. Psychologist,* 34:834–841.

Stechler, G., & Carpenter, G. (1967), A viewpoint on early affective development. In: *The Exceptional Infant,* Vol. 1, ed. J. Hellmuth. New York: Brunner-Mazel, pp. 65–189.

Steele, R. (1979), Psychoanalysis and hermeneutics. *Internat. Rev. Psycho-Anal.,* 6:389–411.

——— Jacobsen, P. (1977), From present to past: The development of Freudian theory. *Internat. Rev. Psycho-Anal.,* 5:393–411.

Stern, D. (1974), Mother and infant at play: The dyadic interaction involving facial, vocal, and gaze behaviors. In: *The Effect of the Infant on Its Caregivers,* ed. L. Rosenblum & M. Lewis. New York: Wiley, pp. 187–215.

——— (1985), *The Interpersonal World of the Infant.* New York: Basic Books.

Stone, L. (1954), The widening scope of indications for psychoanalysis. *J. Amer. Psychoanal. Assn.,* 2:567–594.

——— (1961), *The Psychoanalytic Situation: An Examination of Its Development and Essential Nature.* New York: International Universities Press.

——— (1981), Some thoughts on the 'here and now' in psychoanalytic technique and process. *J. Amer. Psychoanal. Assn.,* 50:709–733.

Strachey, J. (1934), The nature of the therapeutic action in psychoanalysis. *Internat. J. Psycho-Anal.,* 15:127–159.

Sulloway, F. (1979), *Freud, Biologist of the Mind.* New York: Basic Books.

Swanson, D. (1977a), On force, energy, entropy, and the assumptions of metapsychology. *Psychoanal. & Contemp. Sci.,* 5:137–153.

——— (1977b), The psychic energy concept: A critique. *J. Amer. Psychoanal. Assn.,* 25:603–634.

Taylor, C. (1971), Interpretation and the sciences of man. *Rev. Metaphysics,* 25:3–51.

Tobin, S., & Lieberman, M. (1976), *Last Hope for the Aged.* San Francisco: Jossey-Bass.

Tolpin, M. (1970), The infantile neurosis: A metapsychological concept and a paradigmatic case history. *The Psychoanalytic Study of the Child*, 25:316–354. New York: International Universities Press.

—— Kohut, H. (1980), The disorders of the self: The psychopathology of the first years of life. In: *The Course of Life: Vol. I. Infancy and Early Childhood*, ed. S.I. Greenspan & G. Pollock. Washington, D.C.: U.S. Government Printing Office, pp. 425–442.

Toulmin, S. (1984), The inwardness of mind. The Helen Ross Lecture, Institute for Psychoanalysis, Chicago.

Turner, V. (1967), *The Forest of Symbols: Aspects of Ndembu Ritual*. Ithaca: Cornell University Press.

Vaillant, G. (1977), *Adaptation to Life*. Boston: Little, Brown.

—— McArthur, C. (1972), Natural history of male psychologic health: I. The adult life cycle from 18–50. *Seminars in Psychiatry*, 4:415–427.

—— Molovsky, E. (1980), Natural history of male mental health: Empirical evidence for Erikson's model of the life-cycle. *Amer. J. Psychiat.*, 13:1348–1359.

Van Gennep, A. (1906), *The Rites of Passage*. Chicago: University of Chicago Press, 1960.

Viderman, S. (1974), Interpretation in the analytic space. *Internat. Rev. Psycho-Anal.*, 1:467–480.

Von Wright, G.H. (1971), *Explanation and Understanding*. Ithaca: Cornell University Press.

Wallace, E. (1985), *Historiography and Causation in Psychoanalysis*. Hillsdale, N.J.: Analytic Press.

Wallerstein, R. (1977), Psychic energy reconsidered: Introduction. *J. Amer. Psychoanal. Assn.*, 25:529–536.

Walsh, W.H. (1951), *The Philosophy of History*. New York: Harper & Row, 1967.

—— (1966), The limits of scientific history. In: *Philosophical Analysis and History*, ed. W. Dray. New York: Harper & Row, pp. 57–74.

—— (1974), Colligatory concepts in history. In: *The Philosophy of History*, ed. P. Gardiner. New York: Oxford University Press, pp. 296–306.

Weber, M. (1904–1905), *The Protestant Ethic and the Spirit of Capitalism*. New York: Scribner, 1958.

Weil, A. (1985), Thoughts about early pathology. *J. Amer. Psychoanal. Assn.*, 33:335–352.

Werner, H. (1926), *The Comparative Psychology of Mental Development*. New York: Harper & Row, 1940.

—— (1957), The concept of development from a comparative and organismic point of view. In: *The Concept of Development*, ed. D. Harris. Minneapolis: University of Minnesota Press, pp. 125–148.

Wessman, A.E., & Gorman, B. (1977), The emergence of human awareness and concepts of time. In: *The Personal Experience of Time*, ed. B. Gorman & A.E. Wessman. New York: Plenum, pp. 4–56.

Wetzler, S. (1985), The historical truth of psychoanalytic reconstructions. *Internat. Rev. Psycho-Anal.*, 12:187–197.

White, H. (1972–1973), Interpretation in history. In: *Tropics of Discourse*. Baltimore: Johns Hopkins University Press, 1978, pp. 51–80.

——— (1978), The value of narrativity in the representation of reality. In: *On Narrative*, ed. J.T. Mitchell. Chicago: University of Chicago Press, 1981, pp. 1–24.

White, S.H. (1965), Evidence for a hierarchical arrangement of learning processes. In: *Advances in Child Development and Behavior*, ed. L. Lipsitt & C. Spiker. New York: Academic Press, pp. 187–220.

Whiting, B., & Whiting, J. (1974), *Children of Six Cultures*. Cambridge: Harvard University Press.

Winnicott, D.W. (1951), Transitional objects and transitional phenomena. In: *Collected Papers: Through Pediatrics to Psychoanalysis*. New York: Basic Books, 1958, pp. 229–242.

——— (1957), On the contribution of direct child observation to psychoanalysis. In: *The Maturational Processes and the Facilitating Environment*. New York: International Universities Press, pp. 109–114.

——— (1958), The observation of infants in a set situation. In: *Collected Papers: Through Pediatrics to Psycho-Analysis*. New York: Basic Books, pp. 52–68.

——— (1960), The theory of the parent-infant relationship. In: *The Maturational Processes and the Facilitating Environment*. New York: International Universities Press, pp. 37–55.

Wolf, K. (1953), Observation of individual tendencies in the first year of life. In: *Problems of Infancy and Childhood: Transactions of the Sixth Conference*, ed. M. Senn. New York: Josiah Macy Foundation, pp. 97–137.

Wolff, P. (1966), The causes, controls, and organization of behavior in the neonate. *Psychological Issues*, Monograph 17. New York: International Universities Press.

Wyatt, F. (1962), A psychologist looks at history. *J. Social Issues*, 26:66–77.

——— (1963), The reconstruction of the individual and the collective past. In: *The Study of Lives: Essays in Honor of Henry Murray*, ed. R. White. New York: Atherton, pp. 305–320.

——— Wilcox, W.B. (1959), Sir Henry Clinton: A psychological exploration in history. *William & Mary Quart.*, 16:3–26.

Zetzel, E., & Meissner, W. (1973), *Basic Concepts of Psychoanalytic Psychiatry*. New York: Basic Books.

Zinberg, N., & Kaufman, I. (1963), *Normal Psychology of the Aging Process*. New York: International Universities Press.

Zubin, J., & Spring, B. (1977), Vulnerability: A new view of schizophrenia. *J. Abnorm. Psychol.*, 86:103–126.

——— Steinhauer, S. (1981), How to break the logjam in schizophrenia: A look beyond genetics. *J. Nerv. & Ment. Dis.*, 169:447–492.

6

Homosexuality in Homosexual and Heterosexual Men: Some Distinctions and Implications for Treatment

RICHARD A. ISAY, M.D.

The purpose of this paper is to provide a clinical perspective that may enable psychoanalysts and other psychotherapists to work more effectively with their homosexual patients. This perspective is based upon two premises. First, that homosexuals can live, as homosexuals, well-adjusted, productive lives with gratifying and stable love relationships. This premise, which is based upon clinical experience, personal observation, and a review of world literature, will not be discussed here, but it has important implications for the therapy of our homosexual patients. The second premise is that the effort to change the sexual orientation of most gay patients is not clinically helpful.[1]

There are some heterosexual men, in distinction to homosexual men, who use homosexual fantasies and behavior primarily as a defense against their conflicts about assertiveness, including heterosexual assertiveness. Since the analysis of such conflicts may be helpful in altering both the homosexual fantasies and behavior in heterosexuals but, in my experience, not

---

A version of this paper originally appeared in *The Psychology of Men: New Psychoanalytic Perspectives*, edited by G. Fogel, F. Lane, and R. Liebert. Copyright © 1986, Basic Books. Reprinted by permission of the publisher.

[1]The term *gay* is used as a synonym for "homosexual," defined later in this paper. "Gay" probably antedates the late nineteenth century term *homosexual* by at least five centuries, and the etymology of the word is reviewed by Bowell (1980, p. 43). I use "gay" in an effort to deemphasize the medical and pathological connotation of "homosexual."

in homosexuals, it is important to make clinical distinctions between these two groups of patients. In this paper, I plan to offer illustrative clinical material and a schema that may be useful in this respect.

The view generally held by psychoanalysts is that homosexuality is a pathological condition. This attitude is derived from the theoretical conception that a homosexual orientation is engendered by faulty parenting, especially binding, engulfing mothering, that results in failure to separate from the preoedipal mother and a consequent fear of closeness to women, and/ or by the inadequate resolution of oedipal-stage conflict and consequent faulty identification. The homosexual object choice is regarded as one attempted solution to the conflicts engendered during these developmental stages. From this perspective those most accepting of their sexuality, the "obligatory" homosexuals, are those who are considered to have severe ego defects and the most severely impaired character structures because of developmental failure during the separation–individuation stage of early childhood (Socarides, 1968, 1978; Bychowski, 1945, 1954).

This view of homosexuality as pathology and the concomitant desire to change our patients' sexual orientation is, I believe, due to the bias that only heterosexuality is normal (Leavy, 1985), and to our internalization of the social prejudice against homosexuals (Isay, 1985). In our work with these men "empirically subjective values are posited as if they were 'objective' and accessible to empirical validation" (Hartmann, 1960, p. 67); thus we find such notions as "there are no healthy homosexuals" (Bergler, 1957, p. 79) or that "all homosexuals suffer from a severe degree of psychic masochism" (Socarides, 1978, pp. 54–55), or that homosexuals are defended, conflicted, or inhibited heterosexuals (Rado, 1949; Bergler, 1957; Bieber et al., 1962; Socarides, 1968, 1978; Ovesey and Woods, 1980).

My earlier clinical efforts to be of assistance to gay patients by helping them to change their sexual orientation through the analysis of early conflict failed time and time again. I noticed that even with motivated patients, behavioral change might occur, but only through the use of such techniques as transference exploitation or positive and negative reinforcement. My later work with homosexual men who had entered a second treatment after unsuccessful efforts by another therapist or analyst to alter their sexuality, has suggested that, while sexual behavior may change (though in most cases only temporarily), sexual orientation remains unchanged in a neutral analytic or therapeutic setting. Clinical depression may be caused by the repression, denial, or suppression of the homosexual impulses and fantasies, and anxiety and depression may result from the disruption of sexual identity formation. These clinical experiences, which I have reported elsewhere (Isay, 1985), have led me to conclude that it is not in the best interest of the gay patient for an analyst or therapist to have the changing of his patient's sexuality as a goal.

My view of the potentially harmful effects of attempting to alter a patient's sexual orientation should not, however, be taken as a nihilistic view of analytic work with homosexuals. Aside from being helpful in the same manner and for the same spectrum of problems as it is with heterosexual patients, analyzing the origin of a gay patient's sexuality may in itself be therapeutic. If such analysis is carried out with appropriate neutrality and with respect and regard for the patient, it may lead to his sexuality becoming less maladaptive, to becoming a better integrated part of his identity, and to enhanced self-esteem. As with any character trait, however, such analysis and understanding by the patient will not, in my experience, make the homosexuality disappear nor will it turn it into heterosexuality. It may, however, modify the sexuality by making it freer of neurotic, self-destructive conflict, if such conflict is present. That sexual orientation is not eradicable, suggests that it has infantile preoedipal origins, that it has a constitutional basis, or, as is likely the case, that its origins lie in a combination of the two. I will return to these issues later in my general discussion.

My definition of a homosexual is one who has a predominant erotic preference for others of the same sex. In adults the erotic preference can usually be recollected as being present from the latency years or early adolescence (ages 9 to 13) and often earlier. There are some heterosexuals who may engage in homosexual behavior for varying periods of time and not be homosexual. This may be for developmental reasons (adolescents), for opportunistic motives (some delinquents), for situational reasons (prison inmates), or in order to defend against anxiety. Most homosexuals do engage in sexual activity, but one need not do so to be homosexual. There are individuals who may be homosexual and are unaware of it because of the repression or suppression of their fantasies (Marmor, 1980, p. 5; Isay, 1985).

I am emphasizing in this definition that it is the erotic fantasy that defines the homosexual and not his behavior, since some homosexuals, like some heterosexuals, may be inhibited by social constraints from expressing their sexuality. I am taking into account that there is a relative preponderance, but not an exclusivity, of homoerotic fantasy. I am emphasizing the tenacity and longevity of the attraction in adults, since the fantasy and sexual impulse are usually recollected from latency or the early years of adolescence. During the course of an analysis or analytically oriented psychotherapy, the recollection of same-sex fantasies or impulses from earlier years of childhood frequently reemerge.

The most frequent form of homosexual-like behavior and fantasy seen in adult heterosexual males serves as a defense against conflicts about assertiveness by the expression of the unconscious wish to be a woman. In these patients, "feminine" is perceived unconsciously as being passive and noncompetitive, and the expression of feminine wishes opposes the dangers inherent in striving to be masculine, seen as being competitive and assertive. The conscious expression of these feminine wishes takes the form of what the patient experiences as homosexual fantasies and homosexual behavior. The expression of the unconscious feminine wish may be derived from "culturally determined attitudes that favor the male. In our society masculinity represents strength, dominance, superiority; femininity represents weakness, submissiveness, inferiority" (Ovesey and Woods, 1980, p. 326).[2] What is also interesting is that the symptomatic expression of these wishes to be like a woman takes the

---

[2]Such defensive homosexual behavior and fantasy has been called "pseudohomosexuality" by Ovesey. While I agree with much of Ovesey's description of "pseudohomosexual anxiety," I do not agree with his view that these same anxieties motivate homosexual behavior (1980, p. 331), although such motives

form of homosexual fantasies at all, and that the nature of the fantasies expresses the unconscious perception of homosexual men as being passive and submissive and heterosexuals as being assertive and dominant.

The phenomenon of defensive homosexuality is seen most frequently in heterosexual male patients whose fathers are perceived as powerful, authoritarian, and frightening and whose mothers are perceived as being submissive, dominated, and demeaned by their husbands. Whether fact or fantasy, such perceptions are used by the child to solidify his oedipal wish to be his mother's ally and rescuer, and they increase his castration anxieties and fears. While the perception of these fathers as being demeaning of their wives is fueled and enhanced by the oedipal child's competitiveness and anger with his father, in my clinical experience it cannot be seen as being exclusively the product of fantasy. I will present two illustrations of defensive homosexual fantasy as seen in my analytic work and then attempt to demonstrate how these predominantly heterosexual men can be distinguished clinically from those who are predominantly homosexual.

Alan was 23 when he began his analysis. He had graduated from college two years before with only fair grades after excelling in high school in both academic studies and extracurricular activities, including athletics. After college he went to graduate school but dropped out during the first year because of his loss of motivation. He then worked for a magazine but quit after six months because of his loss of interest. When he started analysis he was working in a retail store. He wanted treatment because of concern about his lack of motivation and his sexual inadequacy. He had a history of premature ejaculation and impotence with a girl friend of two years, whom he had stopped seeing about one year before beginning his analysis. Currently he was dating hardly at all. His masturbation fantasies were of erect penises, sometimes of performing fellatio, and, less frequently, of having violent heterosexual sex.

---

may be present in some gays. Nor do I believe, as he does, that these same concepts are applicable in the treatment of homosexuals as in the treatment of those who use homosexuality defensively.

Alan's father was a wealthy and highly successful business-man. My patient saw him as competitive, powerful, and emo-tionally detached. As the analysis progressed, he saw him more clearly as being, like himself, ashamed of tender feelings and contemptuous of tenderness in others. He was very aware of his closeness to his beautiful mother, who was sometimes sub-servient to her husband and at other times demeaning of him. Alan became increasingly aware of his sadistic and spiteful rage for her and for other women that arose out of his frustrated sexual longings.

By the third year of his analysis Alan had successfully com-pleted graduate school and was working for a corporation. This period of renewed success was in part motivated by both a strong positive transference and the fear that I would injure him if he did not please me. It was accompanied by renewed experiences of competitiveness and increasing homosexual fan-tasies both in and outside of the analysis. He had the following dream the night after being complimented by his boss for an unusual and innovative solution to a complicated business prob-lem: "I was underneath some blankets with my shorts on. All of a sudden this guy was rubbing his leg against me. I wanted to get out from underneath the blankets but couldn't because my shorts were off and he'd see I had a hard on. He wanted to kiss me and I wanted to kiss him too. I had this sexual feeling even though I was resisting it."

His associations were of sexual feelings for me, feeling small, powerless, and helpless. There was further elaboration of the manifest dream: that his legs were spread like a woman's. He commented that in the dream his penis was small like a clitoris, that he felt helpless and unable to do anything by him-self—just like a woman. He wondered what it would feel like to be anally penetrated by me.

As the analysis continued and Alan was able to permit himself greater success in different areas of his life, including increased sexual pleasure with girls, his anxiety correspond-ingly increased, and he had even more frequent conscious ho-mosexual fantasies of fondling my penis or some other man's, of being anally penetrated, and of performing fellatio. Al-though these fantasies were sexually arousing to him, the only actual sexual activity occurred with some gay neighbors, when he teasingly took down his trousers and let them fondle his buttocks.

On many occasions he called my attention to his erections in a casual, offhand but playfully seductive manner, repeating exhibitionistic childhood sexual play with his mother. He wanted to be like a woman (his mother) in order to get close to a powerful man (his father) by being penetrated by him, and thereby to acquire his father's energy, vitality, and power. He was hoping to demonstrate that he was no threat to me. Throughout this time of intense transference and movement in the analysis, there was no drive to be attached to another man through sexual activity. Rather, he continued to have a pervasive heterosexual drive and increasingly satisfying sexual activity.

Another patient, Benjamin, also illustrates how a basically heterosexual man may have homosexual feelings activated by his aggressive and competitive strivings. He sought help because of his concerns about premature ejaculation, an inability to get close to women, and persistent fantasies of being forced to perform fellatio on men with large penises. His other major concerns were of his inability to do well in graduate school and to focus on any specific vocational goals. His father was perceived as being powerful, authoritarian, and distant. He felt very close to his mother, although he spoke with anger of her being too easily dominated, too weak, and too conforming of her life to his father's needs.

Unlike the previous patient, Benjamin's inhibition in sexual activity gave way to analysis more readily than his work inhibition. During periods of increased sexual activity and improving sexual performance, or when he had unconscious aggressive feelings toward me, he would comment on his frequent and troublesome images of erect penises, and thoughts of anal penetration. He recollected that, as a child of 5 or 6, on occasion he had put on some article of his mother's clothing, but he had no recollection of homosexual fantasies until about age 15. There was little or no impulse to engage in homosexual activity during his analysis, and his heterosexual impulses throughout remained strong.

In both of these patients homosexual fantasies were first activated in late adolescence by the specific threats and dangers inherent in increasingly successful and aggressive strivings. Their symptoms were largely rooted in oedipal-stage conflicts and negative-oedipal identifications as an attempted resolution of these conflicts. In addition, with Alan, there was important unconscious gain in perceiving himself and being perceived as being like a girl, since he felt his mother preferred her daughter from a prior marriage to him. The second patient, the youngest of four sons, felt his father would have preferred a daughter. In both there was a strong drive for heterosexual attachment, and heterosexual activity became enhanced during their analyses without direction, reinforcement, or transference exploitation. Homosexual fantasies decreased in frequency and intensity with the analysis of the transference. In both patients the unconscious fantasy was to be a woman, which was partly gratified through homoerotic thoughts and feelings. Homosexual fantasies, such as being penetrated and performing fellatio, are not primarily motivated to provide gratification for longings for attachment to other men, but to express the fantasies of being in a penisless state like a woman and of acquiring a penis.

The following characteristics may be helpful in distinguishing clinically between the heterosexual man who uses homosexuality defensively or regressively from the true homosexual.

1. In the heterosexual, the homosexual fantasy usually has the unconscious meaning of being womanlike and nonmasculine. The sexual fantasy may have that same unconscious significance at times in some homosexuals, but it is not of exclusive nor predominant significance. The meaning of the homosexual fantasy of homosexuals, like the heterosexual fantasy of heterosexuals, is dependent on many aspects of character and early conflict.

2. Homosexual behavior and fantasy in a heterosexual wards off and defends against heterosexual attachment. The homosexual behavior and fantasy of the homosexual has attachment to another man as its aim, although, as with any heterosexual, that is not the only aim of the sexual behavior and fantasy, nor is it necessarily the conscious aim. Sexualization and hypersexuality may, of course, be used by both homosexuals and heterosexuals to avoid such attachment.

3. Most, although not all, heterosexual men enjoy in their childhood stereotypical male, aggressive "rough and tumble" activities. Most homosexual men have a history of aversion to and avoidance of these activities in childhood (Friedman and Stern, 1980; Bell, Weinberg, and Hammersmith, 1981). They also have a feeling of being different from their same-sex peers, which is most likely based upon the unconscious or preconscious perception of their sexual orientation.

4. In the heterosexual the onset of the homosexual fantasy is usually recollected as starting in late adolescence or early adulthood. The fantasies of the homosexual have their onset in childhood and are usually recollected as starting in the latency years or early adolescence (Friedman and Stern, 1980, p. 431).

5. In heterosexuals, the homosexual fantasy is by and large unwanted and distressing (ego dystonic). To most, although not all, homosexual patients the fantasy and behavior feel natural (ego syntonic).

6. In the heterosexual, the homosexual fantasy either disappears or is greatly mitigated in any therapy conducted in a noncoercive, neutral manner. In the homosexual, fantasy and sexual activity become less conflicted during a properly conducted treatment.

7. In such heterosexual men, the homosexual fantasy is most likely to appear at times of conflict around aggression and competitiveness both inside and outside of the analysis. In gay men, the same-sex fantasies and behavior remain comparatively constant in a neutral, noncoercive analytic experience. The nature of the homoerotic fantasy or the nature of the sexual behavior may, of course, vary at times of heightened transference and may change as the patient's homosexuality becomes less distorted or less inhibited by neurotic conflict.

The clinical task with the homosexual is, as with every patient, to enable him to be as free as possible of conflict that is inhibiting and self-destructive so that he can live as gratifying a life as it is within his grasp to live. Since, in my clinical experience, the sexual orientation of these men is not mutable, this can best be accomplished if the sexuality is accepted as a given. By accepting the homosexuality as a fixed trait the analyst or therapist, I feel, is in the best position to "avoid imposing his self or his values" (Poland, 1984, p. 291) and, by conveying in this manner his regard for the individuality of his patient, to "sustain and nurture the patient's observing ego" (Poland, 1984, p. 285). I also feel that such a stance best approximates Anna Freud's (1936) idea of neutrality as maintaining equidistance between intrapsychic structures. The analyst is then most readily able to recognize and analyze those conflicts that interfere with his patient's capacity to love as a homosexual man. I am not suggesting that the origin of the homosexual object choice, like the origin of other behavior, should not come under analytic scrutiny, for such analysis and the hoped-for insight may itself enhance the patient's freedom to express his sexual impulses in a less self-destructive manner, encourage self-acceptance, and strengthen his homosexual identity. But I do feel that in good therapeutic work with these men, empathic attention must be paid not only to internal conflict of early origin but to conflict both old and new that is caused by the difficult external, social reality that may also interfere with a fulfilling expression of their sexuality.[3]

I view those homosexual patients, who come for analysis or therapy because they are dissatisfied with themselves as homosexuals and with their sexuality, to be responding to the real and immense social pressures and prejudices that face them and to the conflicts engendered by these; to internal conflicts interfering with and inhibiting the acceptance and expression of their sexuality and homosexual identity; and/or to conflicts unrelated to their sexuality but displaced onto it. The analysis of such conflicts should enable them, like the majority of homosexual patients who enter treatment for other than conscious

---

[3]It is important for any therapist or analyst working with gay men to understand that our social structure, prejudice, and legal restrictions contribute to the courting and sexual customs of homosexuals. Social factors contribute to, although certainly do not entirely explain, the proclivity toward anonymous sex on the part of some gays. They also contribute to the perception that homosexuals are only interested in quick sex.

Homosexuals were not allowed to elaborate a system of courtship because the cultural expression necessary for such an elaboration was denied them. The wink on the street, the split-second decision to get it on, the speed with which homosexual relations are consummated; are all products of an interdiction [Foucault, 1982–1983, p. 18].

conflict about their sexual orientation, to live less encumbered, more conflict-free, less inhibited, more gratifying lives as homosexuals. The analysis of Carl, a 26-year-old graduate student, illustrates aspects of the neutral and accepting attitude that is essential in working with these patients, as well as some of the clinical issues that arise in treatment:

Carl is tall, lanky, and clean shaven, with curly dark hair. He is nice looking but he has poorly defined facial features, so he is not conventionally handsome. He has a slightly effeminate walk, but no other feminine features or mannerisms. This was Carl's second treatment experience, having been in therapy while in his last year of high school and first year of college. He left that treatment in part because of a perception of his prior therapist's disapproval of his homosexuality and life-style. He initiated therapy again in his junior year of college because of depression and dissatisfaction with his life. He had very low self-esteem and an inability to form meaningful relationships. He had casual friendships with both girls and boys, and transient, usually anonymous sex with boys. His sexual activity was largely confined to the bathroom of the college library or to the stalls of the pornographic bookstore, performing or being the recipient of oral sex. Occasionally he had dated girls, and had sex on two occasions without enjoying it to see if "he could do it." He would have liked to be able to please his mother by getting married and having children. He felt this was the "right" thing to do, but he most desired to be able to have a loving relationship with another boy. His mother was described as having been very attentive when he was quite young, but at the time of the birth of his younger brother, when he was 3½, Carl was sent to prenursery school, his mother got her first part-time job, and she became abruptly less attentive. His father was felt to be kind and intelligent, but to be weak, dominated by his wife, and not to be living up to his intellectual or economic potential. Throughout grade school Carl did well academically, but he felt different and therefore estranged from other boys his own age. He disliked athletics and other "rough" activities of his peers. He remembered homosexual impulses from age 8 or 9, when he felt attracted to some of his classmates. His first homosexual experiences were mutual masturbation in his junior year of high school. In college he had some further sexual activity that increased after a summer trip abroad before his junior year, and it was in the spring of that year that he started treatment.

My initial clinical impression was that Carl was homosexual. This impression was based upon his history of homosexual impulses from childhood; the continued push, in spite of conflict and social pressures, toward homosexual activities and relationships; his childhood history of feeling estranged and being "different" from other boys of his age; and his aversion to the usual "rough and tumble" activities of boys his own age.

In these early hours he expressed conflict about his homosexual impulses. My attitude was one of interest in him and in the development of his sexual orientation, but a lack of investment in whether he was heterosexual or homosexual. For example, when he revealed dismay about his homosexual impulses and feelings, I avoided asking questions that might reveal any bias toward what his sexual orientation should be. During these early hours I would have viewed any questions or comments about why he did not go out with girls as an expression of heterosexual bias. After a therapeutic alliance was established, questions relating to his conflicted feelings about his homosexuality were appropriately raised in view of the difficulty he was having in forming meaningful attachments other than to men.

As the analytic material developed, it further supported my early hypothesis, based on the initial interviews, about his homosexual orientation. The sexual fantasies and behavior were influenced by transference in the manner in which they were expressed but not in the sex of the object toward whom they were expressed. The initial concern about his homosexuality largely disappeared, as his feelings about getting close to other men became freer of conflict. The persistence of his pursuit of attachment to other men, in spite of his difficulties in forming attachments, indicated the strength of his erotic drive, and there was no evidence of a primary conflict over being close to women. With the clinical material that follows I will illustrate how conflicts about intimacy with other men were presented, how they were manifested in the transference, and convey how the analysis of these conflicts contributed to his enhanced self-esteem and better integrated image of himself as a homosexual man.

Carl longed for boys who were unobtainable: they were either attached to someone else, had previously rejected him, were conflicted about their homosexuality, or were heterosexual and not interested. Anyone who was available was perceived as being like him and became repugnant after the first sexual encounter. After he left college and had expanded opportunities for meeting gay men who wanted relationships, a sexual pattern emerged: if he found someone he developed affection for, he became impotent.

Throughout much of our work the patient articulated and stressed that he was not attracted to "older men," men in their forties, feeling they were "lecherous" and that they would be taking advantage of his youth. He felt anxious and helpless if an older man approached him, a conviction that raised the unsubstantiated hypothesis of an actual sexual experience or the perception of such an experience with an older man (or woman) while he was still a child. He had intense anxiety about being the recipient of anal sex. He was often too tight to permit anal penetration, especially if he felt affection for his sexual partner. He was attracted to passive, effeminate-appearing boys, but had masturbation fantasies of powerful black men with large penises. These symptoms were manifestations of conflicts around passivity, identification with his mother's rage, and his wish to be dominated.

The transference was initially characterized by his appearing to be oblivious of me, in spite of his occasional seductiveness and exhibitionistic behavior on the couch. He would sometimes turn to face me if he had a point that he didn't want lost, fearful that he was too weak and insignificant to be noticed unless he did so. He would ask for advice, guidance, and direction, as though I were a source of power that he needed and lacked. At other times, he would ignore my interpretations or clarifications or focus on a relatively insignificant aspect of what I had said, to defend against feeling overwhelmed or taken over by me. As the analysis progressed, he became more conscious of both his fear and the wish that I totally dominate him. At times this repeated the perceived domination and fear of his mother. At yet other times these conflicted wishes to be dominated expressed his wish for a powerful man who would protect him from his mother. For example, during one period of his analysis he was accused by his mother of siding with his father in a financial dispute. In the same hour he complained about ways in which I was dominating and subjugating him. He became so anxious about his conflicted feelings for me that he thought of looking around to see what I was doing. He recalled during this hour an occasion when his father had spanked him, one of the few signs of his father's dominance, an incident that he turned to frequently thereafter as a reminder of masculine strength and power, when he felt fearful of being overwhelmed by his mother.

The affectional–sexual split gradually began to heal as the transference was analyzed and he became more tolerant of his wishes to get close to a man he perceived as powerful. Transference wishes and fears of getting close to me began to be expressed more clearly in his dreams: "I'm in a room. It looks like a cell. Some guy comes after me. I hear his heavy breathing. I dig my heels into the floor, going backwards, trying to get away."

His associations were to lying on the couch, sometimes being distracted by the noises I made behind him. I interpreted that if he ran away by digging in his heels and going backwards, that he would bump into me. He accused me of "going a bit far." Then he got mad about my silence and how long the analysis takes. "I don't know what I want from you anymore," he stated with considerable longing in his voice. Another brief dream the same week: "I went into a shop to have my bicycle pump repaired. No matter how hard I tried it just wouldn't work."

He felt that he did not get what he needed and wanted from me; that I was not good enough or smart enough to help him. His father was also weak and ineffective. The following week he dreamt: "I was flying my own plane but you were directing it, telling me how to take off. I couldn't get it up and you had to recommend someone, a dentist or doctor to help. To get the plane up there was a strap or something I had to hold onto. I couldn't grab the other end of the strap with both hands. I came close to crashing a couple of times."

He felt that I, like his father, was not strong enough to help him. His mother always complained about both of us. He had a lot of affection for his father but was frightened of getting close to him out of fear of his mother. Getting close to me, feeling I could help him, was a frightening disloyalty to her. A few weeks later he had this clear dream expressive of his attraction and desire for closeness:

> I meet this guy. He's selling something. I'm in a cave or some dark environment. I really want to sleep with him. I don't know if he's gay. He's tall and skinny. He has long, non-styled hair, almost like Tarzan. His pants are open. I reach out and grab his leg. He has a bathing suit underneath. We start making out. I say something like, "Let's take off our clothes; let me suck your dick." There's something on the underside of his dick like a swelling or herpes. It looks like it's been cut and has scar tissue around it. I suck his cock and then I sit on it. I don't remember his coming; just the wonderful feeling. I woke up very hard and jerked off.

He associated to seeing his physician at a gay resort and having spoken with him there. He wondered what he would do if he ever saw me there. He remembers recently reading about an article I had written twenty years ago when I was in the Navy, and comments that I must have looked good in a uniform. Then for the first time he acknowledged some attraction to me.

This dream during his fourth year of analysis, that expressed the least disguised sexual transference wish he had ever had, was followed by affectionate feelings for me and positive feelings about our work together and the progress he was making. It seemed to usher in an even less ambivalent, but still tentative, appreciation of a young man a bit older than he whom he had been going out with for several months, and whom he was now thinking of living with.

Only some of the determinants of Carl's selection of another man instead of a woman as a love object seem clear. The homosexual object choice was in part determined by his need to establish and experience closeness to a longed-for and demeaned father while at the same time he searched for and replicated his mother by selecting androgynous partners (Socarides, 1978). Some aspects of his need early in the analysis to maintain distance and to keep separate by avoiding me in the transference were out of his fear of being overwhelmed or taken over, as he was by his mother if he surrendered to these longings for attachment. In part this anxiety was caused by the fear of closeness to his mother. Furthermore, the birth of his brother and perceived rejection probably contributed to his turning in anger from women to men.

These dynamic explanations of possible determinants of his homosexual object choice are, however, not very satisfying. First, there is nothing either specific or particular to Carl's family constellation or history that one does not find in many heterosexuals. Second, the basis of such explanatory efforts is to understand why he avoids women (i.e., someone like his mother), while the natural flow of a properly conducted analysis with a gay man, who is not encumbered by either realistic or neurotic anxiety about his sexuality, is toward the unfolding of and understanding of the conflict interfering with gratifying relations with other men. This is perhaps comparable to the analysis of a heterosexual man, where we learn little about why he avoids sex with other men. Furthermore, attempting to analyze why the patient has an aversion to sex with women has no mutative value as regards his sexual orientation, though it may alter behavior patterns (Isay, 1985).

At present the evidence that homosexuality is constitutional is not entirely convincing, and what data we do have come largely from animal studies, which are contradictory or methodologically deficient (Hoult, 1984). Nor is there convincing evidence, as proposed by evolutionary biologists, for any advantageous factors that might account for the selective survival of genes for homosexuality, even if such genes did exist. It is true, of course, "that any biological characteristic has a genetic basis, in the trivial sense that it could not develop unless the organism has information—that permits the potential development of the trait." Likewise there must be an "environment in which [the genetic information] is to develop" (Futuyma and Risch, 1983/1984, p. 159). We can, it seems to me, say with certainty, that human beings do have an inherent capacity for flexibility in sexual response, and that under certain environmental circumstances, one or another type of sexuality may become prominent. We can also say that understanding conflict incurred by the familial environment does not change sexual orientation.[4]

---

[4]Since this paper was originally published, my clinical experience with gay men who are comfortable with their sexual orientation has led me to emphasize constitutional factors and to discount environmental factors in the

Before making some summary comments with regard to analytic therapy with the gay patient, I want to briefly mention work with bisexuals, who can gain varying degrees of satisfaction and pleasure with either same-sex or opposite-sex persons. Because of Freud's connection (1905, p. 144) of an inherited bisexual disposition with the development of inversion or homosexuality, some analysts feel that bisexuals are either sick heterosexuals, who use their homosexuality to ward off anxiety-provoking heterosexual impulses, or that they are, in fact, homosexuals and that proper treatment will enable them to become functioning heterosexuals. Although there are, indeed, those who appear to be bisexual who clinically may be defending against one or the other aspect of their sexual orientation, my experience again suggests that the sexual arousal patterns are established from such an early age that only behavior can be modified by therapeutic endeavors. An important distinction between these patients and our gay patients is that the suppression of one or the other of their sexual impulses in order to adapt to a life-style they prefer does not appear to produce the same adverse psychological and social consequences. My experience, however, has only been with bisexuals who wanted to get married or remain married and who entered treatment because they feared that their homosexuality would be harmful to their marriage.

Most bisexual men and women seek treatment because the homosexual component of their bisexuality is unconscious and produces anxiety. In such patients the most important aspect of the therapeutic task is to make such impulses conscious and tolerable. Those who have a strong bisexual orientation may through a traditional, neutral psychoanalytic or psychotherapeutic process be enabled to live a heterosexual life relatively unencumbered by their homosexuality. The comfort of their lives as functioning heterosexuals will, I feel, depend upon the degree to which they are made conscious of and accepting of

formation of male homosexuality (Isay, 1989). Recent empirical studies are also highly suggestive of the biological basis of homosexuality in men (Levay, 1991) and that it is heritable (Bailey and Pillard, 1991). Early parenting and culture, however, are clearly important determinants of the way all sexuality is expressed.

their anxiety-provoking homosexual fantasies and impulses, which can then be used in the service of their heterosexuality and productivity. My impression is that these men have enough emotional gratification and satisfying sexual discharge that their homosexual longings do not need expression at the sacrifice of a satisfying heterosexual relationship. A bisexual may make both a satisfactory emotional and sexual adjustment in a heterosexual marriage, although of necessity it will be one based on compromise and some renunciation. Nevertheless, in our society such an adjustment would appear to be a favorable clinical outcome. However, as is true of the homosexual patient, the bisexual orientation, established early in development, remains, and there will be alterations only in the sexual behavior. The best clinical outcomes are in those patients motivated strongly to maintain a heterosexual relationship, who can tolerate the acknowledgment of their homosexual fantasies and impulses and the frustrations of some renunciation of homosexual behavior. Of course, as with homosexual men who remain in happy marriages, there are marriages where the wife is supportive of and comfortable with the expression of her spouse's bisexuality.

My efforts in this paper to clarify some basic aspects of the treatment of gay men, heterosexuals who use homosexuality defensively, and, very briefly, of bisexuals should not lead to the idea that I feel that human beings can be categorized in the discrete clinical entities of homosexual, heterosexual, or bisexual. The complexity of human development leads to partial identification with both parents in every person as a solution to oedipal-stage conflict. Such partial identifications provide depth, complexity, flexibility, and richness in all aspects of relationships, providing they do not lead to significant internal conflict. As mentioned earlier, homosexual fantasies or behavior that derive from such identifications may be used defensively in heterosexuals, and, when they are, these fantasies are usually manifestations of a wish to be nonmasculine. Homosexual fantasies and behavior may be used by men with a significant bisexual disposition in an attempt to resolve conflict associated with the fear of sex and/or relationships with women; likewise, heterosexual fantasies and behavior may at times be symptomatic and evoked by the transference in some gay patients and bisexuals (Isay, 1985).

The question of the psychology of the homosexual man cannot be answered if the question is posed simply as, What is the nature of the oedipal or preoedipal conflict that determines one's homosexuality or the homosexual object choice? I have seen homosexual men, such as Carl, with family constellations as described in the literature; namely, a strong, binding mother and the father who is perceived as weak. But, I have also seen heterosexual patients with similar family constellations and many homosexual patients who appear to have had "average expectable" parenting (also see Leavy [1985]). There are as many different types of homosexuals as there are heterosexuals, and these include homosexual men and women capable of forming lasting, loving relationships, as well as those whose relationships are conflicted. There are also homosexuals, like heterosexuals, who are sadistic, masochistic, narcissistic, depressed, borderline or psychotic; i.e., who run the spectrum of psychological disturbances. Those patients who are gay who have such psychological disturbances, dynamically resemble their heterosexual counterparts more closely than they do each other. The nature and origin of their object relations, the manner in which they express their sexuality and conflicts about their sexuality, are determined by the nature of whatever pathology may coexist with the homosexuality and by those developmental conflicts that have contributed to this coexisting pathology. The ways in which same-sex love relationships are affected by such conflict deserve the same clinical and theoretical efforts that we have made in our attempts to understand the distortions and inhibitions of our heterosexual patients' sexuality. Questions about the origin of these patients' sexuality and the nature and origin of whatever psychopathology they may also have, must be separated if we are going to gain such understanding and be of adequate therapeutic assistance to our gay patients.

I have avoided the use of the term *fixation* to describe the true homosexual when attempting to distinguish him from the heterosexual's defensive or regressive use of homosexuality. This term carries the implication of being stuck in an immature

developmental stage, a stage which should have been progressed beyond, a stage of developmental arrest. "Fixation" has
the clinical connotation that there is a "persistence of primitive
ways of satisfaction, of relating to people, and of reacting defensively to old, even outmoded dangers" (Moore and Fine, 1968,
p. 47). Like heterosexuality, the way homosexuality is expressed
may evolve, at least in part, as a solution to early conflict, but
this behavior acquires, also like heterosexuality, an autonomy
from early conflict and the defensive role that it may have
initially played.

I want to emphasize in this paper that the appropriately
neutral analytic attitude can be maintained only if the analyst
or therapist has neither the explicit aim nor an implicit interest
in converting the homosexual love object to a heterosexual love
object. It is not conceivable to me that an analyst can accept the
sexual object choice of his gay patient, working empathically
with the neurotic vicissitudes of his relationships, while at the
same time conceptualizing that patient's sexuality as being "perverted."[5] Neutrality with these men can be best approximated,
it seems to me, only if the homosexual arousal pattern is viewed
as being structured so early in life by constitutional factors that
it is conceptualized as a fixed trait.

When it comes to our clinical formulations about homosexuality, we must remind ourselves that value judgments based
upon social mores should play no role in our analytic work
with these patients. The judgment that it is both possible for
homosexuals to become heterosexual and that it is in their best
interest to do so, I feel, reflects a "certain lack of clarity in
distinguishing the sphere of 'health' from the sphere of 'mor-
als'" (Hartmann, 1960, p. 69). It is also a value judgment that
gays should behave like heterosexuals not only in their object
choice but in the ways they enact their homosexuality. The
healthy individual may, but does not necessarily, conform to

---

[5]The word *perverted* derives from the Latin verb *pervetere*, which means
"to deviate from what is considered right and correct" (*American Heritage
Dictionary*, p. 980); i.e., heterosexuality. This term and the noun *pervert* are
frequently used in the psychoanalytic and psychiatric literature. These words
are by definition moralistic and have acquired a pejorative connotation that
reflects social bias.

current social values that often vary from culture to culture (Ford and Beach, 1951) and epoch to epoch (Boswell, 1980). I believe that the essential clinical issues for us as analysts and therapists is the extent to which we may lessen the burden of the sacrifices that society imposes on these men (Freud, 1927) and the degree to which we are able to help them resolve those conflicts that interfere with the fullest and most gratifying expression of their sexuality.

References

American Heritage Dictionary (1969), ed. W. Morris. Boston: Houghton Mifflin.

Bailey, J.M., & Pillard, R.C. (1991), A genetic study of male sexual orientation. *Arch. Gen. Psychiat.*, 48:1089–1096.

Bell, A., Weinberg, M., & Hammersmith, S. (1981), *Sexual Preference: Its Development in Men and Women*. Bloomington: Indiana University Press.

Bergler, E. (1957), *Homosexuality: Disease or Way of Life?* New York: Hill & Wang, Inc.

Bieber, I., et al. (1962), *Homosexuality: A Psychoanalytic Study*. New York: Basic Books.

Boswell, J. (1980), *Christianity, Social Tolerance and Homosexuality*. Chicago: University of Chicago Press.

Bychowski, G. (1945), The ego of homosexuals. *Internat. J. Psycho-Anal.*, 26:114–127.

——— (1954), The structure of homosexual acting out. *Psychoanal. Quart.*, 23:48–61.

Ford, C.S., & Beach, F.A. (1951), *Patterns of Sexual Behavior*. New York: Harper & Hoeber.

Foucault, M. (1982/1983), Interview. *Salmagundi*, 58–59:10–24.

Freud, A. (1936), *The Ego and the Mechanisms of Defense*. Writings 2. New York: International Universities Press, 1966.

Freud, S. (1905), Three essays on the theory of sexuality. *Standard Edition*, 7. London: Hogarth Press, 1953.

——— (1927), The future of an illusion. *Standard Edition*, 21:3–56. London: Hogarth Press, 1961.

Friedman, R.C., & Stern, L.O. (1980), Juvenile aggressivity and sissiness in homosexual and heterosexual males. *J. Acad. Psychoanal.*, 8(3):427–440.

Futuyma, D.J., & Risch, S.J. (1983/1984), Sexual orientation, sociobiology and evolution. *J. Homosexuality*, 9(2/3):157–168.

Hartmann, H. (1960), *Psychoanalysis and Moral Values*. New York: International Universities Press.

Hoult, T.J. (1984), Human sexuality in biological perspective: Theoretical and methodological considerations. *J. Homosexuality*, 9(2/3):137–155.

Isay, R.A. (1985), On the analytic therapy of homosexual men. *The Psychoanalytic Study of the Child*, 40:235–254. New Haven: Yale University Press.

——— (1989), *Being Homosexual: Gay Men and Their Development*. New York: Farrar, Straus & Giroux.

Leavy, S.A. (1985), Male homosexuality reconsidered. *Internat. J. Psychoanal. Psychother.*, 11:155–174.

Levay, S. (1991), A difference in hypothalamic structure between heterosexual and homosexual men. *Science*, 253:1034–1037.

Marmor, J., ed. (1980), *Homosexual Behavior: A Modern Reappraisal.* New York: Basic Books.

Moore, B.E., & Fine, B.P. (1968), *A Glossary of Psychoanalytic Terms and Concepts.* New Haven: The American Psychoanalytic Association and Yale University Press, 1990.

Ovesey, L., & Woods, S.M. (1980), Pseudo-homosexuality and homosexuality in men: Psychodynamics as a guide to treatment. In: *Homosexual Behavior: A Modern Reappraisal,* ed. J. Marmor. New York: Basic Books.

Poland, W.S. (1984), On the analyst's neutrality. *J. Amer. Psychoanal. Assn.,* 32:283–299.

Rado, S. (1949), An adaptational view of sexual behavior. In: *Psychosexual Development in Health and Disease,* ed. P. Hoch & J. Zubin. New York: Grune & Stratton, pp. 159–189.

Socarides, C.W. (1968), *The Overt Homosexual.* New York: Grune & Stratton.

——— (1978), *Homosexuality.* New York: Jason Aronson.

7

The Midlife Crisis

ELLIOTT JAQUES, M.A., M.D., PH.D., F.R.C. PSYCH.

In assessing the psychological state and behavior of an individual, two phenomena are commonly taken for granted which it would be well to identify explicitly. The first is that the types of behavior and of psychological state that are characterized as normal or as abnormal vary enormously with age: what would be considered normal at one stage would be considered decidedly abnormal at another. It is this phenomenon that leads to the age grading in societies which has been described by anthropologists and sociologists (Mannheim, 1928; van Gennep, 1960; Elder, 1975; Brim, 1976).

The second phenomenon is that psychological development does not proceed evenly. It occurs in discontinuous stages, separated by periods of rapid change or transition from one stage to the next. This view of human maturation and development as a series of stages linked by transition crises is well recognized in childhood but not in adulthood. Thus, for example, the early childhood stage is punctuated by the oedipal crisis; there follows the latency stage, broken by puberty and the adolescent crisis; and then the adult stage moves onto the scene—but this stage has usually been seen as one long period unbroken by any generally occurring crises, each individual experiencing his own personal ups and downs as a result of the vicissitudes of his own particular life situation.

There are, of course, exceptions to this widely and implicitly accepted picture of adulthood as one single stage. Erikson (1950), for example, has from his earliest writings pursued the idea of developmental stages as occurring throughout life; Lidz (1968) has taken this perspective of cyclical development in his analysis of the growth of personality; and, more recently, Levinson (1978) has reported on research into the transition from youth to middle age. There have also been several studies of discontinuity in adult career development, as, for example, those by Sofer (1970) and Fogarty, Rapoport, and Rapoport (1971).

My own experience has been that significant developmental stages occur throughout life and that it is a matter of some importance to recognize their existence. I would characterize them as follows. *Infancy*, the critical first year of life is terminated by what might be termed the *depressive crisis*, following Klein's concept (1940) of the transition to the depressive position in the second half of the first year. *Early childhood*, the period of emergence of organized conscious ego functioning and language, is separated by the *oedipal crisis* from the *latency stage* of development, which in turn is ended by the crisis of puberty and adolescence. There then emerges the stage of *early adulthood*, from roughly the late teens to the mid-thirties; then in the late thirties occur the *midlife crisis* and the transition to mature adulthood, which runs from around forty to the middle or late fifties. There then occurs what I would term the *late adult crisis*, leading into *late adulthood*, the period of the sixties and seventies. There is some evidence—as seen, for example, in the flowering of new types of creativity in geniuses such as Verdi—that there is a further maturational step at around the age of 80 if senility does not step in, but we leave this possibility as an open question.

The foregoing hypotheses about critical stages corresponds in part with Erikson's schema of ego development. His stage of "Identity vs. Identity Confusion" encompasses childhood through to adolescence; his stage of "Intimacy vs. Aloneness" corresponds precisely with our early adult stage; that of "Generativity vs. Stagnation" with mature adulthood; and that of "Integrity vs. Despair" with late adulthood. These stages also correspond closely with those formulated by Levinson.

The point about defining stages of this kind is that they represent observable regularities in development. If the observations are valid, the existence of such stages points to discontinuities in maturational processes, even though the underlying reasons for these maturational discontinuities (other than the profound physiological changes of puberty) may not yet be clear. The significance of such stages is that they give a systematic picture of a general order to be found in the psychological development of everyone. As Levinson (1978) put it:

> The life structure evolves through a sequence of alternating periods. A relatively stable, structure-building period is followed by a transitional, structure-changing period. The major developmental tasks of a structure-building period are to make crucial choices, to create a structure around them, to enrich the structure and pursue one's goal within it. . . . In a transitional period the major tasks are to reappraise the existing structure, explore new possibilities in self and world, and work toward choices that provide a basis for a new structure. In the course of a transitional period a man may choose to involve himself in new persons and places, or he may retain his marriage, job and social network but establish different relationships and live out different aspects of the self. . . . The periods occur in a fixed sequence; . . . there are no shortcuts or alternative routes; . . . Developmental impairments and defeats from the past may prevent a man from beginning a new period and working on its tasks. He is then in a state of decline. He is stuck. Developmental blocking of this kind can occur in adulthood, as in childhood, as a result of overwhelming biological, psychological or social insult. Thus, a large percentage of men in some groups may have such difficulty with the tasks of the Mid-life Transition and Entering Middle Adulthood that they cannot create the basis for even a moderately satisfactory life in middle age [pp. 259–261].

The identification and description of maturational stages are important both for psychoanalysis and for the individual. In psychoanalysis, knowledge of maturational stages sharpens the analyst's perception with respect to the structure of normally expected ranges of behavior and of psychic conflict, and the often subtle or obscure boundary beyond which lies the evidence of emotional disturbance.

Every analyst has his intuitively established criteria of what constitutes normal or abnormal psychic states. In particular, he judges the analysand's behavior during each session from the point of view of these criteria. Child psychoanalysts will be readily aware of how much their judgments are affected by assumptions about stages and crises: the expected orderly behavior of the child in the latency stage, for example, as against

the expected normal degrees of disturbance of the 4-year-old
in the middle of the Oedipus complex or the 16-year-old in the
middle of the crisis of adolescence. The gravamen of this chapter is that this discrimination between stages and the occurrence
of normal crises is equally germane to the analysis of adults.

For the individual, whether the adult on his or her own
behalf or the parent on behalf of a child, it is of some reassurance to know that certain crises of development, with their
accompanying uncertainty, anxiety, and stress, are a matter of
normal expectation and not necessarily a sign of serious instability or of mental abnormality. I have been struck repeatedly,
for example, by the extent to which analysts themselves seem
to have experienced, with some considerable relief, my description (Jaques, 1965) of the midlife crisis (this chapter is an extension of that article) as applying personally to themselves and as
helping to explain at least part of the psychological stress and
disturbance they encountered at that point in their lives. The
widespread existence of this kind of feeling is manifested also
in the popularity of the book *Passages* by Gail Sheehy (1974),
which gives a sound journalistic account of the midlife crisis.

It is my intention to illustrate the theme of alternating
stages and crises by reference to the early adult and mature
adult stages and to the midlife crisis which separates them.

The Midlife Crisis in the Highly Creative Person

The existence of a critical stage in development during the
late thirties is particularly noticeable in the lives of highly creative people, especially those of genius. There is a marked tendency toward crisis in the creative work of great men, clearly
expressed by Richard Church (1964) in his autobiography *The
Voyage Home*. "There seems to be a biological reason for men
and women, when they reach the middle thirties, finding themselves beset with misgivings, agonizing inquiries, and a loss of
zest. Is it that state which the medieval schoolmen called *accidie*,
the cardinal sin of spiritual sloth? I believe it is" (p. 139).

Or, as George Bernard Shaw put it: "God ordains that
every genius shall have an illness at 40. The object is to make

him go to bed for several weeks. Sometimes God overdoes it—Schiller and Mozart died of it, but Goethe survived to carry on. I myself did the thing handsomely by spending 18 months on crutches" (Dervin, 1975, p. 271).

This crisis may express itself in three different ways: the creative career may simply come to an end, either in a drying up of creative work or in actual death; the creative capacity may begin to show and express itself for the first time; or a decisive change in the quality and content of creativeness may take place.

Perhaps the most striking phenomenon is what happens to the death rate among creative artists. I had got the impression that the age of 37 seemed to figure pretty prominently in the death of individuals of this category. This impression was upheld by taking a random sample of some 310 painters, composers, poets, writers, and sculptors, of undoubted greatness or of genius. The death rate shows a sudden spike between 35 and 39, the group including Mozart, Raphael, Chopin, Rimbaud, Purcell, Baudelaire, Watteau. There is then a big trough in the death rate between the ages of 40 and 44, followed by a return to a steady death-rate pattern in the late forties. The closer one keeps to genius in the sample, the more striking and clear-cut is this up-and-down spiking of the death rate in midlife.

The fact that there is a very considerable change in creativity which occurs during this period can be seen in the lives of countless artists. Bach, for example, was mainly an organist until his cantorship at Leipzig at 38, at which time he began his colossal achievements as a composer. Rossini's life is described by Stendhal (1824) in the following terms: "His comparative silence during the period 1832–1868 (i.e., from 40 to his death at 74) makes his biography like the narrative of two lives—swift triumph, and a long life of seclusion" (p. 196). Racine had thirteen years of continuous success culminating in *Phèdre* at the age of 38; he then produced nothing for some twelve years. The characteristic work of Goldsmith, Constable, and Goya emerged between the ages of 35 and 38. By the age of 43, Ben Jonson had produced all the plays worthy of his genius, although he lived to be 64. At 33, Gauguin gave up his job in a bank and by 39 had established himself in his creative career as a painter. Donatello's work after 39 is described by a critic as showing a marked change in style, in which he departed from the statuesque balance of his earlier work and turned to the creation of an almost instantaneous expression of life.

Goethe, between the ages of 37 and 39, underwent a profound change in outlook, associated with his trip to Italy. As many of his biographers have pointed out, the importance of this journey and this period in his life cannot be exaggerated. He himself regarded it as the climax to his life. Never before had he gained such complete understanding of his genius and mission as a poet. His work then began to reflect the classical spirit of Greek tragedy and of the Renaissance.

Michelangelo carried out a series of masterpieces until he was 40: his *David* was finished at 29, the decoration of the roof of the Sistine Chapel at 37, and his *Moses* between 37 and 40. During the next fifteen years, little is known of any artistic work. There was a creative lull until, at 55, he began work on the great Medici monument and then, even later, *The Last Judgment* and the frescoes in the Pauline Chapel.

I am not suggesting that the careers of most creative persons either begin or end during the midlife crisis. There are few creative geniuses who live and work into maturity, in whom the quality of greatness cannot be discerned in early adulthood in the form either of created works or of the potential for creating them: Beethoven, Shakespeare, Goethe, Couperin, Ibsen, Balzac, Voltaire, Verdi, Handel, Goya, Dürer, to name but a very few at random. But there are equally few in whom a decisive change cannot be seen in the quality of their work—in whose work the effects of their having gone through a midlife crisis cannot be discerned. The reactions range all the way from severe and dramatic crisis to a smoother and less troubled transition—just as reactions to the phase of adolescent crisis may range from severe disturbance and breakdown to relatively ordered readjustment to mental and sexual adulthood—but the effects of the change are there to be discerned. What then are the main features of this change?

There are two features which seem to me of outstanding importance. One of these has to do with the mode of work; the second has to do with the content of the work. Let me consider each of these in turn. I shall use the phrase "early adulthood" for the pre-midlife phase, and "mature adulthood" for the post-midlife phase.

Precipitate and Sculpted Creativity

I can best describe the change in mode of work which I have in mind by describing the extreme of its manifestation. The creativity of the twenties and early thirties tends to be a hot-from-the-fire creativity. It is intense and spontaneous and comes out ready-made. The spontaneous effusions of Mozart, Keats, Shelley, and Rimbaud are the prototype. Most of the work seems to go on unconsciously. The conscious production is rapid, the pace of creation often being dictated by the limits of the artist's capacity physically to record the words or music he is expressing.

A vivid description of this early adult type of work is given in Gittings' biography (1954) of Keats:

> Keats all this year had been living on spiritual capital. He had used and spent every experience almost as soon as it had come into his possession, every sight, person, book, emotion or thought had been converted spontaneously into poetry. Could he or any other poet have lasted at such a rate? . . . He could write no more by these methods. He realized this himself when he wished to compose as he said "without fever." He could not keep this high pulse beating and endure [p. 178].

By contrast, the creativity of the late thirties and after is a sculpted creativity. The inspiration may be hot and intense. The unconscious work is no less than before. But there is a big step between the first effusion of inspiration and the finished product. The inspiration itself may come more slowly. Even if there are sudden bursts of inspiration, they are only the beginning of the work process. The initial inspiration must first be externalized in its elemental state. Then begins the process of forming and fashioning the external product, by means of working and reworking the externalized material. I use the term "sculpting" because the nature of the sculptor's material—it is the sculptor working in stone of whom I am thinking—forces him into this kind of relationship with the product of his creative imagination. There occurs a process of interplay between unconscious intuitive work and inspiration and the considered perception of the externally emergent creation and the reaction to it.

In her note, "A Character Trait of Freud's," Riviere (1958) describes Freud's exhorting her, in connection with some psychoanalytic idea which had occurred to her, "Write it, write it, put it down in black and white—*outside you*, that is; give it an existence independently of you" (p. 146). This externalizing process is part of the essence of work in mature adulthood, when, as in the case of Freud, the initially externalized material is not itself the end product, or nearly the end product, but is rather the starting point, the object of further working over, modification, elaboration, sometimes for periods of years.

In distinguishing between the precipitate creativity of early adulthood and the sculpted creativity of mature adulthood, I do not want to give the impression of drawing a hard and fast line between the two phases. There are of course times when a creative person in mature adulthood will be subject to bursts of inspiration and rapid-fire creative production. Equally there will be found instances of mature and sculpted creative work done in early adulthood. The *David* of Michelangelo is, I think, the supreme example of the latter.

But instances where work in early adulthood has the sculpted and worked-over quality are rare. Sometimes, as in scientific work, there may be the appearance of sculpted work. Young physicists in their twenties, for example, may produce startling discoveries which are the result of continuous hard work and experimentation. But these discoveries result from the application of modern theories about the structure of matter—theories which themselves have been the product of the sculpted work of mature adulthood of such geniuses as Thomson and Einstein.

Equally, genuinely creative work in mature adulthood may sometimes not appear to be externally worked over and sculpted and yet actually be so. What seems to be rapid and unworked-over creation is commonly the reworking of themes which have been worked upon before or which may have been slowly emerging over the years in previous works. We need look no farther than the work of Freud for a prime example of this process of books, written rapidly, which nevertheless are the coming to fruition of ideas which have been worked on, fashioned, reformulated, left incomplete and full of loose ends, and then formulated once again in a surge forward, through the emergence of new ideas for overcoming previous difficulties.

The reality of the distinction comes out in the fact that certain materials are more readily applicable to the precipitate creativity of early adulthood than are others. Thus, for example, musical composition and lyric poetry are much more amenable to rapid creative production than are sculpting in stone or painting in oils. It is noteworthy, therefore, that whereas there are very many poets and composers who achieve greatness in early adulthood, indeed in their early twenties or late teens, there are very few sculptors or painters in oils who do so. With oil paint and stone, the working relation with the materials themselves is of importance and demands that the creative process go through the stage of initial externalization and working over of the externalized product. The written word and musical notation do not of necessity have this same plastic, external, objective quality. They can be sculpted and worked over, but they can also readily be treated as a mere vehicle for the immediate recording of unconsciously articulated products which are brought forward whole and complete—or nearly so.

Lyrical and Philosophical Contents of Creativity

The change in mode of work, then, between early and mature adulthood is a change from precipitate to sculpted creativity. Let me now consider for a moment the change in the quality and content of the creativity. The change I have in mind is the emergence of a tragic and philosophical content which then moves on to serenity in the creativity of mature adulthood, in contrast to a more characteristically lyrical and descriptive content to the work of early adulthood. This distinction is a commonly held one and may perhaps be considered sufficiently self-evident to require little explication or argument. It is implied, of course, in my choice of the adjectives "early" and "mature" to qualify the two phases of adulthood I am discussing.

The change may be seen in the more human, tragic, and less fictitious and stagey quality of Dickens's writing from *David Copperfield* (which he wrote at 37) onward. It may be seen also in the transition in Shakespeare from the historical plays and comedies to the tragedies. When he was about 31, in the midst of writing his lyrical comedies, he produced *Romeo and Juliet*. The great series of tragedies and Roman plays, however, began to appear a few years later: *Julius Caesar, Hamlet, Othello, King Lear*, and *Macbeth* are believed to have been written most probably between the ages of 35 and 40.

There are many familiar features of the change in question. Late adolescent and early adult idealism and optimism, accompanied by split-off and projected hate, are given up and supplanted by a more contemplative pessimism. There is a shift from radical desire and impatience to a more reflective and tolerant conservatism. Beliefs in the inherent goodness of man are replaced by a recognition and acceptance of the fact that inherent goodness is accompanied by hate and destructive forces within, which contribute to man's own misery and tragedy. To the extent that hate, destruction, and death are found explicitly in early adult creativeness, they enter in the form of the satanic or the macabre, as in Poe and Baudelaire, and not as worked-through and resolved anxieties.

The spirit of early adult creativeness is summed up in Shelley's *Prometheus Unbound*. In her notes on this work, Shelley's wife has written:

> The prominent feature of Shelley's theory of the destiny of the human species is that evil is not inherent in the system of the Creation, but an accident that might be expelled. . . . God made Earth and Man perfect, till he by his fall "brought death into the world, and all our woe." Shelley believed that mankind had only to will that there should be no evil in the world and there would be none. . . . He was attached to this idea with fervent enthusiasm [Shelley, 1838].

This early adult idealism is built upon the use of unconscious denial and manic defenses as normal processes of defense against two fundamental features of human life—the inevitableness of eventual death and the existence of hate and destructive impulses inside each person. I shall try to show that the explicit recognition of these two features and the bringing of them into focus are the quintessence of successful weathering of the midlife crisis and the achievement of mature adulthood.

It is when death and human destructiveness—that is to say, both death and the death instinct—are taken into account that the quality and content of creativity change to the tragic, reflective, and philosophical. The depressive position must be worked through once again, at a qualitatively different level. The misery and despair of suffering and chaos unconsciously brought about by oneself are encountered and must be surmounted for life to be endured and for creativity to continue. Nemesis is the key, and tragedy the theme, of its recognition.

The successful outcome of mature creative work lies thus in constructive resignation both to the imperfections of men and to shortcomings in one's own work. It is this constructive resignation that then imparts serenity to life and work.

The Divine Comedy

I have taken these examples from creative genius because I believe the essence of the midlife crisis is revealed in its more full and rounded form in the lives of the great. It will have become manifest that the crisis is a depressive crisis, in contrast to the adolescent crisis, which tends to be a paranoid–schizoid one. In adolescence, the predominant outcome of serious breakdown is schizophrenic illness; in midlife the predominant outcome is depression or the consequences of defense against depressive anxiety as reflected in manic defenses, hypochondriasis, obsessional mechanisms, or superficiality and character deterioration. Working through the midlife crisis calls for a reworking through of the infantile depression, but with mature insight into death and destructive impulses to be taken into account.

This theme of working through depression is magnificently expressed in *The Divine Comedy*. This masterpiece was begun by Dante following his banishment from Florence at the age of 37. In the opening stanzas he creates his setting in words of great power and tremendous psychological depth. He begins: "In the middle of the journey of our life, I came to myself within a dark wood where the straight way was lost. Ah, how hard it is to tell of that wood, savage and harsh and dense, the thought of which renews my fear. So bitter is it that death is hardly more" (1946, p. 61, lines 1–10).

These words have been variously interpreted—for example, as an allegorical reference to the entrance to hell, or as a reflection of the poet's state of mind on being forced into exile, homeless and hungry for justice. They may, however, be interpreted at a deeper level as the opening scene of a vivid and perfect description of the emotional crisis of the midlife phase, a crisis which would have gripped the mind and soul of the poet whatever his religious outlook or however settled or unsettled his external affairs. The evidence for this conclusion exists in the fact that during the years of his early thirties, which preceded his exile, he had already begun his transformation from the idyllic outlook of the *Vita Nuova* (written when he was between 27 and 29) through a conversion to "philosophy," which he allegorized in the *Convivio*, written when he was between 36 and 38 years of age.

Even taken quite literally, *The Divine Comedy* is a description of the poet's first full and worked-through conscious encounter with death. He is led through hell and purgatory by his master Vergil, eventually to find his own way, guided by his beloved Beatrice, into paradise. His final rapturous and mystical encounter with the being of God, represented to him in strange and abstract terms, was not mere rapture, not simply a being overwhelmed by a mystical oceanic feeling. It was a much more highly organized experience. It was expressly a vision of supreme love and knowledge, with control of impulse and of will, which promulgates the mature life of greater ease and contemplation which follows upon the working through of primitive anxiety and guilt, and the return to the primal good object.

Dante explicitly connects his experience of greater mental integration, and the overcoming of confusion, with the early infantile relation to the primal good object. As he nears the end of the thirty-third canto of *Paradiso*, the climax of his whole grand scheme, he explains: "Now my speech will come more short even of what I remember than an infant's who yet bathes his tongue at the breast." But the relationship with the primal good object is one in which reparation has been made, purgatory has been traversed, loving impulses have come into the ascendant, and the cruelty and harshness of the superego expressed in the inferno have been relieved. Bitterness has given way to composure.

In Dante, the result of this deep resolution is not the reinforcing of manic defense and denial which characterize mystical experience fused with magic omnipotence, but rather the giving up of manic defense, and consequent strengthening of character and resolve, under the dominion of love. As Croce (1922) has observed, "What is not found in the 'Paradiso,' for it is foreign to the spirit of Dante, is flight from the world, absolute refuge in God, asceticism. He does not seek to fly from the world, but to instruct it, correct it, and reform it. . . . he knew the world and its doings and passions" (p. 279).

The Significance of Personal Death

Although I have thus far taken my examples from the extremes of genius, my main theme is that the midlife crisis is a reaction which not only occurs in creative genius but manifests itself in some form in everyone. What then is the psychological nature of this reaction to the midlife situation, and how is it to be explained?

The simple fact of the situation is the arrival at the midpoint of life. What is simple from the point of view of chronology, however, is not simple psychologically. The individual has stopped growing up and has begun to grow old. A new set of external circumstances has to be met. The first phase of adult life has been lived. Family and occupation have become established (or ought to have become established unless the individual's adjustment has gone seriously awry); parents have grown old; and children are at the threshold of adulthood. Youth and childhood are past and gone and demand to be mourned. The achievement of mature and independent adulthood presents itself as the main psychological task. The paradox is that of entering the prime of life, the state of fulfillment, but at the same time the prime and fulfillment are dated. Death lies beyond.

I believe, and shall try to demonstrate, that it is this fact of the entry upon the psychological scene of the reality and inevitability of one's own eventual death that is the central and crucial feature of the midlife phase—the feature which precipitates the critical nature of the period. Death—at the conscious level—instead of being a general conception, or an event experienced in terms of the loss of someone else, becomes a personal matter, one's own death, one's own real and actual mortality. As Freud (1915) has so accurately described the matter:

> [W]e were . . . prepared to maintain that death was the necessary outcome of life. . . . In reality, however, we were accustomed to behave as if it were otherwise. We showed an unmistakable tendency to put death on one side, to eliminate it from life. We tried to hush it up; . . . That is . . . our own death, of course. . . . It is indeed impossible to imagine our own death. . . . in the unconscious everyone is convinced of his own immortality [p. 289].

This attitude toward life and death, described by Freud in another context, aptly expresses the situation we all encounter in midlife. The reality of one's own death forces itself upon our attention and can no longer so readily be shelved. A 36-year-old patient, who had been in analysis for seven years and was in the course of working through a deep depressive reaction which heralded the final phase of his analysis some eighteen months later, expressed the matter with great clarity. "Up till now," he said, "life has seemed an endless upward slope, with nothing but the distant horizon in view. Now suddenly I seem to have reached the crest of the hill, and there stretching ahead is the downward slope with the end of the road in sight—far enough away it's true—but there is death observably present at the end."

From that point on, this patient's plans and ambition took on a different hue. For the first time in his life, he saw his future as circumscribed. He began his adjustment to the fact that he would not be able to accomplish in the span of a single lifetime everything he had desired to do. He could achieve only a finite amount. Much would have to remain unfinished and unrealized.

This perspective on the finitude of life was accompanied by a greater solidity and robustness in his outlook and introduced a new quality of earthly resignation. It reflected a diminishing of his unconscious wish for immortality. Such ideas are commonly lived out in terms of a denial of mourning and death, or in terms of ideas of immortality, from notions of reincarnation and life after death, to notions of longevity like those expressed by the successful 28-year-old novelist who writes in his diary, "I shall be the most serious of men, and I shall live longer than any man."

The Unconscious Meaning of Death

How each of us reacts to the midlife encounter with the reality of our own eventual death—whether we can face this reality, or whether we deny it—will be markedly influenced by his infantile unconscious relation to death, a relation which depends on the stage and nature of the working through of the infantile depressive position, as Klein (1940, 1955) discovered and so vividly described.

Let me paraphrase her conclusions. The infant's relation with life and death occurs in the setting of his survival being dependent on his external objects, and on the balance of power of the life and death instincts which qualify his perception of those objects and his capacity to depend on them and use them. In the depressive position in infancy, under conditions of prevailing love, the good and bad objects can in some measure be synthesized, the ego becomes more integrated and hope for the reestablishment of the good object is experienced; the attendant overcoming of grief and regaining of security are the infantile equivalent of the notion of life. Under conditions of prevailing persecution, however, the working through of the depressive position will to a greater or lesser extent be inhibited; reparation and synthesis fail, and the inner world is unconsciously felt to contain the persecuting and annihilating devoured and destroyed bad breast, the ego itself feeling broken into bits. The chaotic internal situation thus experienced is the infantile equivalent of the notion of death.

Ideas of immortality arise as a response to these anxieties and as a defense against them. Unconscious fantasies of immortality are the counterpart of the infantile fantasies of the indestructible and hence immortal aspect of the idealized and bountiful primal object. These fantasies are equally as persecuting as the chaotic internal situation they are calculated to mitigate. They contain omnipotent sadistic triumph and increase guilt and persecution as a result. And they lead to feelings of intolerable helplessness through a dependence on a perfect object that in turn demands an equal perfection in behavior.

Does the unconscious, then, have a conception of death? The views of Klein and those of Freud may seem not to correspond. Klein assumes an unconscious awareness of death. Freud assumes that the unconscious rejects all such awareness. Neither of these views, taken at face value, is likely to prove correct. Nor would I expect that either of their authors would hold to a literal interpretation of their views. The unconscious is not aware of death per se. But there are unconscious experiences akin to those which later appear in consciousness as notions of death. Let me illustrate.

A 47-year-old woman patient, suffering from claustrophobia and a variety of severe psychosomatic illnesses, recounted a dream in which she was lying in a coffin. She had been sliced into small chunks and was dead. But there was a thread of nerve as thin as a spider's web running through every chunk and connected to her brain. As a result she could experience everything. She knew she was dead. She could not move or make any sound. She could only lie in the claustrophobic dark and silence of the coffin.

I have selected this dream because I think it typifies the unconscious fear and experience of death. It is not in fact death in the sense in which consciously we think about it, but an unconscious fantasy of immobilization and helplessness, in which the self is subject to violent fragmentation, while yet retaining the capacity to experience the persecution and torment to which it is being subjected. When these fantasies of suspended persecution and torture are of pathological intensity, they are characteristic of many mental conditions: catatonic states, stupors, phobias, obsessions, frozen anxiety, simple depression.

The Denial of Death: A Case Study

In the early adult phase, before the midlife encounter with death, the full-scale reworking through of the depressive position does not as yet necessarily arise as part of normal development. It can be postponed. It can be put to one side until circumstances demand more forcibly that it be faced.

In the ordinary course of events, life is full and active. Physiologically, full potency has been reached, and activity—social, physical, economic, sexual—is to the fore. It is a time for doing, and the doing is flavored and supported to a greater or lesser degree, depending on the emotional adjustment of the individual, by the activity and denial as part of the manic defense.

The early adult phase is one, therefore, in which successful activity can in fact obscure or conceal the operation of strong manic defenses. But the depressive anxiety that is thus warded off will be encountered in due course. The midlife crisis thrusts it forward with great intensity, and it can no longer be pushed aside if life is not to be impoverished.

This relationship between adjustment based on activity in the early adult phase, and its failure in midlife if the infantile depressive position is not unconsciously (or consciously, in analysis) worked through again, may be illustrated in the case of a patient, Mr. N, who had led a successful life by everyday standards up to the time he came into analysis. He was an active man, a "doer." He had been successful in his career through intelligent application and hard work, and had a wife, three children, and many good friends. All seemed to be going very well.

The idealized content of this picture had been maintained by an active carrying on of life, without allowing time for reflection. His view was that he had not come to analysis for himself but rather for a kind of tutorial purpose—he would bring his case history to me and we would have a clinical seminar in which we would conduct a psychoanalytic evaluation of the case material he had presented.

As might be expected, Mr. N had great difficulty coping with ambivalence. He was unconsciously frightened of any resentment, envy, jealousy, or other hostile feeling toward me, maintaining an attitude of idealized love for me and tolerant good nature toward every attempt on my part to analyze the impulses of destructiveness and feelings of persecution he was counteracting by this idealization.

When we finally did break through this inability to cope with ambivalence—indeed a pretty complete unfamiliarity with the experience—it emerged that in all his relationships his idealization was inevitably followed by disappointment—a disappointment arising out of failure to get the quality of love he was greedily expecting in return, and nursed by his envy of those he idealized.

It was out of the analysis of material of this kind that we were able to get at the reflection in the analysis of his early adult mode of adjustment. He admitted that he was ill and that unconscious awareness of his illness undoubtedly was the main reason for his seeking analysis. Being active and being over-concerned for others were soporifics to which he had become addicted. Indeed, he confessed, he had resented my analysis taking this defensive addiction away from him. He had secretly entertained ideas of stopping his analysis because, in his words, "all this thinking about myself, instead of doing things, is no good. Now I realize that I have been piling up my rage against you inside myself, like I've done with everyone else."

Thus it was that, during the first year of his analysis, the patient lived out many of the techniques which had characterized his early adult adjustment. It was with the onset of the Christmas holidays that the unconscious depressive anxiety, which was the main cause of his disturbance in midlife, came out in full force. It is this material that illustrates the importance of the depressive position and unconscious feelings about death in relation to the midlife crisis.

He had shown definite signs before the holiday of feelings of being abandoned, saying that not only would he not see me, but his friends were to be away as well. Three days before the end of the holiday he telephoned me and, in a depressed and tearful voice, asked if he could come to see me. I arranged a session that same evening.

When he came to see me, he was at first afraid to lie on the couch. He said that he wanted just to talk to me, to be comforted and reassured. He then proceeded to tell me how, from the beginning of the holiday, a black gloom had settled upon him. He yearned for his mother to be alive, so that he could be with her and be held and loved by her. "I just felt completely deserted and lost," he said. "I sat for hour after hour, unable to move or to do any work. I wanted to die. My thoughts were filled with suicide. Then I became terrified of my state of mind. That's why I phoned you. I just had never conceived it as even remotely possible that I could lose my self-control like this." Things were made absolutely unbearable, he then explained, when one of his children had become nearly murderously aggressive toward his wife a few days before. His world seemed to have gone to pieces.

This material, and other associations, suggested that his wife stood for the bad aspect of his mother and his son for the sadistic, murderous part of himself. In his fear of dying, he was reexperiencing his own unconscious fantasies of tearing his mother to pieces, and he then felt abandoned and lost. As I interpreted on these lines, he interjected that the worst thing was the feeling of having gone to pieces himself. "I can't stand it," he said, "I feel as though I'm going to die."

I then recalled to him a dream he had had just before the holiday, which we had not had time to analyze and which contained material of importance in the understanding of his infantile perception of being dead. In this dream he was a small boy sitting crying on the curb in his hometown. He had dropped a bottle of milk. It lay in jagged, shattered bits in the gutter. The fresh, good milk ran away, dirtied by contact with the muck in the gutter. One of his associations to the dream was that he had broken the bottle by his own ineptness. It was no use moaning and crying over the spilled milk, since it was himself, after all, who had caused the damage.

I related his dream to his feeling of being abandoned by me. I was the bottle—containing good milk—which he destroyed in his murderous rage because I had abandoned him and went dry. He unconsciously felt the Christmas holiday as losing me, as he felt he had lost his mother and the good breast because of his ineptness—his violence and lack of control—and his spoiling me internally with his anal muck. He then felt internally persecuted and torn to pieces by the jagged bits of the bottle, representing the breast, myself, and the analysis; as Klein (1955) has expressed it, "the breast taken in with hatred becomes the representative of the death instinct within" (p. 313).

I would conclude that he had unconsciously attempted to avoid depression by paranoid-schizoid techniques of splitting and deflecting his murderous impulses away from me, through his son against his wife. These techniques had now begun to fail, however, because of previous analytic work with respect to his splitting and denial. Whereas he had been able to deny what in fact turned out to be a pretty bad situation in his home, by perceiving it merely as the product of his own projections, he now became filled with guilt, anxiety, and despair, as he began to appreciate more that in reality the relationships at home were genuinely intolerable and dangerous and were not just a projection of his own internal chaos and confusion.

During the succeeding months we were able to elaborate more fully his attitude toward death as an experience of going to pieces. A connection between his phobic attitude to death and his escape into activity was manifested, for instance, in his recalling one day a slogan that had always meant so much to him—"Do or die." But now it came to him that he had always used his own personal abbreviation of the slogan—simply, "Do." The possibility of dying just did not consciously exist for him.

On one occasion he demonstrated at first hand how his

fear of death had caused him always to retreat from mourning. A friend of his died. The patient was the strong and efficient one who made all the necessary arrangements, while friends and family stood about helplessly; bathed in tears and paralyzed with sorrow. He experienced no feeling—just clearheadedness and a sense of action for the arrangements that had to be made. He had always been the same, had done the same when his father and his mother had died. More than that, however, when I interpreted his warding off of depression by means of denial of feeling and refuge in action, he recalled an event which revealed the unconscious chaos and confusion stirred within him by death. He remembered how, when a cousin of his had suddenly collapsed and died a few years before, he had run back and forth from the body to the telephone to call for a doctor, oblivious of the fact that a small group of people had gathered about the body, and not realizing that everyone but himself was perfectly aware that his cousin was quite dead and had been for some time before he arrived on the scene.

The chaos and confusion in the patient in connection with death I would ascribe to his unconscious infantile fantasies equivalent to death—the fantasies of the destroyed and persecuting breast and of his ego being cut to pieces. Mainly, I think, because of the love he got from his father, probably reinforcing his own innate good impulses and what he has had described to him as good breast feeding in the first five weeks with his mother, he had been able to achieve a partial working through of the infantile depressive position and to develop his good intellectual capacities. The partial character of his working through was shown in the extent of his manic denial and activity and his excessive use of splitting, introjection and projection, and projective and introjective identification.

During the period of his early adulthood—twenties and early thirties—the paranoid-schizoid and manic defense techniques were sufficiently effective. By means of his apparent general success and obsessional generosity, he was able to live out the role of the good mother established within, to nurture the good part of himself projected into others, to deny the real situation of envy and greed and destructiveness expressed by him as his noxiousness, and to deny the real impoverishment of his emotional life and the lack of genuine love and affection in his behavior as both husband and father.

With the onset of mature adulthood in his mid-thirties, his defensive techniques began to lose their potency. He had lost his youth, and the prospect of middle age and eventual death stimulated a repetition and re-working through of the infantile depressive position. The unconscious feelings of persecution and annihilation which death represented to him were re-awakened.

He had lost his youth. And with both his parents dead, nobody now stood between himself and the grave. On the contrary, he had become the barrier between his children and their perception of death. Acceptance of these facts required constructive resignation and detachment. Unconsciously, such an outlook requires the capacity to maintain the internal good object and to achieve a resigned attitude to shortcomings and destructive impulses in oneself, and imperfections in the internal good object. My patient's unconscious fantasies of intolerable noxiousness, his anxieties of having polluted and destroyed his good primal object so that he was lost and abandoned and belonged nowhere, and his unconscious fantasies of the badness of his internalized mother, as well as his father, precluded such detachment and resignation. The psychological defenses which had supported his adjustment in early adult life—an adjustment of a limited kind, of course, with a great core of emotional impoverishment—failed him at the midlife period when, to the persecutory world in which he unconsciously lived, were added his anxieties about impending middle age, old age, and death. If he had had a less well-established good internal object and had been innately less constructive and loving, he might have continued his mature adult life along lines similar to his early adult type of adjustment; but if he had, I think his midlife crisis would have been the beginning of a deterioration in his character and of bouts of depression and psychosomatic illness due to the depth and chronicity of his denial and self-deception and his distorted view of external reality.

As it has worked out, however, the positive factors in his personality makeup enabled him to use his analysis, for which he developed a deep sense of value and appreciation. The over-coming of splitting and fragmentation first began to show in a session in which, as out of nowhere, he saw two jagged-edged right triangles. They moved together and joined to make a perfect square. I recalled the dream with the broken bits of bottle to him. He replied, "It's odd you should mention that: I was just thinking of it. It feels like the bits of glass are coming together."

Reactions to the Awareness of Aging

The circumstances met by this patient at the midlife phase are representative of a general pattern of psychological change at this stage of life. The sense of the agedness of parents, cou-pled with the maturing of children into adults, contributes strongly to the sense of aging—the sense that it is one's own turn next to grow old and die. This feeling about the age of parents is very strong; even in patients whose parents died years before there is the awareness at the midlife period that their parents would then have been reaching old age.

In the early adult phase of life, contemplativeness, detach-ment, and resignation are not essential components of pleasure, enjoyment, and success. Manically determined activity and warding off of depression may therefore—as in the case of Mr. N—lead to a limited success and pleasure. Splitting and projection techniques can find expression in what are regarded as perfectly normal patterns of passionate support for idealized causes and equally passionate opposition to whatever may be felt as bad or reactionary.

With the awareness of the onset of the last half of life, unconscious depressive anxieties are aroused, and the repeti-tion and continuation of the working through of the infantile depressive position are required. Just as in infancy—to quote Klein (1940) again—"satisfactory relation to people depends upon [the infant's] having succeeded . . . against the chaos in-side him (the depressive position) and having securely estab-lished his 'good' internal objects" (p. 348), so in midlife the establishment of a satisfactory adjustment to the conscious contemplation of one's own death depends on the same process, for otherwise death itself is equated with the depressive chaos, confusion, and persecution, as it was in infancy.

When the prevailing balance between love and hate tends more toward the side of hate, when there is instinctual defusion, there is an overspill of destructiveness in any or all of its various forms—self-destruction, envy, grandiose omnipotence, cruelty, narcissism, greed—and the world is seen as having these persecuting qualities as well. Love and hate are split apart; destruction is no longer mitigated by tenderness. There is little or no protection from catastrophic unconscious fantasies of annihilating one's good objects. Reparation and sublimation, the processes which underlie creativeness, are inhibited and fail. And in the deep unconscious world there is a gruesome sense of invasion and habitation by the psychic objects which have been annihilated.

In primitive terms, the process of sculpting is experienced partly as a projective identification, in which the fear of dying is split off and projected into the created object (representing the creative breast). Under the dominance of destructiveness the created object, like the breast, is felt to "remove the good or valuable element in the fear of dying, and to force the worthless residue back into the infant. The infant who started with a fear that he was dying ends up by containing a nameless dread" (Bion, 1962).

The conception of death is denuded of its meaning, and the process of sculpted creativity is stopped. It is the experience of a patient who, having created a work of art by spontaneous effusion, found that "it goes dead on me; I don't want to have anything more to do with it; I can never work on it further once it is outside, so I can never refine it; it completely loses its meaning for me—it's like a strange and foreign thing that has nothing to do with me."

The ensuing inner chaos and despair are unconsciously fantasied in terms akin to an inferno: "I came to myself within a dark wood. . . . savage and harsh and dense." If this state of mind is not surmounted, hate and death must be denied, pushed aside, warded off, rejected. They are replaced by unconscious fantasies of omnipotence, magic immortality, religious mysticism, the counterpart of infant fantasies of being indestructible and under the protective care of some idealized and bountiful figure.

A person who reaches midlife, either without having successfully established himself in marital and occupational life or having so established himself by means of manic activity and denial with consequent emotional impoverishment, is badly prepared for meeting the demands of middle age and getting enjoyment out of his maturity. In such cases, the midlife crisis, and the adult encounter with the conception of life to be lived in the setting of an approaching personal death, will likely be experienced as a period of psychological disturbance and depressive breakdown. Or breakdown may be avoided by means of a strengthening of manic defenses, with a warding off of depression and persecution about aging and death, but with an accumulation of persecutory anxiety to be faced when the inevitability of aging and death eventually demands recognition.

The compulsive attempts, in many men and women reaching middle age, to remain young, the hypochondriacal concern over health and appearance, the emergence of sexual promiscuity in order to prove youth and potency, the hollowness and lack of genuine enjoyment of life, and the frequency of religious concern are familiar patterns. They are attempts at a race against time. And in addition to the impoverishment of emotional life contained in the foregoing activities, real character deterioration is always possible. Retreat from psychic reality encourages intellectual dishonesty and a weakening of moral fibre and of courage. Increase in arrogance and ruthlessness concealing pangs of envy—or self-effacing humbleness and weakness concealing fantasies of omnipotence—is symptomatic of such change.

These defensive fantasies are equally as persecuting, however, as the chaotic and hopeless internal situation they are meant to mitigate. They lead to attempts at easy success, at a continuation on a false note of the early adult lyricism and precipitate creation—that is, creation which, by avoiding contemplation, now seeks not to express but to avoid contact with the infantile experience of hate and of death. Instead of creative enhancement by the introduction of the genuinely tragic, there is emotional impoverishment—a recoil away from creative development. As Freud (1915) incisively remarked, "Life . . . loses in interest, when the highest stake in the game, life itself, may not be risked" (p. 290). Here is the Achilles heel of much young genius.

Working Through the Depressive Position

When, by contrast, the prevailing balance between love and hate is on the side of love, there is instinctual fusion, in which hate can be mitigated by love, and the midlife encounter with death and hate takes on a different hue. Revived are the deep unconscious memories of hate, not denied but mitigated by love; of death and destruction mitigated by reparation and the will to life; of good things injured and damaged by hate, revived again, and healed by loving grief; of spoiling envy mitigated by admiration and by gratitude; of confidence and hope, not through denial, but through the deep inner sense that the torment of grief and loss, of guilt and persecution, can be endured and overcome if faced by loving reparation.

Under constructive circumstances, the created object in midlife is experienced unconsciously in terms of the good breast, which would in Bion's terms (1962) "moderate the fear component in the fear of dying that had been projected into it and the infant in due course would re-introject a now tolerable and consequently growth stimulating part of its personality" (p. 116).

In the sculpting mode of work, the externally created object, instead of being experienced as having impoverished the personality, is unconsciously reintrojected and stimulates further unconscious creativeness. The created object is experienced as life-giving. The transformation of the fear component in the fear of dying into a constructive experience is forwarded.

The thought of death can be carried in thinking and not predominantly in projective identification, so that the conception of death can begin to find its conscious realization. The reality testing of death can be carried out in thinking, separated partly from the process of creating an external object. At the same time, the continuing partial identification of the creative sculpting with the projection and reintrojection of the fear of dying gives a stimulus to the sculpting process because of its success in forwarding the working through of the infantile projective identification with a good breast.

Thus in midlife we are able to encounter the onset of the tragedy of personal death with the sense of grief appropriate to it. We can live with it without an overwhelming sense of persecution. The infantile depressive position can be further worked through unconsciously, supported by the greater strength of reality testing available to the nearly mature individual. In so re-working through the depressive position, we unconsciously regain the primitive sense of wholeness, of the goodness of ourselves and of our objects, a goodness which is sufficient but not idealized, not subject to hollow perfection. The consequent feeling of limited but reliable security is the equivalent of the infantile notion of life.

These more balanced conditions do not, however, presuppose an easy passage through the midlife crisis. It is essentially a period of purgatory—of anguish and depression. So speaks Vergil: "Down to Avernus the descent is light. But thence thy journey to retrace, there lies the labour, there the mighty toil by few achieved" (*Aeniad*, 1953, lines 126–129). Working through again the infantile experience of loss and of grief gives an increase in confidence in one's capacity to love and mourn what has been lost and what is past, rather than to hate and feel persecuted by it. We can begin to mourn our own eventual death. Creativeness takes on new depths and shades of feeling. There is the possibility, however, of furthering the resolution of the depressive position at a much deeper level. Such a working through is possible if the primal object is sufficiently well established in its own right and neither excessively idealized nor devalued. Under such circumstances there is a minimum of infantile dependence upon the good object, and a detachment which allows confidence and hope to be established, security in the preservation and development of the ego, a capacity to tolerate one's shortcomings and destructiveness, and, withal, the possibility of enjoyment of mature adult life and old age.

Given such an internal situation, the last half of life can be lived with conscious knowledge of eventual death, and acceptance of this knowledge, as an integral part of living. Mourning for the dead self can begin, alongside the mourning and reestablishment of the lost objects and the lost childhood and youth. The sense of life's continuity may be strengthened. The gain is in the deepening of awareness, understanding, and self-realization. Genuine values can be cultivated—wisdom, fortitude, and courage, deeper capacity for love and affection and human insight, and hopefulness and enjoyment—qualities whose genuineness stems from integration based upon the more immediate and self-conscious awareness and acceptance, not only of one's own shortcomings but of one's destructive impulses, and from the greater capacity for sublimation which accompanies true resignation and detachment.

Reality Testing and Development

Out of the working through of the depressive position, there is further strengthening of the capacity to accept and tolerate conflict and ambivalence. One's work need no longer be experienced as perfect. It can be worked and reworked, but it will be accepted as having shortcomings. The sculpting process can be carried on far enough so that the work is good enough. There is no need for obsessional attempts at perfection, because inevitable imperfection is no longer felt as bitter, persecuting failure. Out of this mature resignation comes the serenity in the work of genius, true serenity, serenity which transcends imperfection by accepting it.

Because of the greater integration within the internal world and a deepening of the sense of reality, a freer interaction can occur between the internal and the external worlds. Sculpted creativity expresses this freedom with its flow of inspiration from inside to outside and back, constantly repeated, again, and yet again. There is a quality of depth in mature creativity which stems from constructive resignation and detachment. Death is not infantile persecution and chaos. Life and the world go on, and we can live on in our children, our loved objects, our works, if not in immortality.

The sculpting process in creativity is facilitated because the preparation for the final phase in reality testing has begun—the reality testing of the end of life. For everyone, the oncoming years of the forties are the years when new starts are coming to an end. This feeling can be observed to arise in a particularly poignant way by the mid-forties. This sense of there being no more changing is anticipated in the midlife crisis. What is begun has to be finished. Important things that the individual would have liked to achieve, would have desired to become, would have longed to have, will not be realized. The awareness of oncoming frustration is especially intense. That is why, for example, the issue of resignation is of such importance. It is resignation in the sense of conscious and unconscious acceptance of inevitable frustration on the grand scale of life as a whole.

This reality testing is the more severe the greater the creative ability of the individual, for the time scale of creative work increases dramatically with ability. Thus the experience is particularly painful in genius, capable of achieving vastly more than it is possible to achieve in the remaining years and therefore frustrated by the immense vision of things to be done which will not be done. And because the route forward has become a cul-de-sac, attention begins its Proustian process of turning to the past, working it over consciously in the present, and weaving it into the concretely limited future. This consonance of past and present is a feature of much mature adult sculpting work.

The positive creativeness and the tone of serenity which accompany the successful endurance of this frustration are characteristic of the mature productions of Beethoven, Goethe, Vergil, Dante, and other giants. It is the spirit of the *Paradiso*, which ends in words of strong and quiet confidence, "But now my desire and will, like a wheel that spins with even motion, were revolved by the Love that moves the sun and other stars" (1946c, p. 484, lines 143–145).

It is this spirit, on a smaller scale, which overcomes the crisis of middle life and lives through to the enjoyment of mature creativeness and work in full awareness of death which lies beyond—resigned but not defeated. It is a spirit that is one criterion of the successful working through of the depressive position in psychoanalysis.

References

Bion, W. (1962), *Learning from Experience*. New York: Basic Books.

Brim, O.G., Jr. (1976), The male and mid-life crisis. *Counseling Psychologist*, 6:2–9.

Church, R. (1964), *The Voyage Home*. London: Heinemann.

Croce, B. (1922), *Aesthetic: As Science of Expression and General Linguistic*, trans. D. Austies. London: Macmillan.

Dante (1946a), *The Divine Comedy*, trans. J.D. Sinclair, Vol. 1. London: Bodley Head, p. 62, lines 1–100.

———— (1946b), *The Divine Comedy*, trans. J.D. Sinclair, Vol. 3. London: Bodley Head, p. 482, lines 106–108.

———— (1946c), *The Divine Comedy*, trans. J.D. Sinclair, Vol. 3. London: Bodley Head, p. 484, lines 143–145.

Dervin, D. (1975), *Bernard Shaw: A Psychological Study*. Lewisburg, Penn.: Bucknell University Press.

Elder, G.H. (1975), Age differentiation and the life course. In: *Annual Review of Sociology, Vol. I. Annual Reviews*.

Erikson, E.H. (1950), *Childhood and Society*, rev. ed. New York: Norton, 1963.

Fogarty, M.P., Rapoport, R., & Rapoport, R.N. (1971), *Sex, Career and Family*. London: Allen & Unwin.

Freud, S. (1915), Thoughts for the times on war and death. *Standard Edition*, 14:273–302. London: Hogarth Press, 1957.

Gittings, R. (1954), *John Keats*. London: Heinemann.

Jaques, E. (1965), Death and the mid-life crisis. *Internat. J. Psycho-Anal.*, 46:502–514.

Klein, M. (1935), A contribution to the psychogenesis of manic-depressive states. In: *Contributions to Psycho-Analysis*. London: Hogarth Press, 1948.

———— (1940), Mourning and its relation to manic-depressive states. In: *Contributions to Psycho-Analysis*. London: Hogarth Press, 1968.

———— (1955), On identification. In: *New Directions in Psycho-Analysis*. New York: Basic Books.

Levinson, D.J. (1978), *The Seasons of a Man's Life*. New York: Knopf.

Lidz, T. (1968), *The Person: His Development Throughout the Life Cycle*. New York: Basic Books.

Mannheim, K. (1928), The problem of generations. In: *Essays on the Sociology of Knowledge*. London: Oxford University Press, 1952, pp. 276–320.

Riviere, J. (1958), A character trait of Freud's. In: *Psycho-Analysis and Contemporary Thought*, ed. J.D. Sutherland. London: Hogarth Press.

Sheehy, G. (1974), *Passages*. New York: E.P. Dutton.

Sofer, C. (1970), *Men in Mid Career: A Study of British Managers and Technical Specialists*. London: Cambridge University Press.

Stendhal (Pseudonym) (1824), *Life of Rossini*. Willows, Calif.: Orion Press, 1970.

van Gennep, A. (1960), *The Rites of Passage*. Chicago: University of Chicago Press.

Vergil (1953), *Aeniad*, trans. E.V. Rieu. London: Penguin, Book VI, lines 126–127.

8

Developmental Psychopathology of Adult Disorders

W.W. MEISSNER, S.J., M.D.

The emergence of a developmental approach to psychopathology within psychoanalysis is one of the most interesting, clinically fruitful, and challenging aspects of psychoanalysis within the last quarter century. Our understanding of developmental defects, maturational arrests, phase-specific impairments and fixations, and in general the impact of the individual's developmental experience on the shaping of his personality and its functioning—both in its normal adaptive aspects and in its pathological and maladaptive aspects—has added a powerful and unifying dimension to psychoanalytic understanding of adult forms of pathology.

Despite the recent emergence of the developmental perspective and its application within psychoanalytic thinking, it must be recognized that psychoanalysis has been essentially a developmental theory from its earliest inception. Even in his early thinking about hysteria, Freud was struggling with the understanding of how early infantile experiences could come to influence the development of symptoms and patterns of pathology in the adult. By 1905, in *Three Essays on the Theory of Sexuality*, Freud had arrived at a developmental formulation, restricted almost exclusively to the libidinal phases of development, but a theory of development nonetheless, which was loosely related to the patterning of adult psychoneuroses and which served in a general sense as an explanatory schema.

The critical turning point, which gave impetus to Freud's thinking about these matters, came in his realization that the seduction hypothesis may have been faulty and that, in fact, the accounts of infantile seduction he received from his patients may have reflected not actual historical events but rather the production of infantile fantasies determined by drive derivatives. Rapaport (1960) comments on this critical phase in Freud's thinking:

> Freud conceived of these fantasies as wish fulfillments of instinctual drives, particularly sexual drives, and he generalized this conception into the central proposition of psychoanalytic theory, that innate, progressively maturing, unconscious instinctual drives underlie the conscious and experiential determiners of behavior. With this conception of instinctual drives, Freud postulated an *intrinsic* maturational factor independent of prior experience, and thus went beyond the anamnestic relationship between behavior and antecedent experience. The theory of the phases of libido development, which is often regarded as the core of Freud's developmental theory (1905), is simply the specific theory of the development of this particular instinctual drive, which, considered by itself, can be construed as the progressive alteration of the libidinal drive by experience [pp. 822–823].

Rapaport goes on to argue for the role of intrinsic factors in the development of the instinctual aspects as well as in the development of the ego and its correlative psychic structures. The psychoanalytic view of development postulates the gradual emergence of intrinsic maturational factors, on a more or less preset timetable, along with their complex and continuing interaction with experiential factors. Development is thus the outcome of nature-and-nurture and not the result of either to the exclusion of the other. Of particular import in the experiential aspects of development are not merely stimulus inputs (in the sense implied by the rather impersonal "average expectable environment") but rather the specific context of object relationships within which that developmental experience takes place. We can speak here of the interplay between maturational factors and developmental learning, such learning taking place within the context of object relationships provided by the child's significant caretakers.

The so-called "genetic point of view" has been defined as one of the metapsychological perspectives in the classic article by Rapaport and Gill (1959): "The genetic point of view demands that psychoanalytic explanation of any psychological phenomenon include propositions concerning its psychological origin and development" (p. 804). They support this definition by an appeal to Freud (1913):

> Not every analysis of psychological phenomena deserves the name of psycho-analysis. The latter implies more than the mere analysis of composite phenomena into simpler ones. It consists in tracing back one psychical structure to another which preceded it in time and out of which it developed. Thus from the very first, psycho-analysis was directed toward tracing developmental processes [pp. 182–183].

The relationship between constitutional-maturational and environmental-experiential factors was alluded to by Freud (1905) in discussing his notion of a "complementary series":

> It is not easy to estimate the relative efficacy of the constitutional and accidental factors. In theory one is always inclined to overestimate the former; therapeutic practice emphasizes the importance of the latter. It should, on no account, be forgotten that the relation between the two is a co-operative and not a mutually exclusive one. The constitutional factor must await experiences before it can make itself felt; the experiential factor must have a constitutional basis in order to come into operation. To cover the majority of cases we can picture what has been described as a 'complementary series,' in which the diminishing intensity of one factor is balanced by the increasing intensity of the other . . . [pp. 239–240].

An important discrimination in articulating the genetic point of view was contributed by Hartmann and Kris (1945), who emphasized that the genetic or developmental point of view was not concerned simply with recovery of past events but rather with the causal sequencing of developmental effects at various levels of the developmental experience. As they put it, "The genetic approach in psychoanalysis does not deal only with anamnestic data, nor does it intend to show only 'how the past is contained in the present.' Genetic propositions describe why, in past situations of conflict, a specific solution was adopted; why the one was retained and other dropped, and what causal relation exists between these solutions and later developments" (p. 17).

Rapaport and Gill (1959) characterize the developmental hypothesis by four basic assumptions: (1) all psychological phenomena have a psychological origin and development; (2) all psychological phenomena originate in innate givens, which mature according to an epigenetic ground plan; (3) the earlier forms of psychological phenomena, though superseded by later forms, remain potentially active; (4) at each point of psychological history, the totality of potentially active earlier forms codetermines all subsequent psychological phenomena.

As Abrams (1977) has noted, each of these propositions contains two related but substantially different concepts. The first concept stresses the understanding of psychological processes in terms of antecedent determinants, while the second stresses the role of developmental transformations, that is, the influence of progressive and regressive processes on the changing organization of the psyche. They assert the direct effect of the past on current mental functioning, a point Freud had made clearly enough in his statement that "hysterics suffer from reminiscences" (Breuer and Freud, 1893–1895).

The role of antecedent determinants is seen in the effect of infantile fantasies in determining later character and symptom formation. This view of antecedent determinants has particular clinical application in the understanding and interpretation of transference and in the use of genetic reconstructions. However, the transformational view places the emphasis on the consequences of sequential genetic transformations, whether progressive or regressive, as determinants of current behavior. As Abrams (1977) notes:

> Naturally, historical precursors influence the course and outcome of any emerging theme, but each phase reflects a new organizational achievement without the necessity of hypothesizing the existence of specific experiential antecedents. This assumption has clinical as well as theoretical importance. It is recognizable in the analyst's interest in the move toward genital primacy and new achievements (see, e.g., Bibring, 1937). Technically, interventions that aim at lifting inhibitions that impede sublimations lean on the validity of the assumption concerning the inherent potential for transformations [pp. 420–421].

Thus, the genetic perspective within psychoanalysis includes the assumptions of Rapaport and Gill but also views these assumptions within the broader frame of reference which embraces not only genetic precursors as antecedent determinants but, in addition, the capacity for genetic transformations. This transformational capacity is part of the continuing process within the individual's life history that expresses the ongoing dynamism, adapting causal antecedents to current contexts.

In view of these considerations, then, it can be said that the developmental viewpoint within psychoanalysis provides a far-reaching framework for the organization of analytic data and for the genesis of specific explanatory schemata. Our concern, then, is not merely with establishing the current effects of antecedent contexts, circumstances, traumata, affective fixations, etc. on the patient's current conflict and behavior but with seeking a broader understanding of those causal determinants which may have brought about one set of behaviors or responses at an earlier stage of developmental interaction and may correspondingly operate in similar or in modified ways to generate current conflicts and behavioral difficulties. The developmental viewpoint, therefore, provides us a complex schema of understanding, a sort of lens or frame of reference through which we can focus the interplay of important factors in the organization and functioning of the patient's personality.

History

We have suggested that Freud's thinking about psychopathology was genetic from the beginning. If we go back to the earliest stratum of his work with Breuer on the hysterias, we must recognize that the hysterical form of psychopathology provided him a template on which he elaborated his early thinking, which at this period was also highly influenced by Breuer's ideas and tended to emphasize energic and economic concerns. Breuer had advanced an early cathartic model of therapy which presumed that there was an area of the mind that had become dissociated or split off, so that in that area affects which had been stirred up or excited in some previous experience were cut off from the normal channels of discharge and thus became constrained or "strangulated." The cathartic method advised that, by gaining access to the dissociated affect and by bringing back to conscious memory the events associated with it so that the individual could reexperience those events and thus discharge the bound-up affect, the hysterical symptoms would be relieved. Breuer and Freud had considerable success in applying this model and in gaining a significant toehold in the difficult process of curing hysterical patients.

Freud's early divergence from Breuer was based on his dissatisfaction with the model and his emphasis on the role of defense in the genesis of neurosis. He saw at least some of the hysteria as reactive, that is, as defending against some previous trauma. Material provided by his patients, particularly the revived and reexperienced accounts of early traumatic events, led Freud to believe that the trauma in question had been an early infantile seduction which had excessively stimulated the child libidinally and consequently had overwhelmed the child's rather fragile defenses. This led to defensive splitting of the mind, with pathological consequences. The traumatic material was repressed and thus became unconscious, and it was only when the repressed material found its way to some degree of expression through the symptoms that the hysterical phenomenon arose.

It should be noted that this famous seduction hypothesis, which guided Freud's thinking for many years, was essentially an economic hypothesis, even though it dealt with the antecedent determinants of pathological behavior. In other words, it draws on a theory of the damming up, redirection of flow, and transformation of psychic energies which found their way into symptomatic expression on the basis of economic principles of discharge. Similar thinking underlies the notion of the repetition compulsion, that is, the general tendency to repeat painful experiences. Although the repetition compulsion is at times used as a basis for genetic explanation, in the sense that it provides an account of the influence of past experience on present behavior, the principles involved in the repetition compulsion remain essentially economic.

It took some time before Freud began to question the supposition and, indeed, the factuality of the seduction hypothesis.

His calling into question of this basic principle of his understanding of the neuroses is one of the critical turning points in the early history of the development of Freud's ideas. He began gradually to realize that the suppositions underlying the seduction hypothesis were indeed questionable, and he became increasingly aware of the possibility that he might be suggesting this hypothesis to his patients rather than confirming it.

This latter point was extremely important because it arose out of Freud's gradual disenchantment with hypnosis as a therapeutic technique and his casting about for alternative methods of dealing with the patient's illness. He tried various methods, all modifications of the "talking cure," the most noteworthy of which was his concentration method. In this approach he would press firmly on the patient's forehead and tell the patient that when he did so the idea or thought or memory that the patient was unable to retrieve would then occur to him. This was, of course, blatant suggestion, which Freud soon came to realize. He finally abandoned the concentration method and adopted the method that was to definitively stamp the approach of psychoanalysis, namely, free association.

However, as Freud withdrew from hypnotic suggestion and gradually abandoned other forms of more subtle suggestion, more and more of the patient's psychic functioning became available to his observation. The phenomenon of resistance made a particularly significant impression on him. He had been aware all along of the struggle involved in trying to regain lost memories—the so-called reminiscences from which hysterics suffered. But it was only when he was finally dealing with the fully conscious and relatively unmanipulated patient that the dimensions and intensity of these resistances became apparent. What also became increasingly apparent was that in large measure such resistances were unconscious.

The result of these developments was that there was a definite shift in Freud's interest from the repressed material which he had previously thought to lie at the etiological root of hysteria to an emphasis on the repressive mechanisms which he felt were related to the patient's defensive organization and particularly were responsible for the resistances he was experiencing in his patients. It was the abandonment of the seduction hypothesis that provided the critical breakthrough, since it brought with it Freud's realization that the accounts given by his patients of traumatic seductions were not in fact historical recountings but were more likely to be fantasy productions and distortions that reflected the operation of infantile sexual wishes. Consequently, there was a shift of emphasis in his thinking from external events to internal events, from the content of what was repressed to the repressing mechanism itself, and from antecedent determinants to genetic transformations. This was a first step in the direction away from dealing with earlier experiences merely as antecedent determinants of subsequent behavior and to seeing them as part of a series of developmental transformations which underlie behavioral manifestations in different yet related ways at particular phases of development.

As Freud became more familiar with and more experienced in dealing with the patient's resistances, he came increasingly to realize the importance of defenses, particularly the variety of defenses at the patient's command. Early in his thinking, defense had been equivalent to the notion of repression, but, as he came to deal with the broader spectrum of the patient's defenses, it became clear that repression was only one modality of defense among many. Freud also became much more aware of the dynamic significance of defenses and of their motivation.

In this context it was not long before he became aware of the role of narcissism as a motive of defense and repression. The emphasis on narcissism pointed to much earlier levels of the infant's developmental experience than had previously been considered. By the time Freud (1914) published his seminal paper on narcissism, he had already developed a fairly elaborate hypothesis dealing with the genesis of the neuroses as well as psychosexual development in general. The theory not only embraced levels of libidinal development (the oral, anal, and phallic periods) but also included concepts dealing with the development of narcissism (primary narcissism, autoerotism, and secondary narcissism). It should be noted that the theory up to this point was essentially a theory of the development of psychopathology, both of the neuroses and the psychoses, or, in Freud's terms, the transference neuroses and the narcissistic neuroses. Moreover, it was specifically a theory of instinctual development dealing with the developmental vicissitudes of both object libido and narcissistic libido.

In 1923 came another significant breakthrough, prompted by Freud's dissatisfaction with the libido theory and by his increasing awareness that the resistances and defenses, which stood in opposition to the expression of libidinal impulses and which could not be associated with the wish and drive dynamics of the unconscious itself, were also largely unconscious. In addition, Freud had become increasingly aware of the dynamic of unconscious guilt as a motivation of resistance in treatment. Both these factors led him to revise his thinking about the organization of psychic structure and to abandon the topographical model.

In its place he provided a structural model of the psychic apparatus which has become the standard template of psychoanalytic thinking ever since. The understanding of intrapsychic functioning was no longer in terms of the relation to consciousness, that is, according to the division of the mind into unconscious, preconscious, and conscious levels. Rather, Freud devised a model based on the organization of psychic functions as the principle of division. This took the form of the well-known tripartite theory of id, ego, and superego, which is still the primary analytic model of the organization of the mind.

Subsequent study by psychoanalysts and developmental psychologists has provided an impressive body of knowledge about the origins of developmental defects, impairments, and failures in the organization and functioning of both ego and superego. Our understanding of developmental psychopathology has been enormously enriched by the clarification of such developmental deficits, the type and quality of developmental experience which contributes to them, and the rich complexity of environmental influences which contribute to the relatively normal, healthy, and nonpathological emergence of such structural formations and, conversely, the negative influences which tend to contribute to their inadequate formation or even failure to form.

One of the important diagnostic discriminations that has emerged out of such considerations is the distinction between

developmental failure and regression as the basis of pathological manifestations. The patient who has failed to achieve certain
developmental levels and suffers from inherent developmental
defects in the organization of psychic structures is in a considerably different position from the patient who has been able to
make such developmental achievements and who has, in fact,
reached a relatively higher level of developmental organization,
but who, under certain developmental or contextual stresses,
has regressed to a lower level of functioning. The clinical situation in such cases involves diagnostically important differences
and dictates quite different clinical approaches and modalities
of treatment.

Along with the intense interest in the study of such developmental impediments and failures over the past three decades, there has also been an increasing interest in the clinical
definition of more primitive forms of personality organization.
This shift in interest has to some extent been determined by
shifts in the patient population treated by psychoanalytic therapists. There is some question whether the shifts involved are
wholly a matter of changes in the patient population, whether
they are the result of as yet unidentified selection processes, or
whether they may be attributed to an increasing sophistication
and awareness on the part of psychoanalysts toward the phenomena in question. Most observers, however, have agreed that
psychoanalysts today tend to see many more of the more primitive forms of character disorder, particularly the narcissistic
disorders and the borderline personalities.

Psychoanalysis through the years had come to see itself as
specifically a theory of the neuroses and as having formulated
a highly sophisticated and finely honed therapeutic approach to
the treatment of neurotic disorders. Gradually over the years,
however, the spectrum of treatment application tended to
broaden to include a variety of character disorders as appropriate subjects for analytic study and treatment (A. Freud,
1954)—this shift being paralleled by the previously noted shift
in theoretical emphasis from instinctual dynamics and conflicts
to a more concerted and intensified study of ego and superego
characteristics. In the course of this evolution it became increasingly clear that those with character disorders suffered not

merely from instinctual vicissitudes but from a variety of defects and failings in the organization and functioning of structured aspects of the psychic organization. These defects became even more apparent and more pressing as the exploration of the more primitive disorders was extended and deepened.

In the course of attempts to articulate and define the fundamental defect in the lower levels of character pathology, the adequacy of the structural theory has come more and more into question. That theory seems best fitted for understanding those forms of pathology in which internal intrapsychic conflict is the predominant characteristic (i.e., in which conflict arises between differentiated and distinguishable psychic entities, as between ego and id, superego and id, ego and superego). The theory presupposes the developmental elaboration of separate and defined psychic entities, particularly ego and superego. But the achievement of such forms of psychic organization is a relatively high order of developmental accomplishment, so that the theory finds its best application in patients whose developmental experience has been relatively successful.

The study of more primitive disorders, however, has focused on that realm of psychopathology in which the decisive and definitive establishment of such intrapsychic entities has by no means been apparent. Rather, the defects seem to lie at a more primitive, even prestructural, level. This has generated within recent years intense interest in the study of narcissistic disorders and defects and, particularly, has issued in the study of object relationships, internalizations, and the organization of the self as vehicles for coming to terms with and understanding the earliest contexts of developmental experience that lie at the roots of both the organization of the psyche and its functioning and in the understanding of the more primitive forms of psychopathology. In this latter area, our understanding of developmental influences and effects is as yet uncertain and is subject to considerable discussion and controversy. Consequently, any formulations regarding these matters must be regarded as tentative and hypothetical, as formulations whose validity is still in question, since our understanding is at this juncture only partial and remains very much open to new data.

An important contribution to our understanding of development was made by Anna Freud (1965) in her concept of developmental lines which can be traced for any given area of the personality and its functioning. They are equivalently developmental scales which trace the child's gradual growth out of dependent, infantile, cognitively less mature and organized, id- and object-determined attitudes or modes of functioning toward increasingly mature, autonomous, differentiated levels and modes of action which reflect increasing ego mastery over internal and external environment. The developmental level achieved by the child in any area reflects the outcome of complex interactions between drive and ego-superego development on the one hand and environmental influences on the other. The developmental line consequently traces the course of interaction between elements of maturation, adaptation, and structuralization.

One of the most important of such developmental lines—even a prototype for other developmental lines—is that which describes the sequence of relationship with objects, reaching from primary infantile dependence to young adult independence and self-reliance. Anna Freud (1965) describes this sequence as follows:

1. The biological unity between the mother-infant couple, with the mother's narcissism extending to the child, and the child including the mother in his internal "narcissistic milieu" (Hoffer, 1952), the whole being further subdivided (according to Margaret Mahler, 1952) into the autistic, symbiotic, and separation-individuation phases with significant danger points for developmental disturbances lodged in each individual phase;

2. the part object (Klein), or need-fulfilling, anaclitic relationship, which is based on the urgency of the child's body needs and drive derivatives and is intermittent and fluctuating, since object cathexis is sent out under the impact of imperative desires, and withdrawn again when satisfaction has been reached;

3. the stage of object constancy, which enables a positive inner image of the object to be maintained, irrespective of either satisfactions or dissatisfactions;

4. the ambivalent relationship of the preoedipal, anal-sadistic stage, characterized by the ego attitudes of clinging, torturing, dominating, and controlling the love objects;

5. the completely object-centered phallic-oedipal phase, characterized by possessiveness of the parent of the opposite sex (or vice versa), jealousy of and rivalry with the parent of the same sex, protectiveness, curiosity, bids for admiration, and exhibitionistic attitudes; in girls a phallic-oedipal (masculine) relationship to the mother preceding the oedipal relationship to the father;

6. the latency period, i.e., the postoedipal lessening of drive urgency and the transfer of libido from the parental figures to contemporaries, community groups, teachers, leaders, impersonal ideals, and aim-inhibited, sublimated interests, with fantasy manifestations giving evidence of disillusionment with and denigration of the parents ("family romance," twin fantasies, etc.);

7. the preadolescent prelude to the "adolescent revolt," i.e., a return to early attitudes and behavior, especially of the part-object, need-fulfilling, and ambivalent type;

8. the adolescent struggle around denying, reversing, loosening, and shedding the tie to the infantile objects, defending against pregenitality, and finally establishing genital supremacy with libidinal cathexis transferred to objects of the opposite sex, outside the family [pp. 65–66].

This particular developmental line is particularly useful in the assessment of object relations in various forms of adult psychopathology.

One of the more useful and fruitful schemata that has emerged from the study of early development has been provided by Mahler and her associates (Mahler, 1968; Mahler, Pine, and Bergman, 1975). To facilitate and bring some clarity to the following discussion, I would like to rehearse the stages of Mahler's developmental schema in some detail. The schema is undoubtedly well known to developmentalists but may not be more generally known to others who have not followed this literature closely. The formulations offered here rest on many years of extensive and careful observation of children from the earliest age levels.

The first phase of development that Mahler describes is the autistic phase:

we will propose to distinguish two stages within the phase of primary narcissism (a Freudian concept to which we find it most useful to adhere). During the first few weeks of extrauterine life, a stage of absolute primary narcissism, marked by the infant's lack of awareness of a mothering agent, prevails. This is the stage we have termed *normal autism*. It is followed by a stage of dim awareness that need satisfaction cannot be provided by oneself, but comes from somewhere outside the self. . . .

The task of the autistic phase is the achievement of homeostatic equilibrium of the organism within the new extramural environment, by predominantly somatopsychic (Spitz), physiological mechanisms [Mahler et al., 1975, pp. 42–43].

As the child develops, he moves from the autistic phase into the symbiotic phase somewhere in the second month. The child becomes dimly aware of the presence of a need-satisfying object. This awareness signals the beginning of normal symbiosis, "in which the infant behaves and functions as though he and his mother were an omnipotent system—a dual unity within one common boundary" (Mahler et al., 1975, p. 44). The symbiotic phase is described as follows:

The essential feature of symbiosis is hallucinatory or delusional somatopsychic *omnipotent* fusion with the representation of the mother and, in particular, the delusion of a common boundary between two physically separate individuals. This is the mechanism to which the ego regresses in cases of the most severe disturbance of individuation and psychotic disorganization, which Mahler has described as "symbiotic child psychosis."

In the human species, the function of and the equipment for self-preservation are atrophied. The rudimentary (not yet functional) ego in the newborn baby and the young infant has to be complemented by the emotional rapport of the mother's nursing care, a kind of social symbiosis. It is within this matrix of physiological and sociobiological dependency on the mother that the structural differentiation takes place which leads to the individual's organization for adaptation: the functioning ego [Mahler et al., 1975, p. 45].

It is out of this symbiotic matrix that the child gradually differentiates himself through the process of separation-individuation. The first behavioral signs of such differentiation seem to arise at about 4 or 5 months of age, at the high point of the symbiotic period. The first stage of this process of differentiation is described as "hatching" from the symbiotic orbit:

In other words, the infant's attention, which during the first months of symbiosis was in large part *inwardly* directed, or focused in a coenesthetic vague way *within the symbiotic orbit*, gradually expands through the coming into being of outwardly directed perceptual activity during the child's increasing periods of wakefulness. This is a change of degree rather than of kind, for during the symbiotic stage the child has certainly been highly attentive to the mothering figure. But gradually that attention is combined with a growing store of memories of mother's comings and goings, of "good" and "bad" experiences; the latter were altogether unrelievable by the self, but could be "confidently expected" to be relieved by mother's ministrations [Mahler et al., pp. 53–54].

As the child's differentiation and separation from the mother gradually increase, he moves on to the second or "practicing" subphase of separation-individuation. The practicing period can be usefully divided into an early practicing period and a practicing period proper. The early phase begins with the infant's earliest ability to move physically away from the mother by locomotion, that is, crawling, creeping, climbing, and righting himself, even though still holding on. Moving away from the safe protective orbit of the mother has its risks and uncertainties, however. In the early practicing phase there is frequently a pattern of visually "checking back to mother" or even crawling or paddling back to her to touch or hold on as a form of "emotional refueling."

The practicing period proper is characterized by the attainment of free upright locomotion. It is marked by three interrelated developments which contribute to the continuing process of separation-individuation. These are the rapid bodily differentiation from the mother, the establishment of a specific bond with her, and the growth and functioning of autonomous ego apparatuses in close connection and dependence on the mothering figure. Mahler, Pine, and Bergman comment:

With the spurt in autonomous functions, such as cognition, but especially upright locomotion, the "love affair with the world" (Greenacre, 1957) begins. The toddler takes the greatest step in human individuation. He walks freely with upright posture. Thus, the plane of his vision changes; from an entirely new vantage point he finds unexpected and changing perspectives, pleasures, and frustrations. There is a new visual level that the upright, bipedal position affords [pp. 70–71].

As this testing of the waters of individuation proceeds, the child enters the third subphase, that of rapprochement, by about the middle of the second year.

> He now becomes more and more aware, and makes greater and greater use, of his physical separateness. However, side by side with the growth of his cognitive faculties and the increasing differentiation of his emotional life, there is also a noticeable waning of his previous imperviousness to frustration, as well as a diminution of what has been a relative obliviousness to his mother's presence. Increased separation anxiety can be observed: at first this consists mainly of fear of object loss, which is to be inferred from many of the child's behaviors. The relative lack of concern about the mother's presence that was characteristic of the practicing subphase is now replaced by seemingly constant concern with the mother's whereabouts, as well as by active approach behavior. As the toddler's *awareness* of separateness grows—stimulated by his maturationally acquired ability to move away physically from his mother and by his cognitive growth—he seems to have an increased need, a wish for mother to share with him every one of his new skills and experiences, as well as a great need for the object's love [pp. 76–77].

The crisis in the rapprochement phase is particularly that of separation anxiety. The child's wishes and desires to be separate, autonomous, and omnipotent are tempered by his increasing awareness of his need for and dependence on the mother. Ambivalence is characteristic of the middle phase of the rapprochement subphase. There is a tension between the child's need to use the mother as an extension of himself, as having her magically fulfill his wishes, and the realization that, with his increasing separateness, she becomes less available and more distant. Thus the mother's availability and the reassurance of her continuing love and support become all the more important.

As the developments of the rapprochement phase are gradually realized, the child enters the fourth and final phase of separation-individuation, namely, the phase of consolidation of individuality and the beginnings of emotional object constancy. At this stage there are significant developments in the structuralization and integration of the ego, as well as definite signs of internalization of parental demands reflecting the development of superego precursors. The development of emotional object constancy depends on the gradual internalization of a constant, well-integrated, and positive inner image of the mother. This constancy implies more than the ability to maintain a representation of the mother in her absence, an acquisition which contributes significantly to the child's ability to function separately despite anxiety and discomfort. It implies also the unifying of partial good and bad aspects of significant objects, particularly the mother, into a whole and integrated representation. The achievement of such emotional object constancy implies the adequate resolution of preoedipal ambivalence, the modification of aggressive and hostile drives by fusion with libidinal elements, the unification of good and bad partial object representations into a whole object representation which is both good and bad. Thus it lays the basis for greater stability of object relations.

In the state of object constancy, the love object continues to be valued and desired, even though it no longer satisfies the subject's needs and even though it has become an object of hostile or aggressive drives. As Mahler, Pine, and Bergman (1975) put it:

> But the constancy of the object implies more than the maintenance of the representation of the absent love object. It also implies the unifying of the "good" and "bad" object into one whole representation. This fosters the fusion of the aggressive and libidinal drives and tempers the hatred for the object when aggression is intense. . . . It has a special bearing on the fate of the aggressive and hostile drives. In the state of object constancy, the love object will not be rejected or exchanged for another if it can no longer provide satisfactions; and in that state, the object is still longed for, and not rejected (hated) as unsatisfactory simply because it is absent [p. 110].

Mahler's conceptualizations have been criticized, particularly by developmental psychologists, for failing to account for developmental observations in the earliest stages of life. The advisability of formulating early phases of normal infant development in terms of pathological states (autism, symbiosis) may be questionable, if not misleading, in view of the demonstrable preadaptedness and object related activity in infants from the very beginning. If such reservations can be accepted as reflecting the uncertain and evolving character of our understanding of early development (Meissner, 1986b) and its implications for psychopathology, the Mahlerian schema has considerable heuristic value and provides a powerful framework for organizing clinical observations.

Recent years have seen the addition of another theoretical perspective, whose implications for the understanding of development (Basch, 1979) and psychopathology remains as yet tentative and exploratory. I refer to the emergence of a psychoanalytic self psychology. Self psychology traces its origin from Hartmann's clarification (1956) of the distinction between self and ego (Meissner, 1986d). Early approaches to a psychology of the self were cast in the context of the structural theory and its related metapsychology. The work of Heinz Kohut (1971, 1977) shifted the ground of the understanding of the self to a more restrictive and exclusively narcissistic basis. Kohut's contributions have amplified certain aspects of the psychology of the self, while ignoring or abandoning others. We must await the further course of theoretical development to see to what extent and in what manner the Kohutian view of the self, particularly the notion of the bipolar self as a reflection of a separate line of narcissistic development, will be rejected or usefully integrated in the progressive march of psychoanalytic understanding (Meissner, 1986a).

With these theoretical perspectives in mind, and with some sense of their implications for development and the understanding of genetic aspects of psychopathology, we can turn our attention to the various forms of psychopathology as viewed in psychoanalytic and developmental terms.

Forms of Psychopathology

In what follows I will proceed in order of increasing psychopathological severity—starting with the neuroses, then considering the other forms of symptomatic neurotic disorder, then the so-called neurotic character types, then the narcissistic personality disorders, the borderline disorders, and finally the psychoses. As we move progressively through this list, we will be meeting forms of dysfunction and personality impairment whose genetic bases lie at increasingly more primitive developmental levels.

Neuroses

Hysteria

Despite the abandonment of "hysteria" as a diagnostic term by DSM-III, the category retains important diagnostic implications within a psychoanalytic framework. Hysterical states are described in two major forms, depending on whether conversion symptoms or dissociative reactions predominate in the pathology. Conversion hysteria tends to occur more frequently, but not exclusively, in women and is characterized by the formation of hysterical symptoms, that is, bodily symptoms which resemble the effects of physical disease or impairment—paralysis, anesthesia, blindness, convulsions, pathological blushing, fainting, headaches, and other forms of painful or uncomfortable bodily experience. These symptoms, however, have no organic or somatic basis.

The dissociative type of hysteria occurs in a variety of complex forms, often difficult to distinguish sharply but characterized by the fact that a group of recent, related mental events, which may consist of memories, feelings, or fantasies, is beyond the patient's power of conscious recall but still remains psychically active and ultimately capable of conscious recovery. The usual forms of dissociative hysteria are somnambulism, various forms of amnesia which can be quite localized or general, a variety of fugue states, and the unusual condition of multiple personality. Other forms of dissociative phenomena that have been described include various trance states, automatic writing, the so-called Ganser's syndrome, and even some forms of mystical states or experience.

It should be remembered that Freud's original thinking about the pathogenesis of neurosis was based on the study of such hysterical patients. With regard to the formation of symptoms, Freud's theory retains a certain validity; the mechanism of symptom production can be regarded as representing a defense against excessively intense libidinal or aggressive stimulation and impulses by a transformation or conversion of psychic excitation into forms of physical enervation or expression. Consequently, the understanding of symptomatic hysteria is based

on the model of intersystemic conflict among structured psychic
entities. Instinctual impulses may be in conflict with other areas
of psychic function governed by the ego and superego, setting
up a conflict which results in repression of the instinctual impulse and its corresponding distortion and reexpression in somatic terms.

Given that model of hysterical process, it was argued that
the hysterical individual must have gained developmentally sufficient access to the oedipal situation to allow for the internalization of relatively integrated parental imagos and the relatively
stable consolidation of these psychic entities in the resolution
of the oedipal attachments. However, greater experience with
hysterical disorders has made analysts increasingly aware of
the extent to which hysterical dynamics express a variety of
pregenital, particularly oral, determinants. Moreover, we have
become increasingly aware that hysterical symptomatology itself is not an adequate guide to the assessment of underlying
character structure. Consequently, while there remains a pre-
sumption that hysterical symptomatology in an otherwise reasonably well-functioning personality suggests that the individual has successfully accomplished the developmental task
leading up to the oedipal formation and that the basic conflicts
lie at that level of psychic organization, caution is called for,
and a more careful assessment of pregenital and other structural aspects of the personality must be made before any definite conclusions can be reached.

Critical issues in this regard are the susceptibility of the
hysterical individual to regression and the degree of vulnerability to depression (Zetzel, 1970). Thus, while such individuals
may be thought of as having successfully negotiated the development issues of separation-individuation and the formation
of a coherent and stable sense of self, analysts remain acutely
aware that the hysterical facade may also cover a variety of
developmental defects and impediments not only affecting the
organization and functioning of the patient's ego but also reflecting a variety of possible narcissistic vulnerabilities. Consequently, it is not at all uncommon for patients who present
as apparently hysterical to turn out to be considerably more

infantile, depressive, and narcissistic than may have been apparent on brief acquaintance.

Phobias

The phobias may be regarded as forms of anxiety hysteria characterized by abnormal fear reactions due to unconscious conflicts that may be related to an increase in sexual excitation attached to an unconscious object or to unconscious aggressive impulses. The resulting fear is avoided by displacing the conflict onto an object or situation outside the self. The ego is able to fight off the anxiety by means of states of inhibition, such as impotence and frigidity, or through the avoidance of the phobic objects that have become associated with the unconscious conflict, either through a historical connection or through their symbolic significance.

The manifestations of phobic anxieties can be quite varied, and often the connection between the fear situation and the original instinctual conflict becomes increasingly concealed as the degree of displacement from the original context increases. The feared situation or object thus may have a specific unconscious significance and comes to symbolize a forbidden gratification, a punishment for an unconscious impulse, or a combination of both. Phobic anxieties are relatively common in young children, particularly in connection with the stirring up of instinctual conflicts. In adults, however, the onset of phobic reactions usually occurs during times of sexual crises and may be contributed to by fixations at the phallic stage, sexual frustrations, the presence of external factors that weaken the ego's ability to manage anxiety, or even increases in libidinal excitement.

The conflict-related nature of the symptoms usually indicates that these patients have achieved a reasonably coherent self-organization and that the internal psychic agencies have been reasonably well established. Consequently, the conflicts are usually regarded as phallic, although phobias about infection and touching often express the need to avoid contamination and suggest that the patient is defending against erotic or sadistic impulses, usually anal in character.

An additional important factor in the assessment of phobias is the extent to which the ego is capable of tolerating and mastering anxiety. A reasonably strong ego may be able to manage the conflict-related anxiety by forming a single phobic symptom complex, but not infrequently phobic anxieties can be seen to generalize and become polysymptomatic. Agoraphobia, the fear of open or public places, may be particularly susceptible to such phobic generalization. This may suggest in such patients a defect in ego development which may reflect impediments in the organization of the ego stemming from pregenital levels of development.

It is interesting to note that behavioral scientists have in recent years developed fairly sophisticated and useful techniques for dealing with symptomatic phobias. Freud himself noted that one of the important issues in the treatment of phobic patients was not only the resolution of their internal conflicts but also their ability to overcome their fear of objects or situations in the real order. From a psychoanalytic point of view, where the phobias are primarily symptomatic and are limited to restricted contexts and do not reflect underlying defects in the structural organization of the psyche, behavioral intervention may be a reasonable and, in many cases, preferable approach. The genetic perspective may be of considerable use in helping to establish this difficult diagnostic discrimination.

Another difficulty with the phobic syndromes is that there can be a subtle shift from the level of externalization connected with phobic anxiety to a more frankly projective distortion of reality of a paranoid order. In this regard, consideration must be taken of the relationship between early phobic anxieties in children and the development of later forms of paranoid psychopathology in adults. The history of adult paranoids often reveals an early childhood history of severe phobic anxieties as well as nightmares. The connections in this progression are not well established, but they seem to involve similar psychic mechanisms and defenses (Meissner, 1978). It is interesting in this regard to compare Freud's two classic cases, that of Little Hans (1909), in which the conflicts were on a phallic level and related to oedipal fears of the castrating father, and that of the Wolf Man (1918), in whom the phobic symptoms were of a more primitive order, reflecting severe ego defects and narcissistic vulnerabilities that later issued in a full-blown paranoid psychosis (Gardiner, 1971; Blum, 1974; Meissner, 1977).

Obsessive-Compulsive Neurosis

The obsessional or obsessive-compulsive neurosis is expressed in persisting or urgently recurrent thoughts (obsessions) and repetitively performed behavior patterns (compulsions) that have little purposive or adaptive use in the patient's real life and are experienced by him as alien or intrusive. Such patients are also characterized by rumination, doubting, and irrational fears. These symptoms may be accompanied by anxiety when the intruding thoughts or repetitive behaviors are prohibited or interfered with. These patients also reveal a strong tendency to ambivalence, a frequent regression to forms of magical thinking connected with the obsessional thoughts, and indications of rigid and severe superego functioning motivated by unconscious guilt and expressing sadistic and destructive drives, usually turned against the self in some degree.

The obsessional neurosis brings about a separation of affects from thought processes or behavior by means of the defense mechanisms of undoing, isolation, or reaction-formation, by regression to anal-sadistic levels of instinctual functioning, or by turning impulses against the self. The defense against a painful, conflict-ridden idea in the unconscious displaces the affect associated with that idea to some indirectly associated and more tolerable thought. This displaced thought then becomes invested with an inordinate quantity of affect and thus becomes preemptory or obsessional.

There are few well-defined obsessional traits that can be established early in childhood before the oedipal period, but it is thought that occasionally such characteristics may arise in the form of premature defenses or development, and closure of structured aspects of psychic functioning earlier in the developmental timetable than is normal or adaptive. As a rule, the obsessional structure arises out of the resolution of oedipal conflicts at a point at which the primary superego defensive system develops in the latency period. This consists of characteristics of general conscientiousness, a sense of shame and self-distrust, and unconscious guilt, usually attributed to oedipal transgressions, wishes, and fantasies.

The obsessional syndrome then is seen as in part a regression to anal-sadistic levels as a defense against intolerable oedipal impulses and conflicts. This regression is classically thought to be motivated by castration anxiety. Consequently, many obsessional mechanisms and behaviors can be seen as secondarily defending against anal-sadistic impulses, and the general behavior of obsessional patients can usually be found to contain indirect sadistic expressions. Thus, the object relations of such patients generally tend to be sadomasochistic in quality. Developmentally, such patients usually have been found to have experienced severe conflicts during the anal stage of development, having to do primarily with toilet training, but in a more general sense involving struggles with controlling parental figures over the child's emerging autonomy. Consequently, issues of ambivalence and control and the need to establish and reinforce a fragile autonomy become predominant elements in the obsessional syndromes.

It can thus be seen that the obsessional patient is one in whom internal structure predominates and provides powerful and often regulatory control over drive impulses and their associated affects. Often, however, in such patients the structure that has been established is excessively rigid and fragile, having been established prematurely on an insecure basis. Defensively, in retreat from castration anxieties, and developmentally, in terms of fixations at the level of anal-sadistic impulses, the basic conflicts in these patients remain prephallic. The extent to which these fixations and conflicts have interfered with ego development determines the extent to which these patients can tolerate regression without severe consequences. Where such ego capacities have been inadequately formed and established, the undoing of obsessional defenses may precipitate rapid regression to near-psychotic levels in which obsessional thoughts become delusional, and compulsive behaviors may reach a level of severe incapacitation and self-destructiveness.

Depressive Neurosis

The depressed patient most frequently presents symptoms which have to do with disturbances of mood, particularly sadness, unhappiness, and hopelessness. He complains of loss of interest in his usual activities or of difficulties in concentration. He feels alone, guilty, empty, worthless, inferior, and inadequate. He craves emotional support and reassurance from those around him, yet his attitude toward himself is highly critical and derogatory. The depressive symptoms often serve the purpose of eliciting sympathy and support from others, but at times his complaints are so hostile and his attitude so irritating that he frustrates his own purpose by alienating those from whom he might gain some feeling of affection or support. Such patients frequently have suicidal ideas and wishes.

The basic dynamics of depressive states were described by Freud (1917) in his classic paper "Mourning and Melancholia." The basic mechanism he described was a turning inward of the ambivalence originally directed toward the lost object and its redirection against the internalized or introjected object which is now part of the subject's own self. This effectively turns the original aggressive impulses, once directed toward the ambivalently loved object, against oneself.

The understanding of depression was later elaborated by Bibring (1953), who pointed out that the common theme in depression is the undermining or diminution of self-esteem. Such patients feel helpless or incapable of controlling or directing their inescapable fate in life. They feel themselves to be victims of loneliness, isolation, and a lack of love and affection. They see themselves as inherently weak and inferior, as failures in life altogether helpless and powerless to do anything to help themselves. Thus, depression must be seen not only as a result of instinctual vicissitudes connected with object loss but also in terms of a sense of inner weakness, vulnerability, helplessness, and inferiority within the ego itself. Neurotic depressions usually involve a reactive component and must be distinguished from the more severe depressive syndromes, such as psychotic depressions or manic-depressive states, in which there is a much greater degree of regression, a deeper and more severely incapacitating depression, and impairments in reality testing and interpersonal functioning.

Neurotic depressions usually involve reaction to loss or failure. The loss may be the death of a loved person or disappointment by a love object. The failures may be in not living up to one's own standards or in not achieving specific personal or vocational goals. Usually, neurotic depressions are accompanied by an overpowering sense of guilt, which may be quite unconscious. The poor self-image and self-esteem of such patients are usually based on early pathological development which took place in an unfavorable or rejecting family atmosphere. Self-esteem may also be diminished as a result of superego aggression, which tends to undermine and critically devalue the self. The discrepancy between behavior and the ideals or values maintained by the superego (ego ideal) and the resulting punishment by the superego is experienced as guilt, but the guilt is associated with diminished self-esteem.

In neurotic depressions, the more prominent the role of guilt in the dynamics of the depression, the more the depression will be seen in terms of superego conflicts. Consequently, such individuals can be regarded as having attained a level of structural formation in the course of their development which allows for the development of structural conflicts but which has resulted in a severe or excessively punitive superego. The superego consequently attacks, devalues, and undermines the self.

Nonetheless, depressive patients as a rule are found to have a considerable degree of oral instinctual and narcissistic underpinnings to their depression, particularly where the excessive demands of the ego ideal are determined by primitive narcissistic wishes which tend to be excessive and sometimes even grandiose. The impossibility of meeting such expectations and ideals sets the stage for the punitive response of the superego. The failure in self-esteem, however, may reflect developmental difficulties and impairments from pregenital levels of development, and this may reflect difficulties from very early levels indeed.

To achieve a positive and healthy sense of self-esteem, a child requires an atmosphere of parental affection and interest that can tolerate his aggressive impulses and can allow him to experience tolerable levels of frustration in reasonably manageable amounts. If the parental atmosphere is accepting, tolerating, and nonfrustrating, it can produce a sense of inner confidence that supports and consolidates the child's self-esteem.

The process of separation-individuation is particularly important in this connection; if the child is able to accomplish this separation without an excessive sense of precariousness, of shame, or of the anxiety connected with the loss of the mother, he is better able to salvage and consolidate his sense of increasing autonomous capacity and self-esteem.

Perversions

The perversions include such behavioral entities as homosexuality, fetishism, transvestism, exhibitionism, voyeurism, and sadomasochism. The general mechanism of the perversions is thought to be a defensive flight from castration anxiety connected with fears of oedipal retaliation. In homosexuality, there is a flight from the positive oedipal configuration, in which the opposite-sex parent is loved and the same-sex parent feared, to the negative oedipal constellation, in which it is the opposite sex which is feared and the same sex loved. In fetishism, anxiety is avoided by displacement of instinctual libidinal impulses to an inanimate object that symbolizes parts of the body of the loved person. Consequently, neurotic interest is attached to an object or body part that is inappropriate for normal sexual gratification. The fetish usually symbolizes the female phallus, and its use is related to a fantasy denying the danger of castration suggested by the anatomical difference between the sexes. Thus, the mind of the fetishist involves a splitting, in which one part is realistically aware of the absence of the penis in the female, but another part of his mind unconsciously asserts the idea that the female does indeed possess a phallus. The transvestite finds sexual excitement in dressing in garments of the opposite sex. For the male, this can represent an identification with the phallic mother; for the female, it serves her wish to deny the lack of a penis. Other perversions can similarly be seen as avoidances of the threat of castration anxiety.

The defense against castration anxiety in the perversions takes the form of a regression to pregenital instinctual levels, so that there is a failure of the normal developmental process by which early instinctual expressions become integrated in the normal heterosexual phallic adjustment. Greater appreciation of the developmental vicissitudes underlying various forms of perverted behavior, however, has impressed on analysts the variety of early developmental failures and fixations that can contribute to the development of perverted behavior. Homosexuality, for example, may be a reflection of genital-level, phallic conflicts, but it can also reflect a wide variety of much earlier and more primitive developmental difficulties, including early, symbiotically based difficulties in separating from the mother, resulting in a relatively intense feminine identification or overwhelming anxiety related to fears of engulfment and loss of a sense of self in any attempt to establish intimate or sexual relations with a woman. Consequently, the diagnostic assessment of the perversions, as in other forms of psychopathology discussed here, requires a careful assessment of underlying ego strengths and earlier developmental achievements, particularly in relation to the problem of separation-individuation (Socarides, 1974, 1988).

Character Pathology

Higher Order Character Pathology

Neurotic character disorders. Character, in the psychoanalytic sense, refers to the individual's habitual mode of bringing into harmony the tasks presented by internal instinctual demands and the external demands of the real world. The analysis of character structure has to do with those more or less enduring qualities of the personality that make it impossible to adjust to the demands of instinctual drives and external reality, and later on to the demands of the superego, in terms of varying degrees, forms, and styles of the functioning and adaptive capacity of the ego.

Contemporary psychoanalysis is concerned with the diagnosis and treatment of character types more than with any other area of psychopathology. It is a frequent experience in the treatment of patients with symptomatic complaints that these symptoms are frequently alleviated relatively early in the treatment, but as treatment progresses the underlying problems related to character structure become increasingly apparent and become increasingly the focus of treatment. Problems on the level of character organization are frequently reflected in difficulties having to do with object relations, the area of adjustment in which the disability and malfunctioning of the character disorder are most apparent.

A given type of character becomes pathological when the patterns of behavior associated with it become exaggerated to the point of being destructive either to the patient himself or to others in his environment, or when the individual's functioning becomes so disturbed or restricted that it becomes a source of distress to himself or to others. Characterological traits tend to be nearly lifelong, and are usually deeply embedded in the organization of the individual's personality. The character types are usually classified in terms of associated symptomatic expression. Thus, *hysterical characters* tend to sexualize relationships and are generally excessively sensitive to affective aspects of their experience. They tend to be suggestible, to have intense emotional experiences and outbursts; their behavior is often dramatic and histrionic in quality, and they tend to show severe emotional distress in the face of intense conflict. Generally, *phobic characters* frequently show reactive behavior in avoidance of fear-ridden situations. External situations are avoided as in neurotic phobic behavior, but, in addition, internal reactions of intense emotion such as rage or love may also be subjected to phobic avoidances.

Obsessive-compulsive characters, like their neurotic counterparts, tend to use defenses of reaction-formation, isolation, and intellectualization in an attempt to control emotional conflicts. They try to conceal an underlying sadism by kindness and politeness. They may show significant degrees of obsessional and compulsive ritualization or even ritual actions. Their habitual isolation results in a lack of affective responsiveness and a restriction in the available modes of feeling which can often be severe. Object relationships in such obsessional characters are usually anal-sadistic in nature and often involve severe struggles over autonomy and control.

The *depressive character* may show all the characteristics of the depressive neurosis, but on a more long-lasting, enduring, and chronic basis. Such individuals feel a chronically low sense of self-esteem along with feelings of worthlessness and victimization. Such individuals often reveal a history of early object loss or deprivation, frequently involving loss of one or both parents. While the depressive neuroses are related to object loss or narcissistic injury, depressive character disorders relate more specifically to deficiencies in ego development and inadequacies of adaptive functioning.

Other forms of character disorder have been variously described, such as the cyclical character, in whom periods of depression are intermingled with periods of elation, or the impulse-ridden character, who tends to deal with inner tension or conflict by impulsive and even self-destructive activity, or the alcoholic-addictive personality, which is characterized by a propensity for addiction to intoxicating substances. These are really secondary categories of character disorder which are generally more usefully described in terms of the characteristics of the more primary divisions. Thus, for example, problems of alcoholism and addiction are a significant and perplexing component of many of the character disorders, particularly the more severe ones. These personalities tend to show a predominance of early oral traits and can often be classified under the narcissistic, schizoid, or borderline forms of character pathology. The strong oral component in such patients may be accompanied by significant depressive components, which may also make it useful to consider some of these patients in terms of depressive character structure.

Lower Order Character Pathology

The above group of character disorders can be regarded as the higher order of character pathology insofar as they generally reflect a reasonably well-organized ego and superego and have conflicts that pertain primarily to the phallic level of instinctual development. It is these higher order forms of character pathology that provide the major area of effective psychoanalytic therapeutic intervention.

There is also a group of lower order character pathologies, in which developmental impediments and failures lie at a much more primitive and predominantly pregenital level. These patients generally show degrees of defect in ego and superego development and have significant difficulties in object relationships. This group includes the narcissistic personality disorders and the spectrum of borderline personality disorders.

Kernberg (1970) has provided a useful schema for describing degrees of character pathology. He includes the hysterical characters, obsessive-compulsive characters, and depressive-masochistic characters in his highest level of character pathology, parallel to the forms of higher order character pathology described above. He describes this level in the following terms:

> At the higher level, the patient has a relatively well-integrated but severe and punitive superego. The forerunners of his superego are determined by too sadistic impulses, bringing about a harsh, perfectionistic superego. His ego, too, is well integrated; ego identity and its related components, a stable self concept, and a stable representational world being well established. Excessive defensive operations against unconscious conflicts center around repression. The character defenses are largely of an inhibitory or phobic nature, or they are reaction formations against repressed instinctual needs. There is very little or no instinctual infiltration into the defensive character traits. The patient's ego at this level is somewhat limited and constricted by its excessive use of neurotic defense mechanisms, but the patient's overall social adaptation is not seriously impaired. He has fairly deep, stable object-relationships and is capable of experiencing guilt, mourning, and a wide variety of affective responses. His sexual and/or aggressive drive derivatives are partially inhibited, but these instinctual conflicts have reached the stage where the infantile genital phase and oedipal conflicts are clearly predominant and there is no pathological condensation of genital sexual strivings with pregenital, aggressively determined strivings in which the latter predominate [pp. 805–806].

The following levels of character pathology correspond to the lower level of pathology presented here. At the intermediate level of character pathology Kernberg emphasizes the defective integration of the superego, which is able to tolerate contradictory demands between sadistic, prohibitive superego nuclei, on the one hand, and rather primitive, magical, and somewhat idealizing nuclei, on the other. He goes on to say:

> Deficient superego integration can also be observed in the partial projections of superego nuclei (as expressed in the patient's decreased

capacity for experiencing guilt and in paranoid trends), contradictions in the ego's value systems, and severe mood swings. . . . The poor integration of the superego, which is reflected in contradictory unconscious demands on the ego, also explains the appearance of pathological character defenses combining reaction formations against instincts with a partial expression of instinctual impulses. . . . Repression is still the main defensive operation of the ego, together with related defenses such as intellectualization, rationalization, and undoing. At the same time, the patient shows some dissociative trends, some defensive splitting of the ego in limited areas (that is, mutual dissociation of contradictory ego states), and projection and denial. Pregenital, especially oral conflicts come to the fore, although the genital level of libidinal development has been reached [pp. 806–807].

In this group Kernberg includes the oral types of character pathology, including passive-aggressive personalities, sadomasochistic personalities, some infantile personalities, and some narcissistic personalities.

At the lower level of character pathology, structural deficits and their developmental consequences are even more severe:

At the lower level, the patient's superego integration is minimal and his propensity for projection of primitive, sadistic superego nuclei is maximal. His capacity for experiencing concern and guilt is seriously impaired, and his basis for self-criticism constantly fluctuates. The individual at this level commonly exhibits paranoid traits, stemming both from projection of superego nuclei and from the excessive use of rather primitive forms of projection, especially projective identification as one major defense mechanism of the ego. . . . The synthetic function of the patient's ego is seriously impaired, and he uses primitive dissociation or splitting as the central defensive operation of the ego instead of repression. . . . His pathological character defenses are predominantly of an "impulsive," instinctually infiltrated kind; contradictory, repetitive patterns of behavior are dissociated from each other, permitting direct release of drive derivatives as well as of reaction formations against these drives. Lacking an integrated ego and the capacity to tolerate guilt feelings, such patients have little need for secondary rationalizations of pathological character traits. . . . Their inability to integrate libidinally determined and aggressively determined self and object images is reflected in their maintaining object-relationships of either a need-gratifying or a threatening nature. They are unable to have empathy for objects in their totality; object-relationships are of a part-object type, and object constancy has not been reached. . . . The absence of both an integrated world of total, internalized objects and of a stable self concept determines the presence of the syndrome of identity diffusion. In fact, identity diffusion is an outstanding characteristic of this lower level of character pathology. The lack of integration of libidinal and aggressive strivings contributes to a general lack of neutralization of instinctual energy, and to a severe restriction of the conflict-free ego [pp. 807–809].

Included in this lowest bracket of character pathologies are the infantile personalities, many narcissistic personalities, antisocial personalities, the more chaotic impulse-ridden characters, the "as-if" characters, and other patients with multiple sexual deviations in combination with drug addiction or alcoholism and pathological object relationships, as well as other forms of schizoid and paranoid personalities. I would regard this lowest level of character pathology as corresponding to the borderline spectrum of personality disorders.

Narcissistic Character Disorders

Most of the narcissistic character disorders form part of an intermediate group whose pathology is more difficult and more severe than the higher order character disorders, but not yet as severe as the lower order character disorders as represented by the borderline personalities. The narcissistic character presents a pathological picture marked by an excessive degree of self-reference in his interaction with other individuals and by an excessive need to be loved and admired by others. Along with this need, there are also apparently contradictory attitudes of an inflated, often grandiose, self-concept and an inordinate need to receive tribute and admiration from others (Bursten, 1973; Meissner, 1984, 1986c).

The narcissistic character disorders can be distinguished from borderline and psychotic states. Narcissistic characters suffer from disturbances in the organization of the self and of archaic objects cathected with narcissistic libido. Consequently, their pathology is based on narcissistic fixations to archaic self-images or representations. These narcissistically cathected introjects have not been integrated with the rest of the personality organization, so that the individual's capacity for mature object relatedness and functioning is impoverished because of the intense investment of psychic energies in the self. Moreover, the realistic adaptation of such individuals is interfered with by the intrusion of primitive narcissistic demands.

The diagnostic evaluation of the narcissistic personality disorders is still a matter of debate among psychoanalysts, but there is a general consensus that they represent forms of psychopathology with more severe levels of developmental fixation than the neuroses, but not as severe or early as in borderline pathology. Narcissistic personalities usually have developed a cohesive self-organization which is structured around relatively archaic narcissistic configurations, and in the psychoanalytic situation have a propensity for forming narcissistic transferences, whether idealizing, mirroring, or both.

The narcissistic personalities can be thought of as reflecting various degrees of pathological severity. The highest level of personality organization is found in the phallic narcissistic personality. Here exhibitionism, pride, show-offishness, and counterphobic competitiveness are characteristic—all in the interest of self-centered needs to gain admiration and approval from others. Relationships often have a quality of arrogance or contempt which masks underlying feelings of inadequacy or inferiority. When compensatory defenses weaken, these patients are vulnerable to depression, marked by diminished self-esteem and a sense of inferiority and shame. The sense of shame and phallic inadequacy are constantly denied by phallic assertiveness.

A more subtle variant of this form of narcissistic pathology has been tagged the "Nobel Prize complex" (Tartakoff, 1966). These individuals are apparently "healthy," socially well adjusted, intelligent, and able, and have usually achieved high levels of academic or professional success. Difficulties arise in contexts of competition or intimate human relationships. Symptoms take the form of reactive depressions or anxiety attacks, and sometimes psychosomatic reactions. They share the conviction from early on that their talents and exceptional abilities will win them success and acclaim, and attaining these goals has become essential to their psychic well-being. Success has usually provided a generous measure of narcissistic gratification, but when narcissistic expectations begin to be no longer fulfilled a narcissistic disequilibrium is created and symptoms result. For such patients, the analysis or therapy is itself drawn into the service of narcissistic needs and becomes a vehicle for achieving success and recognition. Not unexpectedly, the analyst often finds himself the object of idealization with these patients.

At a more pathological level, the narcissistic need seeks not only admiration and recognition, but also feels entitled to exploit or manipulate others for the enhancement and aggrandizement of the self. Such personalities are "manipulative" (Bursten, 1973) and in more developed form approximate the description of psychopathic or antisocial personalities. Dealings with others are marked by contempt and devaluation. Others are valued only to the extent that they serve the subject's needs, and a high premium is placed on putting something over or getting away with something. This exploitative form of narcissistic repair overlies a deeper sense of shame, worthlessness, and narcissistic vulnerability. As long as the resources for narcissistic repair are available, these patients do not experience regression. But their unremitting narcissistic need creates considerable difficulty in maintaining meaningful and mutually satisfying relationships with others.

At more severely pathological levels, narcissism becomes more needy, clinging, and demanding. The need to be given to and taken care of reflects an uncompromising sense of entitlement. These patients often are involved in intensely dependent and needy relationships that have a highly ambivalent and hostile-dependent quality. The significant object is never quite able to satisfy the patient's demands and expectations. As a result, these individuals are constantly in threat of disappointment and frustration, feeling deprived and desperate. In this type of primitive narcissistic character, the clinging dependency and neediness often mask a core of grandiosity and entitlement which gives them a claim on concern, care, and attention from others, however detrimental to the other.

The developmental defect or fixation in such patients takes place at the critical level in which the differentiation of self and objects has been accomplished and the further tipping of the balance away from infantile narcissistic needs and demands toward a responsiveness and interaction with the demands of real objects takes place. Thus, narcissistic characters have attained a cohesive and organized self and are not threatened by the possibility of irreversible decompensation in the organization of the self or of narcissistically cathected objects. Since this form of character structure is able to maintain a cohesive and stable psychic representation, narcissistic characters are able to establish relatively stable transferences, even though these are highly narcissistic in character. It is the presence of these stable narcissistic configurations that marks the narcissistic forms of pathology off from borderline or psychotic states.

The Borderline Spectrum

The lowest level of character organization is occupied by a variety of forms that can be grouped together as the "borderline spectrum." Kernberg's description of borderline personality organization (1967) has led in the direction of an understanding of this level of character pathology as a single entity (Gunderson and Singer, 1975), a view canonized by its incorporation in DSM-III and DSM-III-R. Despite the current acceptance of this approach in general psychiatry, Kernberg's own sense of borderline personality as a form of structural diagnosis lies closer to psychoanalytic concerns. These variants of character pathology represent a collection of entities that encompass a spectrum of borderline disorders (Meissner, 1984, 1988).

The borderline spectrum extends from the psychotic border on one side to the higher order border of narcissistic pathology on the other. It includes the more labile, disorganized, and frequently chaotic forms of personality organization, in which we find patterns of emotional lability, dissociation of ego states, degrees of regressive vulnerability, ego deficits, tendencies to act out, intense anger and rage, and impoverished object relations reflecting poor developmental achievement, the failure of object constancy, the dominance of need-satisfaction, narcissistic vulnerability, and demandingness. It also includes better organized personalities who reveal good ego strengths and adaptive capacity, but who under certain conditions of severe conflict or stress react in a manner to suggest underlying borderline issues.

The following categories represent a preliminary attempt to sort out these components of the borderline spectrum, and must be regarded as tentative at best. As I see it, the spectrum includes two major divisions or clusters of pathological character disorders which I have labeled the *hysterical continuum* and the *schizoid continuum*.

The Hysterical Continuum

The hysterical continuum represents a series of disorders of decreasing pathological severity, extending from the most primitive forms of character pathology, bordering on the schizophrenic, to more highly organized and integrated forms of disturbance bordering on the narcissistic and hysterical. The more severe levels of disturbance within this continuum are marked by increasing affective lability, diminished tolerance for anxiety and/or frustration, increased ego weakness, greater tendencies for externalization and acting out as a means of releasing tension, greater instability or fragility of introjective configurations and a corresponding vulnerability of self-cohesion, higher levels of primitive pregenital aggression, increasingly primitive defensive organization, a greater tendency to regressive states and functioning, increasing tendencies to clinging dependence on objects, and a constant threat posed by fears of abandonment and loss.

Pseudoschizophrenias. The first group of patients reveal primary symptoms which they share with schizophrenia, even though they may be less striking and intense; this includes thought and association disorders both of process and content, disorders of affective regulation, and even disorders of sensorimotor and autonomic functioning. The anxiety is diffuse, chronic, intense, and pervasive. The neurotic symptoms are usually multiple, shifting, and confusing; they include obsessions and compulsions, phobias, hysterical manifestations, hypochondriasis, depression, depersonalization, and a variety of apparently neurotic defense mechanisms occurring simultaneously or successively. The obsessions and phobias may often reach delusional proportions. This pan-neurotic picture may include tendencies to acting out and dramatic or histrionic behavior, or even antisocial and drug-dependent behavior. Sexual organization and functioning is chaotic, both in fact and in fantasy.

Primitive affective personality disorder. These patients may never actually develop psychotic symptoms, but they have a high capacity for psychotic decompensation under certain circumstances. Such transient regressions may be accompanied by a loss of reality testing, but they retain the capacity for ready reversibility of the regression so that psychotic episodes remain transient. In these patients the issues remain psychotic, but unlike the pseudoschizophrenic, these patients have a higher capacity to maintain their functioning on a more or less consistent level during nonregressed periods, so that they remain in reasonably good contact with reality and are relatively more capable of adaptive functioning. However, the propensity for transient regressions, even though relatively brief and reversible, remains a marked aspect of this form of character pathology.

The maintenance of an integrated and cohesive sense of self is a constant difficulty in that the self is continually threatened with dissolution and disintegration, and is plagued by the need to cling to objects, as well as the fear of fusing with them. Where such ego boundaries become porous and uncertain, there is often a preoccupation with identity problems; this is often the case in analysis, where regressive pulls tend to increase the dedifferentiation and defusion of ego boundaries. These patients are closely related to the borderline personality disorder as described in DSM-III-R.

Dysphoric personality. The dysphoric personality represents a step up in the consistency of organization and capacity for functioning from the affective character, even as the affective character also represented a step up from the level of the pseudoschizophrenias. There is a peculiar quality to these patients' subjective experience in interpersonal situations. They seem extraordinarily sensitive and responsive to the unconscious fantasies and impulses, as well as primitive superego contents, in the significant objects around them. The conscious and intentional ego activity of people around them is held with abiding suspicion and mistrust, as though they were somehow deceptions or malicious tricks, while the id and superego elements seem somehow more genuine. There is also a tendency for these patients to feel that the elements of enduring character style, self-organization, and ego functioning in themselves is somehow unreal or phony (Krohn, 1974).

When seen in a regressive crisis, dysphoric personality patients, unlike potentially healthy neurotics, are unable to easily establish a confident relationship with the therapist. Rather, magical expectations, a diminished capacity to distinguish fantasy from reality, episodes of anger and suspicion, and fears of rejection dominate the therapeutic interaction for an extended period. Gradually, however, such patients are able to respond to good therapeutic management and, at least partially, to relinquish their unrealistic and magical expectations, as well as their fears and suspicions, and are able to establish an at least workable therapeutic alliance (Zetzel, 1971).

Nonetheless, the dysphoric personality is able to retain a relatively good level of functioning and adaptation to reality. The regression in these patients is more typically seen either as the result of progressive involvement in the therapeutic relationship and increasing susceptibility to regressive pulls, usually in analysis but also frequently enough in psychotherapy, or in particularly intense relationships with significant objects outside the therapy. Thus, the dysphoric personality may be able to retain relatively good and well-functioning relationships with a wide spectrum of other people in his environment, but may regress to relatively infantile and destructive, if not maladaptive, involvements with particular objects.

The primitive (oral) hysteric. The primitive hysteric often presents with more or less marked hysterical symptomatology, but the character organization tends to be somewhat more infantile. Long-lasting or significant involvement with objects frequently shows a progressively more regressed, childlike, oral, demanding, and frustrated aggressive quality, which is not characteristic of the hysteric. The need to be loved, to be the center of attention and attraction, functions on a less specifically sexualized level, has a quality of greater helplessness, and seems inappropriately demanding and reflective of more primitive narcissistic trends.

The Schizoid Continuum

The schizoid continuum is a rather loosely organized group of character pathology, which represents a variety of resolutions of the basic schizoid dilemma. That dilemma is an expression of the need-fear dilemma in which an intense need for objects is countered by a fear of closeness or intimacy with the same objects. The schizoid defense counters this fear of involvement (which in its more severe manifestations becomes a fear of engulfment) by withdrawal or minimization of the need for objects.

The schizoid personality. The schizoid dilemma and defense are seen most characteristically in the schizoid personality. The schizoid patient complains of feeling isolated, cut off, shut off, out of touch, apart, strange, or complains of life seeming futile, meaningless, empty, and leading nowhere. External relationships seem to be affectively empty and are characterized by emotional withdrawal. Vital and effective mental activity has disappeared from sight into a hidden inner world, so that the patient's conscious self is emptied of vital feeling and capacity for action and seems to have become unreal.

The schizoid character often presents with a mask of depression. His typical complaint is of feeling isolated and out of touch, cut off from any meaningful interaction with his fellows, feeling apart, alien, estranged. He often feels that his life is futile and meaningless. The depression is not a real depression, since it lacks the typical inner sense of anger and guilt; rather, it is a reflection of the schizoid withdrawal from external relationships and libidinal detachment. True depression remains essentially object related, but the schizoid character has basically renounced objects.

The schizoid attitude to the external world is one of noninvolvement and more or less passive observation without any emotional engagement. The major schizoid defense against anxiety is emotional detachment, remaining affectively distant, inaccessible, and isolated. The schizoid condition is essentially an attempt to cancel external object relationships and to live in a detached and isolated world. The depressive dilemma is that of anger directed toward a loved object; but the schizoid dilemma is that of destroying and losing the love object by reason of the intense, devouring, hungry, greedy, and needy desire that can never be satisfied or fulfilled. The schizoid can exist neither in a relationship with another human being nor out of one without risking the loss of both the loved object and himself. Loving relationships in this perspective must be viewed as mutually devouring and destructive.

Consequently, from a genetic point of view, the basic defect of the schizoid character is at the earliest levels of the introjection of primary objects. The schizoid personality is formed around the internalization of severely hostile and destructive introjects, which are buried within the psychic structure, where they remain constantly rejecting, indifferent, or hostile. This negative introject becomes a focus for the patient's feelings of inner worthlessness, vileness, destructiveness, and malicious power.

The schizoid pathology often shows markedly narcissistic characteristics. The cold and isolated self-sufficiency of the schizoid personality often expresses an inner grandiosity which reflects severe pathological roots in the grandiose self. This brand of grandiose self-sufficiency often makes such patients relatively inaccessible to therapeutic intervention. The schizoid disorder may be regarded as a severe form of narcissistic disorder, but an important difference from the narcissistic character is that the narcissistic character remains relatively involved with external objects, even though that involvement is narcissistic. The schizoid, however, is involved only in the world of inner objects, so that his pathology becomes, thereby, more severe and less treatable.

The false self organization. The false self is essentially a schizoid condition which is marked by a form of turning away from interpersonal relationships motivated more by the need to preserve a sense of inner autonomy and individuation than by a specific anxiety regarding intimate contact with objects. The idea was originally introduced by Winnicott (1960), who described a split between the false self, that part of the personality which was involved with the external environment and real objects, and the true self, which inhabited the inner core of the personality and was hidden from the scrutiny of observers.

The narcissistic vulnerability underlying the false self organization relates to the persistence of an infantile grandiose ego ideal or grandiose self. The false self individual feels that his early caretakers and later significant objects do not appreciate or accept his grandiose attempts to preserve a sense of inner spontaneity and integrity, and he thus retreats to an inner world to preserve this sense of vitality and spontaneity. It is a retreat to a kind of grandiose self-sufficiency, which is characteristic of schizoid states (Modell, 1975). This same grandiose self-sufficiency is often what motivates these patients to seek treatment. The goal of the treatment for them is to be able to achieve and maintain such isolation and self-sufficiency without the stigma of loss or abandonment.

The as-if personality. Deutsch's original description of the "as if" personality (1942) focused on the patient's impoverishment of emotional relationships. Such patients may be unaware of their lack of normal affective involvements and responses, in which case the disturbance may be perceived by others or may be first detected in treatment, or they may be keenly distressed by their emotional defect, which may be experienced as transitory and fleeting, or as recurring in specific situations, or may persist as an enduring distressing symptom.

The patient's relationships are devoid of warmth, expressions of emotion are formal, and inner experience is excluded. Deutsch compares it to the performance of an actor who is well trained to play a role, but who lacks the necessary spark to make his enactment true to life. She takes pain to distinguish this inner emptiness from the coldness and distance of a more schizoid adjustment: in one there is a flight from reality or a defense against forbidden instinctual drives, while the other seeks external reality in order to avoid anxiety-laden fantasies. In the as-if personality, it is loss of object cathexis that is involved rather than repression. The relationship to the world is maintained on a level of childlike imitation, which expresses an identification with the environment and results in ostensibly good adaptation to reality despite the absence of object cathexis. The result is passivity to the demands of the environment and the highly plastic capacity to mold oneself and one's behavior to such external expectations.

Identity stasis. Developmental experiences, particularly in adolescence, demand a commitment to physical intimacy, to occupational choice, to competition of various sorts, and to a specific form of psychosocial self-definition. The necessity of choice and commitment gives rise to conflicting identifications, each of which narrows the inventory of further choice; movement in any direction may establish binding precedents for psychosocial self-definition. The failure of this commitment results in avoidance of choice, lack of inner definition of self, and external avoidance, isolation and alienation.

Engagement, whether in terms of friendship, competition, sex, or love, becomes a test of self-delineation. Engagement carries with it the constant threat of fusion and loss of identity, which may result in various forms of social isolation, stereotyped or formalized interpersonal relationships, or even the frantic seeking of intimacy with improbable or inappropriate partners. Such attachments, whether as friendships or affairs, become simply attempts to delineate identity by a form of mutual narcissistic mirroring. Such patients have a characteristic difficulty in committing themselves to any line of action or career choice. Particularly difficult is a commitment in the areas of work and love: they find themselves unwilling or unable to make a definitive choice of life partner, just as they find it extremely difficult to decide upon and commit themselves to any line of life endeavor, such as a profession or career. At times, these difficulties in self-definition and commitment are found in one area but not in others. The patient may have a well-defined work life or career, but be unable to make the defining commitment in an intimate love relationship.

Identity stasis represents a form of character pathology which involves an impairment of meaningful identifications and an inability in self-definition. The pathology does not reside in the ego or even superego as much as in the organization and delineation of the self. There is a complex interplay with object relations conflicts, related to the incapacity to define or commit oneself. On a primitive genetic level, however, the underlying fears have to do with the threat imposed in separation-individuation and the surrender of infantile objects and one's dependence on them. Ultimately, commitment to a life, whether of work or of love, means to accept limitations and change, the surrender of infantile omnipotence and narcissistic entitlement, and the ultimate acceptance of the finitude of human existence and death. Maintaining the self in a posture of persistent uncertainty, lack of definition and commitment, is to maintain a condition of continuing possibility and a denial of the necessity to ultimately come to terms with the demands and expectations of reality.

Borderline Development

One of the critical questions that has arisen with regard to borderline psychopathology is whether the borderline deficits and the failures of developmental integration can be attributed to a single phase of development, or whether they are more usefully regarded as manifesting deficits stemming from a number of developmental phases. Following in the wake of Kernberg's characterization of borderline psychopathology (1967), Mahler (1972) emphasized the splitting, the role of separation anxiety, narcissistic fixations, the condensation of oedipal with preoedipal determinants (unresolved preoedipal aggression, particularly), and severe conflicts in object relations, and concluded that these characteristics seem to reflect a failure to resolve the developmental tasks of the rapprochement period and the "rapprochement crisis."

But in a subsequent consideration, Mahler seems to move away from a unitary view.

> In our assessments of the personality organization of narcissistic and borderline child and adult patients, the overriding dominance of one subphase distortion or fixation must not obscure the fact that there are always corrective or pathogenic influences from the other subphases to be considered [Mahler and Kaplan, 1977, p. 84].

An alternative point of view would regard the pathological outcome in any given individual as the result of developmental deficiencies and conflicts stemming from several developmental levels. The developmental derivatives may thus have an impact on the final pathological outcome; but if major deficits can be traced to the developmental vicissitudes of a given developmental period, it remains equally true, and important in the overall evaluation, to assess the extent to which prior developmental phases may have set the stage and contributed to the pathogenic outcome of a particular later stage, as well as to trace the pattern of subsequent influences as they both come to influence and are modified by the developmental process in later phases. Thus, there is no reason why borderline patients may not manifest significant oedipal level conflicts, just as patients with neurotic disorders may reflect the influence of significant preoedipal defects.

Consistent with this view, the "rapprochement crisis," may represent the point in development where the pathology of borderline structural deficits becomes apparent, rather than reflecting their source or origin. Horner (1979) views as oversimplistic and reductionistic the attempt to conceptualize borderline defects as the result of maternal failures associated primarily with the rapprochement phase. The borderline failure to resolve the rapprochement crisis, then, can be seen as more a matter of the influence of preexisting structural deficits that are already in place as the child enters the rapprochement period.

In terms of developmental etiology, the process of developmental organization and integration can be disrupted by a wide variety of causes, but the pathological influence on the organization of psychic structure is the final outcome. Such causes and their attendant failures can impinge on the developmental process at any point along the way. Generally, we presume that the earlier the failure in terms of the infant's developmental experience, the more severe the impact on structural integration and the more malignant the resulting pathology. From an epigenetic perspective, such deficits will have their precedents in terms of developmental influence and their consequent effects on the ensuing flow of developmental resolutions. The achievement of subsequent developmental tasks is inevitably compromised by residues of unresolved primitive fears, anxieties, and structural impediments.

As the child emerges into the oedipal configuration, splitting and the narcissistic alternatives may effect a triangular involvement between the self, a good externalized object, and a bad externalized object. The dynamics involved with such split and narcissistically invested objects may play themselves out in the oedipal situation, or may be expressed in any triangular involvement in which the good object image can be projected onto one individual and the bad object image onto another. As Horner (1979) points out, this gives rise not so much to the classical oedipal configuration involving rivalry and the fear of punishment, but rather has the quality of a masochistic relationship involving a persecuting and frustrating bad object along with an idealized relationship with a good rescuing object. Thus, preoedipal involvements contaminate the oedipal situation, and both contaminate and impede the oedipal resolution. While the oedipal involvement may be sexualized, it remains one essentially based on preoedipal narcissistic investments in objects that act against a truly oedipal constellation and prevent authentically triangular involvements.

I would argue that the pathology found within the borderline spectrum reflects the residual stigmata derived from various levels of developmental difficulty experienced during the course of separation-individuation. The pathology represented by the borderline spectrum does not derive exclusively from a single phase of this process—as, for example, the rapprochement phase—but rather reflects a combination of difficulties arising with varying degrees of emphasis and intensity from all the phases of this developmental process, and, in the more severe levels of borderline psychopathology, reflects residues of unresolved conflicts at an even earlier level (e.g., that of infantile symbiosis).

Psychoses

Needless to say, the most severe developmental defects are found in the psychoses. Such patients reveal severe structural defects in the organization of both ego and superego, a frequently severe failure in the achievement of self-cohesion so that the organization of the patient's inner world and the correlative sense of self is severely vulnerable to regressive pulls. Such patients suffer from inner fragmentation of the organization of the personality so that the fragments of the personality tend to be organized around residues of archaic narcissistic elements which are often reflected in a cold psychotic grandiosity and isolation existing side by side with a sense of devastating worthlessness and nothingness. The object relationships of such patients have not achieved the integration of whole objects so that intolerance of ambiguity is severe and rudimentary, and the patient's object experience remains on the level of need satisfaction and is unable to move beyond the level of part-object involvement. Such patients remain essentially fixated at the most primitive levels of developmental attainment and have been relatively unable to negotiate even the earliest phases of separation-individuation.

The predisposition of psychosis may be seen as reflecting the tenuous balance between positive introjections (which may contribute to a more or less narcissistic and grandiose ego ideal) and the aggressive and destructive introjections (contributing to severely punitive superego components). This delicate balance is maintained by special ego defenses, by forms of character pathology, or even by disorders in psychophysiological functioning through which conflicts may attain some degree of symbolic expression. Narcissistic defenses may take the form of patterns of denial, projection, and distortion. To preserve its fragile position, the ego must deny the presence of painful sensations and any responsibility for them. This may be accomplished by the loss of ability to distinguish between internal and external stimuli. Denial, projection, and distortion serve to alter sensory perceptions so that they become ego-syntonic.

Schizophrenic or even manic-depressive regression or decompensation is often precipitated by loss or the frustration of object-related needs. The response to loss takes the form of a primitive rage which tips the delicate balance between fragile and fragmentary introjective components in the patient's self-organization. The loss of equilibrium between positive and negative introjects leads to an inundation with diffuse and deneutralized destructive feelings which require regression to the point of deepest fixation. This tends to be a primitive, even primary, narcissistic position, in which there is an inundation with diffuse and deneutralized aggressive and destructive impulses. This regressive disorganization is accompanied by a dedifferentiation of boundaries between self and object. It is only in this regressed condition that the patient can achieve the release of internal self-related and external object-related tensions.

Implications for Treatment

While it seems apparent from these considerations that the emergence of the genetic perspective within psychoanalysis has added a unifying and clarifying dimension to psychoanalytic conceptualizations of adult forms of psychopathology, it should not be overlooked that the developmental viewpoint has had a decisive impact on the psychoanalytic treatment process as well. The four areas in which this impact has been most clearly felt are those having to do with analyzability, the understanding of therapeutic effects, the use of parameters, and, finally, the broadening of the area of application of psychoanalytic principles to psychotherapy.

The developmental perspective has contributed significantly to the assessment of analyzability. There has been a much greater appreciation of the role of pregenital genetic factors and their interrelation with higher level oedipal and postoedipal developments. Likewise, the genetic emphasis on early developmental vicissitudes has brought into much clearer focus an appreciation of the nature and quality of developmental defects in both ego and superego. The defects in ego development have particular relevance to the issue of analyzability, since patients who are able successfully to undertake the analytic process and to withstand and utilize the therapeutic regression in analysis require a significant degree of ego strength. This process requires the capacity to tolerate considerable frustration and significant postponements of gratification, to maintain the integrity and coherence of the self in the face of regressive pulls, and to maintain the important distinctions between fantasy and reality, self and other, which make the therapeutic experiencing and reworking of the transference neurosis possible. To put it succinctly, the successful analytic patient must be able to undergo functional regression without a significant degree of structural regression. The assessment of these aspects

of the patient's personality functioning, along with clear delin-
eations of the developmental level and extent of ego impairments and defects, has become a crucial part of the evaluation
and assessment of patients as possible candidates for psychoanalysis.

The developmental perspective has also significantly modified our understanding of the way in which the therapeutic
effects of psychoanalysis are achieved. For a considerable part
of the recent history of psychoanalysis, the understanding of
therapeutic change was dominated by the model of psychic
functioning based on the ego psychological and instinctual processes as envisioned by analytic theorists of the late 1940s and
1950s. The model essentially called for instinctual regression
to the point of neurotic fixation, which would allow for the
opening up and undoing of the basic neurotic conflicts. The
therapeutic effort was directed toward mobilizing and facilitating the building up of ego resources in order to bring them to
bear on the correction of the underlying conflicts. The main
therapeutic tool in this model was the analyst's interpretation.

However, the emergence of the developmental viewpoint
has brought into much clearer focus the dimensions of neurotic
and character-disordered personalities that stem from much
earlier levels of developmental experience than are available to
the higher order interpretive interventions of the analyst. The
therapeutic model, based on interpretation and rooted in the
tripartite theory of id, ego, and superego, serves very well as the
basis for understanding therapeutic change where specifically
intrapsychic neurotic and structural conflicts are in question—that is, conflicts between well-defined and articulated intrapsychic structures. However, with regard to the aspect of
patients' personalities that have suffered developmental defects
at earlier genetic levels and in which the core conflicts lie at an
earlier, narcissistic level or involve basic and often primitive
object-relations conflicts, the utility of the model began to over-
reach itself. Such early developmental defects were described
by Balint (1968) as the area of the "basic fault." Similar empha-
ses have been made in the work of Winnicott (1965), who emphasizes the necessity for therapeutic "holding" as a correlative

of the necessity for "good enough mothering" in the child's developmental experience.

The general paradigm derived from these influences would say that oedipal level structural conflicts may be available for interpretive correction, and even that in significant degree some preoedipal fixations and conflicts may also be corrected by this classic analytic therapeutic modality. But at the same time, frequently there are relatively primitive areas of developmental fixation or failure in many patients which lie beyond the reach of such interpretive devices and call for parameters of therapeutic intervention which have less to do with what the analyst says and more to do with how he says it, how he acts toward the patient, and how he is with the patient in the therapeutic relationship. Recent emphasis has been given to this aspect of the psychoanalytic process by Kohut (1971, 1977) in regard to the treatment of narcissistic personalities, and by Winnicott (1971) in his analysis of the role of play in therapy.

Consequently, the shift in emphasis to early developmental vicissitudes having to do both with narcissism and with early object relationships has led to the introduction of a variety of parameters in an attempt to modify analytic therapy in order to meet the demands imposed by these inherent developmental limitations. There is considerable debate as to how far this enterprise can proceed and to what extent it can be expected to succeed. The ultimate question is whether some developmental defects are not so deeply seated and irretrievably damaged that therapeutic effort cannot in any meaningful way undo the fundamental deficit.

In any case, it seems safe to say that the developmental emphasis and the clarification of certain aspects of the bases of pathology in developmental vicissitudes have had a palpable impact on the application of psychoanalytic understanding and principles to widening areas of psychopathology. This emphasis has brought clearer understanding and formulation to the psychoanalytic view of the psychoses and, within the last two decades, has contributed substantially to the understanding of borderline deficits and narcissistic disorders. In many of these instances there seem to be clear indications that developmental deficits will not allow these forms of psychopathology to be considered potential objects for psychoanalysis itself, but there has unquestionably been a broadening of the range of psychopathology that can be effectively interpreted and understood in terms of basic psychoanalytic principles. In the case of the borderline disorders, particularly in the work of Kernberg, and of the narcissistic disorders in the work of Kohut, important therapeutic modifications have evolved which have significantly changed the therapeutic approaches to such forms of psychopathology.

Postscript

The present account has sketched in rather broad terms the developmental point of view as it has emerged in psychoanalytic thinking and its application to the understanding and interpretation of a variety of forms of adult psychopathology and personality functioning. There has been no attempt to be detailed or exhaustive in this account, since there is little by way of closure or completeness in the current understanding of these concepts. Rather what we have before us is a continuing challenge to further investigation, deepening experience, and the need for continued and extensive exploration of the implication of these principles in various forms of psychopathology. Our understanding to date can be regarded as little more than fragmentary and preliminary.

The achievements and the fruits derived from the application of developmental principles have been significant—in fact, they rate among the most powerful and decisive contributions of psychoanalysis to modern psychiatric understanding. But that is to say little more than that the process has only begun and that the greatest part of the challenge lies before us. If our efforts at this point have been able to do little more than shed a dim light into the dark continent of psychopathology, we can at least hope that increasing growth in clinical experience and in theoretical sophistication will allow us to build on these slender beginnings and thereby bring greater resources of therapeutic wisdom and technical analytic skill to the service of our troubled patients.

References

Abrams, S. (1977), Genetic point of view: Antecedents and transformation. *J. Amer. Psychoanal. Assn.*, 25:417–425.

Balint, M. (1968), *The Basic Fault: Therapeutic Aspects of Regression*. London: Tavistock.

Basch, M.F. (1979), An operational definition of "self." Paper presented to the Boston Psychoanalytic Society, November 16.

Bibring, E. (1937), On the theory of therapeutic results of psychoanalysis. *Internat. J. Psycho-Anal.*, 18:170–189.

——— (1953), The mechanism of depression. In: *Affective Disorders: Psychoanalytic Contributions to Their Study*, ed. P. Greenacre. New York: International Universities Press, pp. 13–48.

Blum, H.P. (1974), The borderline childhood of the Wolf-Man. *J. Amer. Psychoanal. Assn.*, 22:721–742.

Breuer, J., & Freud, S. (1893–1895), Studies on hysteria. *Standard Edition*, 2. London: Hogarth Press, 1955.

Bursten, B. (1973), Some narcissistic personality types. *Internat. J. Psycho-Anal.*, 54:287–300.

Deutsch, H. (1942), Some forms of emotional disturbance and their relationship to schizophrenia. *Psychoanal. Quart.*, 11:301–321.

Freud, A. (1954), The widening scope of psychoanalysis. *J. Amer. Psychoanal. Assn.*, 2:607–620.

——— (1965), *Normality and Pathology in Childhood: Assessments of Development*. New York: International Universities Press.

Freud, S. (1905), Three essays on the theory of sexuality. *Standard Edition*, 7:123–245. London: Hogarth Press, 1957.

——— (1909), Analysis of a phobia in a five-year-old boy. *Standard Edition*, 10:1–149. London: Hogarth Press, 1957.

——— (1913), The claims of psychoanalysis to scientific interest. *Standard Edition*, 13:165–190. London: Hogarth Press, 1955.

——— (1914), On narcissism: An introduction. *Standard Edition*, 14:67–102. London: Hogarth Press, 1957.

——— (1917), Mourning and melancholia. *Standard Edition*, 14:237–260. London: Hogarth Press, 1957.

——— (1918), From the history of an infantile neurosis. *Standard Edition*, 17:1–122. London: Hogarth Press, 1957.

——— (1923), The ego and the id. *Standard Edition*, 19:1–66. London: Hogarth Press, 1961.

Gardiner, M., ed. (1971), *The Wolf-Man by the Wolf-Man*. New York: Basic Books.

Greenacre, P. (1957), The childhood of the artist. *The Psychoanalytic Study of the Child*, 12:47–72. New York: International Universities Press.

Gunderson, J.G., & Singer, M.T. (1975), Defining borderline patients: An overview. *Amer. J. Psychiat.*, 132:1–10.

Hartmann, H. (1956), The development of the ego concept in Freud's work. In: *Essays on Ego Psychology*. New York: International Universities Press, 1964, pp. 268–296.

——— Kris, E. (1945), The genetic approach to psychoanalysis. *The Psychoanalytic Study of the Child*, 1:11–30. New York: International Universities Press.

Hoffer, W. (1952), The mutual influences in the development of ego and id: Earliest stages. *The Psychoanalytic Study of the Child*, 7:31–41. New York: International Universities Press.

Horner, A. (1979), *Object Relations and the Developing Ego in Therapy*. New York: Aronson.

Kernberg, O.F. (1967), Borderline personality organization. *J. Amer. Psychoanal. Assn.*, 15:641–685.

——— (1970), A psychoanalytic classification of character pathology. *J. Amer. Psychoanal. Assn.*, 18:800–822.

Kohut, H. (1971), *The Analysis of the Self*. New York: International Universities Press.

——— (1977), *The Restoration of the Self*. New York: International Universities Press.

Krohn, A. (1974), Borderline "empathy" and differentiation of object representations: A contribution to the psychology of object relations. *Internat. J. Psychoanal. Psychother.*, 3:142–165.

Mahler, M.S. (1952), On child psychosis and schizophrenia: Autistic and symbiotic infantile psychoses. *The Psychoanalytic Study of the Child*, 7:286–305. New York: International Universities Press.

——— (1968), *On Human Symbiosis and the Vicissitudes of Individuation: Vol. 1. Infantile Psychosis*. New York: International Universities Press.

——— (1972), The rapprochement subphase of the separation-individuation process. *Psychoanal. Quart.*, 41:487–506.

——— Kaplan, L. (1977), Developmental aspects in the assessment of narcissistic and so-called borderline personalities. In: *Borderline Personality Disorder: The Concept, the Syndrome, the Patient*, ed. P. Hartocollis. New York: International Universities Press, pp. 71–85.

——— Pine, F., & Bergman, A. (1975), *The Psychological Birth of the Human Infant*. New York: Basic Books.

Meissner, W.W. (1977), The Wolf-Man and the paranoid process. *Annual of Psychoanalysis*, 5:23–74. New York: International Universities Press.

——— (1978), *The Paranoid Process*. New York: Aronson.

——— (1984), *The Borderline Spectrum: Differential Diagnosis and Developmental Issues*. New York: Aronson.

——— (1986a), Can psychoanalysis find its self? *J. Amer. Psychoanal. Assn.*, 34:379–400.

——— (1986b), The earliest internalization. In: *Self and Object Constancy: Clinical and Theoretical Perspectives*, ed. R.F. Lax, S. Bach, & J.A. Burland. New York: Guilford Press, pp. 29–72.

——— (1986c), *Psychotherapy and the Paranoid Process*. New York: Aronson.

——— (1986d), Some notes on Hartmann's ego psychology and the psychology of the self. *Psychoanalytic Inquiry*, 6:499–521.

——— (1988), *Treatment of Patients in the Borderline Spectrum*. Northvale, N.J.: Aronson.

Modell, A.H. (1975), A narcissistic defense against affects and the illusion of self-sufficiency. *Internat. J. Psycho-Anal.*, 56:275–282.

Rapaport, D. (1960), Psychoanalysis as a developmental psychology. In: *The Collected Papers of David Rapaport*, ed. M.M. Gill. New York: Basic Books, pp. 820–852.

———— Gill, M.M. (1959), The points of view and assumptions of metapsychol-
ogy. In: *The Collected Papers of David Rapaport*, ed. M.M. Gill. New York:
Basic Books, 1967, pp. 795–811.
Socarides, C.W. (1974), Homosexuality. In: *American Handbook of Psychiatry*,
Vol. 3, 2nd ed., ed. S. Arieti. New York: Basic Books, pp. 291–315.
———— (1988), *The Preoedipal Origin and Psychoanalytic Therapy of Sexual Perver-
sions*. New York: International Universities Press.
Tartakoff, H.H. (1966), The normal personality in our culture and the Nobel
Prize complex. In: *Psychoanalysis—A General Psychology: Essays in Honor of
Heinz Hartmann*, ed. R.M. Lowenstein, L.M. Newman, M. Schur, & A.
Solnit. New York: International Universities Press, pp. 222–252.
Winnicott, D.W. (1960), Ego distortion in terms of true and false self. In: *The
Maturational Processes and the Facilitating Environment*. New York: Interna-
tional Universities Press, 1965, pp. 140–152.
———— (1965), *The Maturational Processes and the Facilitating Environment*. New
York: International Universities Press.
———— (1971), *Playing and Reality*. New York: Basic Books.
Zetzel, E.R. (1970), The so-called good hysteric. In: *The Capacity for Emotional
Growth*. New York: International Universities Press.
———— (1971), A developmental approach to the borderline patient. *Amer. J.
Psychiat.*, 127:867–871.

9

The Development of Intrapsychic Structures in the Light of Borderline Personality Organization

OTTO F. KERNBERG, M.D.

The principal objective of this chapter is to present the clinical evidence and theoretical background that have led to my conceptualization of intrapsychic developments. The fact that both my clinical data and their theoretical analyses evolved into a high degree of congruence with the theories of Jacobson (1964, 1971), Kernberg (1977b), and the developmental studies of infancy and childhood of Mahler (Mahler and Furer, 1968; Mahler, 1971, 1972; Mahler, Pine, and Bergman, 1975; Mahler and Kaplan, 1977) strengthens, it seems to me, all three conceptualizations and facilitates presenting them in a common frame of reference. In what follows, I apply this common frame of reference, spelling out where complementarity of viewpoints obtain and where divergencies occur.

Psychoanalytic Views of Borderline Conditions: Historical Perspective

In the 1950s, "borderline" patients were perceived as presenting ego weakness, as reflected in the ease with which repressive barriers broke down, and distortions in their ego structures and functions, reflected in severely regressive transference reactions and acting out. The fact that primary-process material, primitive and normally deeply repressed intrapsychic conflicts, would appear in consciousness without permitting introspection, insight, and working through, was puzzling and could not be fully understood with the psychoanalytic models then prevailing. The transferences of these patients were called "narcissistic" because they used the therapist ruthlessly as a transference object to gratify their needs and because they were unable to achieve object constancy (to maintain the representation of the good object under the impact of experiencing frustration from it). The lack of a clear conception of narcissism as a clinical entity at that time, however, prevented further clarification of these transferences. Borderline patients were variously described as presenting a primitive kind of megalomania, intense aggression, magical thinking, paranoid trends, severe mood swings, and a striking tendency to perceive significant others as all good or all bad. Their weakened capacity for evaluating themselves or others realistically raised questions regarding their reality testing, and this, together with the vague and idiosyncratic thinking processes that had been observed in them, and the primitive nature of their interactions with others, suggested that these patients were "prepsychotic." However, it was difficult to differentiate these patients from those presenting unmistakably psychotic reactions and this led some observers to consider them essentially psychotic (Hoch and Polatin, 1949; Hoch and Cattell, 1959).

The traditional approach to development in psychoanalytic thinking was centered on the stages of libidinal development, and there was general agreement that these patients presented preoedipal fixations. Beyond that consensus was a puzzling awareness that, while these patients showed strong oral trends, they simultaneously presented strong aggressive tendencies related to all levels of psychosexual development, and a particular aggressivization of oedipal strivings. Borderline patients, in short, defied efforts to hypothesize the origin of their psychopathology along the lines of ordinary stages of libidinal development. To make matters worse, not only did clinical observations show ego weakness, but the evaluation of defense–impulse constellations often did not permit a clarification of which agency within the tripartite intrapsychic structure (ego, superego, and id) was defending against which impulse within which other agency.

The theoretical confusions regarding borderline patients were matched by the uncertainties regarding their psychotherapeutic and psychoanalytic treatment. Clinical observations regarding treatment failure of these cases with nonmodified psychoanalytic approaches accumulated in the 1950s and led to Knight's (1954) recommendation that these patients be treated with an essentially supportive approach that would contribute to strengthening their ego functions and defenses. Those psychoanalysts who attempted to maintain a strictly psychoanalytic approach began to consider a modification of techniques that culminated in Eissler's (1953) suggestion of using "parameters" of technique. The contradictions between those who preferred a purely supportive approach and those who attempted to apply modified (or even standard) psychoanalytic procedures could not be resolved under conditions in which clinical observations remained unintegrated with theoretical formulations.

New Clinical Evidence and Theoretical Formulations

The psychotherapy research project of the Menninger Foundation (Kernberg, Burnstein, Coyne, Appelbaum, Horvitz, and Voth, 1972) permitted, for the first time, a study of both the effect of various treatment modalities on patients with "ego weakness" and (by providing the most detailed information available, session by session, on forty-two patients who had undergone many months and years of psychoanalysis or psychotherapy) a clarification of the descriptive, psychodynamic, and structural intrapsychic characteristics of these patients. We found that those patients with ego weakness treated with supportive psychotherapy did rather poorly. (This followed the traditional conceptualization that such patients need to reinforce their defensive operations and that, therefore, resolution of resistances by interpretation is risky.) In contrast, many of the same category of patients treated with expressive psychotherapy did remarkably well but, as predicted, did rather poorly with unmodified, standard psychoanalysis. The analysis of the characteristics of expressive psychotherapy that were most effective with patients presenting ego weakness led me to gradually develop a treatment approach specifically geared to patients with borderline personality organization (Kernberg, 1975, 1976a, 1976b). I reached the following conclusions regarding the intrapsychic structure and dynamic characteristics of these patients (Kernberg, 1975, 1977b, 1978b).

Implications of an Ego Organization Centering Around Splitting

In the neurotic patient (a patient suffering from symptomatic neurosis or nonborderline character pathology), the ego's defensive organization centers around repression and other advanced or high-level defensive operations, such as reaction formation, isolation, undoing, intellectualization, and rationalization, all of which protect the ego from intrapsychic conflicts by means of rejecting a drive derivative or its ideational representation, or both, from the conscious ego. In patients with ego weakness, that is, patients with borderline personality organization, in contrast, splitting and other related mechanisms, such as primitive idealization, primitive types of projection (particularly projective identification), denial, omnipotence, and devaluation, protect the ego from conflicts by means of dissociating or actively keeping apart contradictory experiences of the self and of significant others. Under the predominance of splitting and other related mechanisms, contradictory ego states are alternately activated, and, as long as these contradictory ego states can be kept separate from each other, anxiety related to these conflicts is prevented or controlled. However, these defenses, although they protect borderline patients from intrapsychic conflicts, do so at the cost of weakening the patient's ego functioning, thereby reducing their adaptive effectiveness and flexibility.

These same primitive defensive operations are found in psychotic organization (particularly in patients with acute and chronic schizophrenic illness and during active stages of affective illness) and have the function of protecting these patients from further disintegration of the boundaries between self and object. In other words, in psychotic organization, these primitive defenses dilute or fragment intrapsychic conflicts, so that these patients' experiences of violent conflicts with others are reduced; in this process, the potential fusion of the self experience with that of significant objects is also reduced.

That the same defensive operations can be observed in borderline and psychotic patients and yet serve different functions is demonstrated by clinical evidence. When interpretation of splitting and other related mechanisms is made to patients with borderline personality organization, their ego integrates, and their immediate functioning improves, whereas interpreting these defenses to psychotic patients brings about further regression (if only temporarily) in their functioning. This immediate shift into increased or decreased social adaptation and reality testing can be used for diagnostic purposes: whether the patient immediately improves or deteriorates under the effect of such interpretation contributes crucially to the diagnostic differentiation of borderline from psychotic organization.

The conception of an ego organization different from that of the neurotic patient and the similarity of defense mechanisms to those found in psychotic patients suggested to me the hypothesis that the fixation and/or regression of borderline patients occupies a developmental intermediary position or level between that achieved by psychotic and neurotic patients. In itself, such a hypothesis might be considered trivial, but it becomes important if one considers that, in the process, the psychoanalytic approach to borderline personality organization permits us to sharpen the differential diagnosis between borderline conditions and the psychoses. As a result, the older concept of "ego weakness" is now replaced by that of a different level of ego organization and is not simply an "absence" or "weakness" of defensive operations and ego functioning.

These findings did not by themselves resolve the question of whether ego organization of borderline patients represented an alternative model of ego organization to that of neurotic and normal persons, or a fixation at a normally intermediary stage of development between neurosis and psychosis. At issue here is a qualitative rather than a merely quantitative difference. Another related question to ask is: Does an ego organization centering around splitting reflect an early normal developmental stage or an abnormal deviation? And still another question is: If the fixation and/or regression of borderline patients reflects an early normal period of development, what are the normal time schedules for this developmental process and the conditions under which fixation and/or regression to it obtain? In searching for answers to these questions, I was led to another set of observations, namely, the qualitative characteristics of transferences of borderline patients and the implications of these for the analysis of their pathology of internalized object relations.

Implications of the Syndrome of Identity Diffusion

Patients with "ego weakness" who eventually were diagnosed as presenting borderline personality organization, typically presented the syndrome of identity diffusion originally described by Erikson (1956, 1959). Identity diffusion, or lack of integration of a normal sense of identity, is represented by a poorly integrated concept of the self and of significant others. It is reflected typically in a chronic subjective experience of emptiness, contradictory self-perceptions, contradictory behavior that cannot be integrated in an emotionally meaningful way, and shallow, flat, impoverished perception of others.

Diagnostically, identity diffusion is detected by the patient's inability to convey to an interviewer the patient's significant interactions with others. The interviewer finds he cannot emotionally empathize with the patient's conception of himself and of others in such interactions (in contrast to his ability to detect clearly enough the primitive transference reactions in his current interaction with the patient). There are frequently such gross contradictions in the descriptions the patient gives of himself or of significant others that he and other people sound more like caricatures than like real people.

Similarly, the quality of object relations of borderline patients is severely affected; that is, the stability and depth, as manifested by warmth, dedication, concern, and tactfulness of the patient's relations with significant others. Additional qualitative aspects are his lack of empathy with or understanding of others, and his difficulties in maintaining a relationship when it is invaded by conflicts or frustration. The quality of object relations is largely dependent on identity integration, which includes not only the degree of moment-to-moment integration but also the temporal continuity of the patient's concept of himself and others.

Normally, we experience ourselves consistently throughout time and under varying circumstances and with different people; and we experience conflict when contradictions in our self-concept emerge. The same applies to our experience of others. But in borderline personality organization, this temporal continuity is lost, and these patients have little capacity for a realistic evaluation of others. The borderline patient's long-term relations with others, particularly those with whom he is most intimately related, are characterized by an increasingly distorted perception of them. He fails to achieve real empathy with others; his relations are chaotic or shallow; and intimate relations are usually contaminated by the typical condensation of genital and pregenital conflicts that we shall examine below.

In contrast, patients with neurotic personality structure have a solid sense of self and an in-depth understanding of significant others. The neurotic patient has the capacity for total object relations that reflects an integration of "good" and "bad" aspects of others, as well as an integration of such contradictory aspects in himself.

In diagnostic interviews, such patients have a capacity to convey a live and real picture of themselves interacting with significant others so that the diagnostician can visualize their world. With borderline patients, in contrast, the diagnostician typically gets a chaotic mixture of the patient's and others' behaviors and is unable to re-create the patient's object world in his own mind.

The search for developmental antecedents for this state of affairs in borderline patients at first brought about further confusion. To begin with, Erikson (1956, 1959) had gradually moved the timetable for the consolidation of ego identity to adolescence, thus confusing his own description of the differences between identity diffusion (a profound disturbance originating in early childhood) and identity crisis (a characteristic of adolescence). This raised the question as to what extent borderline patients represent an abnormal solution to the developmental crises that emerge in adolescence.

Careful evaluation of identity diffusion in adolescence led me (1978b) to conclude—in agreement with Masterson's (1967) earlier work—that adolescent patients with various degrees of symptomatic neuroses and nonborderline character pathology do not present the syndrome of identity diffusion, and that, even when an adolescent patient presents with a chaotic life-style or life situation, the diagnostic interview may produce evidence, in spite of severe neurotic conflicts with his environment, of a solid conception of the self and of significant others. In contrast, the syndrome of identity diffusion appears regularly in patients who present all other descriptive, structural, and dynamic characteristics of borderline conditions. In fact, a surprising finding has been how very normal adolescents without borderline personality organization are and how strikingly different their developmental crises are from the chronic chaos and confusion that reflect the syndrome of identity diffusion (Offer, 1971, 1973; Kernberg, 1975).

Beyond this finding, however, the questions remained: What is the relation of identity diffusion to the defensive organization of the ego characteristic of borderline patients? And what developmental stage, normal or abnormal, is involved? Three related findings seemed to clarify this issue. The first was the analysis of superego and ego pathology in borderline adolescent patients carried out by Jacobson (1964). Her findings led her to hypothesize a relation between lack of integration of ego and superego as well as a persistence of nonintegrated internalized object relations as unintegrated components of ego and superego structures. The second finding was the clinical observation of the remarkable differences between the transferences of borderline and psychotic patients, in spite of their both presenting identity diffusion (Kernberg, 1966, 1968, 1975, 1977a). The third was Mahler's description of the differences between the psychopathology of symbiotic psychosis and that of the stage of separation–individuation, particularly the rapprochement subphase (Mahler and Furer, 1968; Mahler, 1971, 1972; Mahler et al., 1975).

My clinical observations indicated a constant relationship in psychotic patients between the loss of reality testing and the development of transferences in which fusion or merger phenomena appeared; a similar constant relationship emerged between maintenance of reality testing, typical of borderline patients, and the absence of merger in the transference of these patients. To focus first on the merger phenomena: psychotic patients, particularly at advanced stages of their psychotherapeutic treatment, present fusion experiences with the therapist; that is, they feel a common identity with him. For example, the psychotic patient may present a delusional conviction that the therapist experiences the same emotions or bodily processes as he does and may automatically assume that any idea expressed by the therapist is the patient's own idea. This development creates a situation in the transference in which there seems to be a confusion between patient and therapist, an absence of any boundary between them, while, simultaneously, external reality seems to fade into the background or to become unavailable. This may be a confusing, disturbing, or painful experience for the therapist who is not prepared to enter into this kind of psychotherapeutic relationship with psychotic patients. The patient may experience intense, rageful panic or messianic fulfillment at such times (Searles, 1965). In contrast, borderline patients, even when they regress to transference psychosis, do experience a boundary of some sort between themselves and the therapist. It is as if the patient maintained a sense of being different from the therapist at all times, but, alternatively, he and the therapist were interchanging aspects of their personalities. By the same token, a primitive "part-object" relationship is activated that can be diagnosed as a "nonmetabolized," dissociated aspect of a total object relation that has been defensively split into opposite components. There is a repetitive, alternating, at times quite chaotic "interchange" of personality attributes partly projected and partly enacted by the patient, but never a true experience of fusion or merger.

The clinical importance of this radical difference between the regressive transferences of borderline conditions and truly psychotic transference was not fully understood until the observations just mentioned and the analysis of symbiotic psychosis and abnormal outcome of the rapprochement subphase by Mahler, together with the clarification of "psychotic identification" by Jacobson (1964), could be integrated into a common

frame. In the process, crucial questions were also clarified regarding the developmental preconditions of borderline personality organization (Kernberg, 1979a).

Jacobson (1954, 1964) suggested that intrapsychic life
starts out as a primary psychophysiological self within which
ego and id are not yet differentiated, and within which aggression and libido are undifferentiated as well. The first intrapsychic structure is a fused representation of self and object which
evolves gradually under the impact of the relationship between
mother and infant. The first few weeks of life, before such a
primary self–object representation is consolidated, constitutes
the earliest—to use Mahler's terms—presymbiotic or autistic
phase of development. Insofar as that fused structure represents the origin of both self and object representations, libidinal
investment in the self and in objects is originally one process.

Mahler (Mahler and Furer, 1968) described the symbiotic
phase of development characterized by the primary fused
self–object representation that gradually differentiates into the
self representation and the object representation. It is this differentiation that contributes importantly to the infant's ability
to differentiate between self and the external world. Jacobson
described the defensive refusion of libidinally invested self and
object representations as the earliest protection against painful
experience, giving rise, when this process is excessively or
pathologically maintained, to what will later become psychotic
identifications characteristic of symbiotic psychosis of childhood, and of affective psychosis and schizophrenia in adulthood (Jacobson, 1954, 1964, 1967, 1971). Eventually, the separation of self and object representations becomes stabilized,
and the stage of separation–individuation (Mahler, 1971, 1972;
Mahler et al., 1975) is characterized by differentiated, but not
yet integrated, representations of self and of objects. Finally,
partial aspects of self and object representations become integrated and lead to the establishment of the next phase, "on the
road to object constancy" (Mahler et al., 1975). Mahler (1971)
proposed that during the final or rapprochement subphase of
the separation–individuation process, children whose normal
resolution of the rapprochement crisis failed may develop a
"bad" introject, which becomes infiltrated with the derivatives

of aggressive drive and may evolve into a more or less permanent split of the object world into "good" and "bad" objects, a process she says is characteristic of most cases of borderline transference.

Combining Mahler's and Jacobson's formulations with my own observations, I concluded (Kernberg, 1975) that the early ego has to accomplish two tasks in rapid succession. It must differentiate self representations from object representations, and it must integrate libidinally determined and aggressively determined self and object representations. The first task is accomplished in part under the influence of the development of the apparatuses of primary autonomy; but it fails for the most part in the psychoses, because a pathological fusion or refusion of self and object representations results in a failure in the differentiation of ego boundaries and, therefore, in the differentiation of self from nonself. In contrast, with the borderline personality organization, differentiation of self from object representations has occurred to a sufficient degree to permit the establishment of ego boundaries and a concomitant differentiation of self from others. The second task, however, of integrating self and object representations, built up under the influence of libidinal drive derivatives and their related affects, with their corresponding self and object representations built up under the influence of aggressive drive derivatives and their related affects, fails to a great extent in borderline patients, mainly because of the pathological predominance of pregenital aggression. The resulting lack of synthesis of contradictory self and object representations interferes with the integration of the self-concept and with the establishment of object constancy or "total" object relations.

The integrated self concept and the related integrated represntations of objects jointly constitute ego identity in its broadest sense. A stable ego identity, in turn, becomes a crucial determinant of the stability, integration, and flexibility of the ego and also influences the full development of higher level superego functions. This is typical of neurotic personality structure and normality. In contrast, failure to integrate the libidinally determined and the aggressively determined self and object representations is the major cause for nonpsychotic ego disturbances, which, in turn, affect analyzability and the general treatment requirements for borderline patients. Although such a lack of integration derives from pathological predominance of aggressively determined self and object representations and the related failure to establish a sufficiently strong ego core, these conditions contrast markedly with the psychoses, in which self representations have not yet been differentiated from object representations.

In borderline conditions, there is at least sufficient differentiation between self and object representations for the establishment of firm ego boundaries and the related capacity for reality testing. The problem is that the intensity of the aggression with which the self and object representations are imbued and the intensity with which the all-good self and object representations are defensively idealized make integration impossible. Bringing together diametrically opposed loving and hateful images of the self and of significant others would trigger unbearable anxiety and guilt because of the implicit danger to the good internal and external object relations; therefore, there is an active defensive separation of such contradictory self and object representations. In other words, primitive dissociation or splitting becomes a major defensive operation. As a consequence, splitting, which is a normal characteristic of very early development, is used actively during rapprochement to separate contradictory ego states; the other defensive operations linked to splitting reinforce it and protect the ego from unbearable conflicts between love and hatred by sacrificing its growing integration.

A further consequence of this development is a chronic overdependence on external objects (in an effort to achieve some continuity in interactions, thoughts, and feeling in relating to them) in the presence of lack of integration of the self concept; that is, the syndrome of identity diffusion. Moreover, contradictory character traits develop, reflecting the contradictory self and object representations, further creating chaos in the interpersonal relationships of the future borderline patient. Superego integration also suffers because the guiding function of an integrated ego identity is missing; contradictions between exaggerated, all-good ideal object representations and extremely sadistic, all-bad superego forerunners interfere with superego integration.

Therefore, superego functions, which would normally facilitate ego integration, are missing, reinforcing the pathological consequences of excessive reprojection of superego nuclei in the form of paranoid trends. Furthermore, a lack of integration of object representations interferes with deepening of empathy with others as individuals in their own right, and lack of integration of the self concept further interferes with full emotional understanding of other human beings. The end result is defective object constancy or incapacity to establish total object relations.

Finally, because of the weakness of ego and superego integration, nonspecific aspects of ego strength (anxiety tolerance, impulse control, sublimatory potential) suffer. The overall outcome, which we see in borderline conditions, is that typical transferences evolve that reflect contradictory ego states; these activate primitive internalized object relations within a psychic matrix that has not achieved a clear differentiation of ego, superego, and id.

Developmentally then, the pathology of internalized object relations and the primitive organization of the ego around splitting appeared as mutually related and as reflecting a stage of development preceding the establishment of object constancy, but later than the symbiotic stage of development. Mahler's proposed timetable for the normal sequence of autistic, symbiotic, separation–individuation, and object-constancy phases thus permits us to link borderline pathology to a stage of development that covers, broadly speaking, the period from the first half of the second year to the second half of the third year of life (Mahler, 1971, 1972; Mahler et al., 1975), and to analyze the antecedents of borderline conditions in observable, behavioral, and developmental terms, as well as in terms of the assumed intrapsychic developments characteristic of these early stages.

Implications of the Presence or Absence of Reality Testing

From what I have said so far, the dimensions of (1) the predominant type of defensive organization of the ego (centering around splitting or around repression) and (2) ego identity

(identity diffusion or identity integration) differentiate border-line personality organization from neurotic organization and normality. In fact, for practical purposes, it is the presence or absence of identity diffusion that most clearly differentiates borderline conditions from nonborderline symptomatic neuroses and character pathology. The evaluation of defensive organization, in contrast, reveals patients with various mixtures of defensive constellations and lends itself much less to a clear differential diagnosis of borderline conditions from neurotic pathology in the initial interviews.

There are, however, exceptions to this rule. For example, narcissistic personalities, who have developed a pathological grandiose self that obscures their underlying identity diffusion, still reflect the predominance of a constellation of primitive defensive operations. Thus, the combination of an apparently solid (yet subtly grandiose) identity and the predominance of a constellation of primitive defensive operations centering around splitting facilitates the diagnosis of narcissistic personality, structurally related to borderline personality organization (although the nonspecific manifestations of ego weakness referred to before are absent in many narcissistic personalities). In addition, to focus on primitive defensive operations in the interaction of the patient and the interviewer contributes to the diagnosis of reality testing, our main point now in question.

Reality testing is an ego function that permits the differential diagnosis of borderline personality organization from psychotic organization. It is a key element in differentiating atypical cases of chronic schizophrenic reaction from borderline personality organization, and an important contribution stemming from psychoanalytic exploration of the personality to descriptive diagnosis in psychiatry. The crucial work of Frosch (1964) in differentiating reality testing from the subjective experience of reality and from the relationship to reality facilitated the descriptive analysis of this ego function. It was then possible, as mentioned before, to observe the constant relation between reality testing and the capacity to develop nonmerger transferences in the middle of severe transference regression. The constancy of this relationship led me to think of reality testing as a general structural characteristic of the ego rather than as a specific ego function.

Reality testing, as I have defined it operationally on the basis of Frosch's work (Kernberg, 1977b), is defined by the capacity to differentiate self from nonself, intrapsychic from external origins of perceptions and stimuli, and the capacity to evaluate realistically one's own affect, behavior, and thought content in terms of ordinary social norms. Clinically, reality testing is recognized by (1) the absence of hallucinations and delusions; (2) the absence of grossly inappropriate or bizarre affect, thought content, or behavior; (3) the patient's capacity to empathize with and clarify the diagnostician's observations of what to him seem inappropriate or puzzling aspects of the patient's affect, behavior, or thought content within the context of their immediate social interaction.

Reality testing, thus defined, needs to be differentiated from alterations in the subjective experience of reality, which may be present at some time in any patient with psychological distress, and from the alteration of the relation to reality that is present in all character pathology, as well as in more regressive, psychotic conditions, and is by itself of diagnostic value only in very extreme forms.

Jacobson (1964) was the first to suggest that the differentiation of self from object representations is a structural intrapsychic precondition for the development of reality testing. The patient's potential capacity for maintaining reality testing, even in the middle of severe transference regression, permits the therapist to maintain an analytic attitude and an essentially psychoanalytic approach to borderline patients. This approach requires that formulations of interpretations with these patients be carried out, beginning with the testing of present reality testing and, if it seems weakened, with an interpretation of the primitive defensive operations that are affecting it. As mentioned before, interpretation of primitive defenses facilitates the restoration of reality testing in the treatment of borderline conditions, but in psychotic structure induces further loss of reality testing and the activation of merger phenomena in the transference.

Viewed in terms of development, the ability to test reality indicates that internalized object relations consisting of differentiated self and object representations have been established; that is, the subject has developed beyond the symbiotic phase and into the phase of separation–individuation. Jointly, reality testing, identity diffusion, and the predominance of a defensive constellation centering around splitting characterize borderline personality organization. These three features are mutually related and point to a definite period of intrapsychic development, namely, the rapprochement subphase within the period of separation–individuation. In the light of developmental studies carried out by Mahler (1971, 1972), borderline structure is particularly related to pathological resolutions of the rapprochement subphase.

On the basis of what has been said so far, borderline personality organization derives from the pathological resolution of the rapprochement subphase of separation–individuation. The borderline personality is fixated at what constituted normal characteristics at an early stage of development; but pathological consequences derived from that fixation, expressed in additional intrapsychic developments ("genetic" sequences in contrast to "developmental" sequences), codetermine the clinical characteristics of the final structural organization. I will now examine these genetic and clinical features and, in the process, reexamine some of the questions raised at the beginning of this paper and not yet accounted for by the structural and developmental analysis presented so far.

The Relationship Between Developmental, Genetic, and Structural Characteristics

I mentioned earlier that patients with identity diffusion have difficulty in conveying to the therapist a realistic in-depth picture of themselves and of significant others in their lives, making it difficult for the therapist to re-create, in his own mind, the patient's internal world of object relations and his external reality. In fact, in the initial diagnostic evaluation, a study of the patient's personality in terms of his functioning at home, in his work or study, his sexual life, family life, and his social, cultural, or other interests with the diagnostician, and, simultaneously, of his interactions in the here and now discloses that nonpsychotic and nonorganic patients tend to fall into two types.

One type, representing the patient with a well-integrated personality, a strong ego, and firm identity integration, permits the diagnostician to shift rapidly from the patient's symptoms to his current emotional life and, upon inquiry about his personality features, to discover important information regarding the patient's present and past interactions with significant others—particularly his family members. The therapist, therefore, finds it relatively easy to link the patient's symptoms and personality with his past history. The immediate transference developments in such a case, however, are subtle; it is often hard to evaluate, in such relatively well-functioning patients, what the immediate predominant defenses are: characterological defenses in these patients are manifest in subtle, yet strong, resistances, which are well rationalized.

In contrast, patients with severe characterological illness, particularly the borderline conditions, tend to bring about a different development in the early hours of diagnostic evaluation, when the diagnostician attempts to evaluate their current personality functioning. Their symptoms tend to merge with diffuse, generalized, chaotic difficulties in living, reflecting serious personality malfunctioning. The difficulty or impossibility of obtaining an integrated view of the patient's personality and of the personalities of the most significant others in his life, as mentioned earlier, reflects the syndrome of identity diffusion and the related serious pathology of object relations of these patients.

At the same time, however, these patients show serious distortions in the immediate diagnostician–patient interaction. Inappropriate behavior, affects, or thoughts, without being psychotic or delusional, reflect the distortion in all of the patients' interactions and the incapacity for tactfulness, subtle self-awareness, introspection, and realistic motivation for change that is found in better functioning patients. Here we find an immediate activation of primitive defensive operations and primitive object relations in the therapeutic interaction and, by the same token, the possibility of rapidly diagnosing early, predominant transference patterns and their current dynamic implications. Here, in other words, intrapsychic conflicts are not repressed or unconscious but are largely conscious and dissociated, and expressed in contradictory transference dispositions and defenses against them.

Paradoxically, therefore, it is relatively easy to have direct access to borderline patients' current predominant intrapsychic conflicts, defensive operations, and transference developments, but these patients' past histories are usually unreliable and highly distorted, owing to the influence of their psychopathology. Therefore, an effort to link current conflicts with past, genetic material is a highly questionable procedure.

What holds true for early contacts with the borderline patient becomes reconfirmed throughout the treatment. Efforts to work analytically with the transference reveal that in borderline patients the genetic links between the transference (current structural organization) and the antecedent childhood experiences (early development) are much less direct, much less available than is true for the standard psychoanalytic case, and reconstructions can be made only tentatively. (This is regardless of whether it takes place in psychoanalytic psychotherapy along the lines I have defined elsewhere [Kernberg, 1975, 1976a, 1978a] or in psychoanalysis proper.) Generally speaking, the sicker the patient, the more indirect and complex is the road from current transference developments to the genetic or intrapsychic history. Early childhood experiences and actual development can be reconstructed only in advanced stages of the treatment of patients who demonstrate such early or premature primitive transference developments. This is why I have stressed the danger of mechanically equating primitive transferences with "early" object relations and have cautioned against the temptation to reconstruct the earliest intrapsychic development on the basis of primitive transference manifestations (1979a, 1979b).

The underlying reason for this indirect relation between current transference—reflecting the predominant structuralization of the patient's internalized object relations—and antecedent developmental features resides, I think, in the vicissitudes of fixated part-object relations. Patients dominated by part-object relations tend to maintain fantastic (in the sense of primitive, early, and diffuse), highly unrealistic affect states reflecting such relations, and to distort later, real interactions with external objects in the light of such earlier split-off internalized object relations. These patients create vicious cycles of projective mechanisms and reinternalization of highly distorted object relations which reconfirm and further distort their antecedent primitive part-object relations.

Two fundamental consequences derive from this progressive distortion of later object relations by fixation at a state of lack of integration of earlier ones. First, a distortion of intrapsychic development occurs that makes it desirable to delay the reconstruction of conflicts of the early preoedipal stages (linked to the origin of borderline personality organization) to the advanced phases of the treatment, after the condensation of preoedipal and oedipal conflicts has gradually been resolved. Therefore, a simplistic application in the early stages of treatment of developmental hypotheses along the lines of Mahler's formulations would do injustice to the complexity and subtlety of her contributions. By the same token, confirmatory evidence of the relationship between early developmental failure in the rapprochement subphase and borderline personality organization can only become available in advanced stages of intensive psychotherapy with adult patients. Second, early pathology of object relations results in an abnormal entrance to the oedipal phase. This leads to a distortion of oedipal processes—the characteristic condensation of preoedipal and oedipal features presented by borderline patients—and explains the failure of earlier attempts to analyze borderline conditions in terms of the classical model of sequential stages of libidinal development.

The earlier the development, fixation, or regression of psychopathology, the more seriously it affects not only the development of ego and superego structures but also the capacity for entering a normal oedipal situation. Under these conditions, preoedipal conflicts, particularly a predominance of conflicts around preoedipal aggression, infiltrate all object relations. In addition to reinforcing and fixating primitive defensive operations centering around splitting, excessive aggression also contaminates the latter object-relations characteristics of the Oedipus complex.

This creates characteristic distortions in the oedipal constellation, reflected in the following frequent findings: excessive splitting of the preoedipal maternal image may be complicated by defensive devaluation, fear, and hatred of the oedipal mother later on, and an unstable idealization of the oedipal father that easily breaks down and is replaced by further splitting of father's image. This reinforces oedipal rivalry in men and penis envy in women and, in both sexes, excessive fear and guilt over sexuality and the search for desexualized and idealized relationships that influence the development of homosexuality. A predominance of sadistic and masochistic components in genital strivings is another consequence of this situation. Under these circumstances, the differentiation of parental images along sexual lines, which is typical for triangular oedipal relationships, may be complicated by splitting mechanisms, which make one sex good and the other bad, or by pathological fusion of the idealized or threatening aspects of both sexes, so that unrealistic combined father–mother images develop; the "phallic mother" is only one example of these developments.

I am stressing that the consequences of severe preoedipal conflicts include pathological development of oedipal conflicts, but not an absence of them. I believe that the controversy regarding the predominance of oedipal versus preoedipal conflicts in borderline personality organization really obscures some of the significant issues. The question is not the presence or absence of oedipal conflicts but the degree to which preoedipal features have distorted the oedipal constellation and have left important imprints on character formation (Blum, 1977). As I mentioned before, it is only at advanced stages of resolution of severe psychopathologies stemming from the preoedipal period that one may, indeed, find a "clearing up" of the condensed oedipal–preoedipal transference. Only then are early dyadic relationships with the preoedipal mother reactivated in relatively undistorted ways; only then do conflicts between the search for closeness and even merger and the need for autonomy (or even differentiation) appear relatively directly in the transference.

In this connection, it is important to distinguish between actual regression to modes of functioning that predate object constancy and patients' fantasies about such regression (Kernberg, 1979b). For example, patients' fantasies about "merger" with the analyst may have many meanings and do not by themselves indicate that a regression to a symbiotic or an early stage of differentiation of self has taken place. Such "merger" fantasies may regressively express wishes for total dependence, or sexual impulses, or efforts to escape from guilt feelings by blurring the responsibility of patient and analyst.

The Central Role of Internalized Object Relations in Structural Development

The analysis of the relationships between the structural characteristics of borderline personality organization and its developmental and genetic origins has led us to an object-relations approach within a psychoanalytic framework. Object-relations theory, a general term for this special approach within psychoanalysis, examines metapsychological and clinical issues in terms of the vicissitudes of internalized object relations. Object-relations theory considers the psychic apparatus as originating in the earliest stage of a sequence of internalizations of object relations.

The developmental stages of internalized object relations I have referred to here (i.e., infantile autism, symbiosis, separation–individuation, and object constancy) reflect the earliest structures of the psychic apparatus. Discrete units of self representation, object representation, and an affect disposition linking them are the basic substructures of these early developmental stages and will gradually evolve into more complex substructures (such as real-self and ideal-self, and real-object and ideal-object representations).

This process, which, roughly speaking, covers the first three years of life, includes the earliest substructures of the psychic apparatus that will gradually differentiate and eventually become integrated into ego, superego, and id.

In this context, Jacobson's, Mahler's, and my own conceptions have in common the assumption that the earliest internalization processes have dyadic features, that is, a self–object polarity, even when self and object representations are not yet differentiated; by the same token, all future developmental steps also imply dyadic internalizations, that is, internalization not only of an object as an object representation but of an interaction of the self with the object, which is why I consider units of self and object representations (and the affect dispositions linking them) as the basic building blocks of further developments of internalized object and self representations, and later on, of the overall tripartite structure (ego, superego, and id).

Psychoanalytic object relations theory, as defined, is an integral part of contemporary ego psychology. It is not an additional metapsychological viewpoint, nor is it opposed to the structural, development–genetic, dynamic, economic, and adaptive viewpoints. Rather, it represents a special approach or focus within the structural viewpoint that links structure more closely with developmental, genetic, and dynamic aspects of mental functioning. It occupies an intermediary realm between psychoanalytic metapsychology, on the one hand, and direct clinical formulations in the psychoanalytic situation, on the other. I have attempted here to illustrate one use of this approach, namely, the linkage between the structural characteristics of borderline personality organization and its genetic and developmental antecedents.

References

Blum, H. (1977), The prototype of preoedipal reconstruction. *J. Amer. Psychoanal. Assn.*, 25:757–785.

Eissler, K.R. (1953), The effects of the structure of the ego on psychoanalytic technique. *J. Amer. Psychoanal. Assn.*, 1:104–143.

Erikson, E.H. (1956), The problem of ego identity. *J. Amer. Psychoanal. Assn.*, 4:56–121.

——— (1959), Identity and the Life Cycle. *Psychological Issues*, Monograph 1. New York: International Universities Press.

Frosch, J. (1964), The psychotic character: Clinical psychiatric considerations. *Psychiat. Quart.*, 38:91–96.

Hoch, P., & Cattell, J.P. (1959), The diagnosis of pseudoneurotic schizophrenia. *Psychiat. Quart.*, 33:17–43.

——— Polatin, R. (1949), Pseudoneurotic forms of schizophrenia. *Psychiat. Quart.*, 23:248–276.

Jacobson, E. (1954), Contribution to the metapsychology of psychotic identification. *J. Amer. Psychoanal. Assn.*, 2:239–262.

—— (1964), *The Self and the Object World*. New York: International Universities Press.

—— (1967), *Psychotic Conflict and Reality*. New York: International Universities Press.

—— (1971), *Depression: Comparative Studies of Normal, Neurotic, and Psychotic Conditions*. New York: International Universities Press.

Kernberg, O. (1966), Structural derivatives of object relationships. *Internat. J. Psycho-Anal.*, 47:236–253.

—— (1968), The treatment of patients with borderline personality organization. *Internat. J. Psycho-Anal.*, 49:600–619.

—— (1975), *Borderline Conditions and Pathological Narcissism*. New York: Jason Aronson, pp. 227–343.

—— (1976a), Transference and countertransference in the treatment of borderline patients. In: *Object Relations Theory and Clinical Psychoanalysis*. New York: Jason Aronson, pp. 161–184.

—— (1976b), Technical considerations in the treatment of borderline personality organization. *J. Amer. Psychoanal. Assn.*, 24:795–829.

—— (1977a), Clinical observations regarding the diagnosis, prognosis, and intensive treatment of chronic schizophrenic patients. In: *Long-term Treatments of Psychotic States*, ed. C. Chiland & P. Bequart. New York: Human Sciences Press, pp. 332–360.

—— (1977b), The structural diagnosis of borderline personality organization. In: *Borderline Personality Disorders*, ed. P. Hartocollis. New York: International Universities Press, pp. 87–121.

—— (1978a), Contrasting approaches to the treatment of borderline conditions. In: *New Perspectives in Psychotherapy of the Borderline Adult*, ed. J. Masterson. New York: Brunner/Mazel, pp. 77–104.

—— (1978b), The diagnosis of borderline conditions in adolescence. In: *Adolescent Psychiatry, Vol. 6, Developmental and Clinical Studies*, ed. S.C. Feinstein & P.L. Giovacchini. Chicago: University of Chicago Press, 16:298–319.

—— (1979a), The contributions of Edith Jacobson: An overview. *J. Amer. Psychoanal. Assn.*, 27:793–819.

—— (1979b), Some implications of object relations theory for psychoanalytic technique. *J. Amer. Psychoanal. Assn.*, 27(Suppl.):207–239.

—— Burstein, E., Coyne, L., Appelbaum, A., Horwitz, L., & Voth, H. (1972), Psychotherapy and psychoanalysis: Final report of the Menninger Foundation's psychotherapy research project. *Bull. Menn. Clinic*, 36:1–275.

Knight, R.P. (1954), Borderline states. In: *Psychoanalytic Psychiatry and Psychology*, ed. R.P. Knight & C.R. Friedman. New York: International Universities Press, pp. 97–109.

Mahler, M. (1971), A study of the separation-individuation process and its possible application to borderline phenomena in the psychoanalytic situation. *The Psychoanalytic Study of the Child*, 26:403–424. New York: Quadrangle.

—— (1972), Rapprochement subphase of the separation-individuation process. *Psychoanal. Quart.*, 41:487–506.

—— Furer, M. (1968), *On Human Symbiosis and the Vicissitudes of Individuation, Vol. I, Infantile Psychosis*. New York: International Universities Press.

—— Kaplan, L. (1977), Developmental aspects in the assessment of narcissistic and so-called borderline personalities. In: *Borderline Personality Disorders*, ed. P. Hartocollis. New York: International Universities Press, pp. 71–85.

—— Pine, F., & Bergman, A. (1975), *The Psychological Birth of the Human Infant*. New York: Basic Books, 1975.

Masterson, J. (1967), *The Psychiatric Dilemma of Adolescence*. Boston: Little, Brown.

Offer, D. (1971), Rebellion and anti-social behavior. *Amer. J. Psychoanal.*, 31:13–19.

—— (1973), *Psychological World of the Teen-ager: A Study of Normal Adolescent Boys*. New York: Harper & Row.

Searles, H.F. (1965), *Collected Papers on Schizophrenia and Related Subjects*. New York: International Universities Press.

10

The Problem of Suicide Throughout the
Course of Life

PAUL C. HOLINGER, M.D.

Introduction

It is difficult to overestimate the importance of suicide as a clinical and societal concern. In the United States, the current number of suicides is over 30,000 per year. When one considers the number of years of life lost through suicide; that suicide may be probably underreported by as much as two to three times; that there are five to ten times as many suicide attempts as there are suicides, the numerical enormity of the problem seems to be beyond one's emotional and cognitive grasp. In addition, other less overt but nonetheless self-destructive behaviors are related to suicide, such as many accidents and homicides.

Yet these numerical analyses can leave one feeling distant from the problem and the tragedy. As clinicians we feel much closer to the emotional impact of suicide when we consider just a single case, and when we become aware of the immediate and long-term impact of the suicide on family, children or parents, friends, community, and therapist.

The purpose of this paper is to present a brief examination of suicide throughout the various developmental phases of the life cycle. An attempt will be made to describe the epidemiologic data and a biopsychosocial understanding of suicide by various developmental stages, but it will not be a comprehensive literature review (e.g., see Blumenthal and Kupfer [1990]).

Much pioneering clinical work on suicide was accomplished by Freud (1917), Zilboorg (1937), Menninger (1938),

and Shneidman (1975). The major breakthrough in understanding suicide on an epidemiologic level was accomplished by
Durkheim (1897). Increasing attention is being paid to both
macroanalyses as well as microanalyses of suicide, as epidemiologic and clinical understanding of suicide have attained greater
sophistication. It now appears possible to achieve some degree
of integration of dynamic and epidemiologic data, i.e., of psychoanalytic and epidemiologic frameworks. As Klerman and
Weissman (1984) noted: "Projecting into the future, we will
likely see a further convergence between epidemiology and
clinical psychiatry, personality research, and developmental approaches to the life cycle" (p. 342).

Epidemiologic Advances and Data

Four issues will be addressed in this section on epidemiology: cross-cultural data; age and period effects; demographic
effects; and high-risk groups. A number of important methodologic problems are involved in the use of national mortality
data for epidemiologic studies. These include under- and over-
reporting and data classification problems. Cross-cultural data
and data on suicide among youth are of particular methodologic concern, as detailed elsewhere (Brooke, 1974; Roy, 1986a;
Holinger, 1987).

Cross-Cultural Data

The suicide rates for virtually all age groups in the United
States lies approximately in the middle of those countries reporting such data to the World Health Organization. Hungary
(in 1989: 61.4 [males] and 23.1 [females] per 100,000 population), Finland (46.4, 11.5), and Austria (36.1, 14.7) recently had
among the highest suicide rates; Greece (5.6, 2.1) and Portugal
(11.0, 3.7), the lowest; and the United States (19.9, 4.8), midway
(World Health Organization, 1991, 1992; National Center for
Health Statistics, unpublished data).

Another pattern emerging from cross-cultural data relates
to the increase of suicide rates with age. While it is well known
that suicide rates in the United States increase with age

(Kramer, Pollack, Redick, and Locke, 1972; Blazer, Bachar, and Manton, 1986), this trend is also remarkably consistent for a variety of countries and cultures. This pattern occurs regardless of the overall rates of the countries, and it appears to be independent of ethnic and racial differences as well as reporting differences (Holinger, Offer, Barter, and Bell, in press). It is unlikely that the trend is based on underreporting of suicides among the young, for underreporting has been noted in the older as well as the younger ages (Blazer, Bachar, and Manton, 1986; Holinger and Offer, 1981).

Age and Period Effects

The concepts of age and period effects are particularly useful in understanding longitudinal epidemiologic data on suicide. Age effects involve changes in age-specific rates of mortality or illness over the life span of the individual (Holford, 1983). Period effects refer to changes in rates of mortality or illness during a particular historical period (Holford, 1983).

Regarding the age effects for suicide in the United States during the twentieth century, the suicide rates (total) tended to increase with age, from very low rates among 5- to 14-year-olds (in 1989: 0.7 per 100,000 population) to the highest rates for 75- to 84-year-olds (23.1) (National Center for Health Statistics, 1992). This pattern of suicide rates increasing with age is seen especially for white males. However, for the other race and sex groups there are differences in the age patterns. For white females, rates tend to peak in the middle-age groups and then decrease in older age. For nonwhite males, rates tend to be highest in the young adult and older adult age groups. The nonwhite females show highest rates among the young adults. Thus the tendency of total suicide rates to increase with age can be seen to be primarily a function of the high rates among white males. Recently, age effects in the United States have shifted somewhat, with some younger age groups demonstrating rates as high or higher than those of some younger adult groups (Holinger, 1987).

Comparing race and sex groups, rates for males are higher than for females. White males have the highest suicide rates for every age group, followed by rates for nonwhite males, white females, and nonwhite females respectively.

Period effects for suicide in the United States, i.e., shifts in rates over time, range from about 10 to 16 per 100,000 and include: decreases in nearly all age groups in the years just prior to and including 1920 (World War I), increases during the early 1930s (the economic depression), decreases during the early 1940s (World War II), and increases from the mid-1950s to mid-1970s. It is also worth noting that within the male and female groups, the period effects occur in virtually every age group, i.e., period effects are strong enough to overcome any influence of age with the exception of the low rate for 5- to 14-year-olds (Kramer et al., 1972; Holinger, 1987).

Demographic Effects

There is increasing evidence that population trends may be useful in understanding a variety of social phenomena (Easterlin, 1980). Recently, two different types of studies have begun to evaluate demographic variables for their possible explanatory and predictive power on suicide rates in the United States and other countries. These two types of investigation have been termed cohort studies (Solomon and Hellon, 1980; Hellon and Solomon, 1980; Murphy and Wetzel, 1980) and studies utilizing a population model (Holinger and Offer, 1982, 1987).

Cohort effects refer to differences in rates of mortality or illness during a particular historical period (Holford, 1983). Cohort analyses enable one to follow over time a group of people born during specific years. Cohort studies enhance the epidemiologic data above in documenting the recent increases in suicide among the young. Solomon and Hellon (1980) and Murphy and Wetzel (1980), studying Canada and United States suicide rates, respectively, identified five-year age cohorts during the 1950s through 1970s and followed the suicide rates as the cohorts aged. Suicide rates increased directly with age, regardless of gender. Not only did each successive birth cohort start with the higher rate, at each successive five-year interval it has a higher rate than the preceding cohort had at that age. Klerman, Lavori, and Rice (1985) noted a similar cohort effect in their study of depressed patients.

The second set of studies investigating suicide and demographics has been termed a population model. Data suggested that as the proportion of adolescents increased (and decreased) over time, the suicide rates for that age group increased (and decreased, respectively) (it should be noted that while one would expect the *numbers* of suicides to increase with an increased number in a specific age group, the *rates* should not necessarily increase). The opposite trend was found for adults: virtually all adult groups showed decreased suicide rates with increased population (Holinger and Offer, 1982, 1987).

The importance of the demographic perspective lies in the capacity for prediction. Inasmuch as the numbers and proportions of various age groups can be determined years in advance based on the numbers in younger age groups, it may be possible to predict the suicide rates over time. If such epidemiologic predictions are substantiated over time, effective interventions can be established based on the relationships between population changes and suicide rates.

High-Risk Groups

Psychiatric patients and those who have previously attempted suicide represent high-risk groups for completing suicide, with rates far higher than those found in the general population. Those patients with diagnosis of affective disorders (major depression, bipolar illness), schizophrenia, severe character disorders, and substance abuse are particularly at risk (Sainsbury, 1982; Diekstra, 1982; Kreitman, 1982; Pokorny, 1983; Blumenthal and Kupfer, 1990). The question as to how this knowledge can be used in prevention is far more complicated than it would first appear. For example, Kreitman (1982) has shown that if one screens even a large high-risk population for follow-up, one will catch relatively few suicides and at high expense; if one concentrates on smaller, higher-risk populations the yield is so low that the overall reduction in the total number of suicides is minimal. The technical derivations of these findings and relative risk figures have been demonstrated by Kreitman (1982).

Biopsychosocial Aspects of Suicide Throughout the Life Course

Suicide is such a multidetermined and complex phenomenon that one risks becoming simplistic when going beyond an in-depth single case study. Yet enough detailed clinical studies of suicide have been conducted to allow some focus on potential vulnerabilities during the developmental phases of childhood as well as periods through the life course. In an attempt to deal with the difficulty of generalizing about suicide from individual cases, a biopsychosocial approach will be taken in the various developmental phases under investigation.

This section will focus on the biopsychosocial aspects of suicide by the age of various developmental tasks: childhood and latency, adolescence and young adulthood, adulthood, and older adulthood. A historical development of the dynamics of suicide along a developmental line can also be noted. Freud (1917) discussed suicide from an oedipal framework, describing the now well-known dynamics of loss of object, followed by identification with the object, and concluding with hostility turned inward onto the self. Others later stressed the preoedipal aspects of suicide. For example, Anthony (1970) stressed the importance of shame and humiliation, ego vulnerabilities, lack of self and object differentiation, and symbiotic ties to the mother. Novick (1984) further elaborated the separation–individuation issues as the key element in pathological regressions culminating in serious suicide attempts. Adler and Buie (1979) utilized Piaget's work to suggest that maternal deprivation may lead to extremely vulnerable evocative memory development, with a suicidal outcome. The self psychology perspective (e.g., Kohut [1971, 1977], Kavka [1976], Reiser [1986]) has emphasized the rapid regressions and fragmentations of the self in suicidal acts; self psychology has also added formulations that suggest suicidal acts may reflect an attempt at consolidation of the self, such as through heroic acts in war.

Childhood and Latency

There are strikingly few data on suicide in childhood and latency. There are usually less than 10 suicides per year recorded among children 9 years old or less. Pfeffer (1986) has written extensively about children who have expressed suicidal ideation or behavior, but systematic data on children who have completed suicide are lacking (Brent and Kolko, 1990). The rarity of suicide in children prompts one to reverse the question of why children commit suicide and ask: what protects children from suicide?

With respect to the biologic component of suicide, far more evidence exists in adults than in children. However, as Pfeffer (1986) has summarized with respect to children:

> Dexamethasone suppression test response, cortisol hypersecretion, and hyposecretion of growth hormone in insulin-induced hypoglycemia have been documented for children and adults with major affective disorders. . . . The importance of these findings is that these factors can be used to diagnose risk for depression. Since depression is associated with suicidal behavior, these biological variables may be important clues for suicidal risk. These findings also suggest that there is a valid neurophysiological basis for affective disorders and that there may be a biologic basis for suicidal behavior in some individuals [p. 79].

In terms of the psychological, three aspects will be considered: cognition, concept of death, and ego capacities. With respect to the development of cognitive structure, Piaget's work (Piaget and Inhelder, 1969) is of particular importance. During the span under study, two major transformations in cognition take place: the shift from the preoperational period to the concrete operation period (at approximately 6–7 years), and from concrete operations to formal operations (at about 11–12 years). The concrete operational period, from about 6 to 7 years to 11 to 12 years, covers most of the years in the 5- to 14-year-old age group. Basch (1977) has noted the importance of this period: before concrete operations, "a time beyond the immediate past was difficult to evoke, the future difficult to anticipate" (p. 237). With the onset of concrete operations: "this distancing-and-awareness (decentering) becomes possible as a result of the merging ability to reach out symbolically and go beyond each activity in time and space" (p. 237). Or, as Shapiro and Perry (1976) have described, "the greater stability and invariance of mental process and the new cognitive structure at 7 also permit the *inhibition and control of drives* and the postponement of action" (p. 97). An increasing capacity to conceptualize death during these years is also relevant (a brief summary of this is presented below). Thus, with these increasing cognitive abilities, the child has a greater chance for anticipating, and avoiding, potentially destructive situations; on the other hand, these cognitive capacities, combined with a more realistic conceptualization of death, also make it more possible to think up and carry out a self-destructive act such as suicide which may aid in an understanding of the beginning of significant numbers of suicides during the later years of childhood.

Another body of literature which needs to be examined in terms of its relationship to overt self-destructiveness is that dealing with the conceptualization of death. Earlier studies (Piaget, 1926; Schilder and Wechsler, 1934; Anthony, 1940, 1971; Bender and Schilder, 1937) suggested that children did show an interest in and fantasies about death, and Anthony's work indicated that, contrary to popular opinion, death was a common topic for young minds. In a developmental study of the child's conceptualization of death by Nagy (1959) three major stages were described: the first stage (about 3 to 5 years of age) highlights the denial of death as a regular and final process (death as a departure, temporary, with living and lifelessness not yet distinguished); the second stage (about 5 to 9 years) suggests death is personified (death is an eventuality, but outside us and not universal). The third stage (after 9 to 10 years) indicates death is recognized as a process which takes place in all of us, and it is seen as inevitable. Although the consensus seems to be that the bulk of the data tend to support Nagy's findings, many critiques and modifications of her work exist (Kastenbaum, 1977; Feifel, 1977). In addition, increasing literature on children with terminal illnesses (Bluebond-Langner, 1977) suggests that even young children who are terminally ill have conceptualizations of death thought to occur only in older children. Haim (1974) stressed the discrepancies in the studies, noted that even young children often showed a solid conceptualization of death, and suggested that adult denial plays an essential role in the apparent absence in the child of a preoccupation with death.

Pfeffer (1986) described children at high risk of suicide as those who manifested sadness or depression, a preoccupation with death, and whose family had depressive or suicidal tendencies. However, Pfeffer (1986) noted that children can be suicidal without having a sense of the finality of death; rather, what was important is that they have some concept of death. She noted that death has a specific meaning to a child, and that this meaning was associated with a solution to the child's perception of overwhelming distress. Orbach and Glaubman (1978) studied normal, excessively aggressive, and suicidal children. They found that normal children knew that death was final significantly more often than the suicidal or aggressive children. Suicidal children gave significantly more responses about the possibility of returning to life after personal death than the two other groups. However, suicidal children had an appropriate understanding of the finality of impersonal death. In addition, normal children thought they would die of old age and illness, whereas aggressive and suicidal children gave brutality more often as a cause of death.

With respect to this issue of concept of death in children, it is of interest to examine Pfeffer's (1986) data on suicidal children. Of more than 25 suicidal children who were 8 years old or younger, approximately half had suffered the loss of a parent (through death, divorce, or separation). Many of those children overtly expressed wishes to join the dead parent or to be rescued by the parent who had left.

In terms of ego capacities, very little data are available on suicidal children and their character structure and ego function, and even less data on children who have completed suicide. Pfeffer (1986) has described interrelationships between stress and internal vulnerabilities which can result in suicidal outcomes for children, but she too notes the paucity of data. However, she does suggest that suicidal children may be more prone to use such ego defenses as introjection, regression, and denial to manage stress, while nonsuicidal children may use predominantly other ego defenses such as repression and intellectualization.

Adolescence

With the increase in adolescent suicide rates from the mid-1950s to the 1980s has come an increase in scientific literature on the subject. Seiden's (1969) comprehensive literature review for the years 1900 to 1967 noted approximately 200 articles and books on youthful suicide. Subsequent literature reviews (Sudak, Ford, and Rushforth, 1984; Holinger and Offer, 1981) indicate that between 1968 and 1983 the number of publications had more than doubled. Further evidence of the emergence of youthful suicide as a specific field of scientific inquiry is seen in two other publications: the Health and Human Services Secretary's Task Force on Risk Factors in Youth Suicide (1987), and the American Psychiatric Press's *Suicide Among Youth: Perspectives on Risk and Prevention* (Pfeffer, 1989).

With respect to biological aspects, there are few biologically oriented hypotheses or studies that address the issue of suicide specifically in adolescence; however, several literature reviews on this topic should be noted. Petzel and Cline (1978) described the controversial nature and paucity of biochemical investigations related to adolescent suicide (e.g., steroids, neurotransmitters, menstruation, pregnancy), but they did note that a higher risk of adolescent suicide might be associated with evidence of structural neuropathology (e.g., electroencephalographic changes and epilepsy). Ambrosini, Rabinovich, and Puig-Antich (1984) have been able to assemble some objective evidence for the existence of a biological disorder, underlying major depressive disorder in childhood and adolescence, which they felt was closely similar to adult depression. They noted that family history suggests that there may be a genetic component to depression in children and adults. An abnormal growth hormone response to hypoglycemia is frequently observed in depressed children and adults, and abnormalities of cortisol secretion can be demonstrated fairly consistently in both age groups. Goodwin and Brown (1989) have recently reviewed these biological factors in adolescent suicide. It might also be noted at this point that affective disorders (major depression and bipolar disorder) and schizophrenia appear to have a biological component, and these disorders are seen in adolescence.

Patients with affective disorders and schizophrenia are at higher risk of suicide than is true for the general population.

With respect to the psychological perspective, many theories of suicide in general exist, but less familiar are the works of several authors who have discussed suicide in adolescence per se. Recently, Hendin (1991) ably reviewed many of the psychodynamic issues involved in youth suicide: rage; hopelessness, despair, desperation; guilt; rebirth and reunion; retaliatory abandonment; revenge; and self-punishment and atonement.

Zilboorg (1937), one of the first to address suicide specifically among youth, noted data that showed marked discrepancy between low suicide rates in children and higher rates in adolescents. He contended that the age of puberty seems to be the crucial factor as far as the development of active self-destructive drives are concerned. He suggested that at puberty the task of the ego is to assert itself as quickly and as fully as possible by means of asserting the instinctual drives with which it must make or is inclined to make an unconditional alliance. Should the ego fail in this task, the suicidal outcome would offer itself as its paradoxical substitute. Zilboorg also noted that only those individuals who appear to have identified themselves with a dead person and in whom the process of identification took place during childhood or adolescence, at a time when the incorporated person was already actually dead, were most probably the truly suicidal individuals.

Gould (1965) maintained that the psychodynamics of suicide must be differentiated between children, adolescents, and adults, with physical, intellectual, and physiologic levels of development being of particular importance in understanding the psychodynamics of suicide in children and adolescents. Gould suggested that although the conscious reason for the suicide attempt seems to be that it is an escape from a situation too difficult to face, the common theme underlying the precipitating events is rejection and deprivation, which results in loss of love and support. This may even be felt by the child or adolescent as a threat to her survival, and Gould felt that the core factor in the formation of a suicidal personality in adolescence was the felt loss of love. The role of hostility from significant others has been studied less in suicidal adolescents than the patient's hostility turned inward. Sabbath (1969) proposed the expendable child concept which presumed a parental wish, conscious or unconscious, interpreted by the child as a desire to be rid of him. Rosenbaum and Richman (1970) found more extreme hostility and less support in families of suicidal patients than nonsuicidal patients.

Andre Haim (1974) noted from his clinical data that adolescents usually can perform the work of mourning that results from narcissistic wounds, damage to the ego ideal, and object losses. However, the inadequacy of two defense mechanisms seems to be one of the most constant features of all suicidal adolescents: mobility of investments and the projective mechanism. Regarding the mobility of investments, Haim asserted that in all suicidal adolescents there is an inability to disinvest the disappointing or lost object. Despite that pain they maintain their investments, repeat their behavior, and brood on their disappointment. In terms of the projective mechanism, Haim noted that when the adolescent is confronted by the gap between his ideal aspirations and reality he reacts by making a projective defense; the adolescent constructs projects and theoretical systems with the ultimate intention of bringing reality into line with his own ideal image of it, or he reacts by attempting at once to alter reality. Haim suggested that in the case of the suicidal adolescent this mechanism is either disturbed, inadequate, or absent altogether.

Anthony (1970) described two types of adolescent depression. In type I the psychopathology would be mainly preoedipal and based on a marked symbiotic tie with the omnipotent need-satisfying mother. In this type the discrepancies between the ego and ego ideal, with resulting changes in self-esteem, are of primary focus. The type II depression as discussed by Anthony is more oedipal in nature, with a great deal of guilt and moral masochism associated with a punitive superego. The detailed psychoanalytic case studies of suicidal adolescents in the literature tend to support the idea that both preoedipal and oedipal problems can lead to a suicidal outcome in adolescence (Kernberg, 1974; Laufer, 1974; Hurry, 1977, 1978; Novick, 1984).

Novick's (1984) group review of seven psychoanalytic cases of suicidal adolescents deserves special attention. Novick presented extensive data on the psychoanalysis of seven suicidal adolescents. They were nonpsychotic adolescents who made medically serious attempts. The patients consisted of three females and four males with an age range of 14 to 19 years of age when they started treatment. Novick's group found evidence in each case for a steplike suicide sequence: the suicide attempt in each of the cases was not a sudden act but the end point in a pathological regression. Novick detailed 13 steps in the suicide sequence. First, for a considerable period prior to the attempt the adolescents had felt depressed, sexually abnormal, and had suicidal thoughts. Second, they took a step that represented breaking the tie with the mother. Third, in all cases the adolescent failed to make such a step. Fourth, they were thrown back onto an intense infantile relationship with their mother. Fifth, in this state of dependency there was anxiety due to sexual and aggressive preoccupations, and there was evidence that the adolescents had some sense of awareness of the incestuous nature of their fantasies. Sixth, there was another attempt to break away from mother—this time by appealing to another person, with the appeal taking the form of a suicide threat. Seventh, there was a breakthrough of aggression toward the mother, with guilt and fear of a loss of control of impulses. Eighth, a sense of intense panic and deadlock ensued with suicide seen as a positive solution. Ninth, the adolescent turned to the external world, provoking rejection from a person other than mother, leading to a decrease in guilt. With guilt no longer an inhibiting factor, the suicide plan is put into motion. Tenth, the suicide attempt is seen as having multiple results, e.g., that the world will be sorry for mistreating them. Eleventh, there is the actual suicide attempt and it is seen as an altered ego state, a psychotic state, a total denial of death, as well as a state of peace in which the adolescent is at one with mother. Twelfth, the method itself often has specific dynamic significance. Thirteenth, the adolescent feels a relief of tension and sense of calm. Novick (1984) thus presented the methodology by which to study the psychodynamics of suicidal adolescents. In addition he emphasized that the suicide attempts were not sudden acts but rather the end point in a sequence of a pathological regression.

With respect to the social perspective, family interaction and adolescence have been excellently reviewed by Williams and Lyons (1976) and dealt with uniquely by Cain (1972). The classical sociological theory of suicide is Durkheim's (1897); according to him, suicide rates are likely to be high at one extreme if persons are isolated interpersonally (egoistic suicide) and at the other extreme if individuals are so tightly integrated into a group that they devalue their own individuality (altruistic suicide). Suicide rates are also likely to be high in situations where the norms and standards are unclear (anomic suicide). As Gibbs (1971) notes, the main tenet of Durkheim's theory is that suicide rates vary inversely with the degree of social integration. This theory would lead one to predict that youth from broken families would have a high suicide rate, and there is some evidence in support of this assertion.

However, attempts to understand the relationship between broken homes and suicide in adolescence have proven controversial. One difficulty relates to the various descriptions and definitions of broken homes; for example, broken through divorce, separation, or death of one or both parents at various stages of the adolescent's life. Another problem concerns the paucity of controlled studies in this area. Finally, with few exceptions (Cain, 1972), nearly all the studies examined attempted rather than completed suicide. The relationship between broken homes and psychiatric disorder, depression and suicide is methodologically complex. Dennehy (1966) and Gregory (1966) emphasized the need to control for the year of birth of the patient and the patient's parents and social class. Crook and Raskin (1975) noted that the reported association of parental loss with attempted suicide may be due to a primary association between parental loss and severe depression. Depression could be an intervening variable since it is a variable related both to attempted suicide and parental loss. Crook and Raskin suggested that future study should establish whether there is an equivalence between those who attempt suicide and control groups on severity of depression. Major methodologic problems in retrospective case control investigations which utilize interviews should be noted, i.e., observation bias and a lack of blindness.

In summary, five major areas can be conceptualized as risk factors for youth suicide: psychiatric disorder, psychosocial milieu (life events, environmental factors, and medical illness), personality traits, biological factors, and family history and genetics (Blumenthal and Kupfer, 1990). In addition, substance abuse and the availability of firearms enhance the risk (Brent, Perper, Allman, Moritz, Wartella, and Zelenak, 1991).

Adulthood

A biopsychosocial approach to the problem of suicide will again be utilized in examining the adult age groups. Unlike the situation with adolescents, there is a great deal of data relating suicide in adults to biological aspects. These data can be separated into two somewhat overlapping categories: (1) biologic and genetic studies; and (2) psychiatric disorders and suicide.

First, various studies have shown that biogenic amines and the neuroendocrine system may be related to suicide (e.g., see Goodwin and Brown [1989] and Winchel, Stanley, and Stanley [1990]). Specifically, research suggests that decreased CSF 5-HIAA, and an activation of the hypothalmic–pituitary–adrenal (HPA) axis are associated with an increased risk of suicide. The absence of reports of negative correlations between the two markers suggests that they may be independent and associated with suicide through different mechanisms (Asberg, Nordstrom, and Traskman-Bendz, 1986). The nature of these mechanisms may be different: HPA activation has long been regarded as a consequence of emotional stress, whereas 5-HIAA has been hypothesized to be a marker of vulnerability. Other data have supported the idea that suicide may have a genetic predisposition, with the above biologic factors possibly being involved. In addition, there appears to be a genetic factor favoring suicide which may operate independently of or additively with depression or other major psychosis (Kety, 1986).

Second, extensive data suggest that those with major psychiatric disorders, such as schizophrenia, bipolar illness, and major depression, are at far higher risk of suicide than normal controls (e.g., Roy, 1986b; Sainsbury, 1986; Black, Winokur, and Nasrallah, 1987). Inasmuch as biologic factors have been identified as contributing etiologically to those disorders, suicide has been linked to the biologic factors as well.

With respect to the psychological aspects, many of the dynamic formulations on suicide are well known (e.g., Freud [1917] and Menninger [1938]), whereas others have only recently received increased attention (e.g., those from a self psychology perspective). What appears to be emerging in the literature is a distinction in the dynamics of suicide between those with oedipal and preoedipal disorders. This distinction is somewhat similar to that noted by Anthony (1970) on adolescents. The distinction also appears similar to the hierarchy approach to character and treatment proposed by Gedo and Goldberg (1973).

Freud (1917), in the well-known dynamic of suicide, noted the following sequence: following an initial object choice, there occurs a real slight or disappointment and the object relationship is shattered; there is then an identification of the ego with the abandoned object; the hostility resulting from the loss is then directed upon the ego as though it were the forsaken object. Freud concluded:

> We have long known . . . that no neurotic harbours thoughts of suicide which he has not turned back upon himself from murderous impulses against others . . . the ego can kill itself only if, owing to the return of the object-cathexis, it can treat as an object—if it is able to direct against itself the hostility which relates to an object and which represents the ego's original reaction to objects in the external world [1917, p. 252].

Kohut (1971, 1977) began describing suicide dynamics from a different perspective, i.e., that of fragmented self-cohesion and disrupted narcissistic homeostasis. Kavka (1976) discussed suicide even more specifically from a self psychological viewpoint in his analysis of Edwin Arlington Robinson's poem on Richard Cory. More recently, Reiser (1986) attempted to utilize a hierarchical schema to elaborate upon the value of self psychology in understanding suicide. He noted that those with self disorders may be prone to rapid fragmentation or sudden disintegration in the face of disrupted narcissistic homeostasis, and that these rapid regressions were often characteristic of suicides by people with disorders of the self. He outlined five levels of developmental arrest reflecting different narcissistic vulnerabilities, all of which could lead to a suicidal outcome: the endangered self (schizoid and schizophrenic conditions); the enraged self ("borderline"); the vulnerable self (self pathology originating in the separation–individuation phase of development); the grandiose self (lack of internalization of self–object functions and disintegration of self when needs for admiration are not met); and the mirroring self (arrest at a level of only fulfilling self–object functions for others).

Finally, Kohut (1971, 1977) also described how suicide might be not just the result of a regression and fragmenting self, but could also be due to the attempt at cohesion. In other words, Kohut felt that some suicide, e.g., those performing heroic though self-destructive acts during war, could be seen as consolidating as inner sense of self by giving their lives for an admired leader or goal.

With respct to the sociological aspects of suicide among adults, Durkheim's (1897) classic work will be presented first, followed by brief mention of more recent directions. Studying suicide data in relation to religious affiliation, marriage and family, and political and national communities, Durkheim suggested there were three categories of suicide. "Egoistic" suicide results from lack of integration of the individual into society; the stronger the forces throwing the individual onto his or her own resources, the greater the suicide rate in the society in which this occurs. "Altruistic" suicide results from taking one's life because of greater integration of the individual into society, that is, religious sacrifice or political allegiance. "Anomic" suicide results from lack of regulation of the individual by society, that is, economic crisis having an aggravating effect on the suicidal tendency.

Two researchers recently have greatly enhanced the understanding of two major sociologic variables: economic (Brenner, 1971, 1979) and demographic (Easterlin, 1980). Brenner's major contribution was to use economic variables to elucidate the period effects for suicide and other causes of mortality. Brenner demonstrated that indicators of economic instability and insecurity, such as unemployment, were associated over time with higher mortality rates. The explanation for this association was that the lack of economic security is stressful: social and family structures break down, and habits that are harmful to health are adopted. The effect may manifest acutely as a psychopathological event (e.g., suicide and homicide) or, after a time lag of a few years, as a chronic disease (e.g., cancer or heart disease).

The Easterlin hypothesis (1980) maintains that there is a cause–effect relationship between birth control size and economic, social, educational, and political trends. Specifically, it correlates movements in birth rates and age-specific rates with particular behavioral phenomena (including suicide, although Easterlin did not study mortality rates in detail). According to Easterlin, when the size of the birth cohort increases (as with the "baby boom" cohort), it produces excessive competition for existing and limited resources and institutions, and results in relative deprivation. Easterlin identified three broad social institutions through which the effects of cohort size operate: family, schools, and the labor market. Increased cohort size can strain the resources of all three, resulting in antisocial behaviors such as drug and alcohol abuse, crime, and suicide.

Older Adulthood

Few data exist with specific reference to biologic factors in suicide among the elderly. This paucity of data is of interest, given that older adults have higher suicide rates than any other age groups. There are, however, studies demonstrating the high prevalence of suicide in older people with psychiatric disorders having a biologic basis (e.g., bipolar illness) as well as various organic brain syndromes (e.g., see Miller [1979]).

In exploring the psychological aspects of suicide in older adults, one is again confronted by the paradox of high suicide rates and relatively little data (see Osgood and Thielman [1990] for a review of these issues). The data can be divided into two categories: intrapsychic data on the character structure of older adults who suicide; and data related to the external stresses (e.g., demographic factors) to which these people are subjected. Inasmuch as so little information exists at this point regarding the intrapsychic vulnerabilities of the older adult suicides, this section will focus on the external stresses.

The demographic factors related to older adult suicide are well known: males are at higher risk than females, and whites higher than nonwhites. Nonmarried persons are at greater risk than married. Studies have consistently shown, however, that the elderly who have lost spouses are particularly vulnerable to suicide, especially males. Thus the elderly white widowers represent an extremely high "at-risk" group (see Osgood, [1985] for a summary of these studies).

Several factors in addition to the demographic data above have been shown to be highly correlated with suicide in older adults. As Miller (1979) and Osgood and Thielman (1990) have shown, severe physical illness, mental illness, the threat of extreme dependency or institutionalization, alcoholism and drug abuse, and pathological interpersonal relationships have been found in controlled studies to be associated with elderly suicides.

The sociologic perspective provides more information on suicide in the elderly than on some of the other age groups. Osgood (1985) described how the elderly fit into Durkheim's categories of both "egoistic" and "anomic" suicide. Durkheim (1897) proposed that suicide increases with age because society as a moral force begins to recede from the person, in terms of both goals and commitments, as the person ages and withdraws from various roles and positions. The older individual is less integrated into and less dependent upon society (egoistic suicide). Rosow (1973) had noted that our culture does not provide older members with definitions and meaningful norms, so older persons are left to structure the "aged role" for themselves, with no clear prescriptions as to the appropriate behavior (anomic suicide).

It is interesting to note that the sociologic perspective reaches for an integration of external factors and intrapsychic aspects in order to understand suicide in older adults. Rosow (1973) suggested that old age, unlike other stages in the course of life, may be the first stage of life with systematic status loss. All other stages are normally marked by steady acquisitions of power, prestige, and rewards. In addition, the elderly may realize with increasing intensity that the life goals they set for themselves may never be attained, as the resources for achieving them dwindle before their eyes (Rosow, 1973). As Osgood (1985) stated, older age status appears to be accompanied by decreasing opportunity to function as an effective member of society and by an increasing inability to achieve life goals. The psychological issue raised here, and the one which requires more research, involves the nature of the intrapsychic vulnerability to both the losses occurring with aging as well as to the increasing tensions resulting from conscious and unconscious expectations which will not be achieved. In other words, what are the subtle differences in character structure of those who are able to successfully traverse the older years from those who are not?

Conclusions

In conclusion, it might be noted that the study of suicide over the course of life forces one to adopt additional perspectives to those used when studying only one age period. A developmental viewpoint continues to be essential, in terms of understanding the various arrests, conflicts, and deprivation in the early years which contribute to later problems. But, in addition, it seems that one must also, in conjunction with this developmental framework, take into account the various psychological and physiological tasks at each stage in order to have a more meaningful grasp of why people commit suicide. For example, two remarkably consistent findings in suicide research are that (1) suicide rates increase with age, and (2) male rates increase steadily with age into the oldest groups, while female rates tend to peak in the years 45 to 64 and then begin to decrease again. It would appear that both a developmental framework plus a sensitivity to the tasks of adulthood and older adulthood (and the difference in those tasks between males and females) are necessary to begin unravelling the puzzle.

References

Adler, G., & Buie, D.H. (1979), Aloneness and borderline psychopathology: The possible relevance of child development issues. *Internat. J. Psycho-Anal.*, 60:83–96.

Ambrosini, P.J., Rabinovich, H., & Puig-Antich, J. (1984), Biological factors and pharmacologic treatment in major depressive disorder in children and adolescents. In: *Suicide in the Young*, ed. H.S. Sudak, A.B. Ford, & N.B. Rushforth. Boston: John Wright PSG.

Anthony, E.J. (1970), Two contrasting types of adolescent depression and their treatment. *J. Amer. Psychoanal. Assn.*, 18:841–859.

Anthony, S. (1940), *The Child's Discovery of Death*. London: Routledge.

—— (1971), *The Discovery of Death in Childhood and After*. Harmondsworth, U.K.: Penguin.

Asberg, M., Nordstrom, P., & Traskman-Bendz, L. (1986), Biological factors in suicide. In: *Suicide*, ed. E. A. Roy. Baltimore: Williams & Wilkins, pp. 47–71.

Basch, M.F. (1977), Developmental psychology and explanatory theory in psychoanalysis. *Annual of Psychoanalysis*, 5:229–263. New York: International Universities Press.

Bender, U., & Schilder, P. (1937), Suicidal preoccupations and attempts in children. *Amer. J. Orthopsychiat.*, 7:225–243.

Black, D.W., Winokur, G., & Nasrallah, A. (1987), Suicide in subtypes of major affective disorder. *Arch. Gen. Psychiat.*, 44:878–880.

Blazer, D.G., Bachar, J.R., & Manton, K.G. (1986), Suicide in late life: Review and commentary. *J. Amer. Geriatr. Soc.*, 34:519–525.

Bluebond-Langner, M. (1977), Meanings of death to children. In: *New Meanings of Death*, ed. H. Feifel. New York: McGraw-Hill, pp. 47–66.

Blumenthal, S.J., & Kupfer, D.J. (1990), *Suicide Over the Life Cycle*. Washington, D.C.: American Psychiatric Press.

Brenner, M.H. (1971), *Time Series Analysis of Relationships between Selected Economic and Social Indicators*. Springfield, Va.: National Technical Information Service.

—— (1979), Mortality and the national economy. *Lancet*, 568–573.

Brent, D.A., & Kolko, D.J. (1990), The assessment and treatment of children and adolescents at risk for suicide. In: *Suicide Over the Life Cycle*, ed. S.J. Blumenthal & D.J. Kupfer. Washington, D.C.: American Psychiatric Press, pp. 253–302.

—— Perper, J.A., Allman, C.J., Moritz, G.M., Wartella, M.E., & Zelenak, J.P. (1991), The presence and accessibility of firearms in the homes of adolescent suicides: A case-control study. *J.A.M.A.*, 266:2989–2995.

Brooke, E.M. (1974), *Suicide and Attempted Suicide*. Public Health Papers 58. Geneva: World Health Organization.

Cain, A.C., ed. (1972), *Survivors of Suicide*. Springfield, Il: Charles C Thomas.

Crook, T., & Raskin, A. (1975), Association of childhood parental loss with attempted suicide and depression. *J. Consult. Clin. Psychol.*, 43:277.

Dennehy, C.M. (1966), Childhood bereavement and psychiatric illness. *Brit. J. Psychiat.*, 112:1049–1069.

Diekstra, R.F.W. (1982), Epidemiology of attempted suicide in the EEC. *Biblioth. Psychiat.*, 162:1–16.

Durkheim, E. (1897), *Suicide: A Study in Sociology*, trans. I.A. Spaulding & Simpson. New York: The Free Press, 1951.

Easterlin, R.A. (1980), *Birth and Fortune*. New York: Basic Books.

Farberow, N. (1979), *The Many Faces of Suicide*. New York: McGraw-Hill.

Feifel, H., ed. (1977), *New Meanings of Death*. New York: McGraw-Hill.

Freud, S. (1917), Mourning and melancholia. *Standard Edition*, 14:237–260. London: Hogarth Press, 1957.

Gedo, J., & Goldberg, A. (1973), *Models of the Mind*. Chicago: University of Chicago Press.

Gibbs, J.P. (1971), Suicide. In: *Contemporary Social Problems*, 3rd ed., ed. R.K. Merton & R. Nisbet. New York: Harcourt Brace Jovanovich, pp. 271–312.

Goodwin, F.K., & Brown, G.L. (1989), Summary and overview of risk factors in suicide. In: *Report of the Secretary's Task Force on Youth Suicide*, Vol. 2. DHHS Pub. No. ADM 89-1622. Washington, D.C.: U.S. Government Printing Office, pp. 263–271.

Gould, R. (1965), Suicidal problems in children and adolescents. *Amer. J. Psychother.*, 19:228–246.

Gregory, I. (1966), Retrospective data concerning childhood loss of parents—II. Category of parental loss by decade of birth. Diagnosis and MMPI. *Arch. Gen. Psychiat.*, 15:362–367.

Haim, A. (1974), *Adolescent Suicide*, trans. A.M.S. Smith. New York: International Universities Press.

Health and Human Services Secretary (1987), *Task Force on Risk Factors in Youth Suicide*. Washington, D.C.: U.S. Dept. Health and Human Services.

Hellon, C.P., & Solomon, M.I. (1980), Suicide and age in Alberta, Canada, 1951–1977. *Arch. Gen. Psychiat.*, 37:505–510.

Hendin, H. (1991), Psychodynamics of suicide, with particular reference to the young. *Amer. J. Psychiat.*, 148:1150–1158.

Holford, T.R. (1983), The estimation of age, period and cohort effects for vital rates. *Biometrics*, 39:1311–1324.

Holinger, P.C. (1987), *Violent Deaths in the United States: An Epidemiologic Study of Suicide, Homicide, and Accidents*. New York: Guilford Press.

—— Offer, D. (1981), Perspectives on suicide in adolescence. In: *Social and Community Mental Health*, Vol. 2, ed. R. Simmons. Greenwich, CT: JAI Press.

—— —— (1982), Prediction of adolescent suicide: A population model. *Amer. J. Psychiat.*, 139:302–307.

—— —— (1987), Suicide and homicide in the United States: An epidemiologic study of violent death, population changes, and the potential for prediction. *Amer. J. Psychiat.*, 144:215–219.

—— —— Barter, J., & Bell, C.C. (in press), *Suicide and Homicide Among Youth*. New York: Guilford Press.

Hurry, A. (1977), My ambitions is to be dead. *J. Child Psychother.*, 4:66–83.

—— (1978), Part II: Past and current findings on suicide in adolescence. *J. Child Psychother.*, 4:69–82.

Kastenbaum, R. (1977), Death and development through the lifespan. In: *New Meanings of Death*, ed. H. Feifel. New York: McGraw-Hill, pp. 17–45.

Kavka, J. (1976), The suicide of Richard Cory: An explication of the poem by Edward Arlington Robinson. *Annual of Psychoanalysis*, 4:479–500. New York: International Universities Press.

Kernberg, P.F. (1974), The analysis of a 15½-year old girl with suicidal tendencies. In: *The Analyst and the Adolescent at Work*, ed. M. Harley. New York: Quadrangle.

Kety, S.S. (1986), Genetic factors in suicide. In: *Suicide*, ed. A. Roy. Baltimore: Williams & Wilkins, pp. 41–45.

Klerman, G.L., Lavori, P.W., & Rice, J. (1985), Birth-cohort trends in rates of major depressive disorder among relatives of patients with affective disorder. *Arch. Gen. Psychiat.*, 42:689–693.

———— Weissman, M.M. (1984), An epidemiologic view of mental illness, mental health, and normality. In: *Normality and the Life Cycle: A Critical Interpretation*, ed. D. Offer & M. Sabshin. New York: Basic Books, pp. 315–344.

Kohut, H. (1971), *The Analysis of the Self*. New York: International Universities Press.

———— (1977), *The Restoration of the Self*. New York: International Universities Press.

Kramer, M., Pollack, E.S., Redick, R.W., & Locke, B.Z. (1972), *Mental Disorders/Suicide*. Cambridge, Mass.: Harvard University Press.

Kreitman, N. (1982), How useful is the prediction of suicide following parasuicide? *Biblioth. Psychiat.*, 162:77–84.

Laufer, M. (1974), The analysis of an adolescent at risk: With comments on the relation between psychopathology and technique. In: *The Analyst and the Adolescent at Work*, ed. M. Harley. New York: Quadrangle.

Menninger, K.A. (1938), *Man Against Himself*. New York: Harcourt, Brace.

Miller, M. (1979), *Suicide After Sixty: The Final Alternative*. New York: Springer.

Murphy, G.E., & Wetzel, R.D. (1980), Suicide risk by birth cohort in the United States, 1949–1974. *Arch. Gen. Psychiat.*, 37:519–523.

Nagy, M.H. (1959), The child's view of death. In: *The Meaning of Death*, ed. H. Feifel. New York: McGraw-Hill, pp. 79–98.

National Center for Health Statistics (1992), Advance report of final mortality statistics, 1989. Monthly Vital Statistics Report, 40/8: Suppl. 2. Hyattsville, Md.: Public Health Source.

Novick, J. (1984), Attempted suicide in adolescence: The suicide sequence. In: *Suicide in the Young*, ed. H.S. Sudak, A.B. Ford, & N.B. Rushforth. Boston: Wright PSG.

Offer, D., & Sabshin, M., eds. (1984), *Normality and the Life Cycle*. New York: Basic Books.

Orbach, I., & Glaubman, H. (1978), Suicidal, aggressive, and normal children's perception of personal and impersonal death. *J. Clin. Psychol.*, 34:850–857.

Osgood, N.J. (1985), *Suicide in the Elderly*. Rockville, Md.: Aspen Publication.

———— Thielman, S. (1990), Geriatric suicidal behavior: Assessment and treatment. In: *Suicide Over the Life Cycle*, ed. S. Blumenthal & D. Kupfer. Washington, D.C.: American Psychiatric Press, pp. 341–479.

Petzel, S., & Cline, D.W. (1978), Adolescent suicide: Epidemiological and biological aspects. In: *Adolescent Psychiatry*, Vol. 6, ed. S. Feinstein & P. Giovacchini. Chicago: University of Chicago Press.

Pfeffer, C. (1986), *The Suicidal Child*. New York: Guilford Press.

———— ed. (1989), *Suicide Among Youth: Perspectives on Risk and Prevention*. New York: American Psychiatric Press.

Piaget, J. (1926), *The Language and Thought of the Child*, trans. M. Warden. New York: Harcourt Brace.

——— Inhelder, B. (1969), *The Psychology of the Child*. New York: Basic Books.

Pokorny, A.D. (1983), Prediction of suicide in psychiatric patients. *Arch. Gen. Psychiat.*, 40:249–257.

Reiser, D.E. (1986), Self psychology and the problem of suicide. In: *Progress in Self-Psychology*, Vol. 2, ed. A. Goldberg. New York: Guilford Press.

Rosenbaum, M., & Richman, J. (1970), Suicide: The role of hostility and death wishes from the family and significant others. *Amer. J. Psychiat.*, 126:128–131.

Rosow, I. (1973), The social context of the aging self. *Gerontol.*, 12:82–87.

Roy, A. (1986a), *Suicide*. Baltimore: Williams & Wilkins.

——— (1986b), Suicide in schizophrenia. In: *Suicide*, ed. A. Roy. Baltimore: Williams & Wilkins, pp. 97–112.

Sabbath, J.C. (1969), The suicidal adolescent—the expendable child. *J. Amer. Acad. Child Psychiat.*, 8:272–285.

Sainsbury, P. (1982), Depression and suicide prevention. *Biblioth. Psychiat.*, 162:17–32.

——— (1986), Depression, suicide, and suicide prevention. In: *Suicide*, ed. A. Roy. Baltimore: Williams & Wilkins, pp. 17–40.

Schilder, P., & Wechsler, D. (1934), The attitudes of children toward death. *J. Genet. Psychol.*, 45:406–451.

Seiden, R.H. (1969), Suicide among youth: A review of the literature, 1900–1967. *Bull. Suicidol. (Suppl.)*.

Shapiro, T., & Perry, R. (1976), Latency revisited. *The Psychoanalytic Study of the Child*, 31:79–105. New Haven: Yale University Press.

Shneidman, E.S. (1975), Suicide. In: *Comprehensive Textbook of Psychiatry*, Vol. 2, ed. A.M. Freedman, H.I. Kaplan, & B.T. Sadock. Baltimore: Williams & Wilkins.

Solomon, M.I., & Hellon, C.P. (1980), Suicide and age in Alberta, Canada, 1951–1977. *Arch. Gen. Psychiat.*, 37:511–513.

Sudak, H.S., Ford, A.B., & Rushforth, N.B., eds. (1984), *Suicide in the Young*. Littleton, Mass.: PSG.

Williams, C., & Lyons, C.M. (1976), Family interaction and adolescent suicidal behavior: A preliminary investigation. *Aust. N. Zeal. J. Psychiat.*, 10:243–252.

Winchel, R.M., Stanley, B., & Stanley, M. (1990), Biochemical aspects of suicide. In: *Suicide Over the Life Cycle*, ed. S. Blumenthal & D. Kupfer. Washington, D.C.: American Psychiatric Press, pp. 97–126.

World Health Organization (1991), *World Health Statistics Annual 1990*. Geneva: World Health Organization.

——— (1992), *World Health Statistics Annual 1991*. Geneva: World Health Organization.

Zilboorg, G. (1937), Considerations on suicide, with particular reference to that of the young. *Amer. J. Orthopsychiat.*, 7:15–31.

11

A Developmental Structuralist Approach to the Assessment of Adult Personality Functioning and Psychopathology

STANLEY I. GREENSPAN, M.D.
WILLIAM J. POLK, M.D.

The developmental structuralist approach to classification of personality and psychopathology offers a conceptual framework which allows the diagnostician to locate the personality on a spectrum, ranging from adaptive to pathological. In this scheme, the most adaptive personality organizations are those which process and integrate a wide range of age- and phase-appropriate experiences into stable, uniquely personal configurations which are resistant to stress. These adaptive structures, by organizing and differentiating the fullest range of age- and phase-appropriate experiences without resorting to pathological compromises, also facilitate further development. In contrast, compromises that limit the range of phase-appropriate experience interfere with developmentally appropriate functioning and further development. Such compromises may be arranged in order of severity. The most severe involve defects in ego functioning, as in reality testing or affect regulation. A less severe group involves constrictions in the range of experience that can be tolerated, such as the inability to tolerate any emotional interactions or certain types of emotions (such as anger or sadness). Compromises at a third level involve encapsulated limitations. For example, contextually relevant experiences, such as particular memories, or specific types of relationships (e.g., with authority figures) are either not tolerated or

335

are organized in unstable personality structures. Encapsulated disorders, in contrast to basic defects and major constrictions, protect the remainder of the personality, permitting engagement in a wide range of age-appropriate life experiences that also facilitate further growth.

It will be observed that the ordering of personality structures according to the range, stability, resilience, and uniqueness of experiential organization may be derived from an understanding of the developmental progression of personality structure during the course of life.

The developmental structuralist approach, then, is an arrangement of personality organizations from most adaptive to most pathological, based on the capacity to process, organize, integrate, and differentiate age-appropriate experiences. The theoretical, clinical, and research foundations for this approach have been presented elsewhere (Greenspan, 1979), as has its application to constructing personality profiles (Greenspan and Cullander, 1975; Greenspan, Hatleberg, and Cullander, 1976). What follows is a description of this approach and its application to the issue of psychiatric and personality diagnosis.

Traditional Approaches to Diagnosis

Psychiatric diagnosis based on symptoms or etiology has traditionally approached the disordered person along two major pathways. In the first instance, the particular pattern of symptoms defines the diagnosis. For example, the patient who is apathetic, with early morning awakening, anorexia, and feelings of sadness, self-hatred, and hopelessness, presents the familiar cluster of symptoms defining the condition called depression. The diagnosis of schizophrenia is often established by observing characteristic primary symptoms, such as thought disorder, inappropriate affect, and ambivalence, along with secondary symptoms, such as hallucinations and delusions. Diagnoses established by symptom clusters are by far the most common in psychiatry, as they are in general medicine.

As a disease comes to be understood more fully, there is greater likelihood diagnosis will be based on distinguishing the etiological agents. In general medicine, pneumonia was once diagnosed by symptoms and signs such as fever, rales, and consolidation on percussion. Later, more sophisticated technology allowed the doctor to view the pneumococcus and then grow it in a culture. In psychiatry, only a few illnesses are well enough understood to base the diagnosis on etiological agents. Organic syndromes are the best examples of this type. The etiologies of schizophrenia and the schizophrenic spectrum disorders continue to be differentiated, as knowledge about genetic and constitutional factors accumulates.

The etiological and symptom complex approaches to classification and diagnosis, although necessary, are insufficient. The same etiological factors can result in different behavioral outcomes or symptom configurations. Just as allergic reactions to a given agent differ, depending on individual differences in response proclivity (e.g., one individual may become dizzy, a second may develop hives, and a third a gastrointestinal disorder), the same etiological agent (e.g., an environment stress, a biochemical change) produces different behaviors and symptoms in different individuals. At the same time, several different etiological agents may result in the same set of symptoms. Just as a given allergen, infectious agent, or series of stresses can produce a gastrointestinal disturbance, so different environmental events, stresses, or chemical changes may produce the same behaviors or symptoms.

In many areas of medicine we have learned enough about pathogenic or adaptive pathways to understand the process intervening between etiological factors and response patterns or outcomes. Thus, a knowledge of bodily processes allows us to understand that one individual may at different times be experiencing the same allergic reaction, regardless of different symptom complexes, or that another may be undergoing two distinct bodily changes, although the final outcome for both may be a similar gastrointestinal disturbance.

Our approach to adaptive and pathological personality configuration is still at the level of symptom complexes and etiological approaches. We do not yet have a complete framework that looks at the pathogenic and adaptive processes. Evidently, there is a need for another dimension to our classification, one that allows us to use the patient's unique way of processing, integrating, and differentiating experience to understand the particular pathways that result in specific behavioral outcomes. This "final common pathway" connects the influence of multiple etiological factors with varying outcomes and suggests that the organism's manner of organizing experience is of fundamental importance.

A truly useful classification system must also attempt to deal with the quantitative dimension of human experience in terms of pathology and adaptation. Historically, dynamic systems or psychiatric frameworks (other than energic concepts) have not been designed primarily to deal with quantitative assessment of functional capacity. To be sure, many of these traditional concepts have been employed at various times for the assessment of capacity (A. Freud, 1965). Whenever they have been used as assessment tools, however, the results have been a more detailed and systematic explanation but not a clear and accurate quantitative assessment. For the most part, the field of quantitative assessment has been abandoned to other disciplines (e.g., behavioral and symptom-oriented approaches). While approaches that rely exclusively on manifest phenomena may provide an illusion of validity, they are often cut off from the processes that constitute human experience.

What is needed is a conceptual system that, as indicated above, systematically integrates experiential processes with manifest phenomena and, at the same time, maintains a central focus on functional capacity. We propose a conceptual approach to assessment (the developmental structural assessment) that rests on principles developed from an integration of psychoanalytic and Piagetian developmental psychology in the context of current clinical and research experience (Greenspan, 1979). Such a scheme of functional processes and capacities, arranged in hierarchical progression, is presented here.

General Features of the Developmental Structural Assessment

In the developmental structural approach, it is assumed that each person has individual methods of dealing with experience, including "inner" experiences (e.g., feelings and thoughts), which may be considered according to developmental structural characteristics. These include the tolerated range of experience, stability, resistance to stress, and personal uniqueness of the methods used. Desirable structures facilitate progress through the stages and tasks of human development, in part by making possible a range of phase-appropriate experiences without significant compromises in functioning. For example, the infant's ability to regulate himself allows him to begin relating to the world around him. Sometimes compromises are necessary. Some infants, in order to maintain calm, may withdraw by sleeping most of the day. Other infants are able to maintain a state of internal harmony while alert and engaged with various animate and inanimate stimuli in the surround. Similarly, some adults can engage in a broad range of wishes, thoughts, feelings, and relationships and deal with "stress" without compromise to their capacity for human experience. But other adults, in order to contain anxiety, must restrict major areas of engagement (e.g., experience no aggressive or sexual feelings; avoid intimate relationships, success, assertion, etc.). Thus, each individual possesses a unique structural configuration.

The developmental structural approach is based on the assumption that, as the child reaches each new developmental phase, he has the opportunity to develop more adaptive flexible ways of organizing experience. For example, even a healthy child of preschool age must use a great deal of denial and may not as yet be capable of experiencing sadness and loss. In contrast, adults can adaptively integrate a wide range of internal and external experiences, including such feelings as sadness, loss, love, compassion, empathy, sharing, anger, competition, humiliation, etc. The "optimal" adult can experience these in a range of contexts, from an intimate relationship with a loved one to a work setting. The healthy adult with a wide range of phase-appropriate experience also maintains a stable and unique sense of himself, manifested in his personal wishes, feelings, ideals, values, and aspirations (even though these may change with new experiences), and remains engaged with major life areas even under stress. A significant change in the healthy adult's situation does not compromise, except perhaps transiently, his capacity for a wide range of phase-appropriate experience in stable, resilient, uniquely personal organizations.

In contrast to "optimal" adult capacities, there are various degrees of impairment in the range of experience tolerated, the stability of these experienced organizations, and their resilience. Such impairments, to be described in succeeding sections, can be ordered according to their specific configurational limitations (e.g., ego defects, constrictions, encapsulated disorders, etc.).

Before outlining the categories of the developmental structuralist approach, it should be pointed out that this approach is phenomenological in that it derives from directly observable data (albeit requiring a sensitive observer), does not sacrifice clinical validity for quickly attainable reliability, and integrates within its framework the symptom-oriented and etiological approaches.

Outline of the Developmental Structuralist Classification Scheme

This section presents an outline of the Developmental Structural Classification of Personality Organization. Figure 1 shows the developmental structural approach in a three-column system, together with etiological and symptom approaches. Columns 1 and 3 depict etiology-based and symptom-based systems. Column 2 lists a developmental structural hierarchy. As an example, consider a person with symptoms of phobia. From the etiological point of view, he may have suffered a traumatic pattern of experience in childhood, which is now displaced and symbolized. From the developmental structuralist point of view, the picture is more complex. A phobia can exist in the context of different structural organizations, ranging from severe ego deficits to relatively minor, encapsulated disorders. It can also represent a transient reaction in a healthy person. Thus, the clinical significance, in terms of degree of illness, treatment indicated, and prognosis, would differ considerably, depending on the structural picture.

**The Developmental Structuralist Approach to
Classification: Narrative Descriptions of Each Category**

Ego Defects

Ego defects may be found in two forms, as physical damage to the mental apparatus or as impairment in the psychological organization.

Impairment in physical integrity of the personality. The first type of ego defect, damage to the basic physical integrity of the mental apparatus, may be the result of genetic predisposition, or chemical, biological, or environmental factors at any time before, during, or after birth. Damage is done to the organic foundations of the mental apparatus and may be manifested by disorders of perception, motor function, perceptual motor coordination, memory, etc. The symptomatic expressions may be diffuse and subtle, as in minimal brain dysfunction in children and senile loss of memory in the aged, or localized and severe, as in congenital blindness. They may also be acute and overwhelming, as in the acute organic brain syndrome of delirium tremens.

Impairment in psychological organization of the personality. The second type of ego defect, impairment in the psychological organization, is manifested by lack of coherent organization of core ego functions. Let us consider some examples. Basic *reality testing* may be impaired, manifested in severe cases by failure to understand the essential nature of the external environment, with overwhelming hallucinations, confusion, and panic.

Organization of thought may be impaired, as is seen in severe thought disorders (e.g., fragmentation of thought) or in milder forms, as with loose associations, tangential thinking, or illogical wandering from the topic. In a mild form, a woman may begin talking about her son's interest in a new girlfriend. She mentions a restaurant he visited with the girl, then describes the bad experience a friend of hers had at the same restaurant. She goes on to say that the friend is not a reliable judge because she complains about everything. Last week the church sponsored a picnic, and the friend was in charge of it. She is disappointed in the new minister because . . . , etc. A defect in *human affective*

FIGURE 1

Etiological Diagnosis (Some examples)	Diagnostic Categories From a Developmental Structuralist Approach	Symptom-Cluster Diagnosis (Some examples)
	1. *Ego Defects*	
Birth injury Encephalitis Vascular Disease, etc.	A. Basic physical organic integrity of mental apparatus (perception, integration, motor, memory, regulation, judgment, etc.)	Minimal brain dysfunction Senile Psychosis, etc.
	B. Structural psychological defects and defects in ego functions	
Partial Genetic Bases of Schizophrenia	(1) Reality testing, organization of perception and thought, and capacity for human affective engagement	Schizophrenic Disorders
	(2) Perception and regulation of affect	Manic-Depressive Disorders, etc.
	(3) Integration of affect and thought	
	(4) Defect in integration and organization and/or differentiation of self- and object representations	Borderline Disorders
	2. *Major Constrictions and Alterations in Ego Structure* A. Limitation of experience of feelings and/or thoughts in major life areas (love, work, play) B. Alterations and limitations in pleasure orientation C. Major externalizations of internal events, e.g., conflicts, feelings, thoughts	Severe Character Disorders

Etiological Diagnosis (Some examples)	Diagnostic Categories From a Developmental Structuralist Approach	Symptom-Cluster Diagnosis (Some examples)
	D. Limitations in internalizations necessary for regulation of impulses, affect (mood), and thought	
	E. Impairments in self-esteem regulation	
	F. Limited tendencies toward fragmentation of self-object differentiation	
	3. *Moderate versions of 2, above*	Moderate Character Disorders
		Symptom Neuroses
	4. *Encapsulated Disorders*	
	A. Neurotic symptom formations	
	(1) Limitations and alterations in experience of areas of thought (hysterical repression, phobic displacements, etc.)	Conversion Reactions Phobias
	(2) Limitations and alterations in experience of affects and feelings (e.g., obsessional isolation, depressive turning of feelings against the self, etc.)	Depressive Reactions Compulsive Syndromes
	B. Neurotic encapsulated character formations	
	(1) Encapsulated limitation of experience of feelings, thoughts, in major life areas (love, work, play)	Neurotic Obsessional or Hysterical Character
	(2) Encapsulated alterations and limitations in pleasure orientation	Neurotic Sexual Disorders
	(3) Encapsulated major externalizations of internal events (e.g., conflicts, feelings, thoughts)	

FIGURE 1 (*Continued*)

Etiological Diagnosis (Some examples)	Diagnostic Categories From a Developmental Structuralist Approach	Symptom-Cluster Diagnosis (Some examples)
	(4) Encapsulated limitations in internalizations necessary for regulation of impulses, affect (mood), and thought	Neurotic Narcissistic Disorders
	(5) Encapsulated impairments in self-esteem regulation	
	5. *Basically Intact Flexible Ego Structures*	
	A. With phase-specific developmental conflicts	
	B. With phase-specific developmentally expected patterns of adaptation, including adaptive regressions	
Phase-Appropriate Stress Situations	C. Intact, flexible, developmentally appropriate ego structure	

engagement is seen in individuals for whom no special or differentiated engagement in the human world has ever occurred (e.g., the severe, primary, psychopathic, psychotic disorders). Most evident in the interview is the uncanny nonhuman affective tone in such individuals, often alongside competent cognitive functioning.

Organization of *perception* may be impaired; in severe cases this can produce major disorientation, confusion, and anxiety. *Regulation of affect* may be impaired (e.g., manic-depressive psychosis). Such a patient may be swept away by the force of his uncontrolled elation, totally unable to moderate his driven clowning and pressured speech. Another slightly less sick patient, suffering with the same impairment of ego function, may communicate satisfactorily through most of an interview. When certain affectively laden content areas are reached, however, he is caught up in storms of rage which he cannot control and which make the interview setting chaotic and unstable.

Integration of affect and thought may be defective in another person (e.g., in a schizophrenic or manic-depressive disorder). For example, the content may be about death and sadness, while the individual smiles, giggles, and laughs.

Impaired regulation of impulses that might be more evident from a history, may, in the interview alone, be manifested by sudden behavior which is difficult to understand (e.g., a patient jumps up without warning and uses the interviewer's telephone, or has associative trends indicating impulsivity as a solution to life's frustrations: "I don't know why I beat up my child and wife. . . . My child cries at night and my wife gets up and goes to him. I still can't understand it").

Impairment of the *capacity for concentration* produces distractibility and an inability to maintain focus or attention. The patient has great difficulty keeping his attention on the interviewer and finds his associations drawn off in all directions.

A second class of less severe ego defects is often associated with impairments in the *organization and differentiation of internalized self- and object representations* (e.g., borderline conditions). These disorders take many forms, but the central feature is some difficulty with internalized self- and object representations, in either their organization, their differentiation, or their consolidation. There is a wide range of overall level of functioning in persons with these disorders, from severe psychosis at one extreme to relatively minor and subtle defects in otherwise strong personalities at the other. This makes diagnosis and classification somewhat more complicated. In the healthier person, particularly, the part of the mind which is less impaired tends to recognize and suppress the distortions, reshaping their appearance in more adaptive ways. For example, defects in reality testing which arise under stress (as described below) would be recognized and consciously suppressed or incorporated in jokes or playful fantasies. Thus, a woman patient who believes her therapist is in love with her might playfully tease him about it in such a way that there is a question whether her belief in the idea is firmly set. Only with skillful inquiry can the diagnostician determine whether the patient's reality testing is genuinely impaired—i.e., how real her belief is that her therapist is in love with her. A patient's continuing inability, during the interview, to distinguish which feelings are his own and which are the therapist's, together with historical evidence of similar difficulty in other relationships, suggests a defect in differentiating self from nonself. Secondary manifestations of this defect involve affect storms, overwhelming anxiety, and at times inappropriate behavior based on these distorted perceptions.

Defects in organization of internalized object representations tend to produce mental representations of important persons that lack sufficient stability and depth of perceptual or associational detail. In the interviews, and in the person's life in general, if there is not constant reassurance of the interviewer's or other significant person's existence, overwhelming panic and anxiety emerge. It could be speculated that their internalized representations are, in a sense, like underexposed photographs—dim, vague, and sketchy. In situations of strong need states, where they are called upon to protect the person from disorganizing anxiety, they are insufficient. For example, in situations of temporary loss, such as separation from an important person, the individual must contain the fear that he cannot survive alone by calling forth the mental representation of the object. When it is too dimly formed, he suffers from severe separation anxiety, with disorganizing panic. Often this panic is warded off with primitive global defenses, such as denial. Such a person, to feel comfortable, must have constant perceptual reassurance that the important object has not gone permanently.

The organization of the representation of the self may be similarly impaired, manifesting itself clinically in the interview in frequent feelings of depersonalization or frightening loss of a "sense of myself," including fantasies of bodily distortions. An often subtle syndrome of defective intentionality may also be seen, as illustrated by a massive inability to resolve conflicts and make decisions (usually linked with obsessional doubting and/ or omnipotent-perfectionist self-criticism), an inability to take initiative, massive inertia in therapy (often associated with a tendency to intellectualize), massive dependency, and a tendency to externalize.

Defective organization of object representations can also result in distorted or insufficient synthesis of the various elements of the representations. Without proper synthesis of the multitude of perceptions, memories, associations, and affects that make up the representations of another person, these may cluster into separate "good" and "bad" part representations. The individual may then remain locked in oscillating ambivalence toward important people and/or in unrealistic idealizing relationships.

The self-representation may remain similarly unsynthesized, well described by Kernberg (1975) as the borderline phenomenon of splitting, again an oscillation between two separate and contradictory part representations (in this case, of the self). Such a person is literally "of two minds."

In the interview session he may relate to the therapist as if he or the therapist were two different people. On the same day, or on different days, he will be all anger and suspicion, or all-trusting and uncritically loving. Whatever he may be feeling at that time cannot be related by him to the other set of feelings. The key point is that with such individuals there is no logical link between one state and the other, nor is there the capacity to discuss one set of feelings while the other is being experienced. If he is loving at this moment, he cannot say "I was angry at you before because. . . ." A less severe result of inadequate synthesis of the internalized representation of the self is the persistence of separate parts of the self which are not organized in such contradictory polarities that ego splitting is required. Rather, these parts are grouped together to resemble the original objects which were likely their model. In the clinical interview the patient appears to have different unrelated experiential worlds. For example, one day he talks and behaves like his "irresponsible father"; then, a day or so later, he talks and behaves in the session like his "critical, moralistic mother." Missing are the associative links and logical connections between these experiential organizations; the patient cannot relate to them, even with the therapist's help.

Disorders related to failures in the differentiation of internalized self- and object representations may take many forms. The most obvious is a difficulty in accurately separating what pertains to external objects from what pertains to oneself. Manifestations of this defect span a wide range of severity, from the sickest extreme, with early failures in basic ego functions necessary for a sense of reality of the self, to rather subtle disturbances which may be confused with excessive empathy or overidentification. A patient may say to the interviewer, "I *know* you don't like me," and cling to this impression regardless of all indications to the contrary. This is different from a patient who says, "I have a feeling you may not like me." In general, such defects are evidenced in the interview by confusion over which feelings and thoughts are the patient's and which the clinician's.

Severe Character Constrictions

The integrity of basic personality functioning may be maintained at the price of flexibility in the overall character structure. Massive avoidance of dangerous areas of life experience, or massive inhibition of wishes, thoughts, or affects, allows the individual to stay away from situations where his ego functions will break down (e.g., severe schizoid or paranoid characters, primitive depressive characters, severe narcissistic disorders, and negativistic personalities).

Persons with this constricted adjustment do not normally show signs of ego defects. They function adequately, within the constrictions of their characters, without special vulnerability to fragmentation. The price they pay is a serious restriction of their life experiences. Such a person may live a relatively symptom-free life by avoiding stressful experiences. For example, a person with a limitation in the capacity to modulate affect might use avoidance frequently to stay away from (what are to him) dangerous or strong feeling states. He would make elaborate rearrangements of his life to avoid emotion-charged situations. In his career, he would seek out work in which he could be isolated, with minimal human contact. He might take his meals alone to avoid the stress of human interaction, and avoid newspaper, TV, or books, any of which might stir him up to uncomfortable levels. If somehow he had married, he might be totally compliant with the wishes of his wife in order to avoid conflicts. With these adjustments, he could conceivably be "symptom free." In the clinical interview one might notice a very restrictive associative range of thought and affect (e.g., talking only about impersonal details of his work situation). While a broad experience may be constricted in different personalities, we shall be considering only the more clearly defined character constrictions.

A major constriction is that of *limitation of experience of feelings and/or thoughts.* For example, a person does not experience warm, loving feelings and avoids intimate one-to-one relationships, as in the schizoid personality. He may appear distant and aloof in interviews, remaining on an emotionally flat level, in spite of significant time spent with the interviewer. Another person (e.g., the chronically depressed individual) restricts his internal affective experience to the passive or sad and does not experience angry or assertive feelings. Behaviorally, he is limited to apathetic, mildly withdrawn actions. Yet another may not tolerate the experience of dependent wishes and externally manifests an overly self-reliant, somewhat unconcerned manner.

Another constriction is *alteration and limitation of pleasure orientation,* as manifested in the perversions. This loss of flexibility is often accompanied by a stereotyped pleasure orientation, intense but limited to selected areas. Thus, certain kinds of pleasure cannot be experienced. In the interview the associative pattern may have a persistent tone of particular themes, such as sadistic pleasure, without signs of compassionate, warm, empathic pleasure. The person may relate to the interviewer with behavior that expresses this sadistic theme. He is markedly limited (in a subtle form) in relating to certain affect trends, consistent with the restrictions in his behavioral flexibility and experience of pleasure in life (e.g., he is unable to experience heterosexual pleasure).

Major externalization of internal events, such as conflicts, feelings, and thoughts, is another character distortion. The person who externalizes hostile internal wishes or feelings may perceive aggression persistently coming at him from the outside. This is seen clinically (e.g., the paranoid syndrome) where, in the interview, themes of "they are out to get me" dominate. Another syndrome of externalization, less severe, is seen in persons who externalize perceptions about themselves (such as low self-esteem) onto others (e.g., in the interview, "I know you find me boring") or who act out their internal conflicts by polarizing their views onto one side and provoking others to speak for the opposite side. For example, a person might externalize his self-criticism by acting in a way to provoke his spouse—or, in the interview, the clinician—to be critical of him. Such individuals may be chronically suspicious, never forming comfortable, close, mutually dependent relationships or may tend to link up with a partner who is willing to act out the reciprocal position.

Another constriction is the *limitation of internalizations necessary for regulation of impulses, affects, and thought*. To the person with an underlying difficulty in internal regulation, impulsivity is not regarded as a symptom. It would, however, become apparent in the interviews, as, for example, when he describes feeling upset after a separation and immediately associates to an instance where he has gone out, gotten drunk, and picked a fight. In the process of the clinical interview, such a person may demonstrate little patience for self-reflection. Instead, he continually prefers to relate potentially gratifying aspects of his life story or current functioning.

Limitations in self-esteem maintenance, as illustrated by the narcissistic disorders, are another type of constriction. Such an individual manages to maintain a surprisingly stable and competent personality superficially (albeit with intolerance for failure and with impaired object relations, as manifested by problems with empathy and intimacy). With the interviewer, he may present a shallow quality of engagement, while, through his associative trends, he attempts to impress the interviewer with how worthy or important a person he is. In the interview he may show little capacity for genuine warmth or empathy and, after a few interviews, vacillates between reliance on the interviewer for a sense of self-worth or self-esteem on the one hand, and on the other, unrealistic grandiose fantasies. If the interviewer is able finally to engage such a patient, the patient may one day verbalize a deep sense of emptiness and vulnerable self-esteem, as well as tremendous fears of loss. Such individuals are constricted in their capacity to experience self-worth, self-esteem, and a range of compassionate and empathic feelings with regard to others.

Persons with a mild *instability in self-object differentiation* are vulnerable to a limited breakdown of that capacity, followed by a capacity for reorganizing. For example, these people may, under stress, lose some control of affect or depersonalize. Their lives are not generally unstable, because they constrict their experiences to avoid stress, but they can regress toward dedifferentiation. Such individuals may, when pressed in an interview, present mild fragmentation in their thinking. For example, such a person may talk about his passive submission toward someone he is involved with. The interviewer may ask if he becomes submissive when he is feeling angry. In response, the associations may become "loose" for a time but then return to the point. Or the individual may associate for a few minutes to how he feels unreal, or the world feels unreal, and then reorganize himself.

Moderate Character Constrictions

Disorders consisting of moderate character constrictions (e.g., moderate obsessive-compulsive or hysterical personality patterns; some limited impulsive behavior; a tendency toward externalization) involve the same categories of inflexibility of personality (characterological constriction) as above, but to a lesser degree. Only certain aspects of the personality evidence chronic repetitive limitations, rather than the entire personality, as in more severe disorders. For example, an individual may demonstrate a rather flexible, wide range of emotional engagement and be emotionally rich in the interview. The clinician feels this person has a sense of developmentally phase-appropriate emotion, interest, and curiosity. However, the individual noticeably omits any description of compassionate or empathic feelings in describing his life. Although he has a wife and family, his description of his home life is matter-of-fact and impersonal. When the interviewer inquires about this, the individual begins to disengage and shift to themes of achievement, talking about how he is concerned with "becoming successful" in work and the importance of "impressing superiors." Later, when the interviewer tries to bring him back to issues of compassion and empathy, he shows no ability to associate in this area and once again returns to the theme of "impressing superiors." At the same time, he again shows some disengagement from the interviewer, manifesting less emotional availability or warmth, and a more impersonal manner. This individual is demonstrating a moderate constriction of areas of affect in an otherwise flexible personality organization.

Encapsulated Disorders

This structural level is characterized by self-contained disturbances of function which are sharply limited in scope and do not involve massive areas of the personality (hence "encapsulated"). Encapsulated disorders protect the flexibility of the personality by producing limited impairments related to symptoms and contextually specific character traits. They differ from characterological constrictions in a very important manner. Persons suffering from these disorders do not avoid broad areas of experience. Encapsulated disorders do not involve chronic repetitive styles of avoidance or limitations of thoughts, wishes, or affects. For example, whereas anger in general is avoided in a character constriction, in an encapsulated disorder only anger directed at a contextually significant other might be avoided (e.g., an authority figure associated with one's father). Similarly, a sexual feeling will be avoided only in contextually relevant situations. While these are usually identified by dynamic hypotheses, they are also phenomenologically evident.

Encapsulated symptom disorders. The major limitations and alterations seen in symptom encapsulations are in thought and affect. The first type, *limitation of thought*, is found, for example, in the "hysterical" symptoms (e.g., periodic dizziness). Aside from this symptom, the individual may function at a very high level, able to engage in warm, loving relationships, to be assertive and accomplished at work, and to experience empathy and concern as well as anger and aggression. What is encapsulated is a particular content area of psychic life, often quite limited, having to do with specific wishes (e.g., of a sexual nature). In the interview, the limitation of thought may become apparent only by its repetitive absence from an otherwise flexible individual who experiences a wide range of ideas and fantasies. The interviewer may need to ask himself how it is that this seemingly open, warm person (who, for example, behaves seductively) cannot verbalize or think about seductive feelings. The interviewer may also note that certain mature heterosexual fantasies are also absent from the otherwise flexible fantasy repertoire of such an individual. The same may be true for certain aggression-related thoughts of a highly specific nature. (The key issue here is the contextual nature of the limitations.) During the course of treatment, limitations may become more dramatic as transference emerges. The classic example of *encapsulated alteration of thought* is hysterical repression, experienced simply as forgetting. A more complex manifestation is the encapsulated phobia.

The second major type of encapsulated symptom disorder is *limitation or alteration of affect* (e.g., an obsessive-compulsive neurosis, manifested in a handwashing compulsion). In the interview, such individuals may evidence the absence of specific affects in certain contextual situations (e.g., they are not angry at the interviewer when such a response would be expected or are unable to evidence associative trends dealing with anger toward certain contextually significant figures).

Encapsulated disorders are usually not difficult to diagnose in an interview with a cooperative patient. The individual shows a broad range of thoughts and affects, good interpersonal engagement with the interviewer, and a richly described life history. However, he is capable of only limited psychic function in certain specific content areas. There is an obvious disparity between the otherwise flexible personality and the encapsulated areas.

Encapsulated character disorders. These disorders present themselves not so much in specific symptoms (as phobias, compulsive rituals, or conversion reactions) but rather as subtle characterological limitations. While not as obvious to the interviewer as encapsulated symptom disorders, they do produce moderate limitation in certain capacities. These disorders differ from severe or moderate character constrictions developed earlier in life, both in the narrowness of the area that is limited and in the mildness of their symptoms. The limitation in these disorders is smaller, less severe, more "stress" related, and more related to contextually relevant thought and affect (e.g., problems with certain types of authority figures).

Although in their manifest form they may appear to be just a milder version of the more severe constrictions, these disorders operate by a different mechanism, more like that of the encapsulated symptom disorders. While severe character constrictions rely on avoidance on a massive scale to ward off a whole type of life experience, these disorders use more subtle character mechanisms (e.g., anger is always rationalized).

They differ in turn from the symptom disorders in that they are not as narrowly focused and often not as intense. An issue may express itself in these disorders in a large number of derivatives over a broader range. For example, an individual with an obsessional encapsulated character might be overly thorough in his attitude toward work details and "getting things completed." He may have trouble being in touch with his feelings and may criticize himself for not being able to feel and express love. (In the interview, he may recognize this limitation and comment on the clinical details.)

A phobic encapsulated symptom would be fixed and relatively intense, such as a fear of heights. By contrast, a phobic encapsulated character disorder would likely have no single symptom as fixed or severe, but would include phobic attitudes of a milder nature, which typically would come and go over time.

In general, neurotic encapsulated character formations may be categorized along the same lines as the more severe character constrictions (with the understanding that the encapsulated disorders are less intense.) Thus, an *encapsulated limitation of feeling or thought* in a major life area is represented in the individual who invariably shies away from the slightest emotional confrontation with male authority figures, while in other areas his emotional experience is not constricted. An *encapsulated alteration in pleasure orientation* might be shown by the woman who has difficulty becoming fully sexually aroused unless her male partner has first been angry and somewhat abusive. An *encapsulated externalization of internal conflict* is seen in the man who wants to purchase a more expensive car but feels guilty about the expense and talks to his wife about it in such glum, self-abnegating terms that she is provoked to argue in favor of the most costly model. An *encapsulated impairment in self-esteem regulation* is seen in the otherwise emotionally healthy professional singer who becomes morose when given a mediocre review.

Although traditional psychoanalytic thinking offers a tremendous depth of understanding of mechanisms, in dealing with the encapsulated character constriction structural diagnoses are advantageous in certain respects, as they are phenomenologically based and do not require the presence of inferred internal phenomena to make the diagnosis. As an example of the structural approach, in an interview an individual with encapsulated obsessional character traits might omit mention of angry feelings in discussing relationships, while otherwise giving access to a broad range of emotional experience. When he might be expected to describe anger, what instead emerges associatively are pleasurable examples of controlling other people. Associations might then move to his anxiety about losing his power, losing control, and not being "top dog." While this associative trend readily lends itself to the formulation of dynamic hypotheses, it is phenomenological in terms of what is and is not associated to.

Diagnosis of an Encapsulated Disorder: A Point of Frequent Confusion

In making a determination of an encapsulated disorder, attention should be given to the functional definition of encapsulation, which states that an encapsulated disorder protects most of the personality for flexible functioning. For example, consider a person with a compulsive handwashing symptom. He restricts his experience of internal feelings because he is afraid of getting germs on his hands and therefore stays away from places where there are people, where he might have to shake hands. He insists he does not have many feelings about people: "If I think of them with feelings, I may want to get together with them and therefore want to shake their hands." Such a person has obviously walled off large areas of experience, in terms of both internal emotions and interpersonal interactions. He rationalizes this walling off as a specific concern with washing hands. The diagnostician might be tempted to say this is an encapsulated disorder of great intensity which has secondarily limited the person's lifestyle. However, in our phenomenological scheme such a classification would be in error. An individual not engaging in certain life experiences, regardless of the reason, we define as constricted or as walling off areas of experience. The symptom involving his hands would be considered minor in comparison to this walling-off of feelings relating to people and interpersonal relationships.

If we examine the evolution of this person's disorder, a superficial history may indicate that it began with what seemed to be an encapsulated disorder which then spread to a constriction. On further inquiry, however, we often find that individuals who have intense focal symptoms that are also associated with general constrictions have, in fact, had long-standing constrictions. Often many symptoms are present, which are used at different times to excuse their limited lives. For example, the hypochondriacal person often uses different complaints at different times as a way of rationalizing a passive, dependent lifestyle.

Intact Flexible Ego Functioning

The next higher level of ego structure is free of difficulties other than phase-specific developmental conflicts and therefore cannot clearly be labeled pathological. The individual at this level can engage in a full range of developmentally appropriate experience, bothered only occasionally with expectable developmental interferences and conflicts. For example, a healthy adult considering marriage may become anxious around issues of intimacy, and not unreasonably; or an adolescent separating from his parents may become somewhat anxious or depressed. These transient episodes are not expressions of permanent structures but are merely reactions to the demands of a particular stage of life. (An important subclass in this group is the phase-specific, developmentally expected adolescent pattern of regression. The surface manifestations here may look like psychopathology, but actually the regression is adaptive, in the service of further growth and development.)

Although personalities at this high level are not structurally deficient, we nevertheless distinguish different levels of functioning, depending in part on the complexity of adaptive transformations available. The flexibility of the personality in its adaptive potential can be categorized in terms of the transformations available to accommodate the full range of phase-appropriate experience and varying degrees of stress. The most adaptive structure has the capacity for *multiple* transformations, which can accommodate a wide range of experience, including conflict, in the context of a viable personality organization that is uniquely personal and developmentally facilitating (Greenspan, 1979).

Practical Issues in the Use of the Developmental Structuralist Approach to Diagnosis

The classification scheme can be used in a number of ways. It can be used to make a judgment regarding the situation the person finds himself in, as well as a classification of preexisting or chronic personality patterns. In assessing functional capacity, these two diagnoses are usually the same, except under rare circumstances such as intense stress, because the developmental structural diagnosis not only takes into account current influences but usually includes a historical perspective which provides a picture of how this individual functions more generally. For example, when we determine that an individual has an ego defect, we do so on the basis of both cross-sectional and historical evidence. We assume that a major functional impairment exists over a period of time. We are dealing with the overall adaptive functional capacity of the personality, and this implies stability. In unusual circumstances, such as disorganization secondary to a toxic reaction, we may see transient ego deficits. Examinations after the episode, however, may point to a less impaired but still morbid level of functioning. Similarly, an individual with a reasonable level of premorbid funtioning may develop a manic episode or series of episodes. In this instance as well, the more permanent personality organization and its vulnerability may be indicated by one diagnosis and the acute disorganization by another. The diagnosis of the more permanent personality organization would of course depend on both overall level of functioning and susceptibility to disorganization, by either biological or psychological precipitants. For example, such an individual may be characterized by a major ego defect in affect regulation or by a characterological constriction whereby affect regulation is rendered vulnerable.

Therefore, while in most cases only one diagnosis is necessary, in special situations this scheme permits flexible diagnoses, including acute and premorbid levels of functioning. Depending on the situation, one might have a double diagnosis.

Further, within a given category (e.g., ego defects), there may be more than one subcategory (e.g., a defect in reality testing and a defect in affect regulation). For clarity of presentation we indicated earlier that in the character constrictions there is either a walling-off of experience or another phenomenon, such as a tendency to externalize. Actually, an individual with a constriction could evince both a walling-off and externalization. Thus, major tendencies can be more finely described with the use of multiple designations.

It should be kept in mind, however, that multiple designations may occur only in the same general category. We would not diagnose ego defects, character constrictions, and encapsulated disorders for the same person at the same time. The person is either flexible enough to manifest encapsulated phenomena only, or he is inflexible and requires a diagnosis of constriction. The two are mutually exclusive at any given time. The diagnostician familiar with traditional nomenclature may ask, What if an individual has phobic symptoms in addition to an underlying depressive character structure? In our scheme, such a person is categorized in terms of the predominant maladaptive level—that is, the depressive character structure implying constriction and intolerance of certain affects and thoughts. The symptomatology atop this constricted state is taken into account in the symptom-oriented classification. Similarly, if an individual has a defect in reality testing and also avoids certain affects, the limitation of affects would be a secondary elaboration in the symptom-cluster column. The structural categories, if they provide the best descriptive tool, can also be used for this purpose.

As indicated earlier, it is useful to conceptualize three columns (see Figure 1) with the developmental structuralist approach in the center, the first column listing the symptom-oriented approaches and the third column the etiological approaches. Thus, a major constriction in the developmental structuralist approach would give the developmental level of the overall adaptive capacities. In the symptom category, the individual may evince phobias, anxiety reactions, obsessive rituals, and so forth. We then have a picture of the predominant symptomatic manifestations evidenced in this depressive character organization.

While this classification scheme suggests qualitative differences between each category (i.e., an ego defect is qualitatively different from a constriction, which is qualitatively different from an encapsulation; and within the ego defects, affect regulation defects are qualitatively different from those having to do with reality testing, etc.), we can use this scheme quantitatively (in a general way) to indicate degree of impairment. We could sketch an illness-adaptation line beginning with the most severe disorders and ending with the most adaptive personality structures (see Figure 2).

· FIGURE 2

Scale* Most Maladaptive

10 Ego Defects

Basic physical organic integrity of mental apparatus (perception, integration, motor, memory, regulation, judgment, etc.)

Structural psychological defects and defects in ego functions

Reality testing and organization of perception and thought and capacity for human affective engagement

Perception and regulation of affect

Integration of affect and thought

7.5 Defect in Integration and Organization and/or Differentiation of Self- and Object Representations

6.5 Major Constrictions and Alterations in Ego Structure

Limitation of experience of feelings and/or thoughts in major life areas (love, work, play)

Alterations and limitations in pleasure orientation

Major externalizations of internal events, e.g., conflicts, feelings, thoughts

Limitations in internalizations necessary for regulation of impulses, affect (mood), and thought

Impairments in self-esteem regulation

Limited tendencies toward fragmentation of self-object differentiation

5 Moderate Constrictions and Alterations in Ego Structure

Moderate versions of major constrictions listed above

3 Encapsulated Disorders

Neurotic symptom formations

Limitations and alterations in experience of areas of thought (hysterical repression, phobic displacements, etc.)

Limitations and alterations in experience of affects and feelings (e.g., obsessional isolation, depressive turning of feelings against the self, etc.)

Neurotic encapsulated character formations

Encapsulated limitation of experience of feelings, thoughts, in major life areas (love, work, play)

Encapsulated alterations and limitations in pleasure orientation

Encapsulated major externalization of internal events (e.g., conflicts, feelings, thoughts)

Encapsulated limitations in internalizations necessary for regulation of impulses, affect (mood), and thought

Encapsulated impairments in self-esteem regulation

2 Age- and Phase-Appropriate Adaptive Capacities with Phase-Specific Conflicts

1 Age- and Phase-Appropriate Adaptive Capacities with Optimal Phase-Expected Personality Flexibility

Most Adaptive

*This framework may also be used quantitatively. For example, a scale from 1 to 10, as illustrated in this diagram, may be used to reach an approximation of degree of impairment. See column at left (scale), where 10 indicates the most severe psychopathology. It should be noted that this particular quantitative scale represents the author's clinical impressions regarding relationships among different levels of impairment, in terms of degree of severity, and is presented for illustrative purposes only.

The diagnostician can use this sequence as a means of seeing where on the continuum of pathology and adaptation a particular patient lies. The sequence also allows the rater to take into account degree of impairment within a given category. Thus, in terms of ego defects, we could rate the person closer to the top or to the bottom of that particular category.

In the next section these categories and the continuum are tied to the sequence of early development and reflect developmental level attained in terms of personality integration and degree of impairment. By "developmental level" we mean level of the arrest in further development in important psychological areas. A major ego defect, for example, reflects a major arrest along a particular line of development early in life. Of course, a developmentally healthy person may have characteristics which can be traced back to infancy, some of which are maladaptive, but these are not arrests in development. For the most part, development continues in such a person along adaptive dimensions. For example, an encapsulated disorder may embody early conflicts, but development in the major sectors of personality functioning has advanced to age- and phase-appropriate levels. In the next section we discuss how these categories and their classifications arise from the various tasks of each stage of early development.

Adult Developmental Structural Categories of Personality and Psychopathology as Derivatives of Childhood Development

In this section we attempt, somewhat speculatively, to connect the levels of personality organization and psychopathology described earlier to a developmental structuralist approach to the stages of early personality development. The stages of development to be used are based on a new model of early development (Greenspan, 1979). To illustrate how this approach to diagnosis can be understood in the context of personality development, the model is presented here in summary and schematic form.

First, the major assumptions of the developmental structuralist approach and its foundations are reviewed briefly. Second, the developmental structural levels emerging at each stage of infancy and early childhood are described. Following this, a schematic outline is presented that suggests the relationship of the derivative adult categories of psychopathology to this scheme of early development.

As indicated earlier, the major assumption of a developmental structuralist approach is that a person is capable of organizing experience from birth onward and that this capacity becomes potentially more adaptive in terms of organizing a wide range of phase-appropriate experience as development proceeds. In addition, this capacity progressively achieves greater stability and resilience, reflecting the integration of unique individual differences. That the infant is capable of organizing experience even at birth and shortly thereafter in an adaptive fashion is now well documented (Sander, 1962; Lipsitt, 1966; Gerwirtz, 1965, 1969; Emde, Gaensbauer, and Harmon, 1976; Klaus and Kennell, 1976; Meltzoff and Moore, 1977). It is interesting to note that this empirically documented view of the infant as capable of organizing experience is consistent in a general sense with Freud's early hypothesis (1911) and Hartmann's postulation (1939) of an undifferentiated organizational matrix early in life. That the organization of experience broadens during the early months of life to reflect increases in the capacity to experience and tolerate a range of stimuli in stable and personal configurations is consistent also with recent empirical data (Sander, 1962; Escalona, 1968; Brazelton, Koslowski, and Main, 1974; Sroufe and Matas, 1974; Stern, 1974a, 1974b; Emde, Gaensbauer, and Harmon, 1976; Murphy and Moriarty, 1976). That these progressively complex capacities to organize experience reflect individual differences in infants present from birth onward is also now well documented (Wolff, 1966; Thomas, Chess, and Birch, 1968; Parmelee, 1972).

The developmental structural levels for infancy and early childhood may be described according to the model referred to above, in terms of the stage-specific tasks and desired capacity in infancy and early childhood. In summary, the first task of the infant can be seen to be the achievement of *homeostasis*.

This involves establishing internal harmony and regulation, including the establishment of rhythms and cycles (Sander, 1962), in the context of a capacity for involvement in the animate and inanimate world. The infant comes into the world with capacities to organize experience in a rudimentary manner and demonstrates individual differences in ways of achieving this initial homeostatic capacity.

Once some capacity for regulation in the context of engaging the world has been achieved with increasing central nervous system maturation, the infant appears to be less governed by internal somatic cues and more attuned to social and interpersonal interaction—e.g., the development of the social smile (Spitz, Emde, and Metcalf, 1970). Between 2 and 4 months, as he becomes more available to responding to the external environment, the growing infant also becomes capable of forming a special relationship with the primary caregivers. Thus, the second capacity that can be delineated is *forming a human attachment*. This task and capacity can be considered in terms of developmental structural characteristics. If an affective and relatively pleasurable attachment is formed (an investment in the human and animate world), then, with growing maturational abilities, the infant develops complex patterns of communication in the context of this primary human relationship. Along with developments in the inanimate world, where basic schemes of causality are being developed—means/ends relationships (Piaget, 1962)—the infant becomes capable of complicated communications (e.g., Charlesworth, 1969; Tennes, Emde, Kisley, and Metcalf, 1972; Brazelton, Koslowski, and Main, 1974; Stern, 1974a) in the context of forming basic schemes of causal relationships in the animate world. Thus, means/ends relationships are established between the infant and primary caregivers, evidenced by his developing ability to discriminate primary caregivers from others and to differentiate his own actions from their consequences behaviorally, somatically, affectively, and interpersonally. A process of somatopsychological differentiation begins occurring along a number of developmental lines (e.g., sensorimotor integration, affects, relationships). Thus, a third set of capacities and tasks may be termed *somatopsychological differentiation*. While schemes of causality are being established in relation to the behavioral, affective, somatic, and interpersonal worlds, it is not at all clear that these schemes exist at a mental-representational or symbolic level. Rather, they appear to exist at a somatic level (Greenspan, 1979).

With appropriate reading of the infant's cues and systematic differential responding by the environment, the infant's behavioral repertoire becomes more complicated, and communications take on more organized, meaningful configurations. We note that the infant is able to begin connecting up behavioral units into larger organizations, as he evinces complex emotional responses such as affiliation, wariness, and fear (Bowlby, 1969; Ainsworth, Bell, and Stayton, 1974; Sroufe and Waters, 1977). We also note, along with this greater organization of complex affective responses, a capacity for forming original behavioral schemes (Piaget, 1962), increased imitative activity, intentionality, originality, and behavioral organization in both the cognitive and the social emotional realm. Thus, a fourth stage and set of capacities can be delineated, that of *behavioral organization, initiative, and internalization.* During this stage there is a type of learning which is evidenced in earlier development but now seems to take a more dominant role: learning through imitation. The growing toddler seems to learn in leaps and bounds through imitating complex patterns.

With further maturation of the central nervous system, as the toddler moves into the end of the second year, we notice the capacity to form and organize mental imagery. What were perhaps internal sensations now become organized in a mental-representational form proper (e.g., Piaget, 1962; Gouin-Décarie, 1965; Bell, 1970). While this capacity for forming mental representations is initially fragile, between 16 and 24 months it appears to become a more dominant mode in organizing the child's behavior. Now the toddler has the capacity for forming, organizing, and manipulating mental imagery. A fifth stage and capacity or task can thus be documented, the capacity for *forming mental representations.*

Now the child develops his capacities for differentiation at a representational level. Just as causal schemes were developed earlier at a somatic behavioral level, now they are developed at the level of symbolic representation. The growing child begins to differentiate feelings, thoughts, and events that emanate from him and those that emanate from others. He begins to differentiate what he experiences and does from their impact on the world. This gradually forms the basis for the differentiation of internal self-representations and internal representations which embody the external world, both animate and inanimate.

Gradually the capacity for differentiating internal representations—including object constancy (Mahler, Pine, and Bergman, 1975)—becomes consolidated. Subsequently, representational capacity becomes reinforced with the ability of the child to develop derivative representational systems. These are tied to the original representations and permit greater flexibility in dealing with a range of experience such as the perceptions, feelings, thoughts, ideals, values, in *stable configurations* (Greenspan, 1979). The substages of representational capacities include *representational differentiation, the consolidation of representational capacity,* and *the capacity for forming limited derivative representational systems and multiple derivative representational systems (structural learning).*[1]

From the earliest stages of infancy to the late stages of adolescence and adulthood, the developing individual has the opportunity to consolidate relatively adaptive structures or varying degrees of compromise. Thus, in the earliest stages of infancy, the infant can form adaptive patterns of regulation whereby his internal states are harmoniously regulated and he is free to invest himself in the animate and inanimate world, setting the basis for rich emotional attachments to his primary caregivers. However, if his regulatory processes are not functioning properly and he cannot maintain internal harmony in the context of being available to the world, the infant or toddler may withdraw. From relatively minor compromises, such as

---

[1] It should be noted that the capacities outlined above do not emerge in an exact sequence. Many of these capacities (e.g., discriminating cues) begin in the earliest months of life. The sequence described above attempts to suggest the time at which each capacity becomes pivotal and dominant in the infant's or toddler's capacity to organize his behavior and further his development.

withdrawing in the face of excess stimulation, to chronic global patterns of withdrawal or hyperexcitability, we can observe the relative degrees to which the infant, even in the first months of life, achieves a less than optimally adaptive structural capacity.

Similarly, early attachments can be warm and engaging, or shallow, insecure, and limited in their affective tone. In the early reciprocal relationships we can observe differences between an infant who reads the signals of the caregivers and responds in a rich, meaningful way to multiple aspects of the communications (with multiple affects and behavioral communications) and one who can respond only within a narrow range of affect (e.g., protest), or who cannot respond at all in a contingent or reciprocal manner (e.g., the seemingly apathetic, withdrawn, and depressed child who responds only to his own internal cues). As the toddler's life becomes behaviorally more organized and complex, patterns appear which reflect originality and initiative in the context of the separation-individuation subphase of development (Mahler, Pine, and Bergman, 1975). We can observe those toddlers who manifest this full adaptive capacity and compare them with others who are either stereotyped in their behavioral patterns (reflect no originality or intentionality), who remain fragmented (never connect up pieces of behavior into more complicated patterns), or evidence polarities of affect showing no capacity to integrate emotions (e.g., the chronic negativistic aggressive toddler, who cannot show interest, curiosity, or love for the human world).

As a capacity for representational organizations is reached, we can distinguish the child who can organize, integrate, and differentiate a rich range of affective and ideational life from the child who either remains without representational capacity, forms a fragmented, unintegrated representational capacity, or who may form and differentiate self- and object representations only at the expense of the extreme compromises in the range of experience tolerated (e.g., the schizoid child). Similarly, we can observe in later childhood (the triangular phase) latency and in adolescence relatively adaptive or maladaptive structural outcomes.

Figures 3 and 4 are schematic outlines of adult psychopathology in the context of the above stages of development, beginning with early infancy and ending with late adolescence.

This outline summarizes the stages of development, adaptive outcomes in infancy and childhood, pathological outcomes in infancy and childhood, and derivative adult pychopathologic personality structures.

In formulating this schematic outline of the stages of early development and hypothesized derivative adult personality structures, we are formulating a speculative model. The phenomenologically based approach discussed earlier is not tied to this model, which is presented to illustrate how a developmental structuralist approach to classification may be derived from understanding early development. It should be expected that refinements in our understanding of early development will lead to further hypotheses and speculations about the relationships between early development and later adaptive and pathological adult derivative personality functioning.

FIGURE 3. Schematic outline of developmental structuralist approach to the relationship between early development and derivative adult psychopathology.

Developmental Structural Levels of Personality Organization

HOMEOSTASIS—Homeostasis involves balancing internal regulation and harmony with investment in the world. This includes taking in sensory stimulation and organizing it with developmentally appropriate capacities (e.g., cycles, rhythms, states of alertness and relaxation).
Illustrative Adaptive Capacities:
Internal regulation (harmony) and balanced interest in the world (animate and inanimate).
Illustrative Maladaptive (Psychopathological) Patterns in Childhood:
Disorders which may involve gross physical or neurological defects, immaturity of the central nervous system, difficulties in early patterns of integration, certain environmental conditions, organ sensitivities (gastrointestinal problems), and allergies are a few of the factors that may contribute to a homeostatic disorder. For example, there is the excitable infant who cannot habituate to stimulation, the infant with specific sensitivities (auditory, tactile), or the infant with immature motor responses who cannot orient or accept soothing from the caregiver. Even in the absence of manifest symptoms (excessive irritability, withdrawal, etc.) and/or in the face of stress, one can observe the degree

FIGURE 3 *(Continued)*

to which an infant fully organizes a homeostatic experience. For example, the infant who is alert, oriented, and engaged in the animate and inanimate world in an organized manner in the context of established patterns of sleeping-wakefulness and eating may be contrasted with the infant who can be calm only at the expense of an optimal state of alertness and engagement. To the former, a mild stress (illness) may result in a temporary change in sleep patterns, while, to the latter, a similar stress may result in intense apathy and lack of engagement in the animate world.

Illustrative Derivative Maladaptive (Psychopathological) Patterns in Adulthood:

Autism and primary defects in basic integrity of the personality (perception, integration, motor, memory, regulation).

ATTACHMENT—An affective relationship forms between the infant and his mother, expressed in the dominance of pleasure in each other and subtle variations of affective relating between the two through multiple modalities (e.g., sensory and motor modalities) and encompassing deep, rich, varied affect.

Illustrative Adaptive Capacities:

Rich, affective multisensory investment in the animate world, especially primary caregivers.

Illustrative Maladaptive (Psychopathological) Patterns in Childhood:

Attachment disorders depend on the relative integrity of the early attachment patterns and the degree to which stress (e.g., infant's hunger, mother's being upset) compromises this integrity. The most severe attachment disorder is autism. Because of genetic or constitutional difficulties or severe early environmental trauma, the autistic youngster never fully achieves homeostasis. He therefore does not move on to the second task, that of human attachment. Disorders of human attachment also arise when depressed mothers cannot reach out to their infants, when their quality of relationship seems shallow and insecure. Another variety comes about when the infant's individual constitutional differences make physical touch or other kinds of human stimulation painful; such a child may be all too vulnerable to a disorder of attachment. Anaclitic depression, psychophysiological difficulties (vomiting, rumination), failure to thrive (metabolic depression, marasmus), and feeding and sleeping disturbances may all be related to this type of disorder.

Illustrative Maladaptive (Psychopathological) Patterns in Adulthood:

Primary defects in the capacity to form human relationships, internal intrapsychic emotional life, and intrapsychic structure.

Consequence Level of Learning

SOMATOPSYCHOLOGICAL DIFFERENTIATION—This represents the first step toward the child's clear separation of himself from his

FIGURE 3 *(Continued)*

actions and the external world. He develops schemes of causal connections, which contribute to the more complex derivative reality testing which emerges later in development. In the animate realm, a process of emotional and interpersonal differentiation occurs which establishes the basic schemes of interpersonal causality (means/ends relationships).

Illustrative Adaptive Capacities:

Flexible, multisystem contingent, reciprocal interactions with animate and inanimate world, especially with primary caregivers.

Illustrative Maladaptive (Psychopathological) Patterns in Childhood:

Disorders in somatopsychological differentiation should be studied in the context of the many phase-appropriate dimensions of differentiation. Some of these are cognition, human relationships, affects, and the flexibility to deal with stress (without compromising developmentally facilitating behavior). An example of an extreme defect in differentiation is the infant who does not respond to different environmental events with different responses of his own and has not developed age-appropriate contingent behavioral and emotional responses (a basic sense of causality as the foundation of reality testing). This may be due either to his own constitutional makeup, to events in his earlier development, or to a withdrawn or overly intrusive (projecting) primary caretaker. A less severe problem exists when only one aspect of emotional differentiation (because of the character of contingent responses) is compromised—e.g., anger is ignored or leads to withdrawal. Many symptoms may be related to disorders of somatopsychological differentiation. These include sensorimotor developmental delays, apathy or intense chronic fear (stranger anxiety), clinging, lack of explorativeness and curiosity, flat or nonresponsive emotional reactions to significant caregivers, as well as specific maladaptive patterns of relatedness, such as biting, chronic crying, and irritability.

Illustrative Maladaptive (Psychopathological) Patterns in Adulthood:

Primary ego defects (psychosis) including structural defects in: (1) reality testing and organization of perception and thought; (2) perception and regulation of affect; (3) integration of affect and thought.

BEHAVIORAL ORGANIZATION, INITIATIVE, AND INTERNALIZA-
TION—The child begins to show greater behavioral and emotional organization. Through imitative behavior, new behavioral patterns are learned quickly. Old schemes are recombined in new goal-directed patterns. There is the use of detours, substitutes, and intermediary devices. Original, organized behavior results in an impression of the toddler as an initiating organized human being.

Illustrative Adaptive Capacities:

Complex, organized, assertive, innovative behavioral emotional patterns.

Behavioral creativity and originality; integration of behavioral and emotional polarities.

Figure 3 *(Continued)*
Illustrative Maladaptive (Psychopathological) Patterns in Childhood:
Disorders in behavioral organization and internalization may compromise the beginning of internal "psychological" life. Behavior remains fragmented, related to somatic or external cues. Intentionality and sense of self are "nipped in the bud," so to speak. Specific disorders of this phase are evidenced by a wide range of problems. These can vary from a complete lack of imitation, intentionality, and organized emotional and behavior systems to circumscribed limitations in certain emotional or behavioral systems—e.g., the child cannot assert himself or has difficulties with affiliative behavior. Symptoms may include chronic temper tantrums, inability to initiate even some self-control, lack of motor or emotional coordination, extreme chronic negativism, delayed language development, and relationships characterized by chronic aggressive behavior.

Illustrative Maladaptive (Psychopathological) Patterns in Adulthood:
Defects in behavioral organization and emerging representational capacities—e.g., certain borderline psychotics; primary substance abuse; psychosomatic conditions; impulse disorders, and affect tolerance disorders.

Representational Level of Learning

REPRESENTATIONAL CAPACITY—The child begins to organize mental representations of inanimate and animate objects. These enable the child to internally manipulate symbols of objects.

Illustrative Adaptive Capacities:
Formation of complex organizations of internal imagery and increased behavioral, emotional, cognitive, and interpersonal repertoire (e.g., the ability to say "no," the development of personal pronouns, ability to recall, ability for organizing mental images and searching for inanimate and animate objects, memory for emotional experience, locating experiences that pertain to self and nonself, the beginning of cognitive insight, combining internalized schemes, being able to identify the various parts of self, relating in a diminishing need-feeling manner, and the beginnings of cooperation and concern for others).

Illustrative Maladaptive (Psychopathological) Patterns in Childhood:
Disorders of this phase are evidenced by the lack of psychological life (internal representations) and may be observed in symptoms involving severe regressive behavior (disorganized emotional and motor responses), chronic unrelenting clinging with complete disruption of explorative behavior, chronic primitive aggressive behavior (biting, scratching, throwing things), chronic fearfulness, and either interpersonal promiscuity or withdrawal.

FIGURE 3 *(Continued)*
Illustrative Maladaptive (Psychopathological) Patterns in Adulthood:
Borderline syndromes and secondary ego defects including defects in integration and organization and/or emerging differentiation of self- and object representations.
REPRESENTATIONAL DIFFERENTIATION—The child makes a major shift away from the somatic and behavioral organization of experience to the internal representational world and differentiates experience at the level of internal imagery.
Illustrative Adaptive Capacities:
Capacity for representational creativity and insight; differentiation of imagery pertaining to self and nonself in context of rich investment in animate and inanimate world. There is a differentiation of various feeling states and behavior, and stabilization of mood. Gradual emergence of basic personality functions. These include reality testing, organization and regulation of impulses, organization and regulation of thought, and integration of thought and affect. Ultimately, there is an ongoing delineation of the sense of self, and it becomes ever more coherent. Eventually it reaches a stage where it is not undermined by brief separations or intense feeling states such as anger.
Illustrative Maladaptive (Psychopathological) Patterns in Childhood:
Disorders of psychological differentiation are seen at two levels. At the more severe level there is a capacity for some organized, internal psychological life, but it is extremely vulnerable to stress (separation, strong feeling states). Magical thinking predominates. This becomes visible in a number of ways. The shift from fantasy to reality is not taking place; under emotional stress, severe distortions in reality-oriented thinking occur; or there is a continued lack of organization and regulation of emotions and impulses; or chronic patterns of disorganized aggressive or regressive behavior are present. The negativism only gets worse; the withdrawal from human relationships increases; the ability to care for bodily functions does not become established; the tendency to blame others becomes more intense; and the fear of loss, security, love, and bodily injury are so severe that progressive development is experienced as dangerous (e.g., intimacy, assertion, curiosity, and self-control are relinquished). At a less severe level, basic differentiation does occur, but at a price. This includes major distortions in personality or character formation—i.e., an overall inability of the personality to engage fully in age-appropriate endeavors. Examples of related disorders are extreme negativism, withdrawal, depression, or apathy.
Illustrative Maladaptive (Psychopathological) Patterns in Adulthood:
Severe alterations in personality structure: (1) limitation of experience of feelings and/or thoughts in major areas (love, work, play); (2) alterations and limitations in pleasure orientation; (3) major externalizations of internal events such as conflicts, feelings, thoughts; (4) limitations in internalizations necessary for regulation of impulses, affect

FIGURE 3 (Continued)

(mood), and thought; (5) impairment in self-esteem regulation; (6) tendencies toward fragmentation of self-object differentiation. Examples are severe disorders such as schizoid, paranoid, depressive, inadequate, or borderline personality.

CONSOLIDATION OF REPRESENTATIONAL DIFFERENTIATION—Differentiation of representations progresses until a stable plateau is reached, where ego functions, and internalized self- and object representations are stabilized.

Illustrative Adaptive Capacities:

Consolidation of basic personality functions, including reality testing, impulse regulation, affect organization, self-esteem maintenance, delineated sense of self, focused concentration, and capacity for learning.

Illustrative Maladaptive (Psychopathological) Patterns in Childhood and Adulthood:

More moderate versions of the above personality constrictions and alterations—for example, moderate obsessional, hysterical, or depressive character disorders.

CAPACITY FOR LIMITED EXTENDED REPRESENTATIONAL SYSTEMS (Representation-Structural Level of Learning)—The child now alters representations for defensive and adaptive purposes, including forming inverse and reciprocal relationships. Derivative representations alter wishes, for example, without compromising the basic integrity of core ego functions or the continuity of the sense of self (i.e., adaptive defenses).

Illustrative Adaptive Capacities:

Enhanced flexibility to conserve and transform complex and organized representations of animate and inanimate experience in the context of new expanded relationship patterns with family, peers, others, and the inanimate world.

Illustrative Maladaptive (Psychopathological) Patterns in Childhood and Adulthood:

Encapsulated disorders including neurotic syndromes: (1) neurotic symptom formations; (a) limitation and alterations in experience of areas of thought (hysterical repression, phobic displacement); (b) limitations and alterations in experience of affects and feelings (e.g., obsessional isolation, depressive turning of feelings against the self, etc.); (2) neurotic encapsulated character formations; (a) encapsulated limitations of experience of feelings, thoughts, in major life areas (love, work, play); (b) encapsulated alterations and limitations in pleasure orientation; (c) encapsulated major externalization of internal events (e.g., conflicts, feelings, thoughts); (d) encapsulated limitations in internalizations necessary for regulation of impulses, affect (mood), and thought; (e) encapsulated impairments in self-esteem regulation.

CAPACITY FOR MULTIPLE EXTENDED REPRESENTATIONAL SYSTEMS—The child makes use of increased cognitive abilities

FIGURE 3 *(Continued)*

now available to develop multilevel systems of transformations. For example, secondary or tertiary defenses may reinforce the initial adaptive defensive manipulation, providing great strength, flexibility, and resilience.

Illustrative Adaptive Capacities:

Optimal flexibility to conserve and transform new expanded experience of animate (emotional) and inanimate (impersonal) world, including developmentally expectable relationship patterns, heterosexual interests, educational and occupational plans, hypothetical considerations, emerging values and ideals, and a more differentiated (independent yet continuous with earlier ties) sense of personal identity.

Illustrative Maladaptive (Psychopathological) Patterns in Childhood and Adulthood:

Phase-specific developmental and/or neurotic conflicts with or without neurotic syndromes. (This pattern can also occur during earlier phases.)

FIGURE 4. Developmental levels and adult psychopathology.

Developmental Structural Levels of Personality Organization	Illustrative Derivative Maladaptive (Psychopathological) Patterns in Adulthood
Homeostasis	Autism and primary defects in basic integrity of the personality (perception, integration, motor, memory, regulation).
Attachment	Primary defects in the capacity to form human relationships, internal intrapsychic emotional life, and intrapsychic structure.
Somatopsychological Differentiation	Primary ego defects (psychosis) including structural defects in (1) reality testing and organization of perception and thought; (2) perception and regulation of affect; (3) integration of affect and thought.
Behavioral Organization, Initiative, and Internalization	Defects in behavioral organization and emerging representational capacities: e.g., certain borderline psychotics; primary substance abuse; psychosomatic conditions; impulse disorders and affect tolerance disorders.
Representational Capacity	Borderline syndromes and secondary

FIGURE 3 *(Continued)*

	ego defects in integration and organization and/or emerging differentiation of self- and object representations.
Representational Differentiation	Severe alterations in personality structure.
Consolidation of Representational Differentiation	More moderate versions of the personality constrictions and alterations: e.g., moderate obsessional, hysterical, or depressive character disorders.
Capacity for Limited Extended Representational Systems	Encapsulated disorders including neurotic syndromes.
Capacity for Multiple Extended Representational Systems	Phase-specific developmental and/or neurotic conflicts with or without neurotic syndromes. (This pattern can also occur during earlier phases.)

Clinical Illustration of the Developmental Structuralist Approach to Diagnosis

The following brief illustration highlights further the differences between the developmental structuralist approach and other approaches.

Case History

Mr. H., a 35-year old man, came for consultation, complaining of feeling "depressed, empty, hollow inside—bad about myself. . . . I can't fall asleep, I wake up early in the morning, and at times I feel so bad, I think life is not worth living." Mr. H. began to talk about himself almost at once, with little hesitance. He spoke clearly and appeared surprisingly undepressed. He was stylishly dressed, well groomed, pleasant, and relaxed, with a warm smile and comfortable eye contact. Paradoxically, there was a great deal of apparent personal engagement yet, at the same time, an impersonal quality.

Mr. H. revealed that a long-standing relationship with a young lady had ended for reasons hard to specify, except that they were fighting and she was complaining that he wasn't committed enough. Subsequently, he had begun to feel empty and hollow and had trouble sleeping. Mr. H. was an advertising executive and was still functioning quite well at his work. He indicated that much of the success of the whole company, in fact, was due to his natural flair for choosing successful promotional themes. He seemed to be the only one who could consistently orchestrate winning campaigns.

After his opening statement, Mr. H. sat with a blank look and after about twenty seconds of silence asked, "What shall I talk about next? What would you like to know?" The consultant asked how it was that, although Mr. H. presented himself so readily and easily, he was unclear on where to go from here. Mr. H. revealed that he was "very good at superficial conversation" but found it hard to really talk about himself. The consultant sympathetically encouraged him to make an attempt. After another silence Mr. H. wondered if the consultant had ever felt depressed and whether or not psychiatry could "be of any help." The consultant empathized that he was aware that one might be reluctant to talk about difficult personal issues when one is not sure how helpful it might be. Mr. H. quickly responded, "Oh, I know I'm supposed to talk about myself. I guess I should tell you about my relationship with my girlfriend." He the went on to describe the relationship in superficial terms of things they had done together (dinner, movies). There was little talk of intimacy or the nature of the emotional involvement. He did observe that he had great difficulty expressing or even experiencing any anger at her. In the last few months, she had repeatedly failed to appreciate what he was accomplishing in his work and at times seemed to be indifferent to him. The consultant found it hard to formulate a vivid or lifelike picture of the young lady.

Following this, Mr. H. commented spontaneously, "Did you see in the newspaper today that there is concern about radiation from energy plants? This is a much graver danger than people realize. I've had headaches and stomach pains, and I am worried they may be caused by radiation." When the consultant inquired about these pains and their relation to radiation, Mr. H. for the first time showed real engagement and involvement, going on to describe a series of "minor physical irregularities which may be due to cancer."

Mr. H. talked about saving money and told the interviewer how much he had made and how much he was saving: "I am afraid of not being able to work and having to support myself; I'd better save my money now." His associations oscillated between "protecting myself for my future" and physical ailments which he suspected were related to radiation in the atmosphere. He said, "I guess I'm going off into an irrelevant area. I should get back to talking about myself." He then glanced toward a plant in the room and said, "You know, occasionally I've seen people being recorded without their knowing it," and followed by asking the consultant, "What do you think of me so far?" The consultant suggested that Mr. H. seemed to feel uneasy about what he was talking about, and that he was also concerned about whether he was being taped and about what the consultant was thinking of him. Mr. H. seemed somewhat relieved and remarked, "I guess I'm being silly. I am very nervous, though."

Mr. H. then said, "I guess I should tell you more about myself. I know psychiatrists are not supposed to direct the patient, but I guess I should start with my childhood history." He then recounted in some detail, though without much emotion, a childhood history in which he was the only son of middle-class parents, his father a bookkeeper, his mother a housewife and part-time nurse. He described having a "normal childhood, with lots of friends, doing well in school, and being a class officer in high school." He did reasonably well in college and "had no emotional problems" until recently. While he observed in passing that he "always had good relationships with people," he did not describe any relationship with much depth, or share with the interviewer the nature of any of his childhood or early adult relationships. The consultant commented that it was hard to get much of a sense of the emotional qualities involved in his growing up. Mr. H. acknowledged, "I'm not a very emotional person, but I do care for people." At this point he appeared to become anxious and looked off in the other direction.

He recalled being depressed periodically but "never like this before." In the preceding ten years, he had had many relationships with women, and frequently after one ended, and before the next one began, he'd go through a period of "loneliness and sadness." But, he repeated, "never like this." Near the end of the interview there were references to people "getting older." He mentioned that his father had died three years earlier, as a relatively young man, of a heart attack. He said little about his mother except that she was now living in Florida and seemed to be enjoying herself.

Other family members included an aunt, who had chronic depressive episodes, and a second cousin, who had been hospitalized with "psychosis." Other than that, "nobody had had any emotional problems in my family."

Case Discussion

While in the ordinary consultative process one might conduct several interviews before reaching a diagnostic impression, it is useful here for illustrative purposes to consider the material in the first interview from different vantage points. From a purely symptomatic point of view, one might diagnose reactive depression with classic symptomatology of feelings of hollowness, emptiness, life not worth living, and early morning wakening. From an etiological point of view, there is no clearcut history of mental illness or, especially, manic-depressive illness in the family, nor clear evidence of cyclical patterns in this man. One would consider it a reactive depression. From a behavioral perspective, one might note that this man had difficulty in getting angry at his girlfriend when she frustrated him. Accordingly, one might recommend assertiveness training or at least show Mr. H. that he needed to be more comfortable with being assertive and angry.

From a developmental structuralist point of view, one would focus on the man's personality structure, those ongoing patterns of organizing experience, internal and external, that characterize his personality. While Mr. H. talked about feeling depressed, presented the classic symptomatology of depression, and gave a history of a recent breakup of a relationship, all suggesting a reactive depression, at the same time he gave a history of—and demonstrated—a shallow emotional life with deep-seated feelings of lonelines and hollowness. Additionally, there were points in the interview at which his capacity to organize his thinking seemed mildly compromised—when, without an appropriate transition, he talked about radiation causing his physical illnesses and, at another point, worried about being tape recorded. On both occasions, however, he was able to reorganize his thinking and say, "I've gotten off on a sidetrack," or, "That's probably a silly idea." Thus, he showed a vulnerability to breakdowns in his capacity to organize thinking logically, with intrusion of fantasy, but usually he could recover and reorganize himself. Near the end of the interview he expressed concerns with physical illness and aging, and worry about dying early like his father.

From the developmental structuralist point of view, then, one would see this man's personality as organized with severe walling-off of most major emotions connected with human experience (intimacy, compassion, joy, sorrow, rage, envy, sadness) but at the same time with awareness of appropriate social adaptation. In addition, one would note that this man occasionally experienced mild breakdown in self- and object differentiation (e.g., the brief intrusions of fantasy into his usual reality adaptation).

One would hypothesize this man as having difficulties deriving from a fairly early stage in development, one in which the organization and differentiation of self from the external world was becoming consolidated (which ordinarily occurs between 2 and 4 years of age). One might further hypothesize, even from the first interview, that this man generally holds himself together well, with good superficial adaptation, but only by severely restricting his participation in distinctly human experience (e.g., the emotions) usually associated with adulthood. Having reached age 35, he became intensely aware of his own aging, in terms of his concerns about illness and an early death like that of his father. (There is some suggestion of an unusual degree of narcissistic vulnerability, making the situation worse.) His typical lifestyle is no longer adaptive, and the recent breakup of the relationship is the precipitant for depressive symptoms and overt signs of vulnerability in the integrity of basic ego functions.

Thus, the problem is seen to be far more complex than a simple reactive depression caused by an object loss. The keys to this formulation were, first of all, the man's indication that he had separated from girlfriends many times before without a depression. Also, the structure and content of his intrusive fantasies about illness and death, and his concerns about how the interviewer was thinking about him, or how people might be looking at him, completed the picture. Because the rigidity of his character structure maintained the constrictions of experience, he could not flexibly bring into play other more adaptive organizational styles, and he suffered a manifest depression and, on observation, a more worrisome vulnerability in the integrity of his personality structure (core ego functions).

An intuitive diagnostician working in the symptomatic or etiological frameworks might readily observe the same manifest phenomena but might be hampered by the lack of a developmental structural conceptualization to integrate these observations.

The developmental structuralist formulation suggests not only the structure of his current illness but also indicates what treatment would have to entail. Although symptom-oriented treatment may help him over the loss of this particular relationship and even his acute depression, and assertiveness training could help him be more assertive, these approaches would not help him cope with his more fundamental difficulty and the developmental issues he never resolved. They would not necessarily stabilize his vulnerability to a breakdown in his reality orientation (differentiation of self and others) and would not help him with his overwhelming inability to tolerate affects associated with human relationships and to deal now with new emotions around loss associated with aging. Just as the patient with occasional mild chest pains may in fact have a severe arterial disease, this patient presenting symptomatically with a "routine reactive depression" evidenced a far more serious structural limitation which requires its own special therapeutic approach. A long-term, developmentally oriented therapeutic relationship, which was to focus on his capacity to experience certain affects, might permit him to stabilize his reality orientation, attain greater flexibility of character organization, and show appropriate growth into middle age.

Discussion: Unique Features and Practical Implications of the Developmental Structuralist Approach to Diagnosis

Phenomenological Basis of the Developmental Structuralist Approach

The developmental structuralist approach is not dependent on inferred internal dynamic processes or psychological abstractions but rather rests on observed data (which nevertheless are organized with more complexity and subtlety than data in a symptom-based nosology). Yet, at the same time, developmental structural concepts readily link up with, and function in a complementary fashion with, dynamic formulations and epigenetic theories of early experience (as they do with other theories of organic or behavioral learning etiologies).

The phenomenological basis of the developmental structuralist approach is perhaps one of its most unique features and deserves special emphasis. Most systems which have taken advantage of subtlety of observation have been related to psychoanalytic appreciation of personality dynamics, and it is not always clear to the general behavioral scientist where phenomenology leaves off and what have been termed "hypothetical" or "inferred internal" states begin. The developmental structuralist classification scheme is based on directly observable phenomena in the interview situation, reinforced with readily obtainable data about historical and current functioning. The difference between the developmental structural approach and more traditional approaches is in the acuity and systematization with which interview, historical, and current functioning data are processed. In other words, the difference is related more to the skill of the clinician during the interview and the hypothetical "magnifying glass" he is using.

A few examples illustrate the point. The most severe compromise in otherwise optimal functioning occurs when there are basic defects in the personality structure, such as impairments in reality testing, the integration of thought and affect, and self-object differentiation. Such defects are observable in the interview situation. First, consider an obvious example of an individual who demonstrates loosening of associations. The interviewer asks, "What brought you here?" to which the person responds concretely with, "The bus brought me here." He goes on to talk about people at work who are unfair and then skips to talk about his parents, all without logical connections. Such an individual is demonstrating a clear-cut loosening of associations.

When the person continually wanders from the topic, he is reflecting a more subtle thought disorder. Such examples, nonetheless, are easily recognized by the skilled clinician. A classification of ego defect is thus easily demonstrated phenomenologically. A more subtle observational capacity would be required to pick up the impairment in self-object differentiation. The clinician, for example, would be required to notice that the patient frequently confuses his feelings about himself with the feelings of the interviewer (e.g., "I can tell you really like me," or "I can tell you want me to leave") and that, under stress, in the interview (e.g., when talking of intimacy or anger) the patient wanders off the topic, switches topics without clear causal links, or brings in an idea "from left field," so to speak, then quickly recovers or rationalizes (e.g., "Are you sure no one can hear what we are talking about? That's silly, isn't it?"). While the construct of an impairment in self-object differentiation is theoretical, the observations that would lead to such a diagnosis are also phenomenologically based. It should be pointed out, however, that to document the more subtle impairments requires more data. The above example is illustrative, and in actual practice more data would be necessary for a confident diagnosis.

The traditional approach would attempt to diagnose a person with an ego defect as being either schizophrenic, manic-depressive, borderline psychotic, having a sociopathic personality disorder, etc. In the structuralist approach, however, the classification sticks to, and is based on, the clearly observable defect. There is no attempt to generalize from a specific defect to a "syndrome." More recently, increased understanding of syndromes has led toward attempts to separate them into subtypes. A better understanding of subtypes would be facilitated by classifying individuals according to the specific phenomenologically based, impaired functions evidenced in interviews (reinforced, of course, by detailed examination of current functioning and past history).

The second broad category of disordered functioning, constrictions in the range of experience tolerated, requires more subtle (but still phenomenological) observations. For example, the individual who comes in and relates to the clinician throughout the interview in a relatively flat, unemotional manner, who sticks to discussion about his interaction with the inanimate environment, is exhibiting an inability to demonstrate his experience of feelings, thoughts, or wishes in relation to human beings. While such an individual traditionally may be classified as a schizoid personality, it is more precise to point out his specific defect in experiencing human engagement.

Another individual may come in, make eye contact, and engage emotionally in a reasonable way, but becomes affectively flat whenever the discussion comes close to assertiveness or anger. While this individual is able to talk easily about other feelings, in this one area he is wooden. He may, for example, shift to somatic complaints, "I am worried about my heart not functioning properly." Such an individual demonstrates an inability to relate to certain dimensions of emotional experience. In this case, we can categorize a specific type of limitation in experiencing certain affects.

A third level of compromise is fairly close to optimally adaptive functioning. Although the individual basically experiences developmentally appropriate phase- and age-expected ranges of human experiences that are stable, organized, uniquely personal, and relatively resistant to stress, he has *contextually* relevant limitations in personality flexibility. Such an individual, for example, may have difficulty experiencing aggressive feelings toward people who are reminiscent of certain persons from the past. In relationships with certain types of authority figures, for instance, he may develop maladaptive patterns. Another example would be that of an otherwise mature woman who becomes "naive" when talking of certain sexual feelings toward men who invoke special meanings for her; or that of an otherwise mature man who may have "no memories" of certain warm feelings toward his father and be unable to relate with warmth to his "understanding" boss, although he is able to relate warmly to the interviewer. These patterns leave the remainder of the personality flexible for the phase-expected range of experiences. The individual in the interview is notable in his capacity for personal warmth and engagement, for experiencing a wide range of feelings, affects, and thoughts, for dealing with anxiety-laden situations without shifting to a more impersonal or a clearly constricted manner of relating. Such an individual also evidences a deepening range of associations over the course of interviews; that is, he talks more richly and deeply, so that one senses a fuller, more complete human being as one gets to know him. By contrast, individuals with major constrictions show the reverse pattern. Their constrictions become more obvious as one gets to know them. Therefore, these more encapsulated disorders (e.g., often thought of as symptom or character neuroses) can also be phenomenologically documented by the overall adaptiveness of the personality, together with limitations in contextually relevant areas of personality functioning.

One point should be further emphasized. The developmentally based clinician should have a clear picture of what constitutes the relative range of age-expected experiential capacities for each age level and each developmental phase. For example, the young adult would be expected to have an experiential world different from that of the latency child or even the late adolescent. Similarly, the middle-aged man is expected to reflect on different sets of issues in different ways than the young adult. In determining the phase-expected experiential range, one should not be thinking in terms of the content or the values of the individual but rather the flexibility of his personality structure to process and integrate a full range of potential phase- and age-appropriate experience. With a normal functioning adult, we would expect a capacity for warmth, love, compassion, and empathy, as well as assertion, anger, jealousy, and rivalry, all existing in a stable configuration and usable in a wide range of interpersonal relationships. In addition, the adult should have a structural capacity for a well-delineated sense of self in the context of stable self-esteem and a capacity for regulating impulses. An individual with major constrictions emanating, perhaps, from an arrest in early adolescence may have unstable self-esteem and an inability to continuously regulate impulses, and may have highly fluctuating values. While the latter may be normal in adolescence, in adulthood it represents a structural limitation.

We are not concerned here whether the individual has a particular political philosophy or set of beliefs. We are concerned only if these philosophies or beliefs reflect a basic constriction, restriction, or defect in the integrating capacities of the personality. For example, the person who believes that the world should circulate around him, that people should do everything for him, could have a certain cultural belief or could be attempting to deal with a sense of inner emptiness and an inability to experience compassion and empathy (e.g., a narcissistic character disorder) or both. We are emphasizing process rather than content, and the clinician must be relatively objective and value-free in looking at the expected structural capacities of individuals of different ages.

Reliability Versus Clinical Validity and the Developmental Structuralist Approach

A direction sometimes taken to increase reliability of diagnoses is the limiting of data to manifest symptoms or behaviors. In so doing, one obtains good reliability but pays the price of ignoring immense amounts of information related to the structural organization of experience. Such reductionistic systems are not only unproductive scientifically but may represent an intellectual regression. Although based on many of the same observable phenomena as manifest-level symptom diagnoses, the conceptualizations of the developmental structuralist approach have far more explanatory power.

The distinction may be clarified with the analogy of different methods for the microscopic examination of tissue. The surface-level symptom approach allows only limited observations by the observer, much as looking through a light microscope allows identification of different tissues limited to their appearance in the plane of the slice. The observer, however, who uses the developmental structuralist approach employs, as it were, the electron scanning microscope to produce three-dimensional pictures exposing the full tissue structure. In addition to the two-dimensional outlines (symptoms), he can organize what he sees in the three-dimensional (structural) picture to yield vastly greater understanding of how the tissue functions, what other structures it interacts with, and what the two-dimensional images (symptoms) really mean in terms of pathological distortions and malformations.

Another effort sometimes made to improve diagnosis is that of evaluating only external environmental adaptive capacities. It is generally true that individuals who are externally successful in the world are reasonably intact and do not often become symptomatically ill. However, external adaptation is only one parameter of health, and to focus on it exclusively is to ignore the way the individual organizes internal experience in relation to the external world. Evaluations which focus excessively on external effectiveness lack the subtlety and explanatory power of the developmental structural assessment. This difference is seen clearly in the evaluations of children and adults who show a superficially solid competence yet have significant deficits in their inner capacity to experience sadness, disappointment, and passivity. When faced with life's inevitable stresses, they run the risk of major psychiatric impairment, including depression, psychosomatic illness, and even psychosis.

For example, in many studies of emotional phenomena in childhood, the hypothetical axis of fearfulness versus self-confidence is often established. The underlying assumption is that the youngster who is a leader and gets A's in school is healthy and mature. However, this bias toward assertiveness overemphasizes external features and ignores entire spheres of the child's inner experience, such as the way he deals with dependent longings, sad feelings, disappointment, humiliation, or other painful affects which are very much part of life. Nor is adequate weight given to his capacity for empathy, sharing, or curiosity about others. Without a complete assessment of the personality, such studies underrate children who may at the time appear frightened, inhibited, or passive but who in fact go on to healthier adaptation at higher levels of organization, in terms of intimate relationships, internal sources of pleasure, and decreased likelihood of mental illness. The superficially adaptive child who becomes depressed or psychotic as an adolescent is an all-too-common phenomenon.

Another example of the misleading bias toward external adaptation is the seemingly healthy adult who is highly successful in work, a good husband and father, capable of assertive behavior and some limited compassion, yet can never tolerate feeling helpless, passive, or weak and surprises everyone by committing suicide in his forties. During an interview, such an individual may be preoccupied with themes reflecting active mastery. He may avoid themes of sadness and defeat and become anxious, even disorganized, if such themes emerge.

Another example of superficially adequate adaptation with underlying structural vulnerability is the self-absorbed individual who gives an outward impression of capacity for intimate involvement with others, but functions internally at a primitive level, intent on gratifying only his own emotional needs. Externally his performance meets the idealistic behavioral expectations he carries with him. He strives to do well and relates effectively and, in fact, meets many of his ideals in family and work performance but does not achieve the pleasure that true reciprocal intimacy brings to others. In many ways, he represents a self-contradicting "shell," with primitive dependency needs operating on the inside and his behavior determined by rigid, idealized values operating outside. In an evaluation of such a person, one sees that his associative style shows little flexibility after an underlying emotion manifests itself. Emotions during the interview reflect primitive needs to "be admired" or "taken care of," with little sign of empathy, curiosity, or interest in others. He may dwell on his high level of accomplishment and success or how his children most surely will be successful. This person is constricted in major areas of phase-appropriate experience and often develops severe symptoms stemming from the routine developmental tasks of adulthood.

In summary, the developmental structural assessment has several advantages over existing diagnostic systems. By focusing on capacity for, and manner of, adaptive integration, it forms a conceptual bridge between etiological factors and manifest symptoms. It is not dependent on inferred psychological abstractions. Yet it complements and easily links up with psychodynamic formulations. Compared to manifest symptom-cluster diagnoses, the structural approach brings an additional dimension of depth and understanding, with greater explanatory power. Where systems based on external adaptation often miss subtle aspects of personality, the developmental structuralist approach highlights these more complex attributes. Finally, it distinguishes strengths in the personality as well as in pathological features.

The Developmental Structuralist Approach Together with Etiological and Symptom-Oriented Approaches

As indicated, the developmental structuralist approach focuses on structures determined by the individual's actual path through development. It deals with a "final common pathway," which is the product of the interaction between many influencing factors that determine the structural characteristics of the personality. All etiological factors (biological, environmental) are therefore integrated in actual personality structures.

The developmental structuralist approach does not exclude either etiological or symptom-complex diagnoses. Instead, it integrates the two with its concept of the developmental stage-specific method used by the person for organizing and processing experience. However, disorders under the conceptual umbrella of optimal expected integrating capacity can also be viewed symptomatically and etiologically. It must be kept in mind that the structural pattern and symptom picture are not always related in a one-to-one correspondence. According to the principle of multiple determination, the developmental level of personality organization and manifest symptoms may be connected in many ways. (This is true even though certain symptom pictures may often be closely and commonly linked to one or another type of developmental structural disorder.) Most useful, as indicated earlier, is a three-column approach to diagnoses whereby each disorder is viewed in terms of its developmental structural characteristics, its symptom clusters (syndromes), and, where unknown, its etiology.

Discussion and Comments on Practical Application of the Developmental Structuralist Approach

The developmental structural assessment has practical applications beyond those already suggested. It does not introduce a totally new terminology. As we have seen, it employs concepts of psychoanalysis, child development, and cognitive development. Thus, the already experienced clinician need not learn a new language nor translate his concepts into another form. The actual application of a developmental structural assessment is not overly complex. For example, if the clinician has formulated his case in psychodynamic terms, further elaboration into a developmental structuralist formulation can be quite straightforward. The essence is the location of the patient's functioning at a particular level in the developmental structural sequence (this can be indicated in two or three sentences). For those familiar with the length of psychodynamic formulation, the developmental structuralist formulations may be misleadingly brief. The complexity is in the implications of the hierarchical arrangement, both theoretical and clinical. Standard associative interviews can easily provide the data necessary for the developmental structural assessment, the additional information coming from the interviewer's approach to conceptualizing the data rather than his use of a different procedure for gathering them.

The developmental structuralist approach is especially useful in evaluating intervention programs. The model provides us a way of looking not only at changes in specific symptoms, behavior patterns, or cognitive styles, but also at the overall level of personality integration. For example, even in evaluating psychotherapeutic approaches that are behaviorally oriented and aim at specific symptom or behavioral changes, we would be able to study changes in the overall integrative capacity of the personality. We could determine whether the individual who has received a particular therapy remains at the same over-all developmental structural level with symptomatic improvement, has regressed to a lower level as a side effect of the symptomatic gains, or has progressed to a higher level of overall personality functioning together with symptomatic relief.

The developmental structuralist approach is also helpful in formulating prognoses. It distinguishes clearly the current acute phenomena from permanent structural capacities of the personality. The developmenal structuralist clinician may make a prognostic statement in which he indicates what can be expected from treatment for the acute phenomena and what might be expected from more ambitious efforts aimed at structural change. To use an analogy, before describing the unique drama an individual is involved in, a determination is first made regarding the individual's structural level, the integrity and flexibility of the stage upon which the drama is being played out. A drama of rivalry is very different and has different prognostic and treatment implications if played on a defective stage, a constricted stage, or a very flexible stage with just some encapsulated bumps.

Justification of progress in treatment for third-party payers may be simplified by the developmental structural assessment. Nonpsychiatrists and especially nonanalysts may be able to use the phenomenologically based concepts of this scheme.

The developmental structuralist approach also provides a conceptual framework for the teaching of psychiatric and psychoanalytic knowledge. It provides a structure on which to hang other concepts and an integrating bridge between global functional level, manifest clinical symptoms, etiologies, and underlying intrapsychic processes.

The developmental structural formulation is potentially useful in research as well. It describes and discriminates particular defects and impairments and therefore may facilitate the subtyping of syndromes. It also describes partially hidden foundations of existing disease entities, which should facilitate exploration of the connections between apparently diverse syndromes. Similarly, it provides a model with which to follow the evolution of full-blown syndromes from precursor states.

The developmental structural assessment may also be useful in screening "healthy" applicants for work placements in which unusual emotional stress is to be expected (e.g., psychoanalytic training, Peace Corps). When the overall developmental structural level has been determined, potentially vulnerable points can be highlighted, although the individual's personality may be functioning well at the time.

Certainly, further study will establish and delineate the full use and limitations of the developmental structuralist approach. In whatever form lines of exploration develop, we anticipate that developmentally based approaches to diagnosis will advance our understanding of the working of the mind.

References

Ainsworth, M., Bell, S.M., & Stayton, D. (1974), Infant-mother attachment and social development: Socialization as a product of reciprocal responsiveness to signals. In: *The Integration of the Child into a Social World*, ed. M. Richards. Cambridge: Cambridge University Press, pp. 99–135.

Bell, S. (1970), The development of the concept of object as related to infant-mother attachment. *Child Devel.*, 41:219–311.

Bowlby, J. (1969), *Attachment and Loss*, Vol. 1. London: Hogarth Press.

Brazelton, T., Koslowski, B., & Main, M. (1974), The origins of reciprocity: The early mother-infant interaction. In: *The Effect of the Infant on Its Caregiver*, ed. M. Lewis & L. Rosenblum. New York: Wiley, pp. 49–76.

Charlesworth, W. (1969), The role of surprise in cognitive development. In: *Studies in Cognitive Development*, ed. D. Elkind & J. Flavell. London: Oxford University Press, pp. 257–314.

Emde, R., Gaensbauer, T., & Harmon, R. (1976), Emotional Expression in Infancy: A Biobehavioral Study. *Psychological Issues* Monograph 37. New York: International Universities Press.

Escalona, S. (1968), *The Roots of Individuality*. Chicago: Aldine.

Freud, A. (1965), *Normality and Pathology in Childhood: Assessments of Development*. New York: International Universities Press.

Freud, S. (1911), Formulations on the two principles of mental functioning. *Standard Edition*, 12:218–226. London: Hogarth Press, 1958.

Gerwirtz, J.L. (1965), The course of infant smiling in four child rearing environments in Israel. In: *Determinants of Infants' Behavior*, Vol. 3, ed. B.M. Foss. London: Methuen, pp. 205–260.

——— (1969), Levels of conceptual analysis in environment-infant interaction research. *Merrill-Palmer Quart.*, 15:9–47.

Gouin-Décarie, T. (1965), *Intelligence and Affectivity in Early Childhood: An Experimental Study of Jean Piaget's Object Concept and Object Relations*. New York: International Universities Press.

Greenspan, S.I. (1979), Intelligence and Adaptation: An Integration of Psychoanalytic and Piagetian Developmental Psychology. *Psychological Issues* Monograph 47/48. New York: International Universities Press.

—— Cullander, C.C.H. (1975), A systematic metapsychological assessment of the course of an analysis. *J. Amer. Psychoanal. Assn.*, 23:107–138.

—— Hatleberg, J.L., & Cullander, C.C.H. (1976), A systematic metapsychological assessment of the personality in childhood. *J. Amer. Psychoanal. Assn.*, 24:875–903.

Hartmann, H. (1939), *Ego Psychology and the Problem of Adaptation*. New York: International Universities Press, 1958.

Kernberg, O.F. (1975), *Borderline Conditions and Pathological Narcissism*. New York: Aronson.

Klaus, M.N., & Kennell, J.H. (1976), *Maternal-Infant Bonding: The Impact of Early Separation or Loss on Family Development*. St. Louis: Mosby.

Lipsitt, L. (1966), Learning processes of newborns. *Merrill-Palmer Quart.*, 12:45–71.

Mahler, M.S., Pine, F., & Bergman, A. (1975), *The Psychological Birth of the Human Infant*. New York: Basic Books.

Meltzoff, A.N., & Moore, K.M. (1977), Imitation of facial and manual gestures by human neonates. *Science*, 198:75–78.

Murphy, L.B., & Moriarty, A.E. (1976), *Vulnerability, Coping, and Growth*. New Haven: Yale University Press.

Parmelee, A., Jr. (1972), Development of states in infants. In: *Sleep and the Maturing Nervous System*, ed. C. Clemente, D. Purpura, & F. Mayer. New York: Academic Press, pp. 199–228.

Piaget, J. (1962), The stages of the intellectual development of the child. *Bull. Menn. Clin.*, 26:120–128.

Sander, L. (1962), Issues in early mother-child interaction. *J. Amer. Acad. Child Psychiat.*, 1:141–166.

Spitz, R.A., Emde, R., & Metcalf, D. (1970), Further prototypes of ego formation. *The Psychoanalytic Study of the Child*, 25:417–444.

Sroufe, L., & Matas, L. (1974), Contextual determinants of infant affective response. In: *The Origins of Fear*, ed. M. Lewis & L. Rosenblum. New York: Wiley, pp. 49–72.

—— Waters, E. (1977), Attachment as an organizational construct. *Child Devel.*, 48:1184–1199.

Stern, D. (1974a), The goal and structure of mother-infant play. *J. Amer. Acad. Child Psychiat.*, 13:402–421.

—— (1974b), Mother and infant at play: The dyadic interaction involving facial, vocal and gaze behaviors. In: *The Effects of the Infant on Its Caregiver*, ed. M. Lewis & L. Rosenblum. New York: Wiley, pp. 187–213.

Tennes, K., Emde, R., Kisley, A., & Metcalf, D. (1972), The stimulus barrier in early infancy. An exploration of some formulations of John Benjamin. *Psychoanal. & Contemp. Sci.*, 1:206–234.

Thomas, A., Chess, S., & Birch, H. (1968), *Temperament and Behavior Disorders in Children*. New York: New York University Press.

Wolff, P. (1966), The Causes, Controls, and Organization of Behavior in the Neonate. *Psychological Issues* Monograph 5. New York: International Universities Press.

Name Index

Subject Index

403